Xinran

CHINA WITNESS

Xinran was born in Beijing in 1958 and moved to
London in 1997 to write for *The Guardian*. She is
author of *The Good Women of China*, a seminal book
about the lives of Chinese women, and *Sky Burial*. Her
charity, The Mothers' Bridge of Love, was founded to
help disadvantaged Chinese children and to build a
bridge of understanding between the West and China.

CHINA WITNESS

CHINA WITNESS

VOICES FROM
A SILENT GENERATION

Xinran

TRANSLATED FROM CHINESE BY
Nicky Harman, Julia Lovell and Esther Tyldesley

Anchor Books
A Division of Random House, Inc.
New York

FIRST ANCHOR BOOKS EDITION, APRIL 2010

The Library of Congress has cataloged the Pantheon edition as follows:
Xinran.
China witness : voices from a silent generation / Xinran; translated from Chinese by Julia Lovell,
Esther Tyldesley, and Nicky Harman.
p. cm.
"Originally published in 2008 in Great Britain by Chatto & Windus,
The Random House Group Limited, London."
Includes index.
1. China—Biography. I. Title.
CT1826.X57 2009
951.0092'2—dc22
2008035840

Anchor ISBN: 978-0-307-38853-7

*Author photograph © Jane Brown
Map by Jeff Edwards*

www.anchorbooks.com

To the Mothers of China
and my mother, Xujun

Contents

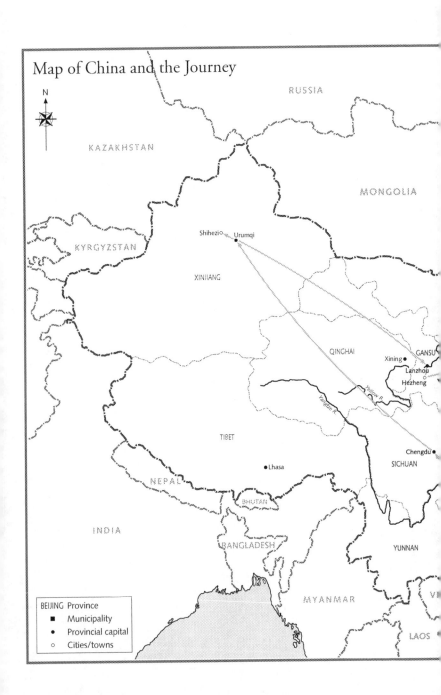

Map of China and the Journey

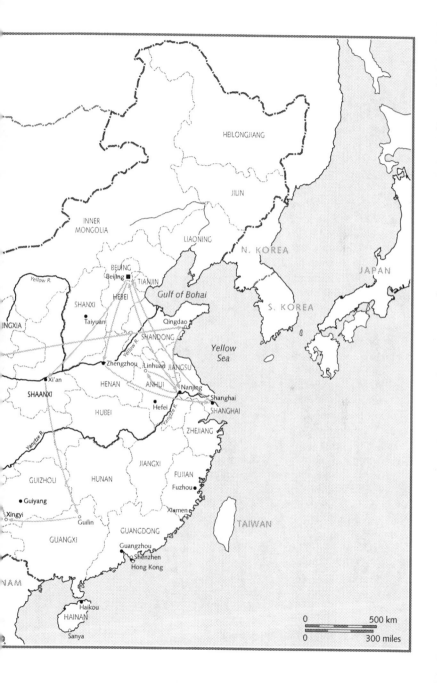

Illustrations

Text Illustrations

Chapter 1: A herb shop, Xingyi, 2006.

Chapter 2: "Double-Gun Woman" with her family.

Her son-in-law, Lin Xiangbei, with daughter and grandchildren.

Chapter 3: Workers of 148 Corps, 1950s, Shihezi.

With survivors of 148 Corps, Shihezi, 2006. *(Photo Kate Shortt)*

Chapter 3: Oil pioneers, north-west China, 1950; and in Hezheng, 2006.

Chapter 4: Acrobats practising, 1950s, and on tour, South America, 1990s.

Chapter 5: The news singer reciting, 2006.

Traditional tea house, 2006. *(Photo Kate Shortt)*

Chapter 7: Lantern workshop, Nanjing, 1950s, and a lantern-maker, 2006.

Chapter 8: A survivor of the Long March, 1947 and 1987.

Chapter 9: General Phoebe as a child, Chicago, 1933, and in Beijing, 2006.

Chapter 10: A policeman with his family, Zhengzhou, 1960s and 2001.

Chapter 11: A shoe-mender woman, Zhengzhou, 2006. *(Photos Kate Shortt)*

Plate Section

1. Funeral for the husband of the "Double-Gun Woman", 1935; inset, Chen Lianshi with her grandson.
2. Fang Haijun, first head of Mao Zedong's guard, and later founder of China's Naval Academy and submarine fleet.
3. Prospecting for oil in northern China, 1950s.
4. Oil prospecting, with Soviet colleagues, 1950s.
5. Family photo of the policeman Mr Jingguan, 1950s.
6. Long-distance coach with factory workers, Jiangsu, 1969.
7. Acrobats performing during the Cultural Revolution.
8. Acrobat Yishujia's husband and son at a military base, 1970s.
9. Painting a lantern in a workshop, Nanjing, 2006. *(Photo Kate Shortt)*
10. Long March survivor, interviewed by foreign media.
11. A crowd in central Urumqi, 2006, watching a film on a large screen.
12. One of the oldest tea houses in China. *(Photo Kate Shortt)*
13. In a Zhengzhou street, 2006, inteviewing with the shoemender.
14. Woman making chopsticks, Guizhou, 2006
15. General Phoebe and her husband, 2006.
16. Monument to the 4 May Movement, Beijing, 2006. *(Photo Kate Shortt)*

(Unless otherwise indicated above in parentheses, photos are from the author's collection and supplied by kind permission of interviewees.)

Glossary and Abbreviations

CCP: Chinese Communist Party, the ruling party of the PRC, founded 1921.

GMD: Guomindang (also Kuomintang/KMT), the Nationalist Party, founded 1912; for many years the most powerful party in China, defeated by Mao Zedong's PLA forces in 1949, when the GMD retreated to Taiwan where it survived as the dominant political party until 2000.

PLA: People's Liberation Army, founded 1927 as the military arm of the CCP to put down GMD rebellion in the Nanchang Uprising of August 1927; originally known as the Chinese Red Army, it was established as the PLA at the end of the Sino-Japanese war in 1945, when China's civil war continued and the PLA finally defeated the GMD in 1949. Comprising all China's military forces, it is now the world's largest standing army.

PRC: People's Republic of China, established 1949, at the end of the Chinese civil war.

Han Chinese: the largest single ethnic group native in China, making up about 92% of the population of the PRC.

Hui Chinese: a mainly Moslem Chinese ethnic group, one of the 56 ethnic groups officially recognised by the PRC.

xiucai: one of the degrees of the competitive imperial examinations for entry to provincial government bureaucracy which survived into the twentieth century.

Three Antis (1951) and the Five-Antis (1952): Mao Zedong's campaigns aimed at rooting out corruption and enemies of the state, particularly in bureaucracy and business; targeting his political opposition and capitalists, these movements consolidated his power base.

Three Red Banners: the 3 principles held up in the 1950s for the building of socialism – the General (Party) Line, the Great Leap Forward and the People's Communes.

Great Leap Forward: Mao Zedong's Second Five-Year Plan, 1958-60, intended to transform China rapidly into a modern industrial society, which resulted in famine and ended in economic and humanitarian disaster, during which millions of Chinese starved to death.

Reform through Labour (Laogai): a slogan of the criminal justice system of convict labour instigated by Mao Zedong in the 1950s, modelled on the Soviet Gulags.

Four Clean-Ups: a movement, also called The Socialist Education Movement, launched by Mao Zedong in 1963 to cleanse reactionary elements from politics, economy, bureaucracy, ideology.

Reform and Opening: the opening up of China and relations with the West under Deng Xiaoping.

Currency:
1 yuan (CNY) = 10 jiao = 100 fen
1 UK pound = approx. 14 yuan (May 2008)
1 US dollar = approx. 7 yuan (May 2008)
1 yuan = approx. 7 pence/14 cents (May 2008)

Oil:
Oil in China has historically been measured in tonnes rather than the more familiar barrels.
1 tonne oil = approx. 7–9 barrels, depending on the type of oil.

Introduction

This book is a testament to the dignity of modern Chinese lives.

It has been not only a personal journey for me through the experiences of my parents' generation, but also – for my interviewees – a process of self-discovery, of revisiting and refining their memories of the past. While I have wondered what questions to ask, they have needed to think about what answers to give; about how to describe a twentieth century that, in many respects, has been full of suffering and trauma. For Chinese people, it is not easy to speak openly and publicly about what we truly think and feel. And yet this is exactly what I have wanted to record: the emotional responses to the dramatic changes of the last century. I wanted my interviewees to bear witness to Chinese history. Many Chinese would think this a foolish, even a crazy thing to undertake – almost no one in China today believes you can get their men and women to tell the truth. But this madness has taken hold of me, and will not let me go: I cannot believe that Chinese people always take the truth of their lives with them to the grave.

Why do the Chinese find it so hard to speak frankly about themselves?

"The concept of guilt by association," Professor Gao Mingxuan, an authority on the Chinese penal code, has remarked, "was always very important in ancient Chinese law. As early as the second millennium BC, a criminal's family was punished as harshly as the criminal himself. Over the next thousand years, this principle steadily tightened its grip on the judicial system. In his canonical history of China, written around 100 BC, Sima Qian recorded that 'after Shang Yang ordered changes in the law [c.350 BC], the people were grouped in units of five and ten households, carrying out mutual surveillance, and mutually responsible for each other's conduct before the law'. If a member of one family committed a crime, the other families in that unit were judged to be guilty by association. By the Qin dynasty (221–206 BC), the principle was applied not only within communities, but also within the army and government. In the case of minor offences, the criminal's family would be exterminated to between three and five degrees of association; with serious offences, to nine or ten. Although the virtues of this penal principle were debated at various points in the imperial past, it remained a mainstay of the Chinese judicial code until the Ming and Qing dynasties (1368–1911)."

China does not have a monopoly on the idea of collective responsibility in criminal law. In 1670, for example, Louis XIV installed just such a principle in France's penal code: entire families – including children and the mentally ill – were to be killed for an individual's crime. Sometimes, whole villages would be condemned, with even the dead posthumously disgraced.

In China, the deep historical roots of the principle of guilt by association gave rise to powerful traditions of clan loyalty, instilling in the Chinese a strong inhibition towards the idea of speaking out openly – out of a fear of implicating others.

None of the cataclysmic changes brought by China's twentieth century – the fall of the Qing dynasty, the chaos of the warlord era, the Sino-Japanese War, the civil war, the Communist revolution – has succeeded in dislodging this strong clan consciousness. The Chinese people still seem to lack the confidence to speak out on what they really think – even as the post-Mao reforms have slowly opened doors between China and the outside world, between China's past and future, and between the individual and government.

The cautionary principle has governed public expression in China too long to be discarded in less than thirty years; China's freedom of speech continues to be hedged with idiotic obstinacy, ignorance and fear.

But I can wait no longer. Thanks to the destruction of the past wrought by the Cultural Revolution, and ongoing censorship of the media and control of school textbooks, China's younger generations are losing touch with earlier generations' struggles for national dignity. The individuals who fought for twentieth-century China are mocked or dismissed for their unquestioning loyalty to now outmoded revolutionary ideals. As they search for new values against the uncertainties of the present and the debunking of the past, many young people today refuse to believe that, without the contributions of their grandparents and great-grandparents, the confident, modernising China they now know would not exist.

After almost twenty years of interviews and research as a journalist, I am worried that the truth of China's modern history – along with our quest for national dignity – will be buried with my parents' generation.

Over these two decades, I compiled a list of around fifty individuals I had encountered, each with astonishing stories to tell. From these, I sifted out a final twenty names to interview for this book. Among my original fifty were numerous national celebrities whose inclusion would have guaranteed my book public attention, even notoriety. I decided, however, that they would have other opportunities to tell their stories, either personally, or through their children. I concluded, instead, that it would be of greater historical value to record the stories of ordinary people, of people who would otherwise lack the fame, money and rank to get their equally astonishing experiences heard. Although I know I cannot hope to summarise the past hundred years of modern Chinese history in the experiences of only twenty people, I firmly believe that these individuals are a part of, and witnesses to, this history – of its notable successes and tragic failures.

The average age of my interviewees was in the seventies; the oldest was ninety-seven. Uncertainties about their physical health gave an added sense of urgency to my project.

Take, for example, the story of Hu Feibao (not his real name), a former bandit along the old Silk Road. After skirmishes with the People's Liberation Army throughout the 1950s, in the early 1960s Hu was finally arrested and condemned to life imprisonment. In the 1980s, he was transferred to a labour camp, where he has worked ever since. When I interviewed him there, from the late 1980s, he spoke to me of the bandit culture he had known along the Silk Road.

The gangs were like clans, he told me, with every bandit sharing the gang surname. Most were of mixed blood – some combination of Chinese, Tibetan, Mongolian and Muslim. No one knew exactly who he was descended from, as there was no concept of normal family life. A bandit knew who his father was, but not his mother, because only boys were kept on in the gang. Girls would be left behind with their mothers – women who had been kidnapped to bear children.

His fellow bandits had never known him as Hu Feibao. Members of the gang were forbidden to tell outsiders – and especially not police – their names. "If they'd known our real surnames, they'd have used them to curse our ancestors." Hu Feibao (literally, Flying Dynamite Hu) was what the locals called him, because of the speed at which his gang moved. Growing up, he'd never heard of the "Silk Road"; he only knew it as the "Cash Highway". After he was arrested in 1963, the policeman who had travelled from Beijing to interrogate him asked him about his "criminal activities on the Silk Road". "Where's the Silk Road?" Hu asked in return.

His confusion was entirely natural: of neither local or ancient provenance, "the Silk Road" was a term invented by the German geographer Baron Ferdinand von Richthofen in 1877, to identify the trade route between classical Europe and Asia.

In 139 BC, Zhang Qian, an envoy of the Han emperor Wudi, led the first embassy from the Chinese capital of Chang'an into the regions of the far west. One of his aides travelled as far as Anxi (Iran) and Shendu (India). All the countries visited sent ambassadors to accompany the embassy back to China. In AD 73, after the Silk Road had been closed by war, another envoy, Ban Chao, led a thirty-six-strong embassy on a second mission out of China, to reopen communications with the West; his aide, Gan Ying, almost reached Daqin (the Roman Empire), then swerved off towards the Persian Gulf, thereby extending the original trade route. This was the "desert" Silk Road, existing alongside the Silk Road of the plateaux, stretching from Chang'an, through the plateaux of Qinghai and Tibet, through to South Asia, and the maritime Silk Road, from Quanzhou, across the Taiwan Strait and through South-East Asia.

Through desert, plains and mountains, this 3,000-mile road – so romantically named by Richthofen after the prized commodity that travelled along it – offered a passage between ancient China and the Mediterranean. And as rivers shifted course and mountains became impassable with snow, so forks developed in it.

The bandit culture that Hu Feibao knew was that of the northern edge of the desert Silk Road: heading north out of Xi'an to Hami, through Jimsa and Urumqi, then on past Shihezi, Huocheng and Ili, before finally ending up on the coast of the Black Sea. His memories of the "Cash Highway" had none of the romantic associations in which Western imaginings of the Silk Road – of its winding, luxury-laden caravans and setting suns – are steeped. The route he had known was strewn with bleached white bones – some of camels, some of humans. "It hardly ever rained," he told me. "During the droughts, you felt like all your blood had been boiled dry. The sandstorms were like shifting graves: they buried men alive. For us, however, they were the best time for ambushes, even though they might kill us, because trade caravans always stopped; they'd never try to move on through them." Hu Feibao and his fellow horsemen lived entirely off their wits: off their ability to exploit often fatally unpredictable local conditions. Born and raised among bandits, as early as he could remember he had always yearned to follow the example of Danbin Jianzan, the "Black Warrior Lama".

After my first interview with Hu, I spent some time researching this mysterious Black Warrior Lama. Back in the early 1990s, there were few computers – and no Internet, of course – in China, and hardly any archives or materials available on modern police history. Although a couple of veteran policemen said they had heard of him, I could find no written sources. Later on, with the help of an army official who had researched the north-western warlord Ma Bufang (ruler of Qinghai in the 1930s and 1940s), I discovered a book by a Danish scholar called Henning Haslung, *Men and Gods in Mongolia*, from which I learned that, towards the end of the nineteenth century, Danbin Jianzan had been a tribal leader in a part of Mongolia under Russian rule. Imprisoned by the Tsar for usurping local power, Danbin Jianzan was subsequently exiled out into the steppe. After the 1911 revolution in China and the collapse of Qing authority in Mongolia, he and his troops overran and occupied the key north-eastern stronghold of Kebuduo. As various factions battled for control of the country, the Mongolian Revolutionary Party, with the help of the Soviet Red Army, encircled his power base. Breaking out, he fled into the wild deserts of Xinjiang and Gansu, where he survived by robbing merchants and traders until, somewhere around the mid-1920s, he mysteriously disappeared. A 1994 Russian monograph, *The Head of the Black Lama*, and a Mongolian newspaper article from 1999 revealed that, in 1924, Danbin and his troops had been wiped out by some six hundred crack troops from a special unit sent by the ruling Soviet faction in Mongolia. Danbin's head now sits, perfectly preserved, in a museum in St Petersburg built during the reign of Peter the Great.

During our last interview in 1996, Hu Feibao refused to accept what I had found out. Although, he told me, locals sometimes tried to frighten their children into good behaviour by telling them "the Black Lama would get them" if they were naughty, he was generally well liked in those parts, because he never robbed the poor, Mongolians or couriers. A few villages along the way to the west even served as his eyes and ears, helping him with information and advance warnings. After his death, Hu went on, the code of bandit practice he had enforced was upheld by all the local gangs, a few of whom still operated even through the 1960s campaign against banditry waged by the People's Liberation Army. This code, according to Hu Feibao, was much stricter than the moral principles preached by the Nationalists, by Ma Bufang or by the Communist Party. He had lived by these rules all his life, and even after decades in prison he wouldn't admit that the robberies he and his fellow bandits had committed had been crimes. "That's how my people had always lived. If we hadn't stolen from the Cash Highway, how would our women and children have survived? How would the local villages have had goods to trade? For centuries and dynasties, we were the only ones who'd ever looked out for these people. We never forced them to work for us, or stole their food and livestock. And we never kidnapped women who were already betrothed, or married with children. We only took unmarried girls, and we treated them much better than the village men; no one was allowed to beat their wives or children. The locals actually sent their daughters out onto the road to wait for us, often leaving them there for days on end. Sometimes they even starved or froze to death. Anyway, if we'd had no women, where would the sons for the gang have come from?"

This was to be our final meeting. We talked, I remember, between packing trucks inside the camp's factory complex, where he was making up bundles of gloves to put into boxes. His hands were trembling with old age. I sat silently to one side, listening to his protestations.

His stories made a deep impression on me. I had never imagined that someone my government had locked up for decades as a bandit, as a menace to society, would still show such courage and spirit; that this withered old man could once have led such an exciting life, or that the communities living by the Silk Road could have so harmoniously coexisted with this strange, apparently criminal society. In Chinese, the word "bandit" has entirely negative connotations. But the bandits along the Silk Road had had their own culture and moral standards. Hu Feibao shook me into re-examining both my own ability to judge right and wrong, and my understanding of Chinese society. Our tendency to judge other societies by our own standards can lead us to punish the innocent.

By the time I had decided to do the interviews for this book in 2006, Hu Feibao had had a stroke. When I telephoned his camp, the warder told me he was no longer able to talk. Suspecting the authorities were trying to stop him speaking to me, I tried again some while later. This time, I managed to talk directly to him. His voice was mumbling, indistinct; it had lost the confident, dignified ring that decades in prison had not succeeded in grinding out. I imagined him holding the phone with trembling fingers, dribbling into the receiver. I knew this was not how this once formidable individual would wish to be remembered. I deleted his name from my list of interviewees.

In the initial interviews I did by phone in May and June 2006, another difficulty that I had anticipated presented itself. When I said that I would like to talk to them in person, my interviewees began to get cold feet; even to pull out completely. More and more subjects became out of bounds; some asked not to be filmed, or taped; others asked me if I knew what might happen after the interviews were published. I could tell that they were torn between the yearning to take this opportunity – quite possibly the last of their lives – to speak out, and anxiety for the possible consequences. Could I get hold of a government permit to speak to them? several people suggested. Or an official "interviewee protection" guarantee? As if the decision to talk about their lives was one for the Communist Party, rather than the individuals themselves, to make.

All of which only confirmed what I already knew from two decades of working as a journalist in China. Even though almost fifty years have passed since Mao's "Liberation" of the country, the Chinese people have not yet succeeded in escaping the shadow of three millennia of imperial totalitarianism and a twentieth century of chaotic violence and oppression, to speak freely without fear of being punished by the prevailing regime.

As I sat in my London home, I had no idea whether these people would really open up to me once I searched them out in China. When we sat down opposite each other, with the video camera running, would they respond by shutting themselves even further away from me? I didn't know whether I would be able to persuade them to talk; whether I would have the skill to tease their memories out of them.

But I knew I had to go forward: not only as a personal document of the work I had done over the past twenty years, but also for Chinese youth today, and especially for PanPan, my son and inspiration – a young man who had grown up between Britain and China. To help him understand the past of the China he knew, this project was a risk I was willing to take.

I began losing sleep, thinking constantly about how I could get my interviewees to trust me, to open up to me; how I could demonstrate to them my sense of responsibility towards their era; how I could persuade them to leave their accounts of what they had witnessed with me.

One June morning, lying in bed in our seventeenth-century cottage in Stourhead, I watched through the window the birds singing and skitting through the trees, their carefree twittering contrasting so markedly with the anxiety I felt at the task ahead of me. I wanted to run away from the project, to take refuge in beautiful, green Somerset, and write escapist fairy stories I'd thought up as a child, or reminiscences about places I had been to, people I had met, friends I had known.

If my mother-in-law, the novelist Mary Wesley, had still been alive, it would have been her ninety-fourth birthday. For some reason, since I had decided to write this book, I had been thinking a lot about her – particularly after a biography of her, *Wild Mary*, had come out. Would Mary have been happy with this document of her life, many people had wondered. Would she have regretted the choices she had made? These were the questions that I wanted to ask my interviewees, and also the questions that Western journalists often asked me: Did I regret anything about the forty years I had lived in China before I moved to the West? Had they been worthwhile?

Though I couldn't explain why, my instinct was always to say yes – they had been worthwhile. Through thousands of years of the Chinese past, so many women have toiled their lives away, bearing children, bringing up their families, gaining nothing for themselves. Would they have said their lives had been worthwhile? I don't even know if they would have asked themselves the question. But I'm sure that towards the end of their lives, a great many Chinese people – both men and women – have thought back over their past, flicking through albums of memories they would never reveal to their children and grandchildren. What, I wonder, might these albums contain? Regret, perhaps? Self-denial? Or joyful affirmation of the life just lived? Perhaps their children and grandchildren would imagine them to contain only blindness and stupidity.

That day, I phoned a woman called Jin Zhi (not her real name). Jin Zhi is an academic authority on the former Soviet Union, specialising particularly on the relations between Mao and Stalin. An outstanding linguist, she speaks fluent English, Russian and German. Despite receiving a Western-style education up to the age of eighteen, she has been throughout her life a passionate supporter of the Communists, firmly believing that the Party will "win back for the Chinese people the dignity that they lost after the Opium Wars". She was an old friend of the family, so we were often in touch.

"Xinran," she had said to me, in her usual forthright tones, months earlier, "I definitely want to be in your book. I want to make my grand-daughter Shanshan understand my past, my feelings, my political ideals. I want her to realise that her generation has something in common with mine."

But now, as we spoke on the phone, she told me that the more she thought about speaking out, the more distressed she felt. She hated herself, she said: the beauty she had lost, the fact that she had never enjoyed a warm, close family life, that even now, past eighty, she felt inhibited, controlled by her husband; that she was still not free. Her only truly happy moments, she told me, were strolling on her own around Beihai Park in Beijing.

"Don't be angry with me," she said, after begging me to let her with-draw. She seemed a different person from the woman who had enthused so excitedly about the project in the past. But after putting the phone down, I knew she was the same Jin Zhi as ever; and that, in her way, she was representative of millions of Chinese. For the last hundred years, the Chinese people have been hesitating between affirmation and denial of the self; her inner struggle was entirely typical. Very few people can under-stand and define themselves as individuals, because all their descriptive vocabulary has been colonised by unified social and political structures. A person can readily respond to external stimuli – to political injustice, to frustrations at work, to the praise of others – but only rarely succeed in making independent sense of themselves.

I thought again of my mother-in-law, who had often been criticised for her individualism. If Mary Wesley had concentrated exclusively on rebelling against convention, on showing other women how they could dare to be different, without writing her novels, would she still be remembered? Might she have faded from view, like so many millions of forgotten old people? Mary had never been willing to be ordinary; she knew better than anything else how to be an individual.

Digging deep into her own life experiences, Mary, who was seventy when her first novel was published, used her writing – a testament to her own determination to swim against the tide – to challenge social and sexual mores. Through her own frankness and self-reflection, she encouraged her readers to re-evaluate themselves. Many older people who have come to hear me speak at bookshops and festivals have told me that reading her books made them feel constricted by their hidebound lives, desperate to

9

rebel, though too timid to do so. But reading the biography – about Mary's self-confidence and wild independence – inspired them.

If these testimonies to the dignity of modern Chinese lives succeed in making some members of China's older generations feel that their lives have not been wasted, and in persuading younger generations that the dazzling landscapes and possibilities of contemporary China have been realised only through the sacrifices and struggles of their forebears, I will feel that I have achieved something for my son and future grandchildren. If we let these old people take their experiences with them to the grave, I feel that we are doing them a serious injustice. They all have stories to tell; and even if these stories strike us as ignorant, foolish, perhaps criminal, they will usefully force us to reflect on progress we have subsequently made.

I realised, that morning in June, I had lost all confidence in myself. I was feeling overwhelmed by the complexities of the lives I had decided to explore – their childhood pleasures, their hopes and ambitions, their loves, friendships, attachments. Had they found happiness? Contentment? How would I begin my interviews? Where would they end?

Planning this journey took me six months; not only was it very difficult to line up interviews but also to structure a "time line" for readers to see the difference between the historical China and today's image of China. From my research, I discovered that it sometimes took more than twenty years for the poorest and westernmost regions of the country to receive the policies and orders from central government departments which were mostly located in the eastern part of China. Improvements in modern living conditions often took as long. For instance, the Single Child policy was initiated in 1979 (it finally became a law in 2004) but many families have large numbers of children in southern and western China, even in the villages near big cities. Therefore, I chose to move between the Yellow River and the Yangtze, the most populated area of China, from west to east, so that readers could follow our journey to see what Chinese lives looked like from the 1980s to 2006.

The witnesses in this book lived in the period that is known to the West as the "Time of Red China", but most Chinese call it the "Time of the Leadership of the Party". For this reason, in this book (which is neither a work of historical research, nor one that comes up to strict academic standards), whether I talk in terms of Red China or of the leadership of the Party, it is necessary for me to tell some of the stories from the history of the Communist Party as plainly, readably and simply as I can. That way, readers, most of whom know nothing of the history of the Chinese Communist Party, will be able to find answers to some of the questions of today's China.

In my search for a witness close to the upper echelons of the Communist Party, I considered several dozens of possible interviewees: I was looking for an eyewitness who has survived the political chaos of China's modern history and come out the other side. This is why I chose Fang Haijun, a victim of a high-level conflict in 1931, the first head of Mao Zedong's personal guard, a man personally selected by Mao in 1938 to be Chief of the Organisation Committee of the Political Office of the Central Military Commission, and a former deputy chairman of the General Party Affairs Office (a body made up of twenty-six high-ranking military leaders, which included such historical figures as Zhu De, Peng Dehuai, Lin Biao, Chen Yi and Liu Bocheng). He was also one of the people who created China's national defence industry after 1949, as well as the founder of China's Naval Academy and submarine fleet. However, his "closeness to history" in the end proved an obstacle, not an opportunity. His story alone requires a book, but our conversation helped me to understand the rules that govern China's political life. When I asked him how he was able to survive the fierce infighting of Mao's inner circle, he told me the following story. In the 1930s, he often played mah-jong with Mao Zedong, Tan Zheng and a few other fellow Hunanese. There are many different systems for mah-jong, but people from the same place play according to the same rules: they did not need to spend a lot of time talking about it, they all understood the strategies, because they had all been raised in the earth and water of the same place. His words were often in my mind as I prepared for the interviews before me.

When choosing accommodation for our research team, I decided that in poorer areas, we would try to stay in the best government guest houses; in more developed cities, we would look for the cheapest single-star hotels. My first consideration in impoverished parts of China was security. Officials in poor areas are for the most part not very educated – particularly with respect to legal freedoms and human rights – and tend to respect only government-run institutions. I thought that if we stayed in the most expensive establishment in the area, the local officials would be too intimidated to interfere with us. In more prosperous parts of the country, I wanted the team to experience as much of ordinary, daily life as they could: to take the everyday temperature of the area through the food that they ate and places they stayed. Through noting local differences, I hoped we would see at first hand the historical fault lines in China's development: the small towns lagging ten, twenty, even thirty years behind the big showcase cities.

But, to be honest, none of us could ever have imagined or expected what we might find on this journey, planned for so long, involving fifty people and based on my twenty years of research.

Before I started, I had no idea. But I knew that I had to complete my journey.

I

Yao Popo, or the Medicine Woman of Xingyi

Sitting on the step of Yao Popo's herb shop.

YAO POPO or the Medicine Lady, aged seventy-nine, *interviewed in Xingyi, Guizhou province, south-western China. When she was four years old, Yao Popo's mother was killed and she was given away to a medicinal herb seller. She was married off to a musician, the foster son of the herb seller, and the three of them travelled around China, from the Yangtze River to the Pearl River between the 1930s and 1960s. She says the Cultural Revolution helped her: she made a home and a life from it because hospitals and medical schools closed down, and people came to her instead.*

At 2.20 a.m., on 27 July 2006, after twenty-eight hours on aeroplanes, from London to Guilin, via Munich, Beijing and Xi'an, I found myself too exhausted to sleep. The two strong sleeping pills I had taken earlier gave me only three hours of troubled rest, full of dreams of getting on and off planes, checking in, reclaiming baggage, and running round and round an enormous circle, searching for its centre – the witnesses I wanted to interview.

The last part of my dream was linked to what my husband Toby and I talked about on the plane: China's century-long quest for a new political and moral centre, following the 1911 revolution. Every time I go back to China, I look for the places that have been important to me in the past, but most of them have disappeared – everything is different. Sometimes, I find it hard to distinguish between my memories and my dreams. If the past is already this blurred for me in middle age, how do older people manage? Do their memories cease to become real? If so, does this cause them pain? Do the stories they hear from other people of their generation also start to seem unreal? How can they convince their uncomprehending or doubting children that stories and events that have left no physical historical trace really took place?

Returning to Guilin in the south – famous for its lush greenness and eerily beautiful limestone formations – for the first time in ten years, my heart grew heavy. As we continued our journey and the moment for approaching my interviewees drew closer, I felt underprepared, hesitant, overwhelmed by the speed at which China was changing. Everywhere I had been a decade ago seemed no longer there. I had nothing with which to orient my memories.

When I moved to Britain in 1997, I was very proud of the speed at which China, and its cities in particular, were changing. But after I saw how careful Europe was to preserve the traces of its past, I began to be troubled by the unseemly haste with which my country was destroying the old to bring in the new. I saw now that this millennia-old empire of ours was being rebuilt by mindless modernisers who took their cultural bearings from McDonald's. In the two decades that Mao had been dead, modernisation had taken a heavy toll on every Chinese city, with arrogant local planners still gleefully bent on continuing this irresponsible destruction of the ancient past.

Xingyi, the capital of the Buyi Minority and Miao Minority autonomous region in the province of Guizhou (south China), is a typical example of a city being transformed by post-Mao modernisation. "Situated at the intersection of three provinces," the local government guidebook informed me, "Xingyi has historically been a key communications, and collecting and distributing centre in the region. Surrounded by undulating hills and intersecting rivers, the area is notable for its limestone formations. With its beautiful countryside and temperate climate, Xingyi – the home of many illustrious historical figures – has much undeveloped potential as a tourist destination."

Arriving in Xingyi, on our way from Guilin to Chengdu, felt like stepping into a time warp. Everything in the city reminded me of early 1980s Beijing and Shanghai: the streets, the clothes, the shops, and especially the municipal government guest house that we stayed in, with its shabby decor, malfunctioning room fittings and leaky bathrooms, its clueless receptionists, chambermaids who never changed your towels, and waiters and waitresses who ignored diners in the main restaurant to minister to raucous private rooms of local officials, its ceaseless din of karaoke and its noticeboards passing off romanised Chinese as English.

What really took me back twenty years was the yard full of high-priced cars and the self-important officials getting out of them. The only way to ensure the attention of the staff in a guest house like this is to impress upon them, the moment you swagger inside, just how important you are. Otherwise, your laundry will disappear, your breakfast token be misplaced, and your personal belongings get "tidied away", never to be found again. Sometimes your room – for which you have already paid – will even be taken away for an official meeting, while your dinner will fail to materialise, because the cooks have knocked off after producing yet another banquet for government bigwigs.

In the two nights and three days that we spent in the city, Toby and I got the full Xingyi experience, with cockroaches, bedbugs and a violent midnight encounter with a roaring drunk, karaoke-singing cadre thrown in as special bonuses.

But, as Nietzsche once said, what doesn't kill you makes you stronger. My original intention had been to start my interviews in Chengdu, in Sichuan province, western China, but while attending the wedding of the friend who translated my first book, *The Good Women of China*, I happened to encounter my first storyteller: the Medicine Woman of Xingyi.

Early one morning, Toby and I – just as we always do in China – were wandering about the streets, people-watching. A couple of hours before 9 a.m., the streets of Xingyi were already bustling with commercial activity: with peddlers and stalls run by local farmers and fishermen, selling various exotic local delicacies, including the mountain mushrooms for which the area is famous. We stepped into a dark, narrow lane running parallel to the main market street, and back through history: past the kind of dilapidated houses and shopfronts I associate with films depicting the "old" (pre-1949) society. What immediately struck me was that most of the shopkeepers and stallholders were women: in addition to those mending shoes, carving chopsticks, selling haberdashery, making burial clothes and paper funeral money, a great number were selling local speciality foods and herbal medicine.

My attention was caught, from some distance, by an old woman whose face shone with a particular, resolute intelligence. She was sitting in an open-front shop talking to a customer. Various kinds of dried herbal medicines were displayed around her: some hanging in bags, some on shelves, tied in bundles; others heaped on the ground at her feet.

I pointed her out to Toby. "She's the only one on this lane who doesn't look worn-down, demoralised by life. I wonder why she seems so different from everyone else round here."

"Go and talk to her, I'll wait. We're not in a hurry." Toby knows that I love these opportunities to chat casually with Chinese women – spontaneous encounters can yield unexpected information.

I waited until the old lady had finished with her customer, then walked over and started up a conversation. "Hello. Are these herbs all grown round here?"

"They are," Yao Popo (Chinese for Medicine Woman) replied in a Hunan accent, without even looking up from the bunch of herbs she was binding.

"What about these? Where are these from?" I asked again, trying to get her to open up.

She finally looked up at me. "I don't pick them myself. Local farmers bring me my stock."

I climbed one of the two low steps in front of her shop. "You must be famous round here, then."

"I'm just an ordinary old woman," she smiled. "I've been here a long time, that's all."

"So when did you start selling medicine?"

"Oh, years ago. Was there anything particular you were looking for?" Yao Popo eyed Toby, standing a little way back from the shop. A foreigner would be a rare sight in provincial Xingyi. "Who's that?"

"My husband," I quickly explained.

The Medicine Woman squinted. "He's tall. And handsome. My daughter married a foreigner too, a Taiwanese." A lot of people in rural China think that anyone from outside the mainland counts as a foreigner – even if they are ethnic Chinese. "He treats her well, but he's not much to look at."

It was my turn to smile. "Are a man's looks so very important?"

"Of course!" she frowned. "Or you'll have ugly children."

I smiled because I knew how to get her to talk to me now. "How many children do you have?"

She was delighted to be asked. "Two sons and five daughters, a dozen grandchildren and four great-grandchildren!"

Yet again, I was reminded of how much importance Chinese women attach to having children. "Goodness me. Lucky you."

"How about you?" Yao Popo asked me, suddenly looking worried on my behalf.

I felt touched by her concern. "Just the one son. He's eighteen."

"Only one?" Yao Popo was unable to conceal her sense of regret. "At least you had a boy, I suppose. Back then, when I was young, we were told to have lots. If you didn't, everyone said you were a bad woman."

In the 1950s, ignoring the warnings of demographers and economists, Mao Zedong encouraged women to have as many children as they could, telling them it was a heroic thing to do. He thought that its enormous population would turn China into a global superpower.

I next asked a question to which I already knew the answer. "You're a woman – do you really think sons are better than daughters?"

She stared uncomprehendingly at me. "It's because we're women that we need to have sons, to protect us. Before 1949, women who didn't manage to have sons really suffered. Girls were always abandoned before boys. I almost starved to death myself. I wouldn't be here today, if my father hadn't taken pity on me."

I climbed the second step. "I'd like to hear about your life."

She batted a hand at me dismissively. "What's there to hear? No one takes notice of what us old people have to say, not even my children. What good would it do you if I told you? Don't waste your time, or your husband's. Off you go, he's waiting for you."

Glancing around to check there were no other customers about, I sat down on a small stool next to her. "I'm not going until you've told me about yourself!"

She looked at me, surprised. "Do you really mean it?" she said, more seriously.

I nodded. "I want to be able to tell my son about people like you. He moved to England six years ago, when he was only twelve. He has no idea about ordinary Chinese people's lives. Whenever I come back to China, I ask people I meet whether they know about their mothers' lives. Most of them don't know their mothers' or their grandmothers' stories. I want to write them down, for later generations to read. I don't want everything your generation suffered to be forgotten. If our children don't know how their grandparents suffered, they won't know how lucky they are. Tell me why you seem so different from everyone else on this street, why you look so happy and calm."

She shook her head. "I've suffered much more than anyone else round here."

She told me she had been born seventy-nine years ago in Hunan. As her mother had died when she was four and the family was very poor, her father gave her and five of her brothers and sisters away to other people. She went to a travelling medicinal herb seller, to whom she was later apprenticed, and who also had a foster son, five years older than her, who could play the huqin, a kind of two-stringed Chinese violin. Because she was quick-witted, a fast learner, her adopted family took a liking to her. At the time, itinerant physicians used music and acrobatics to attract custom to their roadside stalls, and she quickly mastered various gymnastic tricks for the purpose – such as handstands, headstands, spinning jars on the soles of her feet. At the same time, the medicine man began passing on to his children some of his knowledge about herbal prescriptions. At the start of the 1940s, with the country torn apart by war, he decided to move the family over the mountains from Hunan to Yunnan, to escape the fighting. As they were too poor to travel by train, they walked and begged lifts wherever they could, on carts, railway repair wagons, and so on. Worried that, as an unmarried girl, his adopted daughter might be abused by passing soldiers, the father quickly married off his two children. After wandering about the mountains of Guizhou for a few years from 1946, in 1950 they arrived in Xingyi, which at that time had just been liberated by the Communists. The municipal government persuaded them to settle there, and helped them to open a Chinese medicine clinic for the local population, which had almost no access to medical treatment. Barely twenty years old at the time, the Medicine Woman looked after her growing family and sold prescriptions from home, while her father went out on domiciliary visits and her husband ran the clinic.

"Life was hard in those years," Yao Popo remembered, "with seven young children. Every day I worried about what we'd eat the next. Luckily, everyone listened to what Chairman Mao said, about it being good to have lots of children, and the government and the neighbours helped out when things got difficult. It's not like now, when no one trusts anyone else, no one helps anyone. Back then, officials never took advantage of you. Or ever forced us to pass any medical certificate." At the same time, she was gaining a reputation for her medical skills; some people even thought her prescriptions better than her husband's.

"You probably don't believe me, but I can tell what's wrong with a person from the look in his eyes, or the colour of his face – even from the smell of his farts or burps. I'm best at curing headaches, stomach aches and joint aches."

The idea was extraordinary: that she could see straight into you, like an X-ray machine. The fierce certainty on her face made me believe her though.

I very much wanted to know why she thought life back then was so different from China today. "What happened afterwards?" I asked instead.

"When? The sixties and seventies? I made a lot of money!" Yao Popo's eyes glinted mischievously.

"You made money during the Cultural Revolution?" I thought I must have misheard. For so long, I had heard nothing but anger, grief and loss in recollections of this period. I had encountered so many victims that I sometimes wondered where all the perpetrators of this misery – the millions of violent, even murderous Red Guards – could have disappeared off to.

Seeing my incomprehension, she smiled. "I'm telling the truth: I really did! With everyone arguing and fighting and making revolution, the hospitals and medical schools had all shut down. But the revolution wasn't curing their sickness; it was making it worse. So more and more people came to me for medicine. I was revolutionary too; I helped a lot of people who couldn't afford medicine, for free. I made my money from the rebels, from the Red Guards. Because if they'd just taken my medicine, if they'd not paid me for it, they would have been no better than capi-talists. Though I didn't actually want too much of their money. I was worried that if they became poor, they'd make even more revolution. Yes, I made a lot of money in the Cultural Revolution, but I also saw terrible things: people forced to confess things they hadn't done, punished for crimes they hadn't committed; everyone was terrified the whole time. The money didn't make me happy."

Those bright eyes dulled. I changed the subject. "Now that your children have grown up, do they help you out with money?"

She threw her head back. "I don't want their money, I'm richer than they are. Last week, when my great-grandson got married, I gave him 5,000 yuan!"* Thinking of her family again cheered her up.

"How many of your children and grandchildren have studied Chinese medicine like you?" I pictured her lecturing a classroom full of her descendants.

"None of them!"

"Why?"

I could hear no regret in Yao Popo's voice. "They say it's not a proper job, there's no money in it, or respect."

I supposed that their scorn was directed at her acrobatic past. Traditionally, it was thought that athletes and dancers were physically strong because they were mentally weak. Although the Chinese have always liked entertainment, they don't respect entertainers. I was surprised to discover the prejudice had survived into the twenty-first century.

"But you earn more money than them. And you've led such an excep-tional life. Everyone knows you, respects you round here."

She bent over to whisper into my ear: "They don't know anything about my past, about the money I've earned; I've never told them. They don't think I know anything; they think I'm just an odd-job woman. Whenever I give them money, they always think it's from my husband, or my father. But I've earned a lot more money than them over the years. Men only know how to treat old illnesses, they can't adapt to new ones. They're no good at business, either. They're too proud to work on a stall."

"What do you mean by old and new illnesses?"

"Old illnesses are the ones everyone's known about for hundreds and thou-sands of years – the symptoms tell you straight away what they are. Every

---

* At 2007 rates, approximately US$700, €460, £350.

family used to have a grandfather or a grandmother who had a bit of medical know-how in the old illnesses: for example, if a person's stomach was sore, they'd best not take any medicine or eat anything. Just drink warm water, rest the stomach and it would soon get better. Stomach problems are at the bottom of most things: headaches, backaches, sleeping problems. Settle the stomach, and everything else will right itself. But these days, I see more and more new illnesses: sore eyes and back from sitting in front of the computer, or in an office, acne from eating too much McDonald's, stomach upsets from too much travelling, earache from too much karaoke, exhaustion from too much driving . . ."

Looking down at my watch and seeing that Toby had been waiting almost an hour, I decided to interrupt Yao Popo's list of modern complaints. "After working hard for so many years, are you planning to retire?" My bottom was numb from sitting on that small wooden stool. I could barely imagine how she could have sat there for seven or eight hours every day for most of her working life.

"Why would I do that? My foster-father's well over ninety and he's still treating patients; his eyes and ears are still good – he's probably healthier than I am. My husband and I are rushed off our feet with the business – we now stock four hundred different herbs. Every day we sell at least thirty or forty different varieties, sometimes over a hundred. That's tens of thousands every year . . . Is he taking a photograph of us?" On discovering Toby aiming his camera at us, Yao Popo suddenly drew herself up and sat facing forward, rigidly straight-backed on her stool, hands folded neatly on her knees. "Has he finished yet?" she whispered to me as she posed. "Has he finished?"

When I told her Toby was done, she relaxed back into her usual posture. While she was clearly in good health, her shoulders had the inevitable hunch of old age.

"Tell your husband to photograph me straight-on. I broke my nose when I slipped doing acrobatics in my youth. My children never got to see how pretty I once was."

Her vanity took me by surprise. The Chinese prize modesty above all other virtues. If we work with other people, we're always trying to pass the credit for successes and achievements onto them; if we do a thing on our own, we'll say we did it badly. A mother will say at her own daughter's wedding how ugly her child is, or how much less clever than other people's children. Her regret for her lost beauty was the first time I had encountered such frankness in twenty years.

I told her I had to go because my son and two other students were waiting for me, but that I wanted to bring PanPan to see her after lunch. She clearly didn't believe she'd see me again. "Come back if you've time," she shrugged. "You look like a busy person."

A little while after noon, PanPan, a couple of female students and I reappeared in front of her shop. "So you really did come back," she beamed at us. "And with these fine young people! Sit down, I've stools for all of you."

She seemed to have just finished her lunch: an empty bowl and pair of chopsticks were lying in the bamboo basket next to her, along with a handful of spring onions and some wild mountain peppers. The Hunanese can eat furiously spicy food. Perhaps she was taking advantage of a lull in business to prepare dinner. An ancient Thermos flask stood next to the basket, alongside a rubbish-filled shopping bag.

I told her that PanPan wanted to give her a poster of London. Also, one of the students, Y, wanted something for her skin allergy, while the other student, K, wanted to take some professional-quality photos of her. Though I'd expected her to refuse to be photographed, she seemed delighted and immediately agreed, even thanking us for our time.

She was very taken with the poster of Tower Bridge. "What a beautiful building!" she exclaimed to herself. "The bridge opens, you say? I've never seen anything like it! What country is London in? Why's it called London? What does it mean?" As I had no answers to her questions, I pushed Y forward. "Could you take a look at her?"

Y pulled up her shirt. Her skin looked terrible, covered in great patches of suppurating lumps and bumps. Without blinking an eye, Yao Popo beckoned her inside. "Three doses of my medicine and it'll be better."

Y and I followed her doubtfully into the shop, where she got down from a shelf a wooden box filled with ground walnuts, peanuts and red dates, on which a number of small brown-winged insects were feeding. Yao Popo then got Y to pick out twenty-one of the fattest, liveliest insects, which she deftly caught and divided between three blue-and-white medicine capsules. She instructed the student to take the three capsules over the course of a single day – checking that the insects were still alive before swallowing them – and to take the first now. "Don't be afraid," she told Y as she passed her the first capsule, "I've fed them only on nuts and fruit. They're much cleaner inside than us."

Y looked first at the insects wriggling inside the capsule, and then questioningly at me. I didn't know what to say to her. After a brief hesitation, she asked me to pour her a large cup of water. She took a deep breath then, still rather nervously, swallowed the capsule down. I was impressed by her intrepidity – a rare quality among her generation of cosseted only children.

She obeyed the Medicine Woman's instructions to the letter, swallowing the remaining two doses over the next twelve hours, checking both times that the insects were still alive. Very soon, her itching stopped; a couple of days later, her scabbed skin miraculously healed over.

Just before we said goodbye, Yao Popo told us about the unhappiest and the happiest times in her life. Her first great source of unhappiness had been growing up without parents, without a home of her own, and with only a damp mud floor to sleep on. The second hardest thing had been bringing up seven children in a tiny room of only twelve metres square. While they were small, she'd not had a moment's peace, day or night. The third had been breaking the bridge of her beautiful nose. A good nose, she said, was a woman's most important feature. The single thing that brought her greatest happiness was that all her children had survived the famine of the 1950s and '60s in which so many millions had died, and that her grandchildren had gone to school and had children of their own. The second great blessing for which she was thankful was that her husband had never hit her. Her third source of pleasure over the years had been sitting in front of the shop, day in, day out, watching the world changing around her.

"In the thirty or forty years I've been sitting here, the city centre's changed every time someone has taken over the local government," she said, pointing to the buildings towering over her poky lane. "Those houses to your left date from the 1950s. Hardly anything was built during the Cultural Revolution, but the ones opposite are from the 1980s, while the buildings to the right went up within the last two years. Now I hear the new mayor wants to rip them down and start again! As soon as they have a bit of cash in their pockets, officials always want to show off, changing everything too quickly for anyone to catch up. But no one's ever thought of fixing this crumbling old lane of ours, even though hundreds of people live here. I'll retire when they finally do something about that," she laughed.

We waved goodbye to Yao Popo, but every straight nose I have since seen has made me think of her – an old woman whose yearning for beauty had not been ground out of her by poverty.

2

Two Generations of the Lin Family: The Curse of a Legend

From left, the "Double-Gun Woman", her husband, her son-in-law Lin Xiangbei, and his wife.

Mr Lin with his daughter and grandchildren.

LIN XIANGBEI, aged eighty-nine, son and son-in-law of revolutionary martyrs, *interviewed in Chengdu, the capital of Sichuan province in south-western China. Lin's father called him "comrade" when he was ten, and Lin joined the Communist Party before he was twenty. But he was branded a counter-revolutionary because he married the daughter of Chen Lianshi, the legendary "Double-Gun Woman", a Chinese revolutionary, and because his father had been Chen Lianshi's lover. He spent over twenty years as a political prisoner and lost family members on both sides during the struggle between the Communist Party and the Nationalist Party from the 1930s to the 1970s. Six of his seven children survived more or less as orphans.*

In China, the "Double-Gun Woman" is a national heroine: a legendary female revolutionary, ruthlessly dispatching enemies and traitors with a gun in each hand, dry-eyed even at the deaths of her husband and children – as fast as a bandit, as tough as a peasant.

In the Archives of the Imperial Academy stored in Beijing Library (which, by some miracle, survived the Cultural Revolution), we can trace the family history of the Double-Gun Woman, Chen Lianshi, back through several generations. Her earliest traceable ancestor on her mother's side is an imperial academician from Sichuan called Kang Yiming, who served during the reign of the Qing emperor Jiaqing (1796–1820). Her father's forebears were equally illustrious, many of them scholar-officials or high-ranking military men.

After the foundation of the Republic in 1912, several members of the family left Sichuan to study elsewhere, some heading to Japan, some joining Sun Yat-sen's revolutionary Tongmeng Society. Having been, in the last years of the Qing, a high-ranking official renowned for his justness and benevolence, and for his work in helping the poor and needy, her father was selected as member of parliament for the area.

Sources that emerged during the 1980s state that, as a girl, "the Double-Gun Woman demonstrated exceptional intelligence, covering in two and a half years the curriculum that took most students seven. After enrolling at the local women's Normal College, she then passed the entrance examination to one of the country's top universities in Nanjing, where she hoped to help her country by studying to become a teacher. She excelled also at painting." The Double-Gun Woman was clearly neither a poor peasant, nor an illiterate bandit.

In Communist China, the designation of national heroes has been a fiercely controlled business. Under Mao, in particular, only members of the proletariat – workers or peasants – were officially permitted to be heroic. More or less since Chinese history began, the country's great patriotic heroes have been mostly male: unflinching individuals permitted to shed tears in only two cataclysmic sets of circumstances: at the death of their mother, or the loss of the motherland. With the rise to power of the Communists – and of the idea that "women hold up half the sky" – women, too, were allowed to become national heroes, but only in the superhuman, patriotic male mould. When I was very small, I saw *Red Crag*, a classic revolutionary film of the 1960s featuring the Double-Gun Woman. In a 1995 book about her published in China, Chen Lianshi wasn't allowed to behave like normal women – weeping at the execution of her husband, or at the death of her daughter. She had to be invulnerable: a Party killing machine devoted to robbing the rich to help the poor.

A few years ago, while researching the possibility of publishing a book about the Double-Gun Woman outside China, I was lucky enough to meet her son-in-law, Lin, her grandson and her five granddaughters. After I had heard them talk about their mother and grandmother, she began to take shape in my mind. In particular, three things furthered my understanding of this national heroine and of the historical period she lived through.

The first was a 1926 painting by her, *A Fish Rises to Jiang Taigong's Bait*. At the time, her husband had been seriously wounded in an armed uprising against a local warlord, in which a great number of their comrades-in-arms had been lost and many others had gone over to the enemy. In these bloodily uncertain circumstances, the unit to which the Double-Gun Woman belonged found itself under constant threat of annihilation. Studying the delicate strokes of the fish scales and the ripples in the water, together with the relaxed lines of the fisherman, it seems incredible that the painting was completed in such dire circumstances. It is equally hard to imagine that the hand capable of such refined brushwork could, hours, or even minutes later, take up a gun and open fire with ruthless impunity. How could a single individual be made up of two such contradictory impulses? The turmoil of twentieth-century China has forced its people – its artists included – to coexist for long periods of time alongside the near constant threat of violence. While war has not succeeded in annihilating modern Chinese culture, it has left an indelible imprint on its development.

Second, I learned that the Double-Gun Woman had had two lovers. The first had been her husband, killed by the Nationalists. What had attracted Chen Lianshi – so exceptional in both looks and talent, a woman who could have had any man she chose – to an obscure young man from the countryside? It was not only his looks and abilities, but also his courage: the courage to stand in the vanguard of his era, to wake – in a people numbed by the suffering of war – a new sense of national pride and dignity. The second was Lin's father, an unconventional idealist who stood by her for the rest of her life though she would never marry him. As a surrogate for the married life they could never enjoy themselves, they eventually betrothed their two children – Lin, and Chen's daughter, Jun. Chen's husband was her inspiration, a soulmate to whom she would remain loyal till her death by refusing ever to remarry, while Lin's father provided her emotional ballast, willing to efface himself almost completely to give her the unconditional love and support she needed.

These two different presences in her life – the great love to whom she devoted herself, and the emotional prop from whom she drew the devotion she herself required – comfortably complemented each other. A great many people feel the need for similar kinds of close, complementary relationships in their lives. But for thousands of years, right up until the 1980s, Chinese women who required ballast outside their marriages were condemned as faithless "bad women", and were punished, even murdered by their fathers and husbands for forming such attachments. Like so many chaste widows of the Chinese past, the Double-Gun Woman, widowed at thirty-five, put up with decades of lonely nights after her husband's death, in order to protect her reputation. I don't know how she stood it. At no point in Chinese history was it ever suggested that remaining virtuously loyal to a dead husband's memory was a form of tyranny, or self-harm. Even the Double-Gun Woman – in all other respects, a liberated, educated modern Chinese woman – found herself unable to shake off the shackles of tradition, demonstrating the slow pace at which civilisation changes and progresses.

The third thing that I discovered concerned the death of the Double-Gun Woman in 1960.

Chen Lianshi died in 1960 of anger and regret, after the failure of the last uprising – involving some thousand people – she organised and led against Nationalist Forces, on Huaying Mountain in Sichuan. In the waves of political campaigns that started in the 1950s, the leaders of the Huaying Mountain guerrillas were condemned by China's Communist rulers as "bandits", "traitors" and "counter-revolutionaries", their failure blamed on treachery. As a result of these groundless charges, not long after 1949 the Double-Gun Woman and her comrades-in-arms were forced out of the Party. The woman who had sacrificed everything – for the Party – including her husband and daughter was denounced as a traitor.

Some said that she died of sorrow and resentment because her Party membership was never returned to her. Party membership was not only a source of personal validation and identity, it was also a promise she had made to her husband, who had also devoted his life to the Party and wished that she should remain faithful to it until her final breath. And yet the Party had rejected her. Some said that she died of despair, because the cause to which she had devoted herself – the Party that was supposed to be for the People – turned its back on hundreds of thousands of innocent victims of the Huaying Mountain Uprising. Why had it abandoned them? The damning official verdict on the uprising turned the children of the "treacherous" guerrillas into orphans and beggars. And yet the Double-Gun Woman silently left this world without pronouncing final judgement on the Party that had dominated her life.

In July 1960, Chen Lianshi lay alone in hospital, dying of cancer, her relatives – punished for her own political disgrace – scattered far and wide. A woman who had denounced her came to visit – perhaps because she had been tormented at night by the ghostly cries of those who had been persecuted to death, or perhaps because she had seen for herself children who had lost their parents in political campaigns picking food out of rubbish, or perhaps because the grief and anger of the Double-Gun Woman had woken her conscience. No one really knew why the woman secretly approached the Double-Gun Woman's bed to beg her forgiveness. She took the skeletal hand of the Double-Gun Woman in both her hands. On the Double-Gun Woman's wrist was the dark green jade bracelet that, all those years before, her husband had given her. Face to face with the revolutionary heroine that she had denounced, the woman wept. In the ten years that had passed since the political trauma to which she had subjected Chen Lianshi – organising a small group charged exclusively with collecting a dossier of materials against her and orchestrating a succession of progressively more frenzied denunciation meetings – a great many other campaigns had taken place. By 1960, the woman herself had suffered from political violence and had long since regretted her actions. But there is no medicine to heal the pain of regret.

By this point too weak to speak, the Double-Gun Woman placed the woman's hand on her bracelet, indicated that she should remove it, then tremblingly placed it on the woman's own wrist. She smiled, a single tear rolling down her cheek, then closed her eyes again. The woman could sense the gesture was a kind of pardon, and on learning later that the family were looking for the bracelet, she was even more moved by the Double-Gun Woman's generosity of spirit.

Chen Lianshi's grandchildren were shaken when they found out. They had thought they'd understood their grandmother at the end; they thought that she had died angry and resentful. Instead, she had died forgiving her bitter enemy. By placing this family heirloom on her enemy's wrist, Chen Lianshi had embraced her as a member of her own family.

I cried every time I heard this story. In the two decades I have worked as a journalist, I've frequently been moved by the ease with which China's old people forgive. Some people cite this generosity as proof of their numbness and lack of spirit. I can't agree. You can see the sorrow they still feel: in the tears they shed as they tell you their stories; in the twitching of their hands as they unearth painful memories. But, somehow, many of them manage to forgive the terrible things that history has done to them, the callous, unjust treatment they have received at the hands of the Party – as easily as they forgive the mistakes of children. But while we should commend their refusal to pass the bitterness of their tragedies down through the generations, we still need to commemorate their suffering.

On 3 August 2006, I arrived in Chengdu, intending to interview the surviving family of the Double-Gun Woman: her son-in-law Lin and her grandchildren. This was the fifth trip I'd made to Chengdu. I still remembered very clearly how poor and run-down it had looked on my first visit at the end of the 1970s, how primitive and backward. In the 1980s, incomes in Chengdu seemed on average several times lower than in other Chinese cities. But the Chengdu I now saw was a refreshing contrast: clean, well ordered, no longer cluttered with ramshackle old hotpot and dumpling stalls – clearly a place on the up.

My awareness of the changes that time had brought intensified during the time I spent with the Lin family, especially as I flicked through albums of photos taken between the 1950s and 1980s. I could sense a deep sadness in the expressions of the people I saw pictured, even in the children. The 89-year-old Lin, in particular, seemed to be carrying a heavy weight inside him. Even though he would laugh and joke when talking about China and about his life, you could sense the reserve in him, typical of many Chinese people: an unwillingness to discuss personal things or political views. It was, it seemed, only in his poetry that Lin truly revealed himself. He seemed to have shut himself firmly away in a box, as so many Chinese have done and continue to do. I wanted to find out what lay inside.

Because of the work Lin had done as a young man helping survivors of the Huaying Mountain Uprising, and because he was married to the daughter of the "traitor" Chen Lianshi, the government branded him a dissident – "a Rightist" – when he was barely thirty. Having joined and offered outstanding service to the Communist Party before he was twenty, he was hit hard by the label of counter-revolutionary. "Chairman Mao," he had sobbed to himself, "why don't you come and save me?" Accused and reaccused throughout every political campaign of the Maoist period – the Four Clean-Ups, the Anti-Rightist movement and the Cultural Revolution – he ended up spending the best part of thirty years in and out of prison, during which time he lost his mother-in-law and great mentor, the Double-Gun Woman, and his wife, her daughter. His six children were forced to survive alone, wandering the streets like beggars, scorned and humiliated by society. But, as his acerbically satirical poems reveal, his spirit survived and was even strengthened by his tragic experiences.

After the Cultural Revolution, he wrote his autobiography at the age of seventy with the help of his daughter, Lin Xue. Reading it, I was once more reminded of the generosity and vitality of the Chinese. I saw in it an innocent, though doggedly determined child refusing to accept defeat, even at the hands of his own father; a rebellious teenager, unhappy at his father's choice of second wife; a young man falling in love, at the same time as his father, with the legendary Double-Gun Woman, though this was no blind, youthful hero-worship; a mature adult constantly searching for the truth, reflecting on the best means of saving China, adoring his wife, and weeping over his children's suffering. Perhaps the most remarkable thing of all was that, even after decades of political persecution, he remained a free man, capable of independent thought and perfectly at ease with himself because – like his legendary mother-in-law – he had remained throughout all his ordeals a man of honour.

When I asked if I could interview him, he requested that we meet outside his home. I agreed, as sometimes overfamiliar surroundings and associations can inhibit the process of remembering.

And so I met Mr Lin in my hotel room. I also asked his relatives to let us speak alone, for I knew that people often disclose secrets to strangers that they conceal from their children. I guessed that there were at least two

Lins, on the one hand a father and grandfather respected by his family for his dignity and self-control; and on the other a fiery, uninhibited, passionate revolutionary. Later, when he showed me a picture of his new wife, I had said how pretty she still was in her sixties. Turning away from his daughters, Lin winked at me. "I wouldn't have married her if she'd been ugly!" he whispered, revealing the exuberance that none of his sufferings had been able to subdue. I wanted to discover who the real Lin was.

Below is an excerpt from our talk in the hotel.

*

XINRAN: Some people say that a person's life is decided by their personality. Would you agree?

LIN: Yes.

XINRAN: Why? Could you describe your personality to me?

LIN: Your personality causes you to make choices. Take me: I've always been competitive, always hated losing – even to my father. We used to skim stones together, across the river by our house. You got a point every time the stone bounced on the water. When we started, he'd always win a lot more points than me because I hadn't got the hang of it, but quite soon I began to beat him. His stones would sink halfway across, while mine often got to the other side, fifty or sixty metres away. I still remember how surprised he was when I first managed it. I practised and practised, just because I didn't want to be beaten by someone else.

*

At this point, Lin – suddenly a teenager again – gave me a quick demonstration of his throwing technique. I had no idea how he had maintained his joy in life through those three lonely prison-like decades. How had someone as competitive as him tolerated so many years of public disgrace? For the time being, I didn't dare put such a sensitive question to him.

*

XINRAN: What shaped your personality?

LIN: I think I've been influenced by three people: my father, my aunt and my mother-in-law, the Double-Gun Woman. It was my aunt who first taught me never to accept defeat. Because my mother died while giving birth to me, my father sent me off to live with his older sister. She was incredibly good to me, treated me like her own son. From time to time, she even lectured her own children that they shouldn't bully me, because I didn't have a mother. She was very sensitive to complaints from her parents-in-law that I was getting free board, so at the start of each month, she would

33

secretly give me five or ten yuan then get me to give it to her in front of everyone else and say my father had sent it to pay for my food. One summer, I remember, when my cousins all had white linen waistcoats to wear, my aunt gave me an extra two yuan, then got me to give it back to her in front of her husband and say my grandmother had sent it to pay for some summer clothes. The next day she produced the white waistcoat she'd already bought me. She would often say to me when we were alone that as long as I worked hard, I'd have a good life. But if I didn't work hard, if I didn't do something with my life, it would reflect badly on her. From that moment on, I struggled constantly to be the best at everything I did.

It was my father who gave me my belief in the Communist Party. I remember once, when I was still very small, seeing my father looking out over the river by our house, deep in thought. I walked over and asked him what he was thinking about. "All sorts of things," he answered. "I'll tell you when you're older."

"Don't worry," I said to him. "When I get bigger, I'll be a filial son and earn plenty of money to look after you and Granny."

Father shook his head. "I want more than a filial son," he said seriously. "When you're older, I want you to be a revolutionary, a comrade."

Though my teachers at school talked a lot about China's national crisis, about the heroes who were working to save the motherland, I didn't really understand much of it, and certainly didn't know what a comrade was, or why it was so important to my father.

"Comrades struggle together towards a common revolutionary goal," he told me. "Being a comrade is more important than being filial, because a filial son is loyal only to his family, while a comrade is loyal to his motherland."

"Let me be your comrade, Father! Tell me what you were thinking about just now."

Father smiled, then thought for a while. "Do you think I'm mad?" he said eventually.

"Only the local officials say you're mad. Ordinary people say you're a good person, and my teachers and classmates all say you're a good father."

Father smiled again. "You're sounding more and more like a comrade."

And then there was Chen Lianshi – my teacher, my surrogate mother almost. It was mainly through her guidance that I became the person I am today. It was through a winter coat that I first came to hear of her.

One evening, while I was eating dinner, a courier came to tell me that a big parcel had arrived for me. Hurrying to the post office to pick it up, I immediately saw it was postmarked Chongqing, which was where my father was, though his name wasn't on the parcel. Inside, I found a brand-new herringbone wool coat, but no message. Because it had been the middle of summer when I left home, I'd only brought thin clothes with me. Now, though, the weather had turned cold. A friend of my father's had given me a cotton-padded army coat, but it was too big – so long it reached down to my feet. Afraid of being laughed at, I only used it as a quilt at night. The friend's wife had also given me an old cotton jacket. Though it was warm enough, I was embarrassed to wear it, because I'd just started courting, and what I really wanted was a properly smart winter coat in which to parade up and down the streets of the small county town I was then living in. And now I had one: but who was my mysterious benefactor?

That evening, I dreamed my mother stood before my bed, her eyes red from crying. "It's so cold outside," she said, "and you've so few warm clothes. Your grandmother used to look after you when you were small, but now, you're all on your own, away from home. Why isn't your father looking after you? Here, try this warm coat I made you. Does it fit?"

The mother in my dream was so young, so pretty and kind. I buried my head in her warm, comforting chest, then looked up to see her smiling and crying. I began laughing with joy that I had such a beautiful and loving mother. My own laughter woke me, and I realised the whole thing had been just a dream – apart from the coat, which I was still lying under.

Unable to go back to sleep, I made up a poem in my head:

> I was saved by a lucky star,
> In the darkness, I saw a light.
> A coat brought me warmth,
> And my mother back to me.

The next day, I wrote to Father, asking him who had sent the coat; he was as surprised to hear about it as me. Much, much later, I finally received a letter telling me that a revolutionary heroine called Chen Lianshi had sent it to me. I began to imagine to myself what the great Chen Lianshi was like, wishing I could have had a mother like her. The first time I met her was with my father. By this point, I'd heard any number of stories and legends about her: about her incredible marksmanship, and about her generosity and concern for others, for the society around her. She wasn't one of those people who joined the revolution hoping for a better life for themselves and their families – she had a genius for sensing other people's needs. She'd learned honesty and a sense of justice from mountain bandits, simplicity and courage from workers and peasants, her moral principles from religion, and cunning and ingenuity from merchants and traders. She could cut through complexities and difficulties as easily as a fish swims through water. You've heard the jade bracelet story, haven't you? It took an extraordinary person to do something like that.

XINRAN: I read your four volumes of poetry last night. One is entitled *Remembering Jun*, in memory of your late wife. In another, *Regret for My Family*, you mention Hua – was she your daughter?

LIN: Our first daughter. When my wife was heavily pregnant with her, we got a tip-off that we were about to be arrested, that the police would come for us in the middle of the night. We left our home there and then, in a torrential downpour. But we couldn't think where to go: there was a friend of my father's, but we weren't sure he'd dare take us in. There we stood, in the rain, under the umbrella, until I managed to hitch a lift for my wife on a narrow, single-wheeled cart to the friend's house – I ran along beside it. He was very good to us, and hid us somewhere no one would find us. But soon after we'd got there, Jun's labour began. We didn't even have a bed for her to lie on; we just put lots of rice straw on the ground. We didn't have anything for the birth, nothing was sterile; we just had to make do. And even after the child was born, there was fighting to be done and we had to move on. As we couldn't take Hua with us, we left her with a local family. A little later on, she got pneumonia. Though it would be easily treated these days, back then the peasants were very ignorant and superstitious. They all worshipped a dead carpenter, and believed that earth from his grave would cure any sickness. Without proper medical care, forced to eat mud, she died – just two years old. There was no one to blame, really, just ignorance, because the locals thought eating earth from a good man's grave could cure sickness. Thinking about it still makes me sad.

*

His voice died away.

*

XINRAN: I'm sorry. I shouldn't have made you go back over these painful memories.

LIN: Don't worry. I'm used to them.

*

36

He's become used to pain, I thought – another of the legacies of China's traumatic last century of modernisation. But should people have to get used to pain? I now decided to ask him the question I had backed away from earlier.

*

XINRAN: I cried yesterday when I read your books, especially *The Red Monk* and *Happiness in Old Age*. There's such a sense of mourning, of suffering in your books. You've said yourself that you've always been ambitious and competitive. But, for decades, you lived without public acknowledgement or understanding; society turned its back on you. You insist that you love your motherland, that you believe in the Party. You yourself know you're a good person. But when you were persecuted as a Rightist, when your children were suffering because of who their father was, did you ever feel regret at what you'd done? If you could live your life again, would you make the same choices?

*

For almost two and a half minutes, old Mr Lin sat before me, staring up at the ceiling, his face twisted with pain. I didn't press him for an answer. I know my question is one that many elderly Chinese people would like to be able to answer.

After two hours I felt that I had come closer to the real Lin, though I hoped the process had not distressed him too much. I hoped the act of speaking out had lightened the burden of memory for him. Concerned that our conversation had had a bad effect on his blood pressure and heart condition, I rang his youngest daughter, Ping, later that evening to check up on him. She was surprised by my anxiety; since the interview, her father's blood pressure had remained unusually stable.

Lin had seven children with Jun: one son and five daughters, in addition to Hua. The son I only saw three times, and found him to be very shy and introverted. The daughters, however, were a real phenomenon – true granddaughters of the Double-Gun Woman. There was the frank, forthright Xue; the refined, gentle Bo; the thoughtful, artistic He; the tough, stoical Zhi; and the multitalented Ping. When I asked them what they thought about the parentless childhood that their parents' and grandmother's radicalism had bequeathed them, they had no complaints. Xue, the eldest, said that she and her sisters had been too young to have any idea what was happening. They were divided when I asked them whether

37

they thought their elders' revolutionary endeavours had been worthwhile. But when I asked them to name the single most important force determining the course of their family's life and suffering, all five sisters replied: "History." How should we define the force that is history? Who should take responsibility for it?

In a book that Xue edited about her grandmother, I found the following passage:

> Imagine that Chen Lianshi had not fallen in love with the radical young man who became her husband; that they had not gone to university in Nanjing after marrying, or that their student careers had not coincided with the anti-imperialist demonstrations of 1925; imagine that her husband had not become a student leader and that he had not been captured by spies, thereby forcing him to return to his home village. Imagine, again, that the two of them hadn't joined the armed uprising against north Sichuan's warlords, or that they hadn't subsequently fled to Huaying Mountain to continue their struggle for ten long years. Would Chen Lianshi still have become the Double-Gun Woman? Assuredly not. She might have become a teacher, a scholar, or a painter, fulfilling childhood ambitions that remained with her to the end of her life.

I knew that Lin's daughters regretted how events had, in reality, turned out. But if things had turned out otherwise, there would have been no Double-Gun Woman, and no Lin as we now knew him.

Months later, back in London, I learned that, after two years' building work, the Huaying Mountain Uprising Memorial Hall had formally opened on 24 October 2006. Inside was an exhibition about the Double-Gun Woman and 116 of her comrades-in-arms, together with displays of the guns and everyday objects they had used, of works of art and literature describing the history of the uprising, and of a few memorials and poems written by fallen heroes.

I rejoiced that this tragic episode had become a part of public history in China.

I also learned that Lin had now completed his autobiography and was looking for a publisher in the West. I wished this indefatigable old man health and every success.

3

New Discoveries in Xinjiang, the World's Biggest Prison

Workers of 148 Corps in the 1950s (see p.64).

With survivors of 148 Corps, 2006.

TEACHER SUN AND HER HUSBAND, and other ex-soldiers and ex-prisoners of Shihezi Farm and Prison, *interviewed in Shihezi, Xinjiang province, north-west China, the biggest province in China (with various ethnic minorities) which shares long borders with Russia, Mongolia and other ex-USSR countries in Central Asia. From around 1950, the Chinese government transported more than half a million prisoners of war (and later their families) and criminals to Xinjiang, where they set up Xinjiang Military Farm, part of which was Shihezi Farm, a huge prison garrisoned by over 50,000 PLA soldiers. The prisoners built Shihezi, a modern city, out of the desert. No. 148 Corps, one of the military construction corps, helped build the city but they still live in houses made of mud without running water, and more than three hundred families share one public toilet. Teacher Sun was one of the first teachers of the Shihezi Construction Corps. Orphaned at thirteen or fourteen, she graduated from senior school in 1959 and went to Shihezi where she had to do farm work and then build her own classroom. She met her husband, an ex-soldier, there and they had four children.*

When I first visited the Tibetan Plateau in 1981, my route took me close to the north-western province of Xinjiang. It was there I first heard a rumour that for thirty years the Chinese government had been building the world's largest prison. According to local hearsay, nearly 200,000 Guomindang prisoners of war and over 300,000 "Reform through Labour" convicts had been moved there from the east. Guarded by 50,000 People's Liberation Army (PLA) soldiers under the leadership of General Wang Zhen, they were put to reclaiming the Gobi Desert where it met the Taklimakan Desert and the Gurbantunggut Desert.

This plan was said to be Mao Zedong's way of killing five birds with one stone. First, by relocating people who might form part of a counter-attack on the mainland for Chiang Kai-shek, it was nipping in the bud the problem of what to do with prisoners of war from the Guomindang Army. Second, as guarding labour reform convicts was taking up a lot of manpower and resources, moving them westwards could relieve pressure on supplies in the densely populated eastern regions. Third, Mao Zedong had already foreseen the inevitability of a rift with Stalin and the Soviet Union, and the Silk Road that led through Xinjiang was a strategically important link between East and Central Asia; troops stationed there to open up the wasteland and garrison the frontier could form a barrier against the Soviet Union. Fourth, many of Xinjiang's forty-seven ethnic groups had always been Muslims, who had never been greatly influenced by the Han Chinese culture or political system. By stationing troops there to open up the wasteland and garrison the frontier, large numbers of Han people could be brought into the local society, where they would inhibit and dilute Muslim inclinations towards independence. Fifth, by accelerating Xinjiang's economic development, the abundant resources of the region could be sent quickly to supply the needs of the interior.

Ever since my first trip, I had been trying to find some confirmation for this rumour. Nobody close to me had heard anything about it, and Han people who came from Xinjiang were equally vague. All they knew was that after 1950 thousands of people had gone there to open up the wasteland and garrison the border; they rarely discussed their family history prior to 1950. Even if they had, it was quite simply impossible for me to get any kind of permission to go reporting in Xinjiang; even friends in the public security system who would normally have helped said: That place is an independent kingdom without a gate! Although I came across Xinjiang Muslims from time to time, they either didn't speak my language or just answered, "I don't know," to all my questions.

Finally, in 2005 I saw a piece of news in the Chinese media:

> On 16 October this year, a group of Chinese and foreign journalists took their first steps into the "mysterious" Xinjiang Production and Construction Corps ... reporting on an exceptional "army unit" on China's western border. This visit was organised by the News Department of the Chinese Foreign Office and the Xinjiang Autonomous Region Foreign Affairs Office.

And so I began a new round of investigations into the Xinjiang Construction Corps. Compared to the primitive investigation methods of a decade earlier, everything was now much more accessible; stories to do with Shihezi had begun to appear in some small local newspapers and hand-copied literature and novels that were outside the scope of government control, and people from Shihezi were starting to talk about their past on the Internet. But these were all just personal anecdotes. It still proved impossible for me to find a properly authoritative historical summary. Later I discovered that the "authoritative historical summary" I was searching for didn't exist.

According to the introduction on a Chinese government website:

> Xinjiang occupies a sixth of China's area, and is inhabited by forty-seven different ethnic groups. The ancient Silk Route passes through here, and it is an important strategic area rich in energy resources. Historically, its economy was based around agriculture and herding, with factories and mines remaining at the handicraft and workshop level. There was not an inch of railway, and industry was practically zero – the nearest thing was blacksmiths making horseshoes. The peaceful liberation of Xinjiang was completed by

25 September 1949, and later that same year, General Wang Zhen received orders to lead the First Corps of the People's Liberation First Field Army into Xinjiang and reorganise the units involved in uprisings against the Guomindang and the armies of the Three Districts Revolution.* Following this, the People's Liberation Army began to open up the wasteland while continuing to guard the border, concentrating their efforts mainly on production, construction, and acceleration of Xinjiang's economic development. In August 1954, before the foundation of the Xinjiang Uighur Autonomous Region on 1 October 1955, 175,000 of these soldiers were transferred to civilian work by the authority of the Central Committee of the Communist Party and the Central Military Committee, and the Xinjiang Production and Construction Corps was founded.

The Construction Corps was not an army unit. It was made up of desk workers, manual workers in the factories and peasants who tilled the fields, all of whom received a civil servant's pay, although military titles and structure continued for a long time. The Construction Corps is a unique case: a special social organisation planned and administered at central government level. Inside the areas of cultivation under its jurisdiction, it runs its own internal administration and legal affairs under the dual leadership of the central government and the government of the Xinjiang Uighur Autonomous Region. Xinjiang Production and Construction Corps is also known as the China Xinjiang Group.

I also discovered that even the material on websites that were regularly checked by the Chinese government contained conflicting information on the size of the Construction Corps and its origins.

After the peaceful liberation of Xinjiang, a large army of *100,000* stationed in Xinjiang and led by General Wang Zhen, and *nearly 100,000* members of the Guomindang Insurrection Army under Tao Zhiyue, all found themselves faced with a lack of food supplies. Consequently, opening up the land for cultivation became the main task of these units.

China's leaders determined that the PLA First Corps and Twenty-Second Army Corps stationed in Xinjiang would only retain one infantry division on active duty for purposes of national defence. The vast majority of the soldiers *(175,000) were to be collectively transferred to civilian work* in Xinjiang

---

* A revolt against the Guomindang government of Xinjiang.

to engage in industrial and agricultural production, and to organise the Xinjiang Production and Construction Corps, with Tao Zhiyue acting as the first Chief of Staff. At a command from Chairman Mao, they took up their guns and their hoes, and embarked on large-scale production.

In October 1954, *a total of 100,000 people were collectively transferred to civilian work*, and they set up the Construction Corps.

In August 1954, following a directive from Mao Zedong, *105,000 PLA officers and soldiers stationed in Xinjiang were collectively transferred to civilian work, along with over 60,000 family members*, all of whom were organised into the Xinjiang Military Area Production and Construction Corps. Their responsibility was to open up the wasteland and garrison the border.

The figures on government websites differed greatly from what I had learned in my enquiries. They mentioned the Second and Sixth Divisions of the First Corps of the Communist Party's First Field Army, the Xinjiang ethnic minority forces and several divisions of the Ninth Corps of the Twenty-Second Army of the Guomindang, but didn't include any prisoners of war or Reform through Labour convicts. Moreover, nothing I could find in any of the historical literature, the material from the local "Xinjiang Construction Corps Museum" that opened on 10 October 2004, or from the handful of retired people who had returned to the east, could provide me with a complete, definitive list of the policymakers who had led and masterminded the transformation of Shihezi from desert to modern city. Apart from the PLA leader Wang Zhen, and the Guomindang Twenty-Second Army Chief of Staff Tao Zhiyue, many different leaders' names appear and disappear, such as Zhang Chonghan, Zhao Xiguang, Wang Genseng and over a hundred others. I know that all these different inclusions and exclusions were the result of different sets of political requirements, and this is one of the thorniest issues in the last hundred years of China's history, as changes in political climate cause those histories that had already changed to "change anew". I think that this "don't talk politics" and "can't say for sure" must be a Chinese speciality. Who would want to be constantly discovering the errors and loopholes in the history they describe?

A few things did become clear as a result of my subsequent investigation. There were explanations relating to the idea that "since the Xinjiang Production and Construction Corps was directly responsible for acting as a deterrent against the forces of Xinjiang independence, its existence has always come under attack by international human rights organisations and supporters of Xinjiang independence. It has been called an occupying army, haphazardly organised and internally corrupt." These explanations proved to me that at least some of the rumours I had heard were correct.

Then there was another piece of information connected with the women in the corps. From 1950 onwards, nine thousand girls from Shandong, eight thousand from Hunan, a thousand Henan peasant girls, and thousands of women from other places in the interior were brought to Xinjiang so that new generations of pioneers could continue to open up the wasteland. Were these yet more women who had been "married off by the revolution"? When I decided to focus my report for *China Witness* on Shihezi, capital of the Xinjiang Construction Corps' Eighth Agricultural Division, I did not expect that this would be a reporting experience in which joy and sorrow were intermingled.

Shihezi city is located in the middle of the northern foothills of the Tianshan Mountains in northern Xinjiang, at the southern edge of the Dzungaria Basin and on the Lanzhou-Xinjiang Railway. Originally a part of Shawan county, Shihezi is situated on the "Silk Route", and shares its unique western customs and culture. First established in 1950, and officially designated a city in 1976, it is the earliest of the Construction Corps cities. It is managed by the Eighth Agricultural Division of the Fourteenth Division of the Xinjiang Construction Corps, whose Divisional Headquarters is located here. Shihezi city holds the United Nations International Award for Best Practices to Improve the Living Environment. Her location was chosen by soldiers, and she was planned and built by soldiers; her miraculous achievement, "the people advances, the sand retreats", has won her worldwide renown; she is a successful "model military border" for China, and she is known throughout the world by the name "Pearl of the Gobi" for her beautiful surroundings and unique, resplendent culture.

– from China's *People Daily Online,* www.people.com.cn

After several months, we finally found somebody willing to help our "study and investigation" group enter this city where "swords were forged into ploughshares", and I started to believe that I had found the key to Shihezi. However, just four days before we were due to get underway, with our team all packed and ready, I received two emails from Shihezi:

18 July

My teacher has finally returned my call. He says that vigilance in the Old Cadres' Home is running extremely high; even the residents' relatives become wary when foreign issues are mentioned. It is strictly forbidden to give out their phone number. They are afraid of getting dragged in if there are any problems. I can understand why; this is just the way things are in our China. My teacher has told me that any interviews with them must be arranged through the Shihezi United Front Office, the office in charge of non-Communist political parties, but if you come in August to compile materials they can help you with that. This is a really disappointing result after a week's hard labour! But sometimes the final result of a thing is always the opposite of what we wish for.

I sincerely wish that everything goes smoothly!

My other "inside agent" sent an email that read like official correspondence, quite unlike his usual style:

I welcome your visit, and I also support the students' investigation into history. However, as Shihezi has only just opened up to the outside world, the interviewees will require a "government-level letter of introduction" before they can take part in the interviewing process. I would not go so far as to say that there will be no opportunities among acquaintances and passers-by, but I am afraid that they would not dare to get involved, or they may dare to help but be unable to do so, having no idea of what to say. I respectfully ask you to reconsider carefully before you begin your journey.

Although I had been prepared for something of this sort, I still felt a great pressure. First, the buses, trains, boats, planes and accommodation had already been booked, and most of the travel tickets had been issued; second, I felt that I was fighting against time as it snatched from my grasp these elderly people who were trying to speak out, struggling against China's long history of fear-induced inertia. Not wanting to lose a vital opportunity to report on this part of China's history, I determined to rush headlong into danger. Even if nobody could tell me anything, we would still be able to get a feeling for that city that was built up from the desert. Not all dramas take place onstage; you can also see them by the roadside.

On 5 August 2006 at dusk, we arrived at Urumqi, the capital of Xinjiang. Our friend Yi was waiting to welcome us. He was moved by our persistence and determination, and he told us that after much effort he had managed to get hold of the first teacher in the Shihezi Construction Corps, who was also the first person to set up a school there. In addition, he was going to make another attempt with a group of old people he knew who had spent nearly fifty years opening up the land for cultivation. In an instant we had gone from "utter destitution" to a treasure trove.

Mr Yi had arranged a meeting room in our hotel for interviews the next morning. Thirty minutes past the appointed time, the first interviewee had still not arrived, and we were starting to feel uneasy. I had experienced this countless times in the past because of "Chinese flexibility" – last-minute changes of plan due to "illness, traffic jams or urgent family business".

But this time I was wrong: Teacher Sun hurried into the room, sweat breaking out all over her forehead, accompanied by her very tall husband. She said: "You've been waiting for ages, I'm so sorry." The couple then declared that they were reluctant to be interviewed and had only come so as not to disappoint her student. I took more than ten minutes to explain why we were looking for Chinese witnesses, that this was a charitable cultural activity to help our future understand our past history and to let the world know about Chinese people's national pride. Clearly they were impressed by our words, and finally outgoing, confident Teacher Sun sat down in front of me. "I like to deal with people who say what they mean, I like working with people who have a smile on their faces. After your affecting words, I can't let you come all this way in vain! In any case I haven't done anything to be ashamed of, I've got no reason to worry about ghosts coming to knock on my door. Let's talk, then – just don't look down on me for not talking well."

To this day, the media in China bases its reporting on "principles", with facts coming a poor second. Interviewees are often "led" to follow the central ideology of the Party, and to express "personal views defined by principles". Therefore, at the start of an interview, many people will tell you that you must not take it amiss if they can't express things properly. Nobody stops to wonder: how can the media define a personal standpoint as good or bad? Perhaps over a thousand years' cultural restraint has already become an integral part of the way Chinese people express political ideas.

Due to the shared understanding between us, my interviewees felt much more comfortable with a fellow Chinese than they would have been with the same questions coming from a foreign face. For many people, as soon as somebody opens the gates of their hearts a great river of stories flows out; no bank can hold them back, and no dyke can block their way. Teacher Sun was one of those.

*

XINRAN: Teacher Sun, you're a successful teacher, you've raised generations of students, many of whom have gone on to great things. Would you also describe yourself as a mother who can communicate with her own children?

SUN: That's not the same thing.

XINRAN: Why not?

SUN: Our children wouldn't understand, they think we were too foolish, living only for others. Things were different in our day, nobody would think of scheming just to get some advantage for one's family. If you only thought of your own children, people would look down on you, and we all need self-respect, don't we?

XINRAN: So what differences are there between your attitude to life and that of your parents?

SUN: They died when I was very young, I didn't know them. At that time life was very hard for every family. Actually, I was one of the lucky ones, I even went to school.

XINRAN: Where did your good luck come from?

SUN: When my parents passed away I was in the first year of middle school, only thirteen or fourteen, and I was the eldest of four children, with three younger brothers. My grandfather was seventy. He said, "I can take care of the house, but I can't look after you. Best if you take a break from school, stay at home to look after your brothers, try a bit of hard work, do the cooking." When I heard this I cried, saying that I wanted to go to school. My grandfather said, "We're all too old or too young in this family, we've got no income, we're just living off that little bit of money from the government, how can you go to school?" So I cried the whole day: *I want to go to school.* In due course the school got wind of this, and two of the school leaders came to my house, they said to my grandfather: "Her marks are very good. It'd be such a shame if she dropped out of school. The school can give her five yuan a month to support her studies, four yuan to buy food coupons, one yuan for a notebook and pencil, and we'll write off her school fees." And that was how I managed to keep on with my studies. At the end of middle school, when I was preparing for the exams, my teacher tried to persuade me to apply to the teacher-training school: "There are no school fees, the state will support you for three years, and afterwards you can teach." I said I wanted to take the exam for senior school, because senior school was the only way to university. I'd always been very competitive, ever since I was small. I thought: Let's see what happens. I'll get in through my own ability; whether I can study there is another matter. And in the end I got in. One of my uncles said angrily: "You really don't know your limits, do you? Even children with a father and mother can't go to senior school, and *you* want to go?" I said: "If children with fathers and mothers can't go to senior school it's because they're not up to it. I have no father and no mother, but I am up to it. Anyway, whether I go or I don't, it won't be with your money, so what's it to you?" After I started at senior school I applied for help with studies, and because of my family circumstances, I got an eleven-yuan bursary a month. In those days the state could give me a grant, and I treasured it. To this day I'm still very frugal in my daily life. My son's wife complains about me, saying I shouldn't wear cheap ten-yuan clothes any more, or shoes from roadside stalls that only cost a bit over ten. But I've always been very careful. When I came to work in Xinjiang, I cried when I got my first wages; if I'd had that thirty-two yuan at home, I wouldn't have had to worry about school fees for a whole term.

XINRAN: Did you graduate from senior school?

SUN: Yes, I graduated from the Number One Senior School in Wendeng city, Shandong province, in 1959. But then there was no grant for university. The state hardly funded anyone to go to university, just a few children of revolutionary martyrs. An old classmate of mine had come to Xinjiang before me – in the three years of natural disasters, she had to quit school halfway, she didn't even have anything to eat, she ate grass roots and tree bark every day. So she came to Xinjiang without finishing school. At that time Shihezi One Eight Cotton Weaving Factory was recruiting workers, so she got a job. Later on when I left school, she sent a letter asking if I was planning to take the university entrance exams. I replied, I had no income, I had no plans to sit the exams. She said, then come here. I said, all right, I have no family anyway. Volunteering to support the borders sounds pretty good, very revolutionary, so I came of my own free will to support the border regions.

XINRAN: How did you come?

SUN: By bus and train. I travelled for over a week. I could have arrived a few days earlier, but I took a bus to Yantai, where my godmother lived, and she refused point-blank to let me go any further; her whole family were clutching at my hands, they wouldn't let me go. They said: "You're a twenty-year-old girl, they speak Xinjiang language where you're going and you won't understand, they write Muslim characters and you won't be able to read them. If you go you'll just bring down suffering on your own head." *Aiya*, it wasn't an easy decision for me either – I spent two days in Yantai struggling – but in the end I said, no, I still want to go, I can't stay here. They said, "You can find work in Yantai, that's just as good, take your time, you're a senior-school graduate, you can find work here. Get a temporary job, you'll get used to it." But I remembered that just before I set off from Wendeng a fortune-teller had told me I would travel far and fly high. I couldn't stay there, I had to go.

XINRAN: Can you still remember what the trains were like then? What did you eat on them? Were there many people? Were the trains like they are now?

SUN: Back then trains weren't as well equipped as they are now. They were all very old and shabby, there was a lot of noise, and they rocked about a lot. You got a real feeling of "tiredness" from them. Every time the train stopped, we thought, "It'll never get started again!" There were only a few trains a week, but they fairly packed us in. At that time a ticket from Yantai to Xinjiang was seventy yuan. I bought my ticket with borrowed money and boarded the train. I was frightened then, it was my first time away from home in my whole life. In those days you had to have a travel permit to go anywhere, and I hadn't got one. I was terrified. An old man from Shaanxi sitting next to me asked: "Girl, where are you going?" I said I was going to Shihezi in Xinjiang. He said, "Have you got a permit?" I said no, and I was scared to death. He said: "No need to be scared, when they come round to check, just keep quiet." When the inspectors came round, he said, "This is my daughter, I'm taking her home with me." Before he got off the train he asked a soldier in the next seat to look after me – at that time we all believed that soldiers were good people. And that was how I came to Xinjiang. By the time I arrived, I'd long since eaten all the rations I'd brought with me.

As soon as I came to Urumqi, I went straight to the Shihezi Cotton Factory. My classmate took me all the way through the factory, from where the raw cotton came in to where the cloth was checked at the end. She was in the cloth-checking workshop. "*Aiya*," I said, "I can't do it, not with all those machines banging and roaring away!" When I left the factory I wanted to throw up, so I didn't work there. Her friends said,

"If your job search doesn't work out, find yourself a husband." I said, "No way, I've come to Xinjiang to find work, not a husband! I've come to realise my ambition."

Before I found a job, I spent a few days sponging off my classmate. I must have been a real nuisance. Those were the famine years; food was in short supply and everyone had a fixed monthly food ration, so I had to cadge a bit here and a bit there. I thought I was causing my classmate far too much trouble. Luckily one day I met some people from back home who said, "The best place in the Xinjiang Construction Corps is the Mosuowan Number Two Farm in the Eighth Agricultural Division. It's a breadbasket, and our place is the best in the whole corps. Why don't you come with us?" I didn't know what sort of place it was, or what they did there, but I went along with them anyway. When I got there, I went to the labour resource office for a job. The supervisor took one look at me and said, "How old are you?" I said, "Twenty-five." He said, "You're a school-leaver, aren't you?" I was small and thin in those days – I only weighed forty kilos. I said, "Yes, I've just left school." He said, "Go back, you can't cope here, all our work is hard labour in the fields. The Production and Construction Corps is mainly production, and that means field work. In summer it's thirty or forty degrees centigrade; in winter it's thirty or forty degrees below. You won't be able to keep up." I said, "It doesn't matter, it'll toughen me up. There are plenty of people my age in your corps too – whatever other people can do I can do! Wait and see if I'm really not up to it, at least." He couldn't talk me out of it, so he let me stay. I said, "What work unit are you going to send me to?" He said, "Where do you want to go?" I said, "A friend from Shandong mentioned a duty supervision unit. There are a fair few young people there, and a lot of intellectuals." He said, "All right then, I'll put you in the duty supervision unit." At that time there was only one kindergarten in the whole corps. When the head of this kindergarten heard that a lively high-school graduate who liked dancing had come from Shandong, she wanted me as a teacher, and I agreed. But as anyone who's worked in the Construction Corps knows, everybody had to do a year's probation. You couldn't start your specialised job until after a trial year of labour.

I worked in the big fields. Really, farm work is just incredibly tough. I even had to work in the fields in winter. And what did we have to eat when we came home in the evening? *Wowotou*, those steamed corn buns, nothing but *wowotou*. At that time less than 20 per cent was flour or rice – the rest was coarse grains. We used to take a few *wowotou* to eat in the field. They'd be frozen solid, like ice lollies, and we ate them just as they were. We didn't go home at midday. In the winter I carried sand, I carted fertiliser. I've done everything. Picking cotton, too. The night before my first day picking cotton I was too excited to sleep. I came to the field, and the others taught me how to do it. After a while I could pick forty kilos of cotton in a single day. At that time I was one of the most capable workers in the company – everyone said that I'd make it through the trial period.

*

I couldn't detect any sense of hardship in Teacher Sun's narrative. This is a mark of the fortitude of that generation of Chinese; they regard "the things I've done" and "what others said about me" as far more important than "eating in the wind and sleeping in the dew". Their lives are lived on the spiritual level.

*

SUN: There were a lot of intellectuals in that place, relatively speaking, but I was the only girl who'd finished senior school. Four or five of the men were senior-school graduates, but none of them had been allowed to go on to university because of their class backgrounds, and that was why they had come here to make their way in the world. They were kind to me. They used to sneak rice or steamed buns into the big basket I carried on my back when picking cotton, so that I could snatch a bite to eat while I was changing baskets. I never asked who'd left them. Nothing about those people was straightforward. Nobody dared to get too friendly with anybody else. At that time it was tough, to be sure, and tense too, but the days went by very quickly. We used to go to the fields before dawn, eat our midday meal in the fields, and sometimes supper too. Then once it was too dark to see or pick cotton, we went to the maize fields for stalks. You could cut a good bundle of stems from a few rows of maize, and we carried them on our backs over all the fields we'd broken in for cultivation and back to the road, to be taken to the cow or sheep pens as fodder, or sometimes to the kitchen for cooking fuel. Freshly cut maize stems were very heavy. I really was dead on my feet, sometimes I used to weep from exhaustion. It was true hard labour.

XINRAN: Did you all have the same routines and bear the same heavy burdens, with no difference between men and women?

SUN: Oh yes, we all did the same work! Nearly everyone who came to Xinjiang in search of a future had a bad family background. It seemed that out of all the people around me, I was the only educated youth from a good class background.

XINRAN: So were you able to do a bit less than people from bad family backgrounds?

SUN: I didn't think in that way – we were all people. Besides, do you have any control over your family background? How is making children bear the sins of their parents any different from that old feudal punishment, the one where the whole family was punished for the crimes of one of its members? *Aiya*, I didn't say this out loud, though I thought it. If people said I worked well, that was good enough for me. I did that job for a year, and they made me a Five-Good Worker and a Progressive Student of Mao Zedong Thought. Because I'd been educated, I was given the job of keeping a record of all the work points in Shihezi [XXX] Regiment. When all the other comrades were fast asleep I had to go to the office to record everything the people in our squad had done – a dozen or more – and then report it to the central Company Work-Point Recorder. I was an Excellent Work-Point Recorder, as well as a Five-Good Worker and a Progressive Student of Mao Zedong Thought.

I was never afraid of hard work, no matter how tough it was. I didn't build roads, dig canals, or break open farmland, but I'm a witness to the history of education in the Construction and Production Corps. In 1963 when we first built a school, there were very few children – only a handful of old comrades who had married after 1956 had school-age children; before that everyone was breaking open the wilderness. There were no houses or anywhere to sleep, who had the time or energy to get married or have children? Even if they had children back home, bringing them to the Gobi was out of the question – there was nothing here for them. Three work units joined together to set up a school, with just the one class. We had to make the schoolhouse ourselves, too. The Regimental Office assigned two comrades and me to make our own sod bricks and build a classroom from sod bricks and mud. Thick wooden sticks with grass stems tied on and topped off with mud went to make up the roof. We made piles of sod bricks, half a metre high, thirty centimetres wide and fifty long, laid sunflower or sesame stalks on top and smeared them with mud. Those were the school desks. The teacher's podium was made in the same way, and we didn't have a teacher's office at all. When there was a Chinese class, out would come the Chinese textbook. I was the teacher. The next class was sums, the children took out their maths textbooks, and I was still the teacher, then it was time for singing and it was me teaching again. After a while they would go out for exercise, and it was still me. I lived in the workers' dormitory, which was just the same: a big building, the beds piles of sod bricks with sesame stalks on top. I'd just turned twenty-six.

XINRAN: Could you bear so much all by yourself?

SUN: At that time there was nothing I couldn't bear. Teaching wasn't difficult. The hardest part was going to the roadside every morning to collect the pupils, especially when it rained in summer or snowed in winter. People could get blown away or buried by wind or snow in the Gobi Desert, sometimes. If it snowed or rained too heavily, I used to take the children halfway home, and then their parents would take over. Winter was the worst. I had to go to the schoolhouse before daybreak to light the stove for the students – that was an earth stove built like a *kang*, you know, with a flue going through it from the stove. The pupils could sit on it while they had their lessons, but not me. I had to keep moving about and checking up on the children, who were all learning different things. When I got tired I sat on an earth stool, with my two long plaits underneath my bottom.

XINRAN: You used your own hair as padding to keep out the cold?

SUN: That's right. I used to have really long plaits, but one day when I was marking homework I forgot to hold my plaits out of the way while I was stoking up the fire. A swish of my plaits, and whoosh – one of them caught fire. Oh, I cried my heart out for a whole day. Another thing that caused me problems was films. It wasn't easy to put on a film in those days – we used to go a very long time between films, and on a film day none of the students wanted to go home. They said: "Teacher, we want to see the film." "Stay and watch it then," I'd say, so they did. They used to bring their own food supplies for lunch, not very much, so I usually had a bit of my own food put by for their supper when there was a film. It was different in those days, not like now, when you can find out where there's a film with just a telephone call, and you don't need to bring food because there are restaurants everywhere. At that time we were eking out a living in the Gobi Desert.

XINRAN: You must have been all by yourself then. Weren't you scared?

SUN: How could I not be scared? But in fact there was proper social order back then. There were no bad people. It's my belief that nobody had the energy to do anything bad – we were all half dead of exhaustion.

XINRAN: So when did you get other teachers for your school?

SUN: They didn't send us another teacher until the third year. Her husband was in the Security Office. He was in charge of the Reform through Labour teams, and he was away from home a lot.

XINRAN: Didn't you say that the social order was good, that there weren't any bad people?

SUN: I said there weren't any bad people in society, but there were lots and lots of Reform through Labour convicts! It was like all the Reform through Labour convicts in the whole country had been sent to Xinjiang. We were assigned a low little house near the school. There was a partition down the middle; she lived on one side, me on the other. It was much better after she came and there were two of us. I'd take PE while she took singing, and then we could swap for a while, or sometimes two classes would have PE or singing together. We taught that way right up to 1979. Before that it was mostly old comrades coming to open farms and things. Later on there started to be more new people, and more and more children. I began teaching middle school in 1984. I took two classes for Chinese, and I did that till 1994, when there was a shake-up in professional education under orders from the central government. Then the school set up a vocational senior high school, and I was transferred there.

XINRAN: You really are a witness to the history of education in the Shihezi Construction Corps!

SUN: Mmm, I watched the children grow up, I watched the school develop from nothing in the Gobi Desert! Still, conditions were much better when I was teaching in the senior school. We even lived in specially built teachers' flats. Two big rooms, only two bedrooms. There was a communal toilet and water room for washing, and the kitchens were cookstoves built up outside your front door.

XINRAN: And this was in 1994?

SUN: At that time a teacher's wages were only thirty-nine yuan a month.

XINRAN: How much were your wages in 1962?

SUN: Same as all the other teachers: thirty-two-yuan wages in the trial period. After a year when you were made permanent you got thirty-six yuan and twelve fen, and after another year when you got on the teachers' pay scale it was thirty-nine, right up to 1995. They didn't give me a pay rise for nearly thirty years. I started work in '62 and got married in '67. And I had four children. But it was the same for everyone back then

– nobody thought it was hard. I had to supervise self-study in the class-room every day as well – I couldn't look after my own children. Evening self-study finished at eleven, and then I had to see the boarders safely to bed. I couldn't go home until lights out.

XINRAN: You really didn't think it was hard? Later I want to know your secret. Four children, and overtime on top of that!

SUN: Yes, four children! Coming home every day in the evening, making clothes by lamplight . . . I made everything myself, I didn't buy shoes, and the children's clothes were old clothes cut down to size. My elder daughter grew fast, so I added a strip to the bottom of her trousers. The next year she'd grown again, and I added another strip. The bottoms of her trousers were like stairs – I'd added three extensions! When she couldn't wear them they were passed on to the next one. I made clothes and shoes for the children every day after work, it felt like I never went to sleep before three o'clock. Anyway, I had a lot of children, I brought it on myself.

XINRAN: You were so eager to excel in your work – why did you have so many children?

SUN: That was eagerness to excel too; whoever had the most was the best. I didn't know that much then, just that I wanted to be better than everybody else!

XINRAN: So you didn't want to lag behind, even in childbearing! But you show no sign of being worn down by the drudgery of four children.

SUN: That's the kind of person I am – I always want to be the best. My work never fell behind, no matter how many children I had or how exhausting the housework was, right up to when I retired in 1995. Just then the Workers' Medical University was opening a branch college. They were running two clinical classes for level-one administrators and directors of rural hospitals aged over thirty-five. These people were the mainstays of village and county hospitals, but because their generation had been sent down to the countryside as school-leavers, they'd missed out on the chance to get a university qualification. It was impossible for them to get promotion, and their pay and conditions were very bad, so as a special consideration, this group were given a chance to do a one-year course leading to a college degree. At that time the college principal was asking around for teachers, and he came to Shihezi. He said he wanted teachers with the best work ethic, who could manage students, so he set his sights on me, begged me. I couldn't hold out against that, so I said I'd sign a year's contract, and at the end of that time both sides could decide. You see if I'm up to it, and I'll see whether I can get used to the job. In the end I worked until 1998. I only stopped when I got a stomach illness.

XINRAN: Could you never slow down a bit? From 1962, when you were twenty-five, to 1998, did you ever slow down?

SUN: I think that after a year of farm work in the corps, no matter how tough things got, it was still a much easier life than that, bending over the yellow earth all day, down to the fields before daybreak and not coming back until dark. To be honest, the year I spent toughening myself up in the corps gave me my work ethic for thirty years of teaching. It made me unusually serious and responsible, so no matter what class I was given, the leaders didn't have to worry. It's all because I have experienced true toil, like the peasants. When I was teaching, no matter how hard or tiring it was, even if I couldn't go home for twenty-four hours at a stretch, you're still inside. Talking to children and teaching schoolchildren doesn't take a lot of strength, does it?

XINRAN: Now can you tell me your secret? And also, how did you meet your husband?

SUN: You ask him, see what he says.

XINRAN: I want to hear what you say. I'm a woman – it's easier for me to listen to a woman telling her stories than a man.

SUN: Really? I sometimes think that way too.

XINRAN: And let's be practical, don't give me all that stuff about "comrades cherishing the same hopes and ideals".

SUN: You're really funny! I'll talk if you want to listen. In any case we're old, we don't mind being laughed at. My husband came straight to Xinjiang when he left his old army unit in Nanjing. A whole group of demobilised soldiers were sent over together. He wasn't due to be demobbed, but when he heard that group was going to be sent to Xinjiang on leaving the army, well, he didn't know what it was like in Xinjiang, but he put in a request to go. His arrival coincided with a big army skills competition, and his military skills had been exceptionally good in the army. He used to be in a colour guard that put on displays for visiting senior officers. At the end of that competition he was selected as best in his category. When General He Long came here from the central government they even let him have a photograph taken with him.

XINRAN: Do you still have that photograph?

SUN: No, in the Cultural Revolution they said all sorts of things about He Long. We were afraid, so we threw it away. In 1967 the armed guard units sent him to the school to give military and political training. He visited all the middle and primary schools in turn, and just then he happened to be responsible for primary schools. He was staying in the school office, and that was how we got to know each other.

XINRAN: When did you first take a fancy to him?

SUN: He was doing drill exercises, you know? I often saw him on the training ground. I was still quite young. I thought he was really handsome, so quick-witted and capable, I thought the way he went through his moves was just wonderful.

XINRAN: Just that? It's got to be more than that, surely!

SUN [laughs]: Well . . . yes, there's more. I had my own requirements for a husband. First, I'm short, so I wanted a tall man; second, my eyes are small, so I wanted a man with big eyes. He matched my requirements rather well. I'd been introduced to a good few men before him. To be honest, we were all quite particular about class background in those days, I was one of the better ones, so I got a good many introductions, but I turned my nose up at all of them. He had an easy, natural bearing, though; tall, with big eyes, very clean and brisk. Our dormitories were only separated by a road. The office was on this side, and the teachers' dormitory was just over there. He spent several months drilling the pupils, our comrades introduced us, and we got together.

XINRAN: Romantic!

SUN: What about your husband?

XINRAN: When you see him later, tell me how you rate him! Once you started living together, did you quarrel? Did you have fights?

SUN: How could we not quarrel? Not so much in the early years; mostly it was after the children came, when we were so busy. He had a bad temper in those days. He'd see the children eating slowly and lose his temper. He always clears his bowl in five minutes, so he insisted that the children finish their food in five minutes too. He wanted the children to do everything extremely quickly, the way they do in an army skills competition. He said it was to help the children's development.

XINRAN: So, has his temper improved a bit?

SUN: Now it's a little better. The children have all grown up. He says that when he was young he didn't understand, he didn't have much to do with the running of the household. I brought up all the children single-handed really – it was very hard. This is why my health is poor. Now he says he wants to make amends for his misdeeds; he does all the housework, I just read the papers and rest. In the morning, as soon as he gets up, he does some tidying. Then he gets our little grandson dressed, gets his food ready, feeds him, and takes him outside to play. When they come in he makes lunch, we have a nap, he takes the child out to play again, and then he makes supper when he comes back. Now he's experienced it for himself, he understands how tough it was for me bringing up four children.

XINRAN: Do your four children understand you now? Are they proud of you?

SUN: Who knows?! They complain about me all the time: "Being shut up all day in that school has made you stupid. Our family has no money and no connections. Other people used their family connections to do this or that." Actually, I think that people should rely on their own abilities. What, me, no connections? The mature cadre students I saw through college were all over thirty. The lowest were senior doctors or managers of village hospitals. I had an unusually good relationship with the cadre class of 1995. They said, "We were so lucky to meet a teacher like you!" Just before they left, they bought me a notebook and a pen and wrote messages inside for me to remember them by. The older ones said that they were both my students and my friends. The younger ones said: From now on I'll call you Mother.

XINRAN: That's a friendship to cherish all your life.

SUN: Of course. Why do you think I'm never able to slow down?

XINRAN: Do you think it was worth it, this life of yours?

SUN: I often say: there's nobody who has done this before me, and nobody will do it after me. How can I put it? In my life, although I've never been a public figure, I've managed to get one thing out of it: nobody has ever said that I kept the students back. Everybody says that Teacher Sun is extremely strict. Whenever I told the students to be in the classroom, I'd always be there ten minutes beforehand, waiting at the door. It's only the students who are late. I've never been late. In those years many people were like that, our generation, I'm just one of them, a drop in the ocean.

XINRAN: There aren't very many teachers like you. Only a very few women then had such great courage, or such decisiveness, endured such hardship, or did so much. To this day you don't admit defeat, and you are still so sure of yourself. How many people are like that? And another thing, do you agree that all the people of Shihezi – soldiers, teachers, or workers alike – have a responsibility to tell people about this history, to tell our children? Things just like what you said just now: how to make chairs out of clods of earth, how to sit on an earth stool in winter, how to find love in the barren desert, how to bring up children while devoting yourself to your career. But the main thing is that you are aware of your happiness today, you can feel it, and be satisfied with it.

SUN: That's right! I really am extraordinarily content with my present situation, my husband says: I never imagined such a comfortable old age, not even in my dreams. We've come to the big city. We live in a block of flats. I'd never have dreamed it. I'm absolutely content. My husband says that when I dream I wake up smiling. My oldest son has a car. On Sunday when he's at a loose end he says, "Dad, Mum, I'll take us on a drive to the outskirts." When my husband's sitting in the car he's happy inside. You have no idea how happy, he says he'd never even have dreamed of such a thing.

*

At midday, I invited the two old people to have lunch with us in the hotel, and I used this time to ask them a few questions.

*

XINRAN: Tell me, which of you was the first to raise the question of courtship? Your wife has told me about how she fell for you as soon as she saw you, before anyone had introduced you. She'll have talked to you about this, I dare say?

SUN'S HUSBAND: No, she hasn't talked about it.

XINRAN: How did it come about that you agreed to marry her?

SUN'S HUSBAND: I don't really know. [He laughs.]

XINRAN: Ooh, getting married without love or feelings, can this be a Chinese man? Tell us about it. Many young Chinese think their parents don't know anything about emotions. They think they just got married as part of a routine process. Was it really like that?

[He doesn't reply.]

XINRAN: How did you arrange your marriage ceremony?

SUN'S HUSBAND: *Aiya*, life was so hard.

SUN: We didn't have any money when we married. I made everything for my marriage myself, including a set of two quilts. First I had to lug all my things to the school. Then after class I carried everything on my own back to get married, a walk of two kilometres. One of his old comrades had gone back home on a family visit. There was nobody living in his quarters, so the leader said we could use this one room for our honeymoon. There wasn't a stick of furniture. The table they used for meetings became a bed. We covered it with plant stems, plastered them with mud, put in a hot-water bottle, and that was our honeymoon suite! There was a simple meeting hall nearby, and 110 workers came to our wedding. The hall had a mud stage, and we stood on it. The leaders witnessed the marriage, and then we handed out sweets and cigarettes. We bought several kilos of sunflower seeds and several more of sweets, and they docked two months from his salary to pay for them. So after we got married, he had to pay off two months of debt. He was a total pauper, not a penny to his name.

XINRAN: And after the sweets, cigarettes and sunflower seeds?

SUN'S HUSBAND: We all sang a song together.

XINRAN: Can you still remember the song you sang?

SUN'S HUSBAND: "We Come from the Five Lakes and the Four Seas". [He laughs again.]

XINRAN: Oh, I can sing that, too. Have you told these things to your sons and daughters?

SUN'S HUSBAND: No, we haven't.

XINRAN: Why not?

SUN'S HUSBAND: Things were different then.

XINRAN: Were you afraid they'd laugh at you, or afraid they wouldn't understand? I think that sometimes it isn't that the sons and daughters don't understand, it's that the older generation are worried their children won't understand. In fact, once the children reach a certain age, they do understand. Another thing, Teacher Sun said that you didn't take a photograph when you got married.

SUN'S HUSBAND: We don't have any wedding photos, it just wasn't possible to take one when we were first married. Our first family photo wasn't taken until we had our third child, when we could finally afford to take a posed family picture at the door of our ramshackle little house. Afterwards the man who took the picture came under suspicion as a counter-revolutionary because he had a camera, but he managed to escape.

XINRAN: For what reason?

SUN'S HUSBAND: What "reason" could there be in those days? If even a child said a wrong word they'd be made a counter-revolutionary. It was senseless! A camera or a radio could be evidence of being a "secret agent". At that time who could say for sure what had happened? And if anyone did say anything, they would come in for years of torment too! That's why our Chinese scholars and leaders are different from foreigners. The foreigners would never believe "the more knowledge, the more reactionary" like our worker-peasant cadres!

*

We all laughed, but it was bitter laughter.

I hoped to hear the true history of Shihezi from their voices. I could see that Teacher Sun and her husband were getting along well enough with me that we had built up a mutual trust. I wanted to ask them to teach me about the background to "Shihezi people", which I had never been able to get straight in my mind.

*

XINRAN: Teacher Sun, what sort of people was this Shihezi Corps made up of?

SUN: The very earliest corps was a group led by General Wang Zhen, an army that came to Shihezi. They were told to garrison and protect the borders, to guard Xinjiang, and to become self-sufficient. They wanted to engage in production, so they didn't have to depend on the state for support.

XINRAN: Protecting Xinjiang in the Gobi Desert? Production in the desert?

SUN: I really haven't thought about it. People in the 1950s didn't discuss their past lives much, we didn't ask too many questions about that. I thought that asking about people's backgrounds was like holding an interrogation; that's Party business, nothing to do with us. I do know that there was a Unit 925 which had a lot of stuff in its background. All the same, I don't know if it was people from the Guomindang, or an army that had been fighting the Guomindang.

XINRAN: How many people were they?

SUN: I'm not really sure. After them came volunteers to assist the frontier. They were all from poor areas like Henan and Gansu, and after that again it was young people assisting the frontier. In 1964 a group of young people came from Shanghai, and another in 1965 or 1966 from Hunan. Another year they came from Tianjin. One of the teachers where I used to work was one of those city youths who came to assist the frontier.

XINRAN: What proportion of people in the corps have gone back home now, and how many have stayed on?

SUN: The majority of the assist-the-borders youths have gone back. Some stayed, but not that many. Then you have the people who came to join the army, from Hunan and Shandong, one group in '52 and another in '54, women soldiers who came to Xinjiang in the name of joining the army.

XINRAN: Why do you say they came "in the name of joining the army"?

SUN: They came to join the army, with drums beating and gongs banging and red rosettes round their necks. To be frank, most of them were recruited to solve the "personal problems" of the army officers here in Xinjiang.

XINRAN: To be wives? Roughly how many?

SUN: I don't have a definite figure, but this was an open secret. Everybody in the corps knew, and they didn't think it was a bad thing either. People spoke very highly of them sometimes: "Even in marriage, their one thought was to help the Party and the motherland. Now that's what I call self-sacrifice and courage!"

*

When I first heard this reply, I thought that Teacher Sun and her husband did not want to discuss the backgrounds of the people in the corps in public, so I brought the conversation to a close. But after several days of interviews, I became aware that there were no proper records for this part of history, because the old people we met with in the 148 Corps could not say anything for sure either.

Teacher Sun gave me what I had been hoping for in my Shihezi reporting trip, but the old people from the 148 Corps we met through Mr Yi exceeded my wildest expectations.

The following day, on our way to the 148 Corps, I visited the Army Wasteland Reclamation Museum. Its 3,000-square-metre exhibition hall contained more than three hundred photographs, all of which moved me greatly, for they were of people living, fighting and struggling in utter poverty. Old people, children and women were treated alike. There might be biological differences, but everyone's lives were the same: days and nights under the sun, stars and moon, with constant sandstorms all year round. Although no figures were given for the number of deaths, we could sense how feeble the "great good luck" of those "lucky survivors" actually was. As we stood at the exit to the exhibition, we found it hard to believe that the modern buildings all around us had been barren wasteland in the fifties.

In the visitors' book I wrote: *Thank you: you have given us the China we know today, we owe you a debt of gratitude as deep as that which we owe to our parents.*

My husband Toby left a message as well: *Every Westerner who comes here and sees with their own eyes what the Chinese achieved out of nothing in the 1950s, transforming the desert into the modern city of today, will ask themselves: Is there anything that the Chinese cannot do?*

After we left the museum, I showed Mr Yi a copy of one of the photographs from the museum, and told him how much I wished I could find the people in it. They were breaking open the virgin soil, moving sand and stones in a sandstorm, but they were talking and laughing. And there was a child by their side, moving sand and stones in a metal washbasin, who also had a very excited expression. I believe that anyone who could smile in the middle of such desperate poverty must be a survivor.

He glanced at the photograph and smiled: Let me give it a go, let's try our luck.

We drove into the residential area of 148 Corps and suddenly I felt that I had walked into that old photograph. I was introduced to two of the old people, and it was immediately clear that they were two of the people in that selfsame photograph! Good heavens! That Mr Yi must be a prophet – or perhaps a wizard. He turned to me and said that without the smiles of history, there would be no self-belief or self-respect. We all knew that the people in that photograph might have been under orders to smile, but nobody came out and said it because we all wanted that time to be real, and because that was the impression that these old people wanted to leave of the days of their youth.

The two old people were husband and wife. Their home was a world away from the skyscrapers and tall buildings of the city, just one house in a row of one-room houses, with mud and earth walls and a roof of straw and wood.

The 320 families in the village shared a single communal water cistern and one public toilet with five squatting spaces each for men and women. Before and after the reporting, I made two journeys to "experience" that toilet, outside which long queues formed every morning. I had barely stepped onto the road to the toilet, before a cloud of flies circled around me, and inside the toilet every inch of the floor was covered in a layer of wriggling white maggots. You had to crush countless maggots to get your feet onto the two "squatting places": planks balanced over a big pit. My eyes were smarting so badly from the noxious fumes drifting out of the pit that I could not keep them open. I thought I might tumble in at any moment, and would have to claw my way out, with a million maggots for company.

We were led into the old couple's house, where we found them preparing us a welcoming meal. Clearly Mr Yi had done a good deal of prior preparation. This is a custom in many Chinese villages, which serves both to welcome guests and to get the measure of them at the same time. When you sit down to a good meal, they watch to see if you take big mouthfuls of the coarse grains and salted vegetables and gulp down the local moonshine before they can be sure whether they should trust you. So I hinted to my group that they should follow their hosts' example. Apart from the hordes of flies competing with us for the food, this was a sumptuous peasant banquet. There were dishes of all sizes, seven or eight in all, including chicken, pork, tofu and vegetables, as well as steamed twisted rolls, rice and a big basin of egg-and-tomato soup.

This was no time to think of dieting. Restraint was not the road to the old people's trust and cooperation. Before too long, two more old people dropped by for a visit. This is another custom in the countryside where there is no cultural life: old people will go to a neighbour's after supper for a smoke and a chat, not returning home to sleep till after dark.

While all this eating and drinking was going on, I started to chat idly with the old people about a few family matters. Afterwards, my interviews began, and as the old people's enthusiasm grew, they could not resist joining in with more words of their own.

*

XINRAN: You said you came in the group of 1956, one of 57,000 who came from Henan. Were you here to assist the border?

148A (a hale and hearty old man of seventy-seven): We all called it "assisting the frontier". Anything that wasn't Reform through Labour or being a soldier was called "coming from the interior to assist the frontier".

XINRAN: Reform through Labour? How many people? Where did they come from?

148B (an elderly 78-year-old whose pipe never left his mouth): Three hundred thousand Reform through Labour convicts. It started about 1951, one lot after another. They seemed to be mostly from Henan and Shandong – well, actually they were from all over. And then there were 15,000 big onions, big onions from Shandong!

XINRAN: Big onions?

148B: Oh, that's Shandong people. [He laughs.] The Shandong Onions came as soldiers, every one of them with a bag of big onions on his back – they're fond of eating big onions.

XINRAN: So how were these people organised?

148A: At that time the name was "Armies of a Hundred Thousand", though that 100,000 was an inflated figure – there were actually only 80,000. So, 80,000 people in one regiment, which was divided into thirteen divisions. Thirteen divisions, 80,000 people, you can work it out. A division could only be so many people. If you worked according to this system, you really couldn't allocate workers properly, so the commissar and the Chief of Staff sent a report to the centre asking for a few hundred thousand more.

XINRAN: Where did these hundreds of thousands of people come from?

148A: Well . . . from Henan, Shandong, and Reform through Labour convicts. Later it was educated youth going down to the countryside from Tianjin, Shanghai and Wuhan. Didn't Chairman Mao have a policy of sending educated youth down to the countryside?

XINRAN: That would be in the Cultural Revolution after 1966, right?

148A: Yes, and we got our next set of Reform through Labour convicts in the Cultural Revolution as well!

XINRAN: How many divisions are there in all now?

148B: It must be fourteen divisions. All told, a third of the population of Xinjiang.

*

An elder who was holding forth on "leadership skills" told me that if you wanted to survive in Shihezi in the 1950s, you had to remember: Don't obey the sergeant, and don't obey the platoon leader either. Why? It was all hard labour in the fields, and that burns you up. Food rations came in fixed amounts, you couldn't eat your fill. When you're sleeping on the ground without a roof over your head or even a bed, year in, year out, taking care of your health and staying alive is down to your own ability. If you kept yourself in good health, if you didn't work well this year, you could have another go the next. The ones who died just died, and that was the end of them. Who thinks about them now? You absolutely had to keep your health. In a society that didn't know who was who, you had to speak less, and listen less, no good would come of talking, all misfortunes come from the mouth. As a leader, you didn't care who got up each day, who never stood up again.

Listening to him, I realised why I couldn't find out the number of dead there, how many were tried and sentenced to death. We don't know. No one knows – no one in Xinjiang, no one in China.

I had heard that hundreds of thousands of young women had been recruited to go to Shihezi to "carry on the family line" for the soldiers, so that their families could put down roots. But I didn't think that the people who were sitting with us would have "made the grade" to be "allocated a wife". Once again, their marriage history was a new experience for me, and in some cases it gave me a lot of food for thought.

I asked 148C, a man of over eighty who still had a head of black hair, where he found a wife. Was she from his home town or from Shihezi?

*

148C: My wife? At home my wife calls me Uncle, d'you know that?

XINRAN: Were you matched as children?

148C: My elder sister said to her: Go with my younger brother.

XINRAN: Were you already here by then?

148C: I came here long before that, she came in the sixties. She's younger than me – when I came out in '56 she was only fifteen years old. Before that I was too poor to get a wife and didn't offer a better prospect than a lot of suffering.

XINRAN: So now she must be a very happy married lady.

148C: Well, we rattle along. I've never given her any cause for worry in my life. All she has to do is eat. [He laughs.]

XINRAN: So what did she do?

148C: She was a worker in the corps, like me. She retired in '86 when she was forty-five. I didn't want her to suffer any more. We had enough to live on. What more do you need?

XINRAN: Are there difficulties today?

148C: That depends on what you call difficulties. If you've had a few years of sleeping on the ground and not getting enough to eat, after that, so long as you can fill your belly and sleep well, you don't think much about difficulties.

XINRAN: Is this why your hair is so black? I really can't believe you're over eighty!

148C: It's fashionable like this now, isn't it? If I don't make myself a bit more easy on the eye, am I being fair to my wife? I've never made her rich, and I couldn't give my children a big official as a father. If I don't think up a few tricks to improve myself, isn't that even more unfair on the whole family, young and old?!

*

So what were their thoughts on the difference between today's relative affluence and their initial penniless existence?

*

XINRAN: Just now in the museum we saw the changes in Shihezi, from utter poverty to basic self-sufficiency. So, has there been a very big change in relationships between people from when you first came here to open up the wasteland?

148D: It was just so different. Put it this way, at that time everyone was so tired that there was no time to think about anything except getting a good sleep. Sometimes we were so tired we fell asleep in the middle of eating. I think that in those days more people died of exhaustion than illness!

XINRAN: Did many people die of exhaustion?

148D: That goes without saying. For some it was all over in just a few days. It's not easy to talk about, you can't say for sure.

XINRAN: Then let's not talk about it. Were there any disturbances here during the Cultural Revolution?

148D: Well, it was better than in the old days. By then we'd started to have reserves in the granary; there were storehouses for rice and wheat, and sometimes you had vegetables to dry outside. We hung up meat outside too. Every family had a room; there were no courtyards, and many houses didn't have a door either.

XINRAN: So when did you start to have doors?

148D: Oh, I think my door must have been put in by about '68 or '67. Back in those days, lots of people got married in the pigpen – that's just the way it was. Others got a shed, and they just lived in that shed. There was no door, nothing at all.

XINRAN: Then you must all have been very pure-minded?

148D: Even if they gave you something, you didn't have anywhere to stash it. Where could you put it? All you had was a room – it was impossible to ask for anything more. We even ate from a big communal pot.

XINRAN: Now do you miss those days?

148D: This high-pressure economy we have nowadays puts too much mental pressure on the workers. The old way was better. In those days, you not only didn't need money to have kids, they gave you money. In hospital nobody ever mentioned a deposit or medical fees, and there was no such thing as a loan. If you were ill in hospital, the work unit would send money over, the hospital would give you food and a bed, and you'd go home once you were cured. When the time came for the children to get married, they just went right ahead. You didn't need money for school either; none of my sons and daughters paid any school fees. If you were sick you didn't pay, if you went to school you didn't pay, and you didn't have to shell out for somewhere to live either, or pay for your kids to find a job. When the children reached working age they reported to their parents' work unit, and they were in work. When the time came for them to start thinking about marriage? Fine, go ahead and get married, and we'll give you a room. In those days there was no need to worry about work or food. You can see the way things are today. Getting married is a burden on the head of the family, and don't even talk to me about getting them a house, I can't even afford the clothes and jewellery! I'll tell you this much, when I got married, we had two kilos of Mohe pipe tobacco, less than a kilo of sweets and no cigarettes at all; we put down a quilt for my wife and a quilt for me, two quilts together and that was that.

XINRAN: Were there guests at your marriage?

148D: Yes, there were. The others in my squad said: "It's your wedding day, we've bought you a picture." And that was that.

XINRAN: What was the picture? [At that time it was fashionable to give a propaganda poster as a present.] Was it a portrait of Chairmen Mao or . . . ?

148D: Oh, no. Portraits of Chairman Mao came later; before that it was all New Year pictures for luck, or scenery.

XINRAN: Have you kept that picture?

148D: No, it's been so many years, how could we have kept it? We didn't keep anything. Look how easy it was to live when I got married – we didn't even miss a day to get the marriage certificate or the health certificate. We went to work, we went for our tests – they took a bit of blood for the health certificate – and when we knocked off work in the afternoon we stopped by the laboratory for the results slip. Getting our marriage certificate was the same. I saw it was getting late, so I went to the office. My wife hadn't had a chance to go, so I went by myself. I ran into the political instructor, and he asked what I was doing there. I said getting married, and we had a little chat, and then I just took the certificate away with me. Once I'd got the certificate, the political instructor said: "When are you going to hold the wedding?" I said, "You decide." The political instructor said: "Saturday, then." I said fine, the political instructor organised a ceremony, and that was it. Nobody in my family knew. It was the political instructor who told me to bring my family over. I sent a telegram, and later the political instructor had my family brought over. *Aiya*, I'm telling you, those days . . . those days are long gone, but we really did have a very carefree life, it's just that there wasn't much money. Public order was really good back then, there were no problems with thieves or robbers. At that time none of the courtyards had a door; if you rode a bike, you could leave it lying there and nobody would touch it. You could hang up meat in a snowfield and again nobody would touch it.

XINRAN: So do you regret coming here?

148D: No, why should I? If I'd stayed in Shangqiu and never come here, I know for a fact that I wouldn't be around today. I don't work any more – they even call it being retired – and the state gives me five or six hundred yuan every month. In my home town, I wouldn't even get ten! It's so poor there that we still get people coming here – fleeing for their lives.

*

I don't know which of the villagers was passing on the news of our reporting, but once we started our interviews, more and more old people from the village gathered round. They even became talkative, and the space outside the host's inner courtyard filled up with people engaged in heated debate. It seemed like everyone was queuing up to recount their thoughts and experiences. I had not expected this. Why did everybody from the outside world believe that Shihezi people would clam up and refuse to discuss history, when in fact they were like underground magma, held down under pressure, awaiting the chance to come bursting out? Was it because this place had been sealed off for too long? Or was it that the people had been squashed by the weight of history until they were gasping for breath?

Yet another old man squeezed in, adding himself to those already "stacked up" on the small, battered old sofa next to me.

*

XINRAN: Hello! Do you still have people back home? Are your parents still with us?

148E: My mother and father are both here. We were all sent by the state, the whole family, more than a dozen of us.

XINRAN: You all came? Do you all have houses to live in?

148E: Yes. My older brother has the old broken-down 1960s house now. His six children all live in flats, they're all earning over a thousand a month.

XINRAN: So when was the last time you went back to your home town?

148E: I was last in Shangqiu in '79. I came back in 1980, when they were just starting up the household responsibility system.

XINRAN: Do you think it's better with land allocated to individual households? Or was it better when everybody was all working together?

148E: There was a lot of waste with the collective. You got no bumper harvests. It's like when two families keep a horse; I'm not prepared to fork out for feed, and neither are you, so that horse is bound to be thin. Or like several people living in a house; you don't look after it, so I won't bother either, and then it's bound to leak, isn't it? If you live by yourself, you have to keep it in good nick, don't you?

XINRAN: So was it much better after the land was parcelled out in 1980?

148E: You can get a thousand pounds of wheat out of a *mu* of land. A thousand pounds a *mu*, that's pretty impressive. Back home in the 1950s it was eighty or a hundred pounds a *mu* at most, and that was the best wheat. Now it's a thousand pounds, that's quite something, it's doubled several times over. Now we have good food supplies in the corps production areas, but there's too much pollution mixed in. Too many chemical fertilisers, perfectly healthy people have been destroyed by fertilisers!

XINRAN: So when you were just setting out to cultivate the wilderness there was no fertiliser?

148E: It was all piss and shit! Back then the toilets were always cleaned right out, clean as a whistle. There wasn't even time for maggots to grow!

XINRAN: Chemical fertiliser saves time and strength, and it's cheap. That's why it replaced physical labour and the workers' piss and shit, isn't that right?

148E: Yes, you can save your labour to do a bit of business on the side, and earn a lot more money than you get toiling away in the fields all day. Nowadays kids don't care about the taste of food: these days it's all numbers, people and possessions.

XINRAN: Have you told the stories of those years to your children? Stories of coming here, breaking in the ground and cultivating the desert?

148E: How could I tell them? That's ancient history. Nobody listens.

XINRAN: Have you talked?

148E: They don't take it in. You've come and listened so eagerly, but when they listen they get ever so impatient. They don't get to hear anything good, who wants those bitter days now, who wants that hard life? At that time four of us would buy a single steamed bun. We'd break it into four with our hands – break a two-hundred-gram bun into four pieces – and we didn't dare to eat it during the meal breaks either. When it was almost time to go to work we'd each grab a piece, eating as we walked.

XINRAN: So if someone asked you about Chairman Mao, what would you say? Do you think that what Chairman Mao did was good or bad?

148E: *Aiya* ... Well ... Chairman Mao ... Deng Xiaoping's already made a public statement for you, right? – 70 percent good and 30 percent bad. It's been said already, hasn't it?

XINRAN: What do *you* think? You've said it yourself, that's what Deng Xiaoping thinks.

148E: What do I think? I think he was OK. I didn't get hurt, so he was all right. But when you look at it from the point of view of the people who did get hurt, when you look at the big picture, the Chairman did do a few bad things towards the end.

XINRAN: At the beginning didn't the people take him to their hearts?

148E: Yes, but towards the end he did some inappropriate things. It's terrifying, really. When the end came, he didn't listen to the truth, he only listened to lies. And the people around him were boasting wildly, telling him any old thing. The policies were good, but when they were carried out at the lower levels they went off.

XINRAN: How are things now? Do you have hope now? Are things a little bit better now?

148E: *Aiya*, now? Jiang Zemin said it: If you straighten out the Party, the Party may die; but if you don't straighten out the Party, the nation dies. Now everything's fine apart from all those little leaks everywhere, and that's not good, is it? All these leaks in small places, it's terrible. I'm telling you, if we keep on like this, we're finished. It's always been like that, from the Qing dynasty to Sun Yat-sen to Chiang Kai-shek, you know what I'm talking about. Why did the Qing dynasty get that way towards the end? Now people are still saying, *aiya*, bring back Sun Yat-sen. It wouldn't do any good, Sun Yat-sen would be too old. They say bring back Chairman Mao, but could Chairman Mao come back? And why would we want them back? To sort out the corrupt elements who take the people's money away from them. If we don't do that, well, things start to go wrong with people when they get old – and the same is true of political parties. The cracks are already starting to show, we need to take ruthless measures to put things right.

XINRAN: So how are conditions in the corps now?

148E: The corps ... well, we can't say much about anything outside the corps. The corps is divided into leaders and workers now, split into superiors and inferiors. They all stick together. When something happens they all present a united front. They protect each other; no matter how weak or useless an official is, he'll always have a government job to do, officials look after their own. In Chairman Mao's time, the corps was a big collective, it didn't belong to just one or two people. What you had, I had, we all had. Nobody could have any more than anyone else, or any less either. Now it's come to a pretty pass; banknotes have blocked out the sky and we common folk can't see what they're thinking up there. In Chairman Mao's day the officials used to come and ask how we were – full of concern, they were – but who comes to take care of us now? Nobody comes, nobody wants to know. We're halfway into our graves already, and when we go our thoughts will be gone too.

XINRAN: Isn't there the Shihezi Museum? We visited there, it was really moving. Future generations will be able to learn about you from that.

148E: Do you believe what it says in those captions? Oh, the photographs are real enough, and the exhibits in the cases, they're real too. But what about the true stories behind their stories? Journalists aren't allowed to look into the things that went on in our corps, not even national-level journalists. What was this corps doing? How many people were they? How did they get here? Who lived and who died? What was going on? You can't say anything for sure about the people who came in 1951, and the ones who came later can't say for sure either. Try if you don't believe me! You teachers and students, you just try asking what those people did before they came to join the corps, and see what you get. Nothing doing!

*

In Urumqi I met the mother of my friend ZH. ZH's mother was sent to Xinjiang in 1958 when she was just thirteen years old. As she told me her story, it was clear from her voice that words could never express all she felt.

"That day a group of ten of us set off by train, leaving the beautiful mountains and lakes of Hangzhou behind. We arrived in the great, bustling city of Shanghai, where we boarded another train to Xi'an. We were shocked rigid by the bleakness of Xi'an and the poverty and ignorance of the locals. Many of the girls started crying, and some ran off back to the cities in the east. I didn't have the nerve to run away with them, so I got dressed in my army uniform, and became a new recruit. I was only thirteen, I didn't understand anything, it had never occurred to me that anything frightening would happen. From Xi'an I took one of those 'sardine-can' trains they used to transport soldiers in, which took us to Urumqi, changing at every station. Altogether, the journey from Hangzhou to Urumqi took one month and seven days.

"When we saw the Gobi Desert stretching out in front of us, we were all shocked out of our wits. We couldn't imagine how people could survive here. Most of what they ate were milk products, and the toilets were big pits beneath two slabs of wood. There were no streets or roads, and practically no lights, let alone shops. Later on I learned that the suffering and poverty were nothing. The worst part was the physical labour. Everyone who came to Xinjiang had to do a probationary year of labour, and mine was building reservoirs. For a city girl, working every day on the building sites, where I had to dig the ground or carry stones or earth on a shoulder pole, hard physical labour in the blistering heat of the sun . . . I'll never forget it as long as I live. It's also why I will never feel tired or overworked again in my whole life. We built the first Xinjiang Military Hospital in that place, and that was where I met the man who's my husband now. In those days he was the director of the Xinjiang Song and Dance Troupe. He fell ill and ended up on my ward. He liked me a lot, and he took me to visit his two sisters, who had also been sent to work in Xinjiang. But I really couldn't get used to his reserved style of courtship, and I didn't much care for the way he kept combing his hair all the time – it was very unmanly. I didn't dare to make up my mind on my own, so I asked my friends in the hospital, but most of them didn't approve. They said that he couldn't stop fussing with his hair and clothes whenever he came to see me, he was too capitalist, too petit bourgeois, and he was bound to end up a counter-revolutionary. I was very confused, but I still decided to marry him, because he was clean and very polite.

"We got married and had two daughters. Life in Xinjiang was very hard, so I made up my mind to go back home to Hangzhou. I was determined not to bring up two daughters in this cruel place, so I left the army and took my daughters back to Hangzhou on my own, where I got a job as a nurse in a local hospital. My younger daughter was only two then, and the other was nine. Every minute of every day was a struggle, with no help from either set of parents. My husband and I lived apart like this for twenty-three years, with me working and bringing up the children alone, suffering all kinds of hardship to raise my daughters. We could only get together once a year. Often my husband was busy and couldn't come to Hangzhou, so I would have to take the two girls on the long, arduous journey of over three weeks from Hangzhou to Urumqi to see their father.

"After twenty-three years of separation, we were finally able to live together once more, but it didn't take us long to realise we had become incompatible. My husband despised the extravagance and self-indulgence of the interior, and the constant quibbling over trifles. And I was hugely disappointed in the husband I had longed for through all those lonely nights: his crudeness, his constant grousing and shouting, his total intolerance of anybody different. It made me miserable. But we didn't divorce. Both of us thought we should stay together, if only for the sake of our two daughters and our grandchildren.

"My elder daughter has a son called Haohao. He's thirteen now, and he often quarrels with his grandfather. Haohao believes that his grandfather is dragging the dark shadow of history into his life today. He thinks that his grandfather should accept the gifts that modern society has to offer. But his grandfather feels wretched and angry that his grandson has such an affluent lifestyle but understands nothing of the trials and suffering of the older generation, he doesn't know or respect what happened in the past. I don't think this is just a problem for our family, I don't know what it's like for other people."

When ZH's mother finished speaking, her eyes were staring at something far away over the horizon. I guessed that this distant place was somewhere for which she had started to yearn when she was thirteen: the life of a happy young girl, a young woman hotly in love, a tender wife, a mother telling stories in a soft, gentle voice, an old age spent hand in hand, mutual support and comfort . . . These are every woman's dreams, but what has she had of such dreams?

In fact, the family life of ZH's parents, like that of Teacher Sun and her husband, is an exact portrait of hundreds and thousands of Chinese families from the 1950s until today. The very same happiness, anger, grief and sorrow between the generations can be found in so many families, especially the families of the Chinese who turned Xinjiang green, the mothers, fathers, sons and daughters of Shihezi.

The Chinese say that the Great Western Region is a land of mystery. Every handful of earth there is heavy with legends, and the people who have been to the region have all been touched with the dust of those legends. Perhaps this is still true, for people who come back from the west find that there is a great gulf between them and the people they left behind, a river of stories separating them from their old home.

On the Road
Interlude 1:
Interview with a North-Western Taxi Driver

At half past five on 10 August 2006, we boarded a plane from Urumqi in the far north-west to Lanzhou, capital of the mid-north-western province of Gansu. After a few hours we found ourselves on the road from Lanzhou airport to Lanzhou city, a distance, we had been told, of more than seventy kilometres, which was likely to take us over an hour.

This motorway coiled its way in a long, unbroken line between the yellow-earth hills. All we could see in this expanse of unbroken wasteland was row upon row of small saplings struggling to survive. According to Mr Li, our driver, these few small trees had been planted seven or eight years previously by Party and government offices and the masses who were on organised unpaid "voluntary" projects – an attempt to add some greenery to the scenery beside the road from the airport to the city. Looking at these little saplings which were still less than a metre and a half in height, I felt an inexpressible pressure within me. Somewhere between here and Xi'an was a place called Shouting Hill, which I had once visited on a reporting trip (and written about in *The Good Women of China*). The yellow-earth hills and cogon grass turned my mind back to the people in that place, and I saw again the desperate hopes those starving people pinned on this sparse, unpromising plant: on yellow-earth hills like these on the edge of the Gobi Desert, the roots of this cogon grass are the local people's one source of survival, cooking fuel and warmth. I could still remember how the men of Shouting Hill village would trudge long distances in search of this cogon grass. Due to increasing demand, cogon grass is becoming scarce, so people have to travel ever greater distances in order to find it, which takes up more and more of their time.

I hope the planting of forests along the airport expressway can bring some hope to this region of yellow earth. I also hope that this swathe of green will be a single spark that sets all the land aflame, reaching all the way to Shouting Hill.

The following day we were scheduled to take a minibus from Lanzhou to Hezheng county, where we were going to interview one of China's oil experts and his wife, the head of a female prospecting team. The results of the last few days' reporting had far exceeded my expectations. In those few days, the heaviness and depth behind the old stories, the memories that had never been opened or touched, had trickled their way, a little at a time, into my records.

I did not know how future generations would judge the fifty or seventy years' sacrifice of Double-Gun Woman's family and the five thousand people of Huaying Mountain and the millions in the Xinjiang Construction Corps, but I knew that what I was doing now might be the most worthwhile act of my life. It was also a very painful experience, because as each of them was telling me the story of their past, there was suspicion in all their eyes, to a greater or lesser extent – could I understand these experiences? Nobody knew how many painful experiences I had lived through in the Cultural Revolution, nobody knew the humiliations I had suffered, nobody knew how much courage it had taken me to live on to today. I longed to reach the age when it would be permissible for me to tell, because I was afraid that my courage would not hold out to that day.

Again, Mr Li was our driver. From the way he stowed our baggage and his polite manner of giving way to other users of the road, I could see that he was a calm, conscientious person.

Chinese drivers in long-distance haulage and public transport have often been some of my best teachers when I am on a quest for knowledge, because they have seen so much – how this country has changed, the huge difference between west and east China, and gaps between cities and countryside, along the thousands of kilometres of highways they drive every day. I started with a question about the weather, the safest topic in any country to open a conversation with a stranger.

*

XINRAN: Do you know today's temperature?

LI: Today's report was thirty degrees, the last two days have been Autumn Tigers, very hot. It'd be nice to have some rain – Lanzhou's desperately short of rain.

XINRAN: What special products are there in your region?

LI: There's Lanzhou pulled-beef noodles. They're very famous, you can find them all over the country.

XINRAN: And apart from Lanzhou pulled-beef noodles? Is *yang-rou-pao-mo* [stewed lamb with breadcrumbs] also a local thing? Do you think that Xi'an's *yang-rou-pao-mo* is more famous, or Lanzhou's?

LI: They're eaten in different ways, you can't compare the two. Lanzhou uses soft, leavened bread, clear soup, bean noodles and slices of meat, you soak them yourself in the soup, and crumble your own bread, it gets soft as soon as it's in the soup. Over in Xi'an you have to soak your own breadcrumbs too, but they're very hard to crumble, the bread's very tough, and once you're done crumbling them, you have to boil them as well, or they're inedible. In all the times I've been to Xi'an, I've never once eaten Xi'an *yang-rou-pao-mo*.

XINRAN: And is there anything else? Aren't there some Treasures of Lanzhou – or is that Gansu? [Gansu is one of the poorest provinces in China, but I always like to give people the chance to tell me what they are proud of locally. Their answers give valuable insights into how local people see themselves and why.]

LI: There's the Lanzhou lily, you might have heard of it, it takes three years to mature, it's a very good tonic that soothes coughs and moistens the lungs, a real, genuine Lanzhou speciality. Then there's Lanzhou's White Orchid melon, that's a Lanzhou speciality too, but that variety hasn't been doing very well the last couple of years, you don't see so many of them these days. And Anning in the Lanzhou area has a kind of peach called the White Phoenix peach, it's a kind of very, very sweet peach, all the Anning peaches are flown direct to Hong Kong. And then there's that magazine the *Reader*, do you know it?

XINRAN: Yes, I know it. It used to be called *Reader's Digest*, then there was a court case, and they changed it to the *Reader*.

LI: That's right, the Americans took them to court. Anyway, that's produced in Lanzhou as well. It's a big name all over the country, must be one of the top five, no question about it. There's a "Reader Street" in Lanzhou, after the *Reader* magazine. And a bridge called the "First Bridge over the Yellow River", the only bridge to span the Yellow River in this place. It was designed in America, and made in Germany – they guaranteed the bridge would last eighty years. Construction began in 1907, and in 1910 it opened to traffic. I've heard that half the total investment went into the building materials. They were shipped from Germany to Tianjin, then transported to Lanzhou in carts, because they couldn't be carried by water. It cost them 300,000 taels of silver. In the 1980s, a German bridge-building firm sent its people specially to inspect the bridge, and it's still here today, after ninety-seven years. Now the government has preserved it as a cultural artefact – it's been converted into a footbridge, and motor vehicles aren't allowed on.

XINRAN: Is there a historical museum in Lanzhou?

LI: I'm sorry to say that I've never been inside the history museum, or taken any customers there. But we have the Horse and Swallow motif, the one that's the emblem of China's tourist industry, which was unearthed in Gansu. The original Horse and Swallow is a bronze statue of a horse galloping on the back of a flying swallow. It was dug up in Leitai in Wuwei county, which is in Gansu province.

XINRAN: And what else is there? Carry on . . . I'll make sure you get proper tuition fees.

LI [laughs]: Well . . . China's Four Great Caves are the Longmen Caves in Luoyang, the Yungang Grottos in Shanxi, Dunhuang's Mogao Caves and the Maiji Grottos, both of them in Gansu. Half of them belong to us!

XINRAN: As a driver you must have felt the changes in Lanzhou more deeply than people in other professions . . .

LI: That's right! Look at all the 1980s buildings that used to line the street here, more than half of them have been pulled down already.

XINRAN: What do the inhabitants of Lanzhou think of the local government's policy these days?

LI: I couldn't say.

XINRAN: They aren't too deeply opposed to it?

LI: It's the corruption. Many government officials and civil servants are very greedy, they always think the people above them take more than they do, everybody thinks they take a bit less than the others. Don't get me started on that – as soon as they're mentioned I lose my temper!

XINRAN: All right, let's not talk about them. What are Lanzhou's latest population figures?

LI: The official figure is over 3 million, but that must be far short of the actual figure. There are so many outsiders doing temporary work here, the streets and lanes are full of them, nobody knows how many there really are. There's a lot of Zhejiang people in Lanzhou, they run a big shopping centre here, it's called the Yiwu Trade City, and it sells nothing but top-quality goods. Zhejiang people do a lot of business here, Lanzhou has a Zhejiang village in the eastern wholesale market, where practically everybody's from Zhejiang.

XINRAN: It's not just here, you find Zhejiang people doing business all over the world. They have a real eye for making money, very quick brains.

*

Zhejiang is in south-east China, a coastal province with a history of migration going back to the twelfth century. New Zhejiang migrant workers can be found almost everywhere on earth since China opened up in the 1980s.

*

LI: I don't get it, we're all people, we're all part of the same national system, how come *they* get to make a living wandering all over the world, while all we can do is bury ourselves in poverty here?

XINRAN: In Lanzhou city, do you see more rich people or poor people? Is there any help for poor people?

*

Before my journey, I had heard state officials announce that China's central government had failed to restructure social systems including health care, education and pensions since the 1980s. On the one hand I am happy to know the leadership are learning how to be honest in the face of problems. On the other, I would like to know how people feel about this. Obviously, Mr Li hadn't heard about it.

*

LI: I can't say for sure. A fair few people are living on the government's social security money, 202 yuan a month.

XINRAN: About what proportion of Lanzhou people are drawing that basic living allowance? Twenty per cent? Ten per cent? Five per cent?

LI: It's not a big percentage, I don't know the figures.

XINRAN: So how do all those rich people get their money?

LI: Property, running work gangs on building sites, investment, private businesses, that sort of thing.

XINRAN: What sort of incomes do Lanzhou government civil servants get?

LI: Civil servants' incomes are very high.

XINRAN: Over a thousand a month? Over two thousand?

LI: Over a thousand isn't that much; at least two or three thousand, I should think. I haven't had anything to do with civil servants. They're not paid according to results like us, where you get a percentage of the profits if you do a good job; if we were to sit there just waiting for customers to come to us, we wouldn't make much. Drivers like me are doing pretty well if we get 1,100 or 1,200 in the high season.

XINRAN: The winter is the slack season, so how much can you get then?

LI: In the slack season I just go home and sleep, and I do casual work; at most I get 800 yuan.

XINRAN: So do you have any minimum-wage security?

LI: No, I have to go out and find other work – they give you 800 yuan a month, how long can you feed a family of three on that? They calculate that the minimum average income should be 170 or a bit more per person, this 800 yuan will feed your family for a bit over a month. When you haven't got a job, they do calculations about you, put in requests, examine and approve them. What with all those endless forms to fill in, all that running around and getting yourself obligated, it's so much hard work you'd be better off looking for a job!

XINRAN: The government has a specialised service for that, don't they?

LI: Well, they do, but the leaders in some of the backward districts . . . let's just say that if you've got connections they'll sort it out for you, but without connections you'll have to wait a few more months. And if you're drawing the basic living allowance, you have to do what they tell you, and do labour for them once a week. If you don't do the labour service then you don't get anything, it shows that you have work to do, and they strike you off the list.

XINRAN: What labour do the people collecting the basic living allowance do?

LI: They have to sweep the streets, or spend a day patrolling the area.

XINRAN: How much is the average income for a peasant in Gansu province?

LI: Peasants who don't live too far from the city have a pretty good income, they all grow vegetables, the government's bought up all the land close to Lanzhou, so they've all had money from that, and houses and living expenses too, so they just do a bit of business on the side to stop themselves getting bored.

XINRAN: So how about peasants who live further out?

LI: Life's very hard. Places with water are a little bit better, you can plant a few food crops, a few vegetables, some melons and other fruits, enough to feed the whole family.

XINRAN: And what about the places without any water?

LI: Without water? That'd be like our Dingxi, where the government's doing all that poverty alleviation work. Have you heard of the Two Xis? One is Dingxi, one is Longxi – it's so poor in those places, your heart aches to hear about it. A family of seven with just one pair of trousers between them – whoever goes outside wears them.

XINRAN: Even now?

LI: Yes, now! They really are that poor, because there's no water in the mountain areas, and every year they can't even get back the seed they've sown. In the past you weren't allowed to leave to find work, that was even more cruel! Now it's a bit better, as the ones who can do hard labour – and dare to climb over the mountains, cross the rivers and trek long distances – can do casual work away from home, to give the family a bit of support. What with that and emergency rations from the government, a lot less of them starve to death than before.

XINRAN: And what about the ones who can't go out to do labour?

LI: The women, old people, little kids . . . well, they just have to stay at home and put up with it.

XINRAN: So from what you know, how does the state help them?

LI: Every year there are emergency grain rations and work-for-food schemes. The government pays your board and lodging, exchanging the work you do for food for your family. And the last resort is migration, moving them to places where there's water.

XINRAN: Are they willing to go?

LI: The younger ones must be – in those places you can't even keep body and soul together. The older ones always think that it's better to die in their own homes, die in the place they know. The poorer a place is the more ignorant and foolish the people are, they just don't believe the world outside exists!

*

After we got out of the car, and I paid Driver Li his "tuition fees", he said, "You didn't have to be so polite! You've seen the world, how could you still not know about Lanzhou?" You hear things like this very often in China: "He's a provincial-level leader, and yet he can't read a blueprint?" "You can't even look after your keys, how can you be in charge of all those people?" A very typical piece of Chinese folk logic.

4

Pioneers of China's Oil: A Distinguished Husband and Wife

Mrs You, *left*, and Mr You, *right*, poring over an oil exploration map with a Russian expert, north-west China, 1950.

Standing in front of their house in Hezheng, 2006.

MR YOU, aged seventy-eight, and his wife, aged seventy-six, pioneers of oil exploration in China, *interviewed in Beijing and Hezheng, Gansu province, in north-west China. Mr You, a Hero of Labour, was part of the very first group of Chinese oil explorers. In the Cultural Revolution he was "struggled against" because of his contacts with the Soviet Union, but is now a respected authority and influences many aspects of China's oil exploration. Mrs You went from trainee teacher to become the first head of a female oil-prospecting brigade. Their three children were raised mainly by grandparents.*

When I was at university I read a book called *The Command of the Air* by Giulio Douhet, a military strategist who was born in Italy in 1869, and who in 1909 started to challenge the traditional military idea of domination by sea, predicting that the skies would become the century's next battleground. In 1921 he published *The Command of the Air*, on which much modern air tactical theory is based, and followed it with *The Face of Future Warfare*. In due course, the great global slaughters of the 1930s and the Second World War proved the correctness of Douhet's theories. However, his contemporaries seem not to have been aware of oil in the way that we are today: since the year 2000, oil has been both a cause of war and a weapon in the struggle for world domination. Less than a hundred years after the first oil was poured into the first barrel, it has leaked into the skies, seas and earth of humanity, into our clothes, food, homes and transport; it has become a part of the structure of our lives that it is impossible to ignore.

In the years when I was growing up in China, people took pride in their future, but for most people this future involved "limitless high production" of wheat (like the exaggerated reports they were accustomed to hearing), and the Soviet Union's "potatoes cooked with beef" (the Chinese idea of a tasty Russian meal). When the great Daqing oilfields were mentioned, they conjured up an image of a profession that "forged men of steel", but the importance of oil in our daily lives, even in political discussions about China's future, was barely touched on. The first major discovery of oil was made in September 1953 in a town called Landa, located in north-east China. Did the Chinese care about oil? When they founded the New China, did the policymakers who had come from the muddy fields and ditches of the countryside, who had defeated the planes and guns of the American Army and founded the People's Republic of

China with "millet and rifles", understand that in the future Chinese people would need to drive cars and take aeroplanes?

I had tried many times to investigate this issue in the years before 1997, and each time I came away disappointed. I had been warned that this was "a national secret". Nonetheless, I hoped that somebody would help me understand the story of Chinese oil, and give an account of how its significance emerged. Finally, through my own circle of friends, I unearthed a married couple: he was a major figure in China's national oil prospecting, and she had been the first leader of a women's oil-prospecting team. Both husband and wife had been buried in history, retirement and "being a national secret" for a very long time.

On 11 August 2006, my reporting team set out in a twelve-seater Icarus minibus, which we had hired for 150 yuan, and travelled two and a half hours from Lanzhou to Hezheng county, where the two old people had a summer residence.

Hezheng county is located in the south of Gansu province. It has a total area of 960 square kilometres, exactly 1/10,000 of China's territory. Hezheng county is situated in the region where the Tibetan Plateau meets the Yellow Earth Plateau of the north-west: to the south of the county is a ridge of high, stony mountains, whereas the north is a region of gullies and ravines in the yellow earth. It is one of poverty-stricken Gansu's rare scenic areas, where the mountains come together, row upon row, each peak rising higher than the last, to form scenery as beautiful as any picture. The area's population is roughly 200,000, of which minority nationalities make up 57 per cent.

The police officers who had helped us along our route were surprised that we had made Hezheng county part of our itinerary, because Linxia Hui Autonomous Prefecture, of which Hezheng county is a part, has seen one of the biggest intensifications of racial conflict in the country in recent years, especially between the Han and Hui (Chinese Muslim) groups. After nine o'clock residents do not enter the territory of other ethnic groups; if they do they might never be seen again. But as far as we newly arrived outsiders were concerned, apart from Buddhist temples and Muslim mosques by the side of the highway, each village vying with its neighbours for strangeness and beauty, and a feeling that the streets were unusually quiet and deserted, we didn't get so much as a whiff of cordite.

We spent the night in the Hezheng County Guest House. This government-run hotel, crammed between a crowd of new buildings which were still under construction, was used by local officials to hold meetings.

The hotel was reminiscent of the guest houses attached to government ministries in Beijing in the 1950s and '60s, roadside hotels in the big cities in the 1970s and '80s, and "two-star" hotels in the '90s: a three-storey building, with a dimly lit service desk on one side of the ground floor, and rows of aluminium keys marked with red paint hanging on the wall, which showed both the scale of the guest house, and its emptiness. On the other side of the lobby was a long dining hall, in which the huge round tables were as numerous as the keys; without a doubt this place had seen innumerable "battles of eating and drinking". The first and second floors were guest rooms: peeling wallpaper patterned with peonies, mildewed red carpets and rust-speckled iron Thermos flasks for hot water. In the light of all this, it is perhaps not surprising that the building was constantly rocked by deafening blasts of noise from the demolition works and building sites outside, so loud that we couldn't hear each other speak.

It is impossible to escape from building noise, one of China's defining characteristics. My bedroom was equipped with the most luxurious furniture available locally, but in a very mismatched style: a mahogany sofa, metal tables and chairs and a king-size bed with plastic stickers on the headboard, against which was propped a pair of pillows embroidered with the words "Love Song" in English. The bathroom was very big, and boasted a 1.5-metre-high "sauna" box as well as a crude shower head, but since any attempt actually to use any of the functions invariably led to "flash floods", I was resigned simply to admire it as a piece of interior decoration.

In order to get a clearer idea of the role Hezheng county had played in the life of Mr and Mrs You, and to give them a chance to get to know us, we didn't start the interviews straight away, but went for a stroll with them around this small county town. This took less than an hour, after which we went with them and some of their relatives to the Hezheng Fossil Museum, a source of international pride to the locals.

Hezheng Fossil Museum is China's only museum of vertebrate fossils. It is one of China's very few national-level specialised museums, built after the Sichuan Dinosaur Fossil Museum, and the Banpo Neolithic village near Xi'an.

Starting in the 1950s, large quantities of rare fossils have been unearthed in Hezheng county, and today the museum collection comprises over six thousand fossil specimens. Hezheng Fossil Museum contains many different varieties rarely seen anywhere else in the world, preserved in good condition: their three-toed horse fossils and collection of fossil skulls are the best in the European-Asian land mass, superior even to the world-famous three-toed-horse-producing areas of Pikermi and Sarmos; and only the New York Natural History Museum and the Natural History Museum in Beijing have larger collections of shovel-tusked elephant fossils. Several of these creatures were named after this place, such as the Hezheng Goat, which has been found nowhere else in the world. The state invested 15,250,000 yuan to build the 3,850-metre-square museum, which is both a National Youth Education Base and a Popular Science Tourism Unit, as well as a scientific base for researchers from China and overseas. It took us almost two hours to view two of the six subject areas: the three-toed horse and the shovel-tusked elephant.

Among the local Han people, it is possible to tell the background of a family without entering the house or asking the owner's name, from the lintel of the doorway of every household. Those who had some local fame, such as an ancestor who had passed the *xiucai* examinations, would have a brightly painted, gilded lintel; if a family's ancestor had been a major official at provincial level, there would be two rows of even more luxurious lintels; three rows of lintels on the gate of a courtyard were for families whose ancestors had been high scholars or officials serving under the emperor himself. The last few generations of the You family had been important people in the locality, so the family courtyard was a small two-storey horseshoe-shaped building, inside the only three-lintel gate in the whole village, which stood out among the masses of humbler dwellings. We addressed Mr You by the respectful name younger people use for scholars of the older generation: Teacher You. Teacher You pointed to those three lintels and said proudly: "That's several generations of true scholarship and talent; you can't buy that now, not at any price!"

On entering the You family courtyard, the ancestral temple stands on the left and the parlour to the right, the two low buildings on either side being for the use of the three brothers and sisters and their families when they came to visit, with bedrooms upstairs and kitchens and living areas downstairs. We were told that this courtyard was normally managed by Mr You's youngest sister, who lived and worked here.

The broad, spacious ancestral temple attracted my attention, for in it were displayed relics of the changing times through which this family had lived. Against the left-hand wall were a pair of dowry chests of the kind used about sixty years ago when taking a bride into the family, and which in some places served as chests for the bride's personal possessions. Two antique high-backed chairs in yellow chestnut were placed against the main wall, flanking an old-fashioned square table, on which sat a radio with a dial printed in Russian, about the size of a small microwave oven. Teacher You said that his family had suffered a good deal in the Cultural Revolution because of this radio, which he had brought back after studying in the Soviet Union. The table also held a picture of Teacher You, taken on a visit to a missile base in a country I couldn't identify; when I asked what country it was he smiled but didn't reply. On the right-hand side the floor was empty, but several eye-catching calligraphy scrolls displaying large characters were hanging on the wall; these had been written specially for him by several deceased national leaders. An old couple gazed sombrely down from a photograph on the wall over the table on everybody who came in.

When I saw this room, I understood why Teacher You and his wife came to Hezheng every year for their summer holidays. I thought: Here at least there are no historical rights and wrongs, no worries over changes in the political climate and none of the stresses of keeping up with fashionable living. Or, in Teacher You's words: not only is the weather cool, the atmosphere is free.

I had originally thought that the main focus of my interviews was to be Teacher You. However, I have always considered that half of a man is woman, and if you wish to understand the man, you must understand the woman who has shared his life, so Mrs You and I had our conversation first. Before she sat down, Mrs You showed me a selection of outfits, and asked me to help choose the one that "suited her best". My suggestion was a pure silk suit of lake green – I thought that this was a colour full of the gentleness of southern Chinese women, and the dignity of a woman with a successful career behind her. When she had changed her clothes and was sitting in front of me, the delicate beauty and dignity of her expression reminded me of my mother. How I wished this could have been me in conversation with my mother.

*

XINRAN: Mrs You, you can sit a little bit more comfortably if you like. First of all I want to ask you for a few memories of your childhood, then stories of when you were a young girl, after that some stories of you as a wife, then as a mother, then as a grandmother. Is that OK?

MRS YOU: Do I have to talk about being a grandmother as well?

XINRAN: We won't discuss big ideas, or politics, just life, your feelings at that time, experiences that are yours alone and nobody else's. How does that sound?

MRS YOU: That's fine, it's my own things I want to talk about, I don't care about other people's business. First let me say that I'm very happy to see you, with your sweet voice and smiling face. You don't have one of those put-on journalist faces.

XINRAN: Thank you! I know you have a lot of experience of interviews: from the 1950s onwards your name was in all the big national newspapers, you were famous all over the country. But I haven't come here because you're famous – there were many famous people in my lists of possible names, but I didn't really want to talk to them. I could tell over the phone that you were a woman of stature, and I saw your beauty from your photographs. In most Western people's eyes we Chinese have no spirit, Chinese women have no feelings and even no beauty in your generation, so I wanted to interview people with spirit, to show them your elegant beauty and spirit, nurtured by Chinese culture! You must have been very beautiful when you were young.

MRS YOU: Oh no, not me.

XINRAN: Mrs You, people say that the greatest benefit of retirement is having the time and space to recall the past. Do you have many childhood memories?

MRS YOU: I would dearly love to write a book of reminiscences, but I haven't got the time. My daughter-in-law had a child just after I retired, and very soon after that my third daughter had a child too. Because we had no time to look after our children in the past, and our children had a sad life as a result, I want to make it up to them now.

XINRAN: What is the story you most want to write? What are the four or five stories that you most want to tell, from when you were a girl of ten until now?

MRS YOU: There are ever so many, where should I begin? I've never told my stories because nobody's ever wanted to hear them. At first I was afraid that people would say I came from a bad family background, then later on I was worried that the children would laugh at me. I was born and grew up in Jingxiang village in Cang'an county, Zhejiang province, it has over six hundred years of history. It was built when the Ming dynasty general Qi Jiguang fought Japanese pirates there, it has a city wall with four gates and a moat, and there's a group of hills inside the town that looks like a lion, called Lion Mountain, the scenery is very beautiful, and there are a lot of cultured people in the town. But it's a pity, they pulled down the walls and got rid of the ancient buildings during the Great Leap Forward and the Cultural Revolution. The Eastern Sea is close by, it's a land of fish and rice, you could eat freshly caught fish every day there. Girls from the seaside all have big, bright eyes, perhaps because they eat a lot of seafood, fish and prawn skins.

XINRAN: Is this a local legend?

MRS YOU: We didn't understand in those days, but later on I discovered that seafood contains a lot of calcium, which is good for the eyes.

XINRAN: I've heard that Zhejiang girls are very beautiful, but I never thought that it was from eating seafood.

MRS YOU: The girls are pretty there, and it has a good climate, there are no bitterly cold winters, and no sandstorms either. There was this one winter when we were young, there was a sudden, light fall of snow, snowflakes were drifting about in small flurries, not many of them. My brothers and sisters and I were so happy, we got a cotton sheet, and each took hold of a corner to catch the snow so that none would fall on the ground, it was very beautiful. And then there was another particularly cold year, it snowed again, and that time we made a snowman. We never saw snow in winter again after that. We never wore thick cotton-padded clothes, thick overcoats, or even woollen undertrousers, we'd just use an extra pair of unlined trousers.

XINRAN: Tell me about your mother and father.

MRS YOU: My father's family had been scholars for generations, although by his generation they had lost most of their wealth. They always approved of education and supported setting up schools. My grandparents gave several *mu* of family land for a school, it was called the "Awakening Teacher School". My oldest uncle went to Hangzhou Commercial College, but my second uncle and my father didn't get so much schooling. My father started out as an apprentice in a tailor's shop straight out of primary school. He didn't marry until he was thirty, and he was very happy when I came along. It was a feudal society in those days, people only celebrated the first male child, but my father wasn't like other men – he treated me like a boy. My grandmother was widowed when she was still in her thirties, she was very fond of me. Now I don't have very clear memories from when I was very small, but sometimes they still appear vaguely in my brain.

I remember when I was four I often put charcoal bricks in my grandmother's brass stove – my mother used to get everything ready, and then

I'd pop in the charcoal. It was a cold winter day, I hadn't slept all night. I heard the grown-ups crying, and I thought that it was Granny, crying because there was nobody to tend her stove, so I called out to Mummy, "Take the stove over to Granny so she can get warm," but Mummy said that Granny had passed away. Later, I saw the adults crying and I cried along with them. That was the first time I saw grown-ups cry, and it made me wonder why.

Then there was a time when I was five or six, a very cold day in winter. We had a pond in the courtyard of our house, the children all liked playing by that pond and looking at the fish. I went to play by the pond, but somehow I fell in! The pool was quite deep in the middle, though the sides were shallow, and I was wearing a black quilted jacket. That heavy soaked padded jacket was a dead weight, dragging me down, I couldn't move, and I didn't know to call out. Luckily, one of my uncles was over on a visit, he heard the splash from the parlour, and saw a black padded jacket bobbing about in the pool. "*Aiya*," he said, "I've just seen a child fall in!" and he came rushing over to pull me out. I was chilled to the bone. Now whenever I speak of cold, I think of the freezing cold of that black padded jacket.

By the time I was seven or eight, I was already in the second year of primary school. Our family had a big house then, with a central courtyard paved with flagstones. In those days there were no toys, nothing to play with, so in summer we little girls drew houses on the flagstones with chalk and played hopscotch. Just as I was playing happily with a few other girls, all of a sudden there was a roar, the earth and sky seemed to shake, the sky grew dark, and we heard a loud noise. We were frightened out of our wits, we didn't know what was happening, so we hurried out onto the street. We saw people strolling about, enjoying the cool evening air; they were all fine, they'd heard a loud noise, but it was all over quickly, and nobody knew what it was. It was only later that we found out from the grown-ups that this noise was made by something called a bomb. The Japanese had been dropping bombs on China, but we had never experienced it in our part of the world. So we girls slowly made our way back home, where we found that a beam of the house had been broken by the shock, and the two beds underneath the beam were covered in tiles from the roof. They had just fetched my baby brother from the bed.

XINRAN: You were saying that you were already at primary school then. What did you learn at school in those days?

MRS YOU: In the first year we learned a lot of poems and children's folk rhymes. There's a song I still know by heart: "Kitten small, kitten jump, kitten catch a rat, rat run away." In the second year the teacher taught us how to use an abacus to add and subtract – there were rhymes to teach us the rules of the abacus. For activities, we ran races and played with rubber balls, and we played hide-and-seek, and running to a tree for forfeits, the last one to touch the tree had to sing a song.

XINRAN: What was the proportion of male students to female students when you were in primary school?

MRS YOU: Our village was relatively enlightened for the time. A lot of the girls went to school, sometimes a third of a class was girls. All the girls in my extended family went to school. My uncle, who had attended commercial college, became the headmaster of the school my grandparents set up. He only had three daughters, no sons, but he had progressive ideas, and encouraged the villagers to oppose Yuan Shikai and support Sun Yat-sen. All his daughters went on to marry scholars and educated men, and they certainly influenced me.

XINRAN: It's said that in China in the thirties and forties standard middle schools were the only route to senior school and then university, but there were very few schools and the fees were very high, so what kind of middle school did you go to?

MRS YOU: In those days there was only a primary school in the village, so when I started middle school at the age of thirteen, I had to leave home to go to teacher training school. At that time my ambition was to be a doctor. A lot of people died of tuberculosis in those days – my cousin and my oldest uncle had both died of TB, and other relatives too. To become a doctor I would have had to attend the standard middle school, followed by senior middle school and university, but my family's finances couldn't stretch that far, so I had to sit the exam for the teacher training school. At the start of the course the teacher announced that the first essay was on "My Ambition". I said that my ambition had originally been to be a doctor, but now I was at the teacher training school, I had told myself: you should be a teacher, and serve the people. The teacher liked my essay, and I got 99 per cent.

Our home was a few li away from the teacher training school, and in those days there were no cars, and it would take two hours to get from home to school on foot. When I was in my second year, I wanted to go back home to pick up some clothes. I had a classmate, not as tall as me, but a year older, who also wanted to go home for her summer clothes, so the two of us set off early one Sunday morning. The school food wasn't that tasty or plentiful, four small dishes between eight of us, and if you were a slow eater you wouldn't get enough. We'd all stand to attention and then they'd say *"kaitong!"* ["dinner is served"], and everybody would pick up their chopsticks at once, quick eaters would eat their fill, slow eaters got very little, so when I came back home I wanted something to eat. In those years we didn't have any biscuits or bread, just rice; the family had a grinder, my mother ground flour and made a few flat cakes, with spring onions and shrimp flakes added – that was a delicious treat. Because we waited for those tasty shrimp cakes, we didn't set off back to school until four o'clock. In summer, thunderstorms could come at any time, but we were young and thoughtless, and nobody thought to warn us. There were four gates in the town wall, north, south, east and west, we left by the north gate, heading for school, but when we reached a village called Qianche the sky darkened, there was a roll of thunder, and all at once the rain came pouring down in torrents. The flagstone path we were walking on was only a handspan wide, just a row of stone slabs, with paddy fields full of uncut rice plants on one side and a big river on the other. We were walking in single file, and I was holding an umbrella, with a bag of summer clothes on my arm. I was scared I wouldn't make it back to school in time and they'd fine us, so I was getting panicky and flustered. We just kept walking, with her in front and me behind. We couldn't see any peasants working in the fields in their south Chinese straw rain capes, there wasn't even anybody else on the path, no one but ourselves between the vast, empty paddy fields and the river, where many wild water lilies were growing. The other girl was going very fast, she was over a dozen metres ahead of me, and somehow I slipped and fell into the river. Luckily the wild water lilies were very thick there, I dropped right on top of them, with the river water rushing past in torrents next to me. At the time I wasn't scared, and somehow I managed to clamber back up. As soon as I was on the bank I shouted, "Heavens above!" (Southerners shout "Heavens above" whenever anything happens.) But that evening I lay on my bed, tossing and turning, unable to sleep. The more I thought about it the more scared I became; if the water lilies had covered me, I wouldn't have been able to climb back up by myself, and nobody would have come to rescue me, they wouldn't even have been able to find my body. Having nearly drowned twice when I was young, I was always afraid of water and so never learned to swim.

XINRAN: Mrs You, in your memories, what sort of people were your mother and father?

MRS YOU: I can't remember so much about Daddy, he was always busy with his work; besides, I was a girl – he liked me, but he didn't care about my studies as much as my younger brothers'. My mother was a very hard-working, very honest woman, she wasn't afraid of hardship. She was very fond of me when I was a little girl, she taught me to turn up a hem, to cut out cloth and make clothes, to sew and mend. In the past, we even made our own belts for trousers; raising silkworms, weaving cloth, we did it all ourselves. She could do everything: reeling the silk off the individual silkworm cocoons to weave into silk, weaving cotton cloth and embroidery. In the summer and winter holidays I liked to follow her about and give her a hand here and there. I wove on the loom as well, and when I was a bit older I helped my mother make shoes. There were four boys after me, so I helped my mother to sew many shoe soles. Our summer holidays weren't like the ones children have nowadays, with drawing lessons, piano lessons or cramming classes. We had to spend every holiday making shoes, we couldn't afford to buy them. I really don't know how we would have managed without my mother's skill and hard work.

XINRAN: After listening to you, I can "see" your mother, a mother who not only taught you how to be a woman, but how to survive. Do you believe that this is one of the reasons why children nowadays are not as close to their mothers as they were in your generation?

MRS YOU: Of course! Just like I never thought about these things until I became a mother myself, but by that time I wasn't my own master, the times were different, and there were different demands on women.

XINRAN: You were the first head of a female oil-prospecting brigade in China's history. You went from a trainee teacher to that, which makes you a Chinese miracle in your own time.

MRS YOU: I haven't really thought about it. We weren't very sophisticated then, we only thought about building up our motherland, about not letting the American imperialists bully us, not giving the Westerners a reason to look down on us! In 1953 a call went out to train a batch of fast-track teachers to serve the nation. Three years of study were condensed into a single year. When I finished teacher training school I was sent straight on to Wenzhou City Normal School. My idea at the time was that once I graduated as a teacher I'd start making a living as a teacher. But when we were about to graduate and be assigned jobs, the North-West Geology Management College sent a representative from Xi'an to our school in

Wenzhou to select two hundred students to help the great north-western oil-prospecting mission. He said the nation needed this survey more than they needed teachers, so the school encouraged activists to devote themselves to the construction of the motherland. I was very progressive in those days, I was class monitor, and I'd been on propaganda teams.

I liked the thought of seeing the outside world, that had always been an ambition of mine. I had read many books as a little girl, and the story of Mulan in the army was the one that stirred me most deeply. I had learned about the Great North-West in geography and history classes, I knew about the northern Chinese scenery, I knew that it snowed in the north-west, and I knew about things like the Qilian Mountains and Jiayuguan, where the Great Wall ends in the desert. All of these were things I'd heard about in poems, and I wanted to go out and explore it for myself. At that time none of us knew what a geological survey actually was, and we never thought to mention it – the motherland needed us!

I was in Wenzhou, which was a long way away from my home town, and at that time transport was poor, there was no road, and no bridge to cross the river, so I hadn't been back at all since I left for the Normal School. I thought the family wouldn't be that worried, after all I wasn't a boy, so I went straight from the school to Xi'an – my family didn't even know.

First we took the bus to Hangzhou, and then a train from Hangzhou to Xi'an. When we arrived in Xi'an we were all very excited, it was quite backward but we didn't care, and we went to visit the Great Goose Pagoda. The course in Xi'an was an accelerated course, we went very fast. We were put into two classes where we studied everything from the theory of surveying to on-the-spot surveying. I was head of the first class. We studied theory as though our lives depended on it, but we didn't really get to grips with what it was actually like and we had no idea of the hard work that was to come. As part of our training, the school sent our group away for field study and testing, so after several months of theory we went to Yan'an for winter training, on the Yellow Earth Plateau.

It was so cold in Yan'an in winter, there was over a metre of snow. Still, nobody complained, none of us showed the slightest anxiety or worried about the hardship, we felt almost holy, living in a cave house in Yangjialing, a place where Chairman Mao had once lived. I was in charge of three small groups in one subunit, all girls, six to a cave house, with six army canvas travelling cots and a basin of burning charcoal to keep out the winter cold. The quilts were very thin, just light summer quilts, and everyone had a heavy cotton-padded jacket and a pair of padded trousers. They only had millet in Yan'an, they'd never even seen rice, and *mantou* [steamed bread buns] were for field training only. Field training was very tough; we got up before daybreak, and set off carrying a water bottle and a dozen *mantou* in our backpacks. By noon our *mantou* were lumps of ice, sometimes we couldn't get our teeth into them at all, there was no fire to heat them on, and we'd finished all the water, we were so thirsty we had to eat snow, we always had good appetites in those days. Walking around in the ice and snow, tens of degrees below zero, the girls' hair stuck together in icy clumps, and when the boys went out their moustaches went all white. The Yan River had frozen solid, and we had to cross it every day to climb the snow-covered mountain; if you fell into a hollow where the snow had piled up you couldn't climb out by yourself, somebody had to pull you out. At that time we lacked even the most basic necessities for our tasks – we didn't even have warm shoes, just light military summer shoes with rubber soles, and those are very slippery. It was impossible to climb mountains in thick cotton-padded trousers, so we didn't wear them, just two pairs of unlined trousers, and nobody complained of the cold either.

We were young, we were healthy and full of energy, but even so, going out early and coming back late, some of our classmates' hands froze up like the *mantou*, sometimes we couldn't get our socks off because they were stuck to our skin. In the evening, when the cold became unbearable, we had to sleep in pairs, huddled together for warmth. I feel a real nostalgia for our enthusiasm and cheerfulness under those conditions: we used to sing songs while we were resting. Sometimes we'd start to sing on one mountain, and they'd pick up the tune on the next mountain; we sang back and forth to each other. There was the "Song of the Pioneers", and songs from the Soviet Union, "Katyusha", "One Road", I've sung them all. And that was our three months of practical study. Back in Xi'an we spent two or three more months reinforcing what we'd learned, and then we were posted to jobs in the Jiuquan Big Brigade. There were three survey brigades then, two with male leaders, and I was the leader of the third brigade. We were the vanguard of the survey, the advance guard of the oil pioneers; our duty was to draw topographical maps of the areas they were exploring, so we were always first on the scene. At that time trains from Xi'an only went as far as Lanzhou, there was no railway from Lanzhou to Jiuquan, so we set off from Lanzhou in big trucks, with the vast yellow sands of the Gobi all along the route, we could go for a day with nothing but endless yellow sands, no sign of human life, and then another day would come and go without a soul to be seen. All the roads were dirt tracks, all bumps and hollows, we were tumbled about in the trucks until even our insides hurt from all the shaking. Our track was a strip of yellow road under us; behind us was dust like a tail of thick, choking smoke, our throats were burning and dry. We could do nothing about our hair – we all had matted hair and grimy faces. Every time we reached a stop in the evening, there'd be over a dozen of us to one big *kang*, all in a row, one next to the other, with grass mats to lie on, we were stung and bitten all through the night, and we couldn't do a thing about it. What did we burn? Cow and horse dung! It was still very cold indeed in the Great North-West when we first went out in April and May, and we only had dung for fuel, which filled the room with its stink as soon as you lit it, but nobody said a word about the dirt or the harshness of the life. It's very interesting to look back on that time, our generation takes pride in having experienced this memorable part of history.

And that was how our band of girls arrived at the Jiuquan Big Brigade base. It was a single-storey building, we slept on iron beds, and we couldn't have been happier if we had gone to heaven. It was almost International Labour Day when we arrived, and I still remember 1 May very clearly: snow was still falling from the sky – we all sat on the ground in the open air, wearing big thick padded jackets, but no hats, holding an activists' meeting.

*

In post-1949 China, 1 May was a very important festival. First, it was a holiday that belonged to the working people themselves; second, it was an opportunity for propaganda, crusading against the oppression and exploitation of the labourers under capitalism; third, work units or the government would use this day to hold activists' meetings, introducing new schemes or work plans for the summer.

*

MRS YOU: In the activists' meeting the leaders told our group that we were going to leave for the worksite. The following day a long file of more than ten trucks set off in the direction of Jiayuguan, carrying my women's survey team and a few tents. Our worksite was on the far side of the Jiayuguan pass. In the past, many majestic, beautiful epic poems had been written by scholars and poets about this Jiayuguan, but when we got there all we could see was the vast Gobi Desert stretching out boundlessly in all directions, a great, barren desert with no sign of life and no vegetation! There wasn't a living soul to be seen.

But do you know something? When we saw it we were full of pride. I told our group: we too can bring our work to places where the great poets of ancient times have been, this is an honour. Really, at that time that was what I thought.

We put up our tents in a village in Jiayuguan and moved in. The only technicians in the team were me and my classmates, all women. One of the apprentice workers from Nanjing was just sixteen, and I was only eighteen. On outside fieldwork we were split into many small groups: Terrain Reconnaissance, Site Selection, Observation, Mapping. My team were the vanguard of the survey, the people in Mapping would survey and map the terrain based on the control points we had measured.

XINRAN: And was that where you met Teacher You?

MRS YOU: Yes, he was in the Jiuquan Big Brigade too. He came to work in our brigade in 1952, to help us with the technology. He was also responsible for the organisational work of the Communist Party Youth League, and he often came to inspect our work. At that time I was still young, I hadn't started thinking about courtship, marriage or anything of that sort. Then a writer called Yu Ruobin (his pen name was Sha Duoling) came to the site; he'd come to experience life with us in the Jiuquan Big Brigade, and he wrote a lot of poems about our women's survey team and the Gobi Desert. Many journalists from the Xinhua News Agency used to come to report on our team, and they took lots of photographs. This writer Sha Duoling told me about You's background: he was a graduate from the Lanzhou University physics department, a Hero of Labour, and his work was first-rate. He said he'd done a special report on You, a man who struggled fiercely for the sake of the construction of the motherland. He suffered from stomach trouble, and once he'd fainted dead away on the worksite, but when he came round he just carried on as normal . . . he was a man with a very strong work ethic. I began to notice this man, and later on You himself suggested that he would like to make friends with me.

XINRAN: Do you still remember the words he used when he asked you to marry him?

MRS YOU: He didn't say the romantic words you would see in books today, he just asked me if I wanted him to make friends with me, and was that all right?

*

In China before 1990, "lover" was an embarrassing word, even a louche, dissolute word. When a man and a woman were said to be "making friends", this referred to courtship. In the period between 1930 and 1980, a couple who were Party members had to gain authorisation from the Party organisation before "making friends"; from the 1950s to the 1980s this rule was an unwritten law in Chinese society.

*

XINRAN: How did you reply?

MRS YOU: At first I really didn't know what to reply. When I kept silent he said: "It's perfectly simple, just tell me, do we or don't we? Be frank." At that time there were quite a few people who were keen on me, but I agreed anyway. Why did I choose him? This has a lot to do with my family, and the influence of my older girl cousins: they had all married university students in the 1920s and '30s, and they were all very talented men: one was a professor in the Shanghai Finance and Economics Institute, and one had been a student of literature at the Sun Yat-sen University in Guangdong, and after the Liberation he became a teacher, everyone thought he was amazing – at that time people who had been to university were rarer than a unicorn horn or phoenix feathers. So I thought I couldn't do less than them, and I had always admired educated people. At that time I'd never heard of MAs, PhDs or anything like that, and though my ambition had been to be a university student myself, it was impossible then, so I would naturally tend to look favourably on a university graduate as a marriage partner! The best candidates among my classmates were only vocational school graduates, none of us had been to university. So You's educational background and his personal circumstances both met my standards, but actually the most important thing was the man himself. Besides, that writer Sha Duoling, our deputy group leader and the organisational secretary of the Youth League had all told me: "A Hero of Labour is bound to be a hard worker, and a hard-working man is always good news."

XINRAN: So, your marriage was influenced by the Party, and by the Party organisation.

MRS YOU: Oh, at that time an introduction from the Party organisation was as good as a guarantee, many people said yes as soon as the organisation introduced them! In those days we'd only just freed ourselves from arranged marriages – anything that wasn't decided by our parents was a kind of freedom! Besides, I had this notion of marrying a university student, so when other classmates suggested getting together, I turned them down. He was the first one I considered, but I didn't know how to answer him.

XINRAN: So how did you answer him?

MRS YOU: He was a leader – even when proposing marriage he knew a thing or two about leadership. He saw I was unable to speak so he said: "Can we or can't we? If not, we don't have to," just like that. I still didn't reply, but I didn't refuse him either.

XINRAN: And how long did your courtship last?

MRS YOU: Not that long. It was silly of me, he won a Hero of Labour prize (back then prizes were always *The Complete Works of Mao Zedong*) but when the time came for him to collect it he didn't go himself, but sent me to collect it for him, so I went blundering off to collect his prize. All this had a purpose, it was to test whether I was really serious, and to show me that he was a famous Hero of Labour. Afterwards when we returned from Jiuquan to Xi'an, he took my suitcase for me, and put it in the truck for me. He didn't lift a finger to help any of my other classmates, I remember it very clearly. When we were back in Xi'an for theoretical study, we went to the Xi'an restaurant on our rest day to eat snacks, especially their local speciality. Xi'an was very backward in those days. There were no cars or buses – we took a horse and cart from outside the city wall to the city centre.

XINRAN: What was the local speciality?

MRS YOU: Different kinds of Xi'an dumplings, all different types, and there was *yang-rou-pao-mo* – lamb stew with coriander and crumbled flat-bread.

XINRAN: When you ate out together, who paid?

MRS YOU: He paid. I wanted to pay, you know, equality between the sexes and all that, but he wouldn't let me.

XINRAN: What was your marriage ceremony like?

MRS YOU: The marriage ceremony I do remember. Before we were married, the Petroleum Bureau wanted to train a group of people in aerial surveying at the Beijing Central Mapping Bureau, in order to improve the speed and quality of surveying. My name was on the list. But then the leaders said: "You're getting married soon, you don't have to go." At that time I always felt I had never learned enough, I'd always dreamed of a university diploma; given a chance like this, I couldn't not go. So I said:

"It doesn't matter if I'm getting married, I can still go once I'm married. I'll come back when the course is over." I was already China's first head of a women's surveying team, I wanted to be a member of China's first aerial surveying team as well. In those days new training programmes were kept secret, there was no announcement. I'd heard the phrase "aerial surveying" but didn't knew whether it meant flying in the air or walking on the ground. I had no idea. I supposed that if it was aerial, it must be flying in the air, surely? I was determined to fly up to the sky; I wanted to be the first female aerial surveyor of the New China. Since I was going away to study, my colleagues said: "Have your wedding right away, before you leave, a settled relationship is beneficial to study" – and so we got married. We were still wearing our fieldwork clothes, even in our wedding photograph, but I bought us two new scarves for the photo, both the same colour and style, and we wore rosettes, attached to our work clothes. Our colleagues had a whip-round and got us two sets of bedding and some sweets, it was a very simple wedding.

XINRAN: Was there any of the traditional horseplay at your wedding?

MRS YOU: Of course – at that time marriages were the biggest events in our social life. They forced us to sing a song. A few of his geophysicist classmates were a bit more unruly, they were slightly older, they'd seen more of the world. I could sing Shaoxing Opera, and so I sang a bit of that, not very well, just "Liang Shanbo and Zhu Yingtai". When I was young I used to join in the community singing, and I was in the singing group. Later on I had my tonsils out, and my voice turned hoarse.

XINRAN: Did you really go to study as soon as you were married?

MRS YOU: Mmm, I did.

XINRAN: For how long?

MRS YOU: Two years in all. As it turned out he was sent to Moscow for two years while I was studying – he went in 1956.

XINRAN: How long did you live apart?

MRS YOU: Three years, he didn't come back till '58.

XINRAN: Did you go to visit him when he was abroad?

MRS YOU: Go to the Soviet *Union?* No, in those days it was impossible, they were very strict about letting you go abroad. Besides, we had had our first child by then. When You came back from his studies in 1958 he was assigned to the Bureau of Mines in Turfan, in Xinjiang province; at that time the slogan was "Spur on the galloping horse to full speed, march on Turfan". They dug a well for prospecting beneath the Flaming Mountain, the same Flaming Mountain as in Wu Chengen's *Monkey*, the part where the monks borrow the fan of the Iron Fan Princess. We set up camp at the foot of the mountain, where we had a one-room brick house for living quarters. There were no fans or electrical equipment then, and in summer the average temperature was over forty-two degrees, and that was in the shade, impossibly hot, you could cook an egg by burying it in the sand. It was over forty degrees inside too, all our things were scalding hot – you could burn your hand on an iron bedstead. Nowhere was it cool, you had to splash the beds and ground with water and at midday draw the curtain, which was just a piece of black cloth, like in a photographer's darkroom; we had to turn day into night to survive there. At midday when it was hottest, work was out of the question, we women just lay there on soaking wet beds, and even that wasn't enough, we had to cover ourselves with sopping towels. The men went to the irrigation ditches, where they skulked under the little bridges, hiding from the heat of the sun. There was nothing else we could do in the middle of the day. Luckily by then our fieldwork could be taken indoors, but the drawing board was so hot that our maps used to stick to it. During the worst heat of the day all we could do was doodle aimlessly, with sweat streaming down our bodies. And as for the nights . . . it was impossible to sleep indoors. We'd drag our beds out into the big courtyard and sleep in the open air. Every evening in Turfan, at eight or nine, a wind would start to blow, and it would continue until eight or nine in the morning, every day was like this, so if we moved outside because we couldn't sleep, we had to try to sleep in the middle of a sandstorm, surrounded by flying sand and walking stones, just like it says in *Monkey*: "The sand was flying, the stones were walking." When I heard this story as a child I thought the writer was exaggerating, how can there really be stones that walk or grains of sand that fly? But in Turfan we experienced it at first hand. The sand and stones scoured your skin, it hurt, and we couldn't do anything about it, you just had to cover your face with a thin bed sheet, but then it didn't let any air in, everybody was in and out all night . . .

XINRAN: It's hard for us to imagine such hardship, let alone to live and work in those conditions. What did you eat at that time?

MRS YOU: There were lots and lots of grapes and Hami melons. We couldn't eat more than a hundred grams of grain rations in a day, it was too hot to eat, so we lived on fruit. The Hami melons were so sweet that they left a sticky, sugary layer on the table. We didn't eat grapes one by one, but a big handful at a time, like playing the mouth organ. [She laughs.]

XINRAN: How long did you work in Turfan?

MRS YOU: *Aiya*, we were there for years! We came in '59 and left in '64.

XINRAN: Where did you transfer your field of operations to after that? Was it an improvement?

MRS YOU: After that we went to Ningxia. Our living quarters were half in a cellar dug under the ground and half in a tent pitched above it. Ningxia suffers from sandstorms too – in a Ningxia sandstorm you could be sitting a metre and a half from me, and I wouldn't be able to see your face for all the sand blowing about!

XINRAN: I've been to a place there called Shouting Hill – people have to shout loudly even when they are very close to each other, there's so much sand in the air that they just can't see or hear each other when they are out working together.

MRS YOU: When you got out of bed in the morning there, you'd find a thick layer of sand on the plastic sheet, and we often used to find sand in our *mantou*, blown in during the cooking process, it creaked and squeaked in your teeth as you ate, really, you wouldn't believe it if you hadn't lived there. In the big storms, our tents used to get covered in sand, heaped up so thickly that we women couldn't get the door open. A man had to come and help us in the morning. In Ningxia it made no difference how high or low your rank was, the sexes were segregated, there was separate accommodation for men and women.

XINRAN: So how did married couples manage?

MRS YOU: Living arrangements were the same after marriage: men living with men and women living with women. Husbands and wives all lived apart.

XINRAN: So how did you have children?

MRS YOU: You need a room for a child, don't you [laughs], and when we first arrived there weren't any. Then a room was set up for married couples. You had to wait in a queue and book it. [She laughs again.] My three children were all made there – my older son was born in 1958, my second son in 1960, and my youngest, a daughter, in 1963. At that time we all knew that finding oil wasn't really the be all and end all, but you did have to go all out for the revolution.

XINRAN: "Finding oil wasn't the be all and end all, but you had to go all out for the revolution"? So you abandoned your families and spouses?

MRS YOU: We didn't abandon them, but they weren't as important as they are to people nowadays. Besides, anyone who talked a lot about their children and husband and so on would be looked down on, people would accuse you of not having a progressive attitude or of being too petit bourgeois. You couldn't be too fussy about living conditions.

XINRAN: Did you miss home?

MRS YOU: Very rarely, we were all tired out every day, nobody mentioned missing home or anything of that sort. When you got up you'd work with all your might; when you got back to the dormitory you went to sleep as soon as your head hit the pillow. It was very simple, and very happy too! Fortunately we didn't have the children with us at that time, my elder children grew up in You's home town, here in Hezheng. When I was pregnant with my younger daughter I decided to take home leave and go back to my own family. Taking care of the children was too much for You's mother, I needed help from my family.

XINRAN: So you hadn't been home since you left?

MRS YOU: The first time I went home on a family visit was 1964, ten years after I left. On the map it looks like there's a direct line from Xinjiang in the north-west to my home in Dong'an in the east, but at that time there were no roads, not even railway stations, the only transport was in big trucks. When I went home for the first time, I squeezed onto a big truck with the local Xinjiang people. I still remember the strong goaty smell from the old sheepskins they wore. It was freezing on the truck, we all crawled inside our quilts, it was like there was a counterpane covering the truck. I took my daughter home by myself, we went from Hami to Lanzhou, spent a night in Lanzhou, and then set off again, changing trains many times en route from Xi'an to Shanghai. At that time trains from Shanghai to my home only went as far as Jinhua, we had to change to a bus at Jinhua, and then a ferry, but at last we finally made it home!

It'd been ten years, and my mother and father looked at me like I'd fallen from the sky, but they were happy, so happy they cried! I didn't sleep at all the night I arrived home. It was summer, I sat with my mother and father in the central courtyard of the house, and we talked till dawn, just the three of us. I didn't have any gifts to bring them from Turfan, only a couple of bags containing several dozen pounds of raisins.

XINRAN: The most important thing to them would be that you brought their granddaughter to them.

MRS YOU: Oh, yes, my father went shouting all the way down the street: "My daughter's back, my daughter's come back, and she's brought my granddaughter!" All our relatives and friends could hear him.

XINRAN: Did they complain about your being away so long?

MRS YOU: Ah . . . they didn't complain.

XINRAN: They didn't complain? You'd left ten years before without a proper farewell, and hadn't been heard of since?

MRS YOU: My parents knew that I had wanted to leave to join the army in 1949 and 1950, but I didn't go then because my brothers were too small, I was needed at home. My home town was liberated in May 1949. The teacher in our local school was a member of the underground Communist Party, though I didn't know that at the time, I only found out once we'd been liberated. The Party organised a teachers' and school-leavers' propaganda team. I joined the team and we went to the country villages and the fishing villages by the sea, opposing imperialism, local despots and feudalism, and helping liberate women from arranged marriages.

XINRAN: Had the people in your home town seen the reports of you in the papers?

MRS YOU: Yes, in 1954, in the *People's Pictorial News, People's Daily* . . . you could find reports about me in all the youth papers. All my family knew, all the teachers too. The news caused a nationwide sensation at the time, this was the early fifties, remember. The Xinhua News Agency took photographs for propaganda, women going to work in difficult places was big news, they were big pictures too. We got letters encouraging us from all over the country, all the young people wanted to be like us, and went as construction volunteers to the north-west. We were all yearning to sacrifice our youth to the motherland.

XINRAN: You spent your youth toiling so hard, did you ever cry?

MRS YOU: No.

XINRAN: Not once? Why not? You have a woman's body too, don't you?

MRS YOU: No, I really didn't cry, not once. I think it's because I had good health, I never got even a touch of frostbite, or any injury – good health is one of my best traits. Plus I had both a burden and an ambition. When I was a student in Yan'an I read a book, in those days the Soviet Union was a model for China, and this story was set in a very, very cold place that was a long way away from Moscow, it was the story of a woman engineer who toiled, struggled and devoted herself to the motherland. I am a woman engineer too, I was a Bolshevik like her, and I was a long way from Beijing, in the Gobi Desert, the Great North-West, struggling for the sake of my own motherland. I thought I was the Chinese version of her.

XINRAN: Then have you ever been worried?

MRS YOU: Oh, I've had every kind of worry in my work! What did it mean to be a Big Brigade Leader, and how did I set about being one? I just didn't get it, but I was the first, there was nobody to teach me. At the very beginning we had to set up four starting points for prospecting sites in a day, when we went out in the morning the sky might be clear for a thousand miles, but a moment later we'd be in the middle of a thunderstorm, the light was all wrong for surveying, so the observation points weren't accurate, and inaccurate surveying would affect the quality of our work. The plan had been to finish our mission in eighteen days, but we couldn't make the deadline, we were working on it for a month. That was an anxious time, we all cried together, we all commiserated. At that time we took the nation's plans very seriously indeed; failure to complete your plan on time was like committing a crime, so if everyone was unable to complete their mission, they would be very, very guilty, profoundly guilty.

XINRAN: So have you cried over matters to do with the home?

MRS YOU: Over family matters? No.

XINRAN: And you didn't cry for your children either?

MRS YOU: No, I didn't! The children were raised by their two grandmothers, so I didn't worry about them, we couldn't keep the children with us, and the old people were fond of them.

XINRAN: Mrs You, have you told these stories to your children?

MRS YOU: Not in as much detail as this, not yet.

XINRAN: Why haven't you told them?

MRS YOU: Ah . . . well, I said not in as much detail, didn't I?!

XINRAN: Did you not have a chance to talk about them? Or were you unwilling to speak of them? Or did you think there was no need to talk?

MRS YOU: I didn't . . . I didn't really go into it.

XINRAN: Have they asked?

MRS YOU: Not like you. They know a little bit. They complain that their parents didn't bring them up when they were small, they grew up tagging along after the old people, they couldn't even go to school properly.

XINRAN: Why not?

MRS YOU: This was the 1960s, the Cultural Revolution, my husband was "struggled against", and he was relieved of all his duties.

XINRAN: So did you get struggled against too?

MRS YOU: I hadn't had as much pre-Liberation schooling as he had. He was worried that I wouldn't be able to bear to see him punished, so he fixed for me to go and stay in the south for a while. I wasn't with him when the public humiliation and criticism were worst, I felt very guilty that I hadn't taken good care of him – '68 was the cruellest time for him, and I didn't come back until '69. Afterwards we had very poor living quarters, our bed was a narrow slab of wood, we had to squeeze onto it to sleep.

XINRAN: At that time, did you have any regrets? That you had married him? That other people didn't understand you?

MRS YOU: I had no regrets. At the time I thought: What's the worst that can happen? He'll go back home to the countryside, he can till the fields and I'll weave cloth, and we'll never go back to any leaders' jobs again, a peaceful, stable life is best.

XINRAN: Do you understand why it all happened?

MRS YOU: I can understand it. They struggled against him because he had been to study in the Soviet Union. Relations between the Soviet Union and China had been good, then later they deteriorated, and he became a running dog of the Soviet Union, and the knowledge he had studied in the Soviet Union for the sake of the nation became a crime. [She sighs.]

XINRAN: You have experienced so many changes in China. What do you think is the biggest difference between young people now and in the past?

MRS YOU: The young people today haven't let themselves get caught up in political movements. We were witnesses to the whole process, we were the ones who went through it all. First it was suppressing counter-revolutionaries, later it was the Three Antis and the Five Antis, then the Four Clean-Ups, then the Anti-Rightist campaign, one movement after another. They haven't experienced that spiritual pressure, or seen the pathetic figures their parents cut on the stage in those sessions.

XINRAN: Do the young people today have the faith or aspirations you had in those days? As I was listening to your story, I felt it was full of heroic spirit, such hardship, such exhaustion; your expression when you were speaking was so full of pride, treating those arduous conditions like they were nothing special. So what about young people nowadays?

MRS YOU: Young people nowadays . . . judging by our own sons and daughter, they don't have our faith or sense of responsibility. In our day, work came first.

XINRAN: Do they understand you?

MRS YOU: Yes, they do, but now I feel very ashamed and full of regrets. We didn't bring up our three children properly, because we were both so devoted to our own work.

XINRAN: Why do you say you didn't bring them up properly?

*

Mrs You's eyes had started to redden and swim with tears. That face, which had been so full of high morale and fighting spirit, fell, and she stared at her hands, rubbing and twisting them together uneasily. When she spoke again it was in the voice of a child who had done something bad.

*

MRS YOU: When they were the right age for school it was the Cultural Revolution, and because their father was a "bad man", they weren't considered suitable. It wasn't till they were grown up that they went to the adult education school, and they found that really hard going. At that time we both had ambitions, we were both educated people and we had very high expectations for our children, but none of them measured up to our ambitions, not even in education. All this was because we had buried ourselves in our own careers, our careers for the sake of the future they have today, yet our children were rejected by the times.

XINRAN: Mrs You, if you could live your life over again, your career, your family, right up to your present day, would you choose this path in life?

MRS YOU: I . . . I think I have no regrets of any kind about my choice of career, in spite of the illnesses I picked up, the stomach problems and the rheumatism I have now. When I recall the hard work of those days, I feel very proud, I feel I have brought honour to my own life, because a person who has never experienced hard work and suffering will never know how sweet work and life can be afterwards.

XINRAN: If your children or your grandchildren were to ask you sometime what made a girl like you, a girl who was afraid of the dark and afraid of water, into someone as strong and tough, successful and self-confident as you are today, would you say that was because of the times you lived in? Or because of your family? Or your personal ambitions? Or your will?

MRS YOU: This has a lot to do with the education in those days. The idea of women's liberation in those days was very masculinised. I wanted to be able to do anything boys could do. In the propaganda team I wanted to dress up to play the boys' roles. My father told me that he wanted me to have the same success as a boy – whatever a boy could do, he required me to do, his demands on me were very severe. There are other stories of Chinese women too, Hua Mulan following the army, Qiu Jin in the 1911 revolution, and Communist women like Song Qingling and Deng Yingchao. Those women influenced me a lot – in those days we were all imitating heroes.

XINRAN: Do you still believe that it was right to have those kinds of aspirations and beliefs?

MRS YOU: I feel that I was right.

XINRAN: Do you know that many young people say that their parents' generation was very foolish in their loyalty, and, going back another generation, that their grandparents' generation was both foolish and ignorant? How do you see this?

MRS YOU: China's current greatness and strength didn't just fall out of the sky, it's only the hard, bitter struggles and sacrifices of the previous generations, one generation after another, that have given us the China we have today. If you don't believe it, ask You later – our generation just had more spirit than today's young generation.

XINRAN: Are you certain that Teacher You will think the same as you?

MRS YOU: Other things I can't be certain about, but we're of one mind about the price we paid in those years for our work, and for the motherland.

XINRAN: Have the two of you ever had arguments?

MRS YOU: Oh yes, we've had arguments.

XINRAN: What do you argue about?

MRS YOU: Sometimes our opinions are different, or our ideas of family life.

XINRAN: In the family? Over the children? Or about life in general?

MRS YOU: He's a northerner, I'm a southerner, sometimes our tastes in food are different – he likes spicy things, I like sweet things – but we aim for agreement in big matters and agree to differ over smaller issues.

XINRAN: Who gives way most, you or him?

MRS YOU: Well, it's usually me who gives way . . . It's a miracle he's still here, he's had a lot of narrow escapes, he's been in car accidents, *aiya*, several times he's come out safely from some pretty scary situations. Once he was in a truck that turned over – he was on his way to help some other people, and his vehicle turned over in the same place; that big Liberation truck went belly up, all four wheels pointing to the sky, and the people inside all came tumbling out from inside the cab. He's been to that big desert they call the Sea of Death – for every ten people who went in nine never came out again. After the Cultural Revolution he became a big leader again, he must have received honours from every institute of learning in the world, rushing here and there, flying all over the place. He didn't retire till he was over seventy, and he's still climbing up and down the mountains, organising efforts to alleviate poverty.

XINRAN: You really are very strong, with a life like this, full of scares and alarms, but never complaining. If someone were to ask you what kind of man Teacher You is, as a comrade, as a wife, as friend, how would you reply?

MRS YOU: He's very strong, he's a very loyal friend, very practical, and in the time of the Cultural Revolution he didn't make wild statements about other people in order to clear himself.

XINRAN: Is he a good husband?

MRS YOU: Ah . . . [laughs] . . . he's a good husband.

XINRAN [also laughs]: Is he a good father?

MRS YOU: You can only call him just about average, because none of the children have grown up into people of accomplishment. None of them have his deep scholarship, none could ever equal him.

XINRAN: If I were to describe a woman like you in three sentences, what three sentences do you think could give the best picture of you?

MRS YOU: I'm really not very outstanding. I have ambition and I've struggled.

XINRAN: But especially as a woman?

MRS YOU: Ah, hmm . . .

XINRAN: As a woman, as a wife, as a mother, as a grandmother.

MRS YOU: I don't know what to say. I want to make it up to them by being a mother and grandmother to them. And I don't know if they're grateful for what I've given up, coming to live in this out-of-the-way place. I want to go to the Old People's University too; I want to play mah-jong, take part in singing contests, sing songs, go on trips to scenic spots. But because I didn't do a good job of raising them before, now I'm retired I want to repay the debt I owe my children through my grandchildren. These aren't very grand ideals, but they come from the heart.

XINRAN: They are words from the heart that I've come on a journey of thousands of miles to hear. I have two questions – I don't want your answers now but I hope you'll think them over. One is: what are the three most bitter and three most happy things in your life? The second question is: you are so successful, you are one of the people who created an era; in the eyes of people nowadays, in the eyes of the young, was it worth it? Please consider these questions.

MRS YOU: I'll think about them, I won't be able to sleep for thinking about them.

XINRAN: I think you must have already spent more nights than you can count thinking about these questions. In fact, once we've given ourselves an answer, we can relax a bit, and sleep a bit easier, at least we won't be disturbed by dreams full of anxiety or sleepless nights. You have a rest now – I'll see you in a bit when we eat.

MRS YOU: Then you try to rest for a while too, don't wear yourself out.

*

When I invited Teacher You in for his interview, his first act on entering the room was to apologise, in a typical Chinese "great man" way, for his wife: "very naive", "no notion of other people's time", "endless nattering" and a series of similar "errors". Although I did not accept his apologies, I did not contradict him either. The first reason for this was that I no longer had the confidence to debate the rights and wrongs between Chinese men and women; the second was that we didn't have the time to discuss this question of "whether a woman could be great, wise and clever in the eyes of her husband", for which no woman has ever had a clear answer since the beginnings of the women's liberation movement. I was one of the many women who had been "taught" by this kind of very successful man; I knew that no matter who you were, in those men's eyes, you would never, ever be able to distance yourself from their preconceived notions of "women and their bad habits".

Teacher You was a man with many honours after his name, most of which were to do with geophysics and oil, but also including a few government posts. This is another very "Chinese" phenomenon: many name cards in China come folded into three sections, with rows of "honours and positions", high-ranking and important offices jostling for space. Sometimes I used to think that they must have three heads and six arms each – how else could they have enough time in the work unit to live out all these parallel existences? A person with so many titles is bound to be a great achiever. However, sometimes you will notice that the majority of the work units to which those titles belong share an address, and can be found in the same unit of the same block of flats: so does the sitting room perhaps count as an organisation? And the kitchen and the bathroom as two companies?

Teacher You's professional titles were all at a national level, yet I could feel a kind of "emptiness" in all of his titles; a feeling that things didn't quite meet in the middle; a sense that there was no successor to carry on his work. This was the "hunger" of modern China's oil business, the "thirst" of modern China's geophysics.

I don't understand the science or history of petroleum, but since the USA and Britain invaded Iraq in 2003 I have seen the madness and cruelty to which petroleum can drive humanity: the men with guns shouting out for freedom and democracy, with never a thought for the children who cannot say in the morning if they will live to see nightfall, and nobody to console the aged mothers left without help or support in the middle of a racial war; and I have seen those oil-drunk "liberators" racing to divide up the "liberated" oilfields. Humankind has barely progressed from the primitive plundering, religious battles and power struggles of the last century; nowadays the evils that spring from hunger and desire have just learned to dress themselves in names like "justice and democracy". I worry that oil will cause my own rapidly developing country to turn to crime in its turn. So I wanted very much to know what those petroleum titles represented.

*

XINRAN: Teacher You, the first time I heard about you, I learned that you had very many titles. Please tell me something about the ten titles that you personally consider the most important, if you don't mind?

YOU: I'll tell you the simple truth: I only recognise a few of those titles. I have been Deputy Commander and Chief Engineer of the Yinchuan Petroleum Prospecting Command Office, and Deputy Head of the China Petroleum Prospecting Bureau, and then in 1979 Zhao Ziyang made me Head of the China Petroleum Prospecting Bureau. Now, although I wear many "hats", according to national policy I am classed as retired. When I was still in post, there were many local factors involved in some of my transfers. For example, I was once made head of a local law court in the Ningxia Hui Autonomous Region. When the Petroleum Bureau found out, they said: "You can't go to work in the regions – you belong to us! So the boss of the Petroleum Bureau came with me to the Ningxia Hui Autonomous Regional Office and got me transferred back. Later on the government of another province wanted me to head their Fossil Fuel Bureau, but the Party organisation didn't allow it, and I was transferred back out again that same night.

The Chinese system of employing people is far from perfect; there is a lack of professional knowledge and imagination both in the plan as a whole and the way it is regulated and carried out.

XINRAN: But as I understand it, you are retired in name only – in fact, you are not properly retired.

YOU: I retired in 1990, it would have been impossible not to go then; people have to retire so that young people can get a chance at the top jobs – if the nation doesn't cultivate young people it will be too late for us. But what you say is quite correct: after I retired I was a consultant for five years, in fact I was also doing five years of bureau chief work. Before I was in post I thought that nobody dared to take the lead in anything, everything had to go through the bureau chief – I was in that position, so I had power, I could use the National Prospecting Bureau to sort out the issues surrounding prospecting on a national level once and for all, and sort out international cooperation in many different areas. So although I had retired, I made use of this time to make adjustments to the overall petroleum situation.

XINRAN: Can we say that, apart from your own learning, experience and ability, one of the reasons that the nation kept you on to continue your work was the fierce disputes over oil, as well as the lack of gifted people in petroleum in China?

YOU: Something of both. I have always worked in this profession, unlike many officials who were transferred out and had to do all sorts of other things. The result was that they lost their professional ability, and had no chance to improve their knowledge. I was once sent to the Soviet Union, and studied for two years in the Moscow State Geological Prospecting Academy. When I came back, the nation needed people like me, specialists educated abroad. The office I was working in was developing resources for the nation; they desperately needed competent young people who properly understood the right kind of analysis and deduction. That isn't something you can pick up overnight. China has been held back for a long time by political movements; the foreigners are racing ahead to grab whatever they can, and they won't wait for us.

For some time before I retired, I took part in a lot of international global management technology exchange and cooperation projects. I had a pretty close relationship with the SEG, the Society of Economic Geologists, which included academic matters as well as basic training of talented people. We worked together with Russia's European-Asian Association of

Earth Management. I also had contacts with the European Earth Management Association, and represented the official Chinese Earth Management Delegation in fact-finding meetings, foreign academic symposia, international meetings and so on. In all these things and others like them, I was the one in charge of the Chinese delegation.

Because of this, I used to be in charge of the day-to-day running of the Petroleum Association, and headed the specialist committee on Earth Management. China's internal structure doesn't match the international system, which doesn't recognise organisations like ours. The state had to consider the fact that once I stood down there was no one to take over a lot of the international work, so I was asked to carry on for a few more years. But the third reason is just that I was still in pretty good health then – if I was left idle, what was I supposed to do with myself? I said that just having fun would be pointless, better to write a few essays, perhaps do a little bit of scientific research. The work needed me, so I carried on working, and I didn't stop after my five years were up, I still keep up with new developments.

XINRAN: As a child, did you ever think you would become the man you are today?

YOU: Never. I was born right here, in this county. Although Hezheng is a very small place, it has produced seven provincial governors and nine army commanders, thirty or forty colonels, over a hundred battalion commanders, and more besides. Some of these took a firm line with the rich and distributed their wealth to the poor, but there was another group who were capitalist bureaucrats or traders in government monopolies. Never mind that this place is small and very poor, all the horse caravans carrying goods to India and Pakistan had to pass through here! Islam is a powerful force here, we are known as China's Islamic county – in the old days everyone used to be Muslims, nowadays we don't see so much of it. In the past, the locals often used to use racial conflict as an excuse for battles and other disturbances – people could barely make a living! That's just the way things were in those days. I used to look at those bureaucrats, dealers in government monopolies and corrupt officials, and tell myself that it was impossible for me to punish them, the best I could do was to become a teacher, to educate the children, so that they could change our lives through education. In our generation the fashion was: "Study maths, physics and chemistry, and you'll never lack food to eat or clothes to wear!" At that time there was no middle school in the whole district, there were only two schools in the whole county for all ages. I had to go to the county town for senior school, and that was over fifteen kilometres away. I used to set off carrying a cloth-wrapped bundle of steamed buns, so I wouldn't have to go home for a week. The Anti-Japanese War was at its height, and the teachers in the school had very strong ideas; they were a fairly progressive lot. They had all come from places where there was fighting, so they taught us that we had to study hard for the sake of our own futures.

XINRAN: So was the course you studied at university one you chose for yourself? Or were you assigned it?

YOU: I graduated from senior school in 1949, when my home town was liberated, and I got into the physics department of Lanzhou University. There were no buses in those days, or any proper roads, it was all little tracks through the mountains. You had to ask your way as you went, and it took me a month to get to the university on foot from Hezheng to Lanzhou. I chose my course myself; I studied physics, but then I moved into geophysics. Geophysics and physics are two completely different concepts: physics is a relatively practical thing, but geophysics is a part of geology. When we went to university it was the time of the Korean War. We all put our names down to join the army and "Fight America and Defend Korea"; we wanted to go to the front. But the university wouldn't allow it. No students studying physics, maths or chemistry were allowed to enlist, though students from other departments could. In 1952, China urgently needed to develop the petroleum industry, and the search was on in China's few universities for skilled people to do geophysical prospecting. So all the graduates from all the physics departments in the country were gathered together in Beijing for specialist training, except for a few who were kept on by the universities to teach. There were only ninety of us in the whole country (in those days there only used to be seven or eight students in a university department): forty-five of us were sent to the Geological and Mining Production Department, which was called the Geological Bureau then, and forty-five were allocated to the Petroleum Bureau.

The Petroleum Bureau tested every aspect of our knowledge, and we were given forty days of specialist training. At the time I really resented it. Where were all the things I'd been studying? It was perfectly simple: my choice of subject and the subject I was using when I started work were totally different, but the nation needed this technical knowledge, so we had to offer our support; besides, we did whatever the Party told us to do! That was our attitude when we set off, and once we got there the leaders told us that the nation was developing petroleum, and our services were required for the task of geophysical prospecting for oil resources. So that was how I came to oil prospecting and became "a finder of oil, whose feet have trod to the north and the south of the motherland's great rivers" – like in the old song.

XINRAN: At that time, did you know much about the current oil situation in China?

YOU: I only knew that China's oil industry had been in a terrible state before Liberation. Oil was a strategically important war material, and if there was another war we'd be finished without it. So "seeking oil for the nation" became our patriotic duty. Prospecting for oil entails a big investment, long periods of work and high risk; it's complicated, and very hard work. I have personally been involved in China's search for oil in west Jiuquan, the Turfan Basin in Xinjiang and the E'erduosi Basin, and I have been in charge of geophysical prospecting in the Tarim Basin in Xinjiang, the Erlian Basin in Inner Mongolia and the Jilin Basin in northeast China.

XINRAN: Had the Daqing oilfield become a household name yet?

YOU: No, this was 1952. Daqing wasn't until 1957.

XINRAN: Just now you said that oil prospecting was extremely hard work, can you give me an example?

YOU: When we were fresh out of training in Beijing, there were four big brigades: the Chaoshui, Minhe, Turfan and Jiuquan Brigades. I was allocated to the Jiuquan Brigade, which at that time was centred on the Yumen oilfield in Jiayuguan; there were no people at all in that place, not even grass grew there. They say: "Leaving Jiayuguan, your eyes will be bright with tears, behind you the Ghost Gate Pass, ahead of you the Gobi Desert." That area was still out of bounds then, there were bandits in the mountains. In order to avoid an encounter with bandits we entered the base area under the protection of a squad of People's Liberation Army soldiers, in big Soviet-style trucks. We all wore bulky cotton-padded clothes, black and dirty, with electric wires tied tightly round our waists to keep the dust from blowing into our clothes. On the few occasions when we encountered any locals, they assumed we were Labour through Reform convicts under escort by the PLA –

there were often convoys of trucks on that road, taking convicts to Xinjiang.

Lunch at noon was two *mantou* a head, which we toasted on a fire. There was nothing to burn, so we burned cow dung, which we had to bring ourselves; we'd heat a bottle of water and then just tuck in. When we came back in the evening we slept in tents – there was nowhere to stay – but our spirits were high in those days, nobody minded a little hardship. We put up the tents in the best places we could find by the side of the road. The drivers who went past on the road had a lot of bad habits, they'd try it on with the women comrades if they could, so the women slept in the middle, and the young male comrades slept on the outside.

We were very pure and idealistic; no matter how tough things were, nothing mattered so long as it did not hold back the work. Later I was made Prospecting Team Leader. I was very strict in my demands of the people under me: courting before the stipulated age was out of the question – marriage was nature's way, of course, but there was no accommodation for married couples, husband and wife could not be together, you might as well be in prison. So the rule was that anyone who got married had to be posted elsewhere, in that way there was no housing problem and no question of children. After all, in the army soldiers were never allowed to marry at all.

XINRAN: People always have the seven feelings and six desires; when they reached the standard age and got married, could they be together then?

YOU: No, normally they couldn't; if they had children, we'd send the children back to their old home. Look at my three children, one child went to her maternal grandmother in Wenzhou, and the other two here, and education here was appalling in those days! The children were left at home with no one to take charge of them. Now my children think badly of me because they had no chance to go to school, they missed out because of me . . .

*

Teacher You's head was bowed and he spoke the last few sentences in a hoarse, low voice, which I could barely catch, as if talking to himself. Once again I saw the deep pain and guilt which those who had sacrificed themselves in those days feel towards their children. There are many people like this in China's older generations, and these feelings could be seen to a greater or lesser extent on the faces of almost every old person I interviewed: a callus on the heart rubbed raw by days and nights of guilt. Their children had become the victims of their parents' devotion to duty, their innocent years of childhood sacrificed on the altar of politics. I am one such child; my father and mother have always been so taken up with their careers that to this day we have never managed to gather the whole family together to celebrate my birthday.

*

XINRAN: Teacher You, as I understand it, before 1980, you all had to request approval from your superiors before you could form a relationship or get married. How is it that a strict team leader like yourself chose a wife from within your own ranks? Wasn't your choice of wife a step beyond the bounds of propriety, a misuse of your authority?

YOU: Oh no, it was a very neat solution to the problem. I was responsible for technology within the brigade, so I had the power to check up on work everywhere, and that was how we got to know each other. She was very fond of studying, but there were almost no books, and you couldn't get magazines either. I worked in the city area, where there was a limited supply of books and newspapers, so I often brought newspapers and magazines out to her.

XINRAN: There were very many girls in the prospecting team; why was Mrs You the only one who caught your fancy?

YOU: She was slightly older, all the rest were younger than her. At the time there was a rule, wasn't there, that you had to be over a certain age, otherwise you would face disciplinary action.

XINRAN: I don't believe it! There must be some other reason, how could you only consider age when taking a wife?

*

Privately, I was quite put out by this typical "Chinese male" tone, unable to admit that his choice had been based on true feelings. His words were spoken in the patronising tone of a "husband" to his wife, as if making his excuses for his regrets in their marriage.

*

YOU: It's true, at that time she was a year or two older than the other girls, otherwise she couldn't have been a team leader. She was also extremely serious and responsible in her work, so when I went to check up on them, I got a good feeling about her.

*

I felt hugely indignant on Mrs You's behalf: in the eyes of the husband she admired so much, their marriage seemed not to have risen from mutual feeling, but to be a part of nature, as spring comes after winter, and summer follows spring. As a woman who has lived and worked in China for over forty years, I should be used to men passing such judgements by now, but it is more than I can manage; I cannot get "used" to it.

*

XINRAN: Do you still remember how you asked her to marry you?

YOU: *Aiya!* That . . . [He laughs.] What's the point of listening to this stuff?

XINRAN: I want to know how your generation lived your daily lives, people like you who devoted yourselves to the motherland, obeying the Party in everything.

YOU: In those days everybody was very simple, we weren't like people today, we didn't understand romanticism – people who worked well and were ideologically advanced were the first to touch our hearts. She was our nation's first ever female Prospecting Team Leader, that was a very tough job, and she did it very well. So, one time she got ill, she had a cold, I bought a few things and went to visit her, to look after her, and so we gradually came to have feelings for each other. I didn't say any words about wanting to get married, just wrote her a letter. In the letter I said: we both need to look after each other; if you're willing for me to look after you, I will take care of you all your life. We were relatively simple-minded, not sophisticated like people nowadays, with their talk of feelings and romance.

XINRAN: That's not simple-minded, it's called persistent devotion to duty, isn't it? The work above all else?

YOU: Well, yes.

XINRAN: You had been so determined, when they "struggled against" you in the Cultural Revolution, did that lack of understanding and denial of what you stood for cause you pain?

YOU: *Hai*, it was painful, it's true. In the Cultural Revolution the Red Guards searched our house as we stood there looking on, and we didn't dare say a word. I felt that it was morally wrong, and I didn't understand what it was in the name of. But at the time we just believed that whatever Mao Zedong said had to be right! And the longer it went on, the worse it got, nobody dared to speak out, and the denunciations were very severe. They had two problems with me, one was that I had brought back a radio from my study in the Soviet Union; nobody had a radio in those days, not even a watch, so these worker-peasant cadres all thought I was a secret agent, using that radio marked in Russian to communicate with enemy stations.

XINRAN: And you didn't explain?

YOU: Explain? Those people hadn't had more than a few days' schooling, they didn't understand what I was saying. That really was "a scholar meeting a soldier, in the right but can't make himself understood". In due course they sent me down to be a mechanic, they made me repair buses and trucks, and I came to understand motor vehicles very well, I was able to do things with engines that other people couldn't. I was a very good motor-repair man.

XINRAN: For how long were you under attack?

YOU: More than two years.

XINRAN: Do you think that you changed after you were denounced?

YOU: A little. Before I was denounced I used to be a straight talker, I always said what was on my mind; I dared to criticise everything, even the Three Red Banners [the general Party line on building up socialism, the Great Leap Forward, and the People's Communes], all of that. Afterwards, I told myself: I haven't committed any crime, they were unfair to me, but I won't betray my Party because of this. So for a long time after I was denounced, I very seldom spoke.

XINRAN: To this day?

YOU: Nowadays I'm a bit better. Sometimes I'm none too pleased with some of the policies, but I still have to take the same line as my superiors while talking to the workers; as a leader and a comrade I must do this.

XINRAN: What do you think are the three biggest differences between China before the Liberation, the fifties to the eighties, and the eighties until today? If young people today asked you how they should view this history, what would be your advice?

YOU: Well, now . . . The time is not ripe, you can't say for sure as yet. This is what I think: people should exchange opinions with former Red Guards and their generation, and they should accept the lessons of the Cultural Revolution. We have a responsibility to guide them, because we have experienced more aspects of life than they have; young people only come into contact with the surface layers of society, but my experience is not just of the surface, but of the cross section. Our generation should exchange views on China's development with the former Red Guards and the new generation of officials.

I'll tell you a bit of what I think about your three periods of history. A great change took place in our country after the Liberation – there can be no comparison between the pre- and post-Liberation systems of government. Firstly, the system of ownership is different: under the Guomindang it was a capitalist system of ownership, but after the Liberation we had ownership by the people. Secondly, relationships between people are different. After Liberation, why did the common people immediately stand up to answer the call of the Communist Party? Before, relations between people were those of capitalist slave owners and slaves, that is the big difference between the capitalists and the Communist Party. The third thing was the change in the means of production: in the past people worked for the capitalists, but now we work for ourselves. So in the period after Liberation, people believed that Chairman Mao was leading China to overturn the Three Great Mountains of imperialism, feudalism and bureaucratic capitalism; enthusiasm was high throughout society, so trust in the nation increased; if nothing else, the common people found self-belief.

After this period a series of major policy changes took place, which led to a series of tragedies that caused China to lag behind internationally and the people's standard of living to fall. In fact, the most significant damage to China was caused by ignorant, narrow-minded political movements, which eroded the self-respect that China had only just rediscovered after the Opium War. This is also one of the reasons why today's Chinese have this unhealthy obsession with things foreign.

XINRAN: Do you think that this situation was the result of limited knowledge, or political expediency, or was it due to economic conditions?

YOU: The damage done to the people and to China's non-state-run enterprises between 1958 and the end of the Cultural Revolution is impossible to calculate. I believe that this historical mistake was primarily due to limited knowledge on the part of the leaders. After a long period of making revolution, class struggle was all they knew, they knew nothing about production, and in the end political mistakes were made. I can't say much about anti-rightism, rightist tendencies and the rightist movement, I didn't have much to do with those, but my guess is that it was a political struggle, a struggle for power. The main reason was the major leaders lacked the knowledge necessary to manage a country – at that time hardly anybody in the government had any real understanding of economics. Deng Xiaoping and others like him had studied abroad in France, but they did not hold the dominant positions, and in my personal opinion Zhou Enlai never held a dominant position either. There are all kinds of reasons why China suffered an identity crisis after the Three Great Mountains were gone, but what it boils down to is a lack of sufficient knowledge on the part of the leaders. Nobody dared to say it in the past, but there was a tacit understanding; actually we have not yet opened up sufficiently to discuss this issue now either.

Chinese people still have their Chinese strength of will: if mistakes have been made, then they rectify them. China's luck hasn't been that bad really; once Deng Xiaoping was released, he took facts as his starting point, and reversed all the wrongful verdicts on the people who had contributed so much to the revolution.

XINRAN: From the vantage point of a high-level national manager, do you still have the same concerns about development now? Are the management and policymaking levels of government limited by their lack of international knowledge?

YOU: In my view there are limitations – I'm not saying with everybody, but they are making an effort to put things to rights. In my estimation, it won't require too much work to put matters straight. For example, Deng Xiaoping implemented the Reform and Opening [the opening up of China to the West], which made a great contribution to China's economic development, but in terms of the nation as a whole, imbalances have emerged, and many places still have a lot of problems. Take the heavy industrial areas of the north-east, and the big expansion of the economy in the western region, these are all long-term matters, not something you can sort out in a day. The new generation of leaders has great resolve; they have enlarged the Great North-Western Region, incorporating the big, wealthy cities of Chongqing and Chengdu into the western regions. Urumqi used to be a tiny city with just two streets, now it's the biggest city in the north-west, and after Urumqi they're going to start opening up Yinchuan [the capital city of Ningxia, one of the very poor, arid areas where the Yous prospected for oil]. In other words, by following the policy guidelines laid down by Deng Xiaoping, Jiang Zemin has achieved a certain level of development, and we now have a chance to re-establish the national pride we lost in the political movements and the Cultural Revolution.

But objectively speaking, the ability of Jiang Zemin and the leaders and cadres who came before him to plan the economy was severely limited, they lacked knowledge of global society. I have more confidence in the system of the current leaders, Hu Jintao and Wen Jiabao. Why? Because they are tackling the issues that the people really feel they need. First there is the "Harmonious Society",* a concept that has already been extended to foreign relations; how much time we Chinese have wasted with our internal squabbles and external conflicts, how many wasted lives. The second thing is their idea that "people are the key": in our thousands of years of history it was always power that was the key, this is why we have never had true, meaningful respect for the common people. But it's the third thing that has won the most hearts: solving the problems of China's peasants.

In the past the Party and government used to make a song and dance about how peasants were the key, but in fact it was still the peasants who suffered most! Now it's much better, they have solved a good many of the peasants' problems in small places like Hezheng. There has been a widespread change to high-yield fields here, whereas in the past they would have sown low-yield wheat, beans and the like; oilseed rape used to sell for a few jiao, and now it's three and a half yuan a kilo. This has improved the standard of living for the peasants who grow the crops. Many city people believe that peasants are nothing to do with them, but that's not so! In the cities it's peasant migrant workers who build houses and do all the low-status work. If you don't take the peasants, the vast majority of the population, into consideration when attempting to solve China's problems, then it's never going to work. You won't catch me going with the cadres to view those "advanced experimental areas", listen to "model reports" or any of that stuff. I just want to visit the grass-roots levels, to hear what those peasants who can never leave their land have to say. China is a big agricultural nation; without the peasants as a stable foundation, the landscape of the nation which we have developed with such suffering will not be stable or harmonious. If the peasants don't have a decent life, our national self-confidence is vain and empty. It is the responsibility of a nation to bring harmony, wealth and equality to its people.

XINRAN: I have three final questions. First, young people nowadays

---

* The idea of "Harmonious Society" was introduced by China's president, Hu Jintao, in an attempt to address some of the increasingly serious inequalities and divisions of Chinese society.

consider that of the last two generations, one generation was foolish and ignorant and the other was foolishly loyal. What do you think? Are they right?

YOU: What angle should I look at this from? Have these people studied any advanced cultural knowledge? How much do they know about history, and what is necessary to set up a nation? I think that those young people are wrong.

XINRAN: Second, if you could choose, would you have your time over again?

YOU: Let's leave that one, you're talking about something impossible.

XINRAN: Third question then. Can you tell me about one or two things you remember best from your childhood?

YOU: This is an easy question for me; to this day I've never forgotten the things from my childhood. I'll give you two examples. When I was in primary school, our school only had fourteen uniforms, so anyone who wanted to be in the Boys' Army had to be a good student, one of the top ten in the class, they had to love study, and they had to love labour. I really wanted a uniform; it was made of khaki cloth, similar to foreign clothes, the kind the American soldiers wore. But to wear that uniform I had to pay a deposit of three yuan. I thought hard about it, and finally I begged my family for the three yuan, with tears in my eyes. It was a fine feeling, putting on that army outfit! Every day when school was out, the Boys' Army left first, leading the way, with the ordinary students following on behind, it really gave you a feeling of achievement. When I got home I used to quickly take it off, fold it up very neatly and put it away. This is one of the deepest impressions of my childhood.

The second was during the Anti-Japanese War, when we held a collection for the soldiers at the front line, and every family made an effort for those soldiers. But later on I saw the head of our police bureau giving a speech, ranting and waving his arms around, and he was wearing some of the things we had donated. I thought: *Aiya*, we've been had, they never sent our gifts to the front line, they took them for themselves! At that moment I decided: if I'm a big official some day, I will never, ever be corrupt. These are the two deepest impressions from my childhood.

XINRAN: Teacher You, do you have any unfulfilled wishes?

YOU: Ah, unfulfilled wishes . . . personally, yes. I'm more ashamed and guilty about my children than anything else. I never gave them a chance to get a proper education. This is my greatest regret.

XINRAN: Now there's hope for your grandchildren.

YOU: Yes! There's hope for the grandchildren! We devote our time to them now, but that's my biggest regret!

*

At that moment we heard a voice in the courtyard calling out for supper.

And so we concluded that day's interview. I prayed for this elderly couple, hoping that these confidences could bring them a measure of peace and comfort. They truly had given their all to China – their own youth, their children's chances in life; how many mothers and fathers in the world would sacrifice their own children's happiness on the altar of a political party or a nation?

The following morning, before we took our leave, I had two more long discussions with Teacher You, in the course of a morning walk and a picnic at noon. This mainly involved me listening to his analysis of the current state of China's petroleum.

*

XINRAN: Teacher You, within the limits of what is permitted, can you tell me in a simple way about China's earliest oil resources?

YOU: Before 1949, China had very little oil; there were only three oilfields in three places. One was the Yanchang oil deposit in northern Shaanxi, an old oil deposit, started in the last years of the Qing dynasty. Another was the Yumen oilfield in Gansu, and the third was the Dushanzi oil deposit in Xinjiang, which we had only just started to develop with Soviet help, we hadn't started extracting. The total value of all three was less than 150,000 tonnes a year.

Before the Liberation we relied mainly on the American company Mobil; as a nation we were dependent on them. After Liberation we only imported Soviet oil for political reasons. The Soviets helped China develop a petroleum industry; they were the ones to suggest recruiting China's physics students as geological prospectors for oil, and the Chinese government did as they suggested, so production levels were somewhat higher in the first ten years after Liberation; with the discovery of the big Kelamayi oilfield, production rose from 150,000 tonnes to 500,000 tonnes.

At that time, when the Petroleum Ministry held its yearly Oil Prospecting

Conference in Beijing, there would barely be a hundred key workers present. Many geologists were posted to Daqing in the north-east; at that time oil work was really tough, it's impossible to describe how hard that time was. The centre told us to stick it out for four more years, and bring Daqing to heel! It was tough, but we just kept on working.

After opening up Daqing, we discovered the Shengli oilfield in Shandong, and the North China oilfield. This was when Chinese geological prospecting really took off and China's petroleum started to develop; come the sixties, China was no longer dependent on oil imports, and we didn't start importing again until after the eighties, when we found ourselves developing too quickly. In the seventies our production increased again, to nearly 700,000,000 tonnes. We could easily supply our own needs, and we started to export petroleum to North Korea and Japan.

XINRAN: I saw a news report recently on the possibility that a Russo-Japanese oil pipeline will pass through Chinese territory. Am I right in thinking this is closely connected with the future of our oil supply?

YOU: The best option for China would have been transportation by pipeline, that is, using a pipeline to transport the oil resources of neighbouring countries, thereby lessening China's dependence on oil from the Central Asian region and transportation via the Malacca Straits. The Arkhangelsk-Daqing Line that would have linked China and Russia collapsed in mysterious circumstances at the last moment, and this cast a heavy shadow over prospects of a pipeline in China's oil strategy.

XINRAN: Do you believe that this "loss" was due to pressure from America and Japan, or was it a Russian manoeuvre? Or was it a problem with our negotiators?

YOU: You could say that it's all of these. Oil is a part of politics now, this is clear to see from international relations, and it's very dangerous.

XINRAN: When did China start having plans for prospecting in Africa? And when did we begin diplomatic relations with the Middle East? When did we start to concern ourselves with Middle Eastern oil reserves?

YOU: Over 50 per cent of our oil imports come from the Middle East; very early on that region became an area of high demand for both oil and weapons. Central Asia accounts for about 30 per cent, and then comes Africa, which produces approximately 20 per cent of China's total crude oil imports. We are now officially trying to get into a few "sidelined and occupied areas". Our main attack is on two fronts: one is Africa, in particular North Africa; the other is the South American region, that's places like Cuba.

In a few months' time China will hold a summit with the heads of forty-eight African nations in Beijing. This will be a forum for Chinese-African cooperation, in which plans will be made for the period between 2007 and 2009, to ensure the future of Chinese-African oil cooperation. The fiftieth anniversary of China's opening diplomatic relations with African countries is in 2006, and it is also the tenth anniversary of the China Petroleum Corporation officially entering Africa on a large scale to develop oil and gas. China's leaders hope to create as quickly as possible a situation in which the African economy will be inseparable from China's oil investment. Africa's oil reserves can safeguard China's energy reserves.

XINRAN: Why are all the brains in the oil world thinking up plans for Africa?

YOU: If you follow the Gulf of Guinea south on an atlas you will see a group of African countries all marked with the sign for oil – that includes Equatorial Guinea, Gabon and the Congo, all the way down to Angola in the south. A whole series of new oilfields with rich potential have been discovered in the Sahara Desert in North Africa, Sudan in East Africa and Chad in Central Africa.

In Africa's history, petroleum came after gold, ivory and slaves; it was seen as another of the "black" treasures of the African continent. Over a period of decades, just about all of the Western oil magnates have invested large sums in Africa. China Petroleum has had forty-four prospecting and development projects in twenty countries in ten years, with thirteen of those countries in North and West Africa.

Just before oil prices started to rise, Africa became another storehouse of oil for the whole world, a possible successor to the Middle East. But, after decades of prospecting, how much virgin territory is there left in Africa to open up? Between oil giants like ExxonMobil, Shell, Total and the others, what opportunities will China Petroleum still be able to find? This is actually a challenge to China's prospecting technology and transportation capability.

XINRAN: Are you worried about China's prospecting capability?

YOU: In many aspects of prospecting and development, China Petroleum has already reached the world standard (in areas such as passive rift valley basin natural gas theory, integrated prospecting technology, fine-scale imaging of oil reserves and so on. China's oil prospecting is still at the middle-mature stage, and our oil reserves are still in the high basic value, stable growth period), but the difficulty of prospecting is increasing all the time. Generally speaking, China's top oilfields are entering a period of decline, and achieving stable production is becoming increasingly difficult.

China's oil needs are skyrocketing, and this has been perceived as a key reason for the major inflation of international oil prices in recent years. China has already replaced Japan as the world's second biggest consumer of oil (second only to the United States); it is estimated that in less than ten years China's oil needs will have increased from 6,000,000 tonnes a day to 11,500,000 tonnes a day. Our oil reserves are seriously inadequate, and in fourteen years' time China's oil may very well be exhausted. This dramatic transformation from the oil exporter of former years to a major oil-importing nation has already become a "bottleneck" in our development. It is predicted that by 2020 at least 60 per cent of our oil will have to come from imports. To bring our prospecting ability up to a level where it can contend with the world's established high-tech oil nations in fourteen years will be no easy task.

XINRAN: If we can't make it in time on the harvesting front, do you worry about the transportation of oil imports?

YOU: Our country's fleet of oil tankers in the Far East is pitifully small; this does not sit well with constantly increasing oil imports. Over 90 per cent of our country's oil imports have to be transported by sea, and 90 per cent of this seaborne oil is transported in foreign tankers. This leads to another even more serious question: the human factor – it is people who are in charge of our nation's oil security. In order to safeguard our nation's energy reserves, China Ocean Shipping (Group) Company is currently building a world-class oil tanker fleet.

XINRAN: Apart from worries about prospecting, harvesting and sea transportation, do you consider that there are any more urgent tasks for Chinese oil?

YOU: I'm not worried about our oil diplomacy with other nations; we can stand aside and let them fight it out between them. But our internal structure and systems of organisation are cause for concern. In 1998, as part of our country's reforms of the petroleum industry, the original single company was split up into the three companies we have today, in the hope of stimulating competition. But today there is no sign of the results they predicted, a state of competition did not develop, quite the reverse, it created a monopoly, with the three companies carving up their fields of influence between them. The government should be on the alert to prevent this; the oil groups could manipulate the market, to coerce the government.

*

Just as we were completing the *China Witness* interviews, I saw a news piece on CNN: on 27 August 2006, Chad, which is one of Africa's emerging oil nations, suddenly ordered two of the world's oil giants – America's Chevron-Texaco Company and a Malaysian oil company – to quit the country. This report stated that the Chad government's true motive was to clear the way for the Chinese oil company Sinopec; in all probability this was "reserving a seat" for Sinopec to enter Chad. Analysts were quoted, saying that if this was correct, it would constitute an enormous change in the political relations of the entire African continent. I hope that this is not setting up the battlefields of the Middle East all over again, and that this area will not become the next place of "urgent need" in the development of the arms industry.

When the time came for me to phone Mrs You to check my final draft, she told me that she was still thinking about my two difficult questions: What are the three most painful things and the three happiest things of your life? You are so successful, you created an era, but in modern people's eyes, in young people's eyes, was it worth it?

5

Acrobat: From Counter-Revolutionary's Daughter to National Medal Winner

Yishijua, *top*, practising, 1950s.

On tour in South America, 1990s.

YISHUJIA, aged sixty, a renowned acrobat, *interviewed in Qingdao, Shandong province on the eastern coast of China, a lively harbour colonised by Germany before the First World War and later Japan. Yishujia's father was branded a counter-revolutionary and detained for five years, leaving her mother to bring up a family of five, so Yishujia joined a travelling acrobatic troupe before she was twelve. The Cultural Revolution changed the nature of their performances but the art survived. She became a first-class National Acrobat, performed around China as "a valuable artist" and travelled to many countries as a Chinese acrobat and cultural ambassador. Her son, Hu, is a professional magician and musician working in Britain.*

Hu is a professional magician, and also a performer on the Western saxophone and a Chinese folk wind instrument called the *suona*. In your first minute of conversation with him you get the feeling that China's three thousand years of etiquette have not yet vanished from the world: he is all polite enquiries after acquaintances, graceful thanks and becoming modesty. By the second minute you have difficulty following him: you have to concentrate hard to follow the tortuous route of his speech, carefully peeling away the adjectives and arranging all his conditional sentences into a logical sequence before the "naked goal" of his verbs comes into view. But in the third minute, all suddenly becomes clear, you want to follow his words, and he has already prepared a space in his thoughts for the words you want to say to him. This is what he has spent the last two minutes feeling for, preparing the ground with all those courtesies. I had never imagined that modern Chinese society, ravaged and made barren by politics, could produce such an "authentic Chinese" man who was not yet out of his thirties, a young man in whom Chinese folk customs remained pure, who could walk among the slurry of Western fast food and emerge unsullied.

I talked to Hu about some of the feelings and losses Chinese experience on coming to the West, hoping I could learn something about the values of the new generation of young Chinese who were making a living overseas. But he left me only with an unforgettable feeling of responsibility: guilt at having been unable to keep his father alive, anxiety at being unable to fulfil his responsibilities to his widowed mother, shame that China's fine, true elegant culture had gained no recognition in the West. In truth, in the decade and more since I moved to Britain, I have rarely met a young Chinese person with such a sense of responsibility.

I had been searching for some time for an opportunity to decrypt this "authentic Chinese" friend, but it was very hard. To me, there was a fortress of personality, made up of his age, his era and his gender: it was difficult for a woman of his mother's generation to enter his "kingdom of causes and effects". Then one day he told me that his mother was coming to Britain to see him, she did not understand English or have any idea how to get around London on her own, and he wondered if it would be possible for me to introduce a few Chinese friends to her.

Hu's mother, Yishujia, was a Chinese National Level One acrobatic performer and one of the few winners of the women's 8 March Red-Banner Pacesetter* medal. It was hard to believe from her limber, agile walk that she was a woman of over sixty, the youthful energy and interest that came from her years of training as a young woman were immediately noticeable. The first time we met, her smile and calm manner made me imagine a comfortable, tranquil life, which was a very rare form of good luck in the last century in China. I completely failed to detect what lay behind those smiles and jokes.

I invited mother and son to spend Christmas with us in London. At dinner, after the roast goose, we brought out a cheese plate. I was worried that Yishujia would not be able to cope with the taste, which Chinese people often find close to unbearable, but I watched her cut off a small piece of cheese, put it on her plate with a smile, partition off an even smaller sliver and place it in her mouth, still smiling. At this point I stopped worrying, and turned to the other guests, but when I glanced back at her place, she was missing. I hurried after her to the toilet, from which issued suppressed sounds of vomiting. I waited quietly outside the door until she came out, tears still glistening on her cheeks. "I'm fine, I was being greedy, I got something stuck in my throat, so I came to clean myself out. I've caused you a lot of worry for nothing." When I heard these words it suddenly hit me: this is a woman of remarkable self-control. That evening, as I said goodbye to her and her son, I fixed a time for her to come to my home for tea. She came as agreed, and brought me her real self: a daughter who had spent every day longing for her mother; a traditional Chinese woman whose husband was dead and whose son lived far away; a National Level One acrobatic performer

---

* A valued medal given to outstanding women workers, awarded each year on 8 March (International Women's Day) at different levels: national, provincial, county and city.

who had struggled for a future of her own, with a father accused of being a counter-revolutionary, and who had grown up along with acrobatics in China as the status changed from amateur to professional; a mother who had raised a pure, authentic Chinese child. This was a Chinese story with no political window dressing, without the gilding and ornamentation of vanity.

Yishujia was the youngest person whom I interviewed. She agreed to come to Qingdao, which was some distance from her home in the city of Jinan, because she did not want the "past things that floated up from the bottom of the sea" to cloud the waters of her daily life. I hoped that by finding a space where she could distance herself from it all, she would be able to allow the unhappiness and griefs to settle.

We arrived in the summer coastal resort of Qingdao, on the Shandong peninsula in east China, on 14 August. It was unusually hot in Qingdao, which is as famous for its pleasantly cool summers as for its Tsingtao beer, with temperatures as high as thirty-nine degrees. However, this did not have any noticeable effect on the annual International Beer Festival: hundreds of thousands of beer lovers from all over the world were celebrating all through the night despite the heatwave, to the point where some people mistook a heaven-sent night-time fall of rain for "rivers of beer in the streets".

We held our interview with Yishujia in a government-run guest house by the sea. She had changed into a person who was both very strange to me and very familiar: this was no longer the lively, vivacious Teacher Yishujia whom the years had passed by, full of smiles and laughter. Instead, she was "standing ready for battle", as if for a political interrogation, with all her answers prepared and ready. This is a classic expression and posture in video interviews in China, and also a very tricky "bottleneck" stage through which you must pass before you can enter into a heart-to-heart dialogue.

I adopted a slow, measured tone, and asked the first question in a seemingly casual way.

*

XINRAN: Teacher Yishujia, after you retired, what did you think about the most?

YISHUJIA: I went over past memories, a bit of everything.

XINRAN: What's the earliest thing you remember?

YISHUJIA: That must be my mother taking me to visit my father. At the time my father was working on a building somewhere outside Jinan, and my mother took me and the eldest of my younger sisters over the mountains on donkey-back to see him.

XINRAN: Can you still remember where you father was?

YISHUJIA: I can't remember what place it was, I just remember that in the evenings you could hear wolves howling.

XINRAN: Do you know what kind of families your parents came from? I'm still rather hazy about my own family background, even now. I know my great-grandfather ran restaurants, as far afield as Malaysia, Japan and Singapore, though it wasn't called Singapore in those days. But nobody in my grandfather's generation wanted to run a restaurant, they all went to work in banks or for Far Eastern companies, so the restaurants were all sold off. In my father's generation, that big family split into two groups: one group went to America with the Western companies, another followed the Communist Party and stayed in China. So what kind of family was yours?

YISHUJIA: I can only remember that my paternal great-grandfather's family was from Hongsong village in Zhouping county, in Shandong. My great-grandfather died young, he was just fifty, and my great-grandmother lost her sight through illness, but she raised my grandfather and a great-aunt without remarrying. In those days widows remained faithful to their dead husbands by never remarrying. The fulfilment of duty was the only way their children could hold their heads up around other people. The impression I got when I was small was that my great-uncle had been to college, and that was why the whole family got an education. My great-uncle was a schoolteacher. My great-grandmother was supporting the family at that time, it was really hard for her. Once my great-uncle started teaching, he took all the boys in the family with him to Jinan to go to school, my great-aunt's boys, my father and uncles from our family. In our extended family, all the males in my father's generation went to school.

XINRAN: About how old were you when you went to primary school?

YISHUJIA: I was seven.

XINRAN: What was the school like?

YISHUJIA: My school was the best in Jinan – my great-uncle taught there.

XINRAN: How many boys and girls were there when you started school?

YISHUJIA: There were forty or fifty children in my class, a lot more boys than girls.

XINRAN: So many people in your family had been to school, did you experience hardships in the political movements after Liberation?

YISHUJIA: In those days our family owned a big, rambling house; we had livestock too, and hired hands to work our land. Just before Liberation, my great-uncle sold a lot of the family property. My great-grandmother was livid, she beat and cursed him, but later on she found out that he had been quite far-sighted: because our family property had all been sold, when the government determined class status after Liberation we were classified as middle peasants, otherwise we would have been classed as landlords and attacked. It wasn't just a question of a few houses, it was life and death.

XINRAN: It always surprises me, the way those old people could see the way society was going. My maternal grandfather donated a sizeable portion of his property to the government after the Liberation: banks, grain stores, shipping fleets, hardware factories, he gave them all to the common cause without a murmur. A good many of the people who had been classified as capitalists along with him came under attack, their children were implicated in their crimes, and this often ended in suffering or death; but in my grandfather's case, apart from the decade of the Cultural Revolution, which he spent in prison, he lived in peace until he died aged ninety-seven, without a stain on his character, and all his children alive and well.

YISHUJIA: Hmm, that's no easy thing.

*

I felt that Yishujia was very guarded in the face of my questions, so I tried to elicit some fellow feeling with stories of my grandparents' generation: after my grandfather died, crowds of people came to express their condolences, nearly a thousand in the course of a week. My aunts and uncles were flabbergasted, none of them knew why so many people who knew my grandfather would come.

*

YISHUJIA: Oh, I know why even your family didn't know.

XINRAN: Why? [I thought she had started to open up, but I was wrong.]

YISHUJIA: You say it, I like to listen!

XINRAN: Many of the people who came to pay their respects knelt in front of his picture and talked to him, telling their stories. Afterwards, my aunt said that when she saw all this she was filled with regret, she said she should have listened more to my grandfather's stories when he was still alive. But members of the younger generation never dared to ask their elders about their history, and old people seldom talked much about their past, especially those who came up from nothing through hard work, who had been manual workers, they believed that they were a lower class than others. There are also people who find it hard to get the words out, especially those who had a history of capitalism after the fifties – most of them avoid mentioning the past entirely.

YISHUJIA: You're right there, and those people are in the majority.

*

I didn't wait for her to say more, but continued to talk about my own family.

*

XINRAN: Kneeling in front of my grandfather's portrait, several elderly ladies who had been prostitutes in the 1940s had told my aunt that my grandfather had saved their lives when the Guomindang were rounding up economic criminals [which included prostitutes] and cleaning up society. He had let them enter one of his handicraft factories, giving them an opportunity to turn from their old ways and learn a few skills, otherwise they would have been shot like many other prostitutes under the Guomindang.

YISHUJIA: I've heard the old people say that the Guomindang were very harsh when they first came to power – they shot people dead in Nanjing, and called it "strict social cleansing". And afterwards our Communist Party used the same word and did similar things. A lot of women who had been prostitutes before 1949 were persecuted to death.

XINRAN: Actually, between the 1940s and the 1990s, both the Guomindang and the Communist Party had some very harsh policies. I think that perhaps 25 per cent of the population of China was treated unjustly or sentenced wrongly in that period, and more than half of those were educated people.

YISHUJIA: My father was branded an active counter-revolutionary just because of a little thing. When my father left home to go to school in Jinan, he became friendly with an underground member of the Party. He couldn't tell my father that he was a Party member, but he did tell him: "If a time comes when you don't see me, don't hang around, go back home." But my father forgot. Afterwards the Eighth Route Army came to Jinan, they had the city surrounded, he couldn't get out, but he had to eat. At that time the Guomindang had set up a San Qing Tuan – the Three Youth League – anyone who joined up would have work to do and food to eat. So, many young people in Jinan whose families didn't have a lot of money joined that society.

XINRAN: The San Qing Tuan, the one that was defined as counter-revolutionary in the fifties? That's serious.

YISHUJIA: He was just a naive student in those days, he didn't understand politics, he joined because he was afraid he would starve. Jinan was liberated after three months, but my father suffered a lifetime of bitterness because of those three months in which he didn't go hungry.

XINRAN: A lifetime of suffering just because of three months in the San Qing Tuan?

YISHUJIA: He hadn't done anything bad, he couldn't shoot a gun or fight, he was an architecture student, but just because of that San Qing Tuan, he became a "wicked man" who could never say anything right. To this day I don't know what exactly the San Qing Tuan was, I've no idea what was so terrible about it.

XINRAN: The Communist Party has a Communist Youth League, right? The Youth League was the first step to joining the Communist Party, and after 1949 you had to join the Party to get any of the important government posts. Similarly, the San Qing Tuan was the Guomindang's version of the Youth League, the first step to joining the Guomindang, which naturally made it the enemy of the Communist Party.

YISHUJIA: Yes, but even if it was a political organisation, it was all over in just three months, it was disbanded as soon as the city was liberated. My father really regretted it; if he'd just remembered what that man had told him, that if he couldn't see him he should leave, then he'd have been fine . . . Then he got in trouble again just after Liberation, when they were building the big City Government building. He was the project supervisor, checking that the work was carried out according to the blueprint, but he discovered that the stairs to the basement had been designed without a handrail, and the waterproofing hadn't been designed to deal with subsidence, so he reported it to his superiors, requesting modifications. But the leaders at that time were peasant cadres who'd fought their way to Jinan, they didn't understand, all they cared about was "more, better, faster, cheaper" and making revolution. My father asked them to stop work to put things right, but that was delaying the revolutionary task, out of the question! Then in the final inspection, a higher-ranking cadre who'd come to sign off the project almost slipped and fell into the cellar – and that staircase without a railing became evidence of my father's crime, a plot to injure revolutionary cadres. On top of that, leaks soon began to appear in the waterproofing, and that was deliberate sabotage! Nobody dared to testify on behalf of a counter-revolutionary in those days, so they arrested my father! I'll never forget that day. All these policemen came into our home, and there were more standing in the courtyard. My father didn't say a word, they just took him away, and I just didn't have a clue why. My mother didn't know the reason either, because my father had never discussed work matters with her. At that time everyone was very particular about "organisational discipline", it was forbidden to discuss work between husband and wife or family members.

XINRAN: After your father was detained in front of all those people, how did your neighbours and people like that treat you?

YISHUJIA: Some were pretty good, and still had dealings with us, but whenever there was the least sign of trouble I'd get called a jailbird's brat.

XINRAN: How long was your father detained?

YISHUJIA: Five years, I suppose, though he was sentenced to twenty. My father never accepted it, he appealed, and finally the high-ups sent someone down to examine the scene of the crime and recheck the plans. In the end he was rehabilitated.

XINRAN: When your father was in prison, how did your mother manage to make a living while bringing up you children?

YISHUJIA: She was a gatekeeper at a neighbourhood-run chemical factory; later on she did embroidery. We only had twelve yuan a month for a family of five, for food, clothes and everything else, it was very hard.

XINRAN: Was this the reason why you started work so young?

YISHUJIA: My mother had no choice – once I'd left home to work there was one burden less on the family.

XINRAN: After you left, how did the family keep going? Did your mother discuss this with you?

YISHUJIA: I know for certain that my mother had a very hard time, but she was a strong woman, she never talked about it. [Tears stream down her face.] Whenever I talk about my mother I feel so awful, she suffered so much! She suffered all her life, and she died early too . . .

*

We sat in silence for a while, but I didn't stop the video recorder. Seeing her weeping in front of me, thoughts of many other women I had interviewed welled up in my mind: how many women in China worked day after day, night after night, toiling away to raise their children in this desert of human culture? We Chinese use our mothers like candles, they melt themselves away to shine their light on others.

I didn't continue with the question of her mother. I knew it was a very, very painful subject.

*

XINRAN: I know you joined an acrobatic troupe before you were twelve – can you tell me something about your first few years? What was your training like? Where did you perform? What were your leaders like? I think it must be etched deeply in your memory.

YISHUJIA: At the very beginning I didn't perform, I just had lessons and practised my acrobatic skills – the waist, legs and the crown of the head are very important in Chinese acrobatics. I got up very early every day; in the morning after breakfast we had professional practice and lessons; sometimes in the afternoon we had school, or sometimes the school lessons were in the evening. In those days we could never get enough sleep, everyone was constantly nodding off – one time in somersaulting class I turned a few somersaults and then went to sleep on the spot. The first time I performed I was thirteen. It was the dance "Catching Butterflies" – I can still remember it. I turned three somersaults and very nearly somersaulted myself off the stage. In those days it was very dark at the bottom of the stage – once the stage lights were on you couldn't see anything below the stage.

XINRAN: What sort of places did you mostly perform in? How did the audience react?

YISHUJIA: We mostly went up into the mountains and to the countryside. The peasants had no cultural activity at all from one year's end to the next, and they loved acrobatics, which you could understand whether you'd been to school or not, so just about every family came to watch, lots and lots of people. There was no electric light in the countryside in those days, we used big hanging hurricane lamps to light the performances we held to bring cultural entertainment to the peasants, and to promote the Party's policies. Sometimes we'd move on very quickly; we'd put on two shows and then leave, then another two shows and off again. All our things went in two big horse-drawn carts, sometimes we even slept on the carts – from time to time there'd be a thump, and that would be someone falling to the ground. We often slept on the ground; if we did get a room there'd be no windows, you'd sleep over here, and over there the worms would be wriggling in and out. After a while conditions improved a bit – we got a tractor, later on it was trucks, ferries and trains, and in the 1980s, after the Reform and Opening, we even got to take a plane. When we retired we joked that we Chinese acrobats had been on everything except submarines and the *Shenzhou VI*.* Ha!

XINRAN: You said your troupe went to many villages to perform – how

* Shenzhou VI was the second human spaceflight of the People's Republic of China, launched on 12 October 2005 on a Long March rocket from the Jiuquan Satellite Launch Center in the Gobi Desert.

did you do those performances? I think it must be impossible for many young people to imagine: no theatre, no lights, no proper stage, how did you put on a show?

YISHUJIA: In the countryside we used the threshing grounds. Some of those big threshing grounds had an earth platform, others didn't.

XINRAN: What was the earth platform for?

YISHUJIA: I don't know, singing opera perhaps? The countryside was very poor, but you still used to get people who went there to sing traditional opera, trading and singing opera at the same time – I think it was a bit like going to market.

XINRAN: I've seen that too, a big acrobatic display on market day – hardly ideal conditions for a performance!

YISHUJIA: Too right! Take juggling stools with your feet: if there happened to be a strong wind, the stool would be blown to one side with one gust, and then, whoosh, it would turn over onto the other side, it was really difficult! If you were juggling umbrellas with your feet, whoosh, one puff of wind and you couldn't find your umbrella at all!

XINRAN: If you fluffed your performance, what would the locals do?

YISHUJIA: You'd have to have another go. If you got it right the second time there'd be clapping from the floor, otherwise they'd curse you for a clumsy fool – peasants are very down to earth, you know.

XINRAN: Did you get used to going to live in the countryside?

YISHUJIA: At that time I only knew to follow the troupe everywhere it went, I didn't feel anything really. It wasn't that comfortable in winter. I've always had pains in the joints on this leg, and why? It's from one year when it was snowing heavily outside, there was only a grass curtain at the window, we were all very tired, we just went to sleep wherever we fell, huddled in pairs for warmth. One quilt couldn't cover four legs, so our legs stuck out, and my leg got frozen, it itched and hurt like mad, and now I'm old it gives me trouble.

XINRAN: What did you do for food?

YISHUJIA: We brought our own kitchen along with us, pots, bowls, ladles, oil, salt, soy sauce and vinegar, the lot, and we bought whatever vegetables they had locally.

XINRAN: Where was the poorest place you went?

YISHUJIA: There were no rich places in those days. Shangqiu in Henan would have been the poorest. The wife of one of the troupe's members lived in Shangqiu, her children never had a chance to eat any meat, or to buy fish. The winters were bitterly cold, and for New Year she'd make the children grope for small fish in the ditches, and their New Year feast would be the whole family clustered around a pot of simple fish soup.

XINRAN: How long did circuit tours like this go on for?

YISHUJIA: Right up to the Cultural Revolution. Before that we went to the countryside at fixed times every year to put on shows for the peasants, but after the start of the Cultural Revolution we slowly stopped going to the countryside, and stuck to doing revolutionary performances in the city. In any case, our wages from the state were the same wherever we were – I got 29.5 yuan every month for ten years, which nowadays is barely enough for a cheap family meal out!

XINRAN: When you think about the revolutionary operas, does it seem ridiculous? I find it very strange. I thought a lot about this before I came to hear your story. I suppose you can insert revolutionary slogans into things like opera, ballet or plays, but how do you add revolutionary slogans or quotations from Chairman Mao into acrobatics?

YISHUJIA: It was ludicrous really, we were all idiots. We acted out battles, or things like "catching a spy", or taking American soldiers prisoner, that kind of revolutionary stuff, all fighting and killing. Some of the acrobats had good voices, so they'd sing a revolutionary song while making showy gestures, but I couldn't sing. Sometimes we did fancy work with staves, and that was the PLA fighting a battle. And tumbling? Boys would do the big somersaults, girls would do the fill-in parts in the background, cheering "Ten thousand years of long life to Mao Zedong!" Basically, all the acrobatic skill was lost. When we went to the army units to show our support, we'd perform "In Praise of Men He", because we wanted to stick to the revolutionary model. This Men He was a hero of the Liberation, he died a hero's death to help the common people. Those of us who were playing the common people all had to wear Red Guard armbands.

XINRAN: During the time of the Cultural Revolution, nobody in China could avoid making a public statement of their position, including foreigners. Those who went along with it survived, those who went against it perished. What were your feelings when you had to change from performing in your national costume to Red Guard costumes?

YISHUJIA: Nobody dared to have an opinion in those days, we just knew we had to go along with the revolutionary image, it was the Cultural Revolution, you couldn't do anything else. And we really felt that national costume was old, we should smash the old and embrace the new, so we ought to wear something new. It's no different from young people these days who wear those rubbishy clothes to keep up with the fashion, at the time that's what we thought.

XINRAN: So what was the difference between what you performed then and the things you did before?

YISHUJIA: Originally it was pure skill and art. During the Cultural Revolution it was just revolutionary gestures, and you had to force words into the acrobatic numbers, to promote Mao Zedong Thought.

XINRAN: So our traditional acrobatic arts were just actions put to music, then in the Cultural Revolution you started talking, like in a play?

YISHUJIA [laughs heartily]: Yes, it was all talk.

XINRAN: I can't imagine what kind of acrobatic performance that would be! Who did the talking? How did they speak? Don't you need breath control for acrobatics? Could you control your breath while you were talking?

YISHUJIA: The movements didn't matter, the important part was shouting slogans and making revolutionary gestures. For example, when I was doing fancy work with a stave, after I'd completed a set, I'd say: "*Revolution is not a crime, rebellion is just!*" before I went on to the next part. Thinking about it now, it was truly ridiculous. At that time everyone was a lunatic, some were genuinely crazy, some pretending to be crazy; if you weren't crazy you didn't come up to the demands of politics, or match the current ideology.

XINRAN: You're a National Level One performer, what is your greatest accomplishment in the field of acrobatics?

YISHUJIA: How much do you know about acrobatics?

XINRAN: I don't understand it, I've only seen it, it's very mysterious to me.

YISHUJIA: Some people say that acrobatics is a catch-all designation for every kind of art that involves the human body surpassing its normal limits. Actually that's inaccurate. Acrobatics includes art, animal training, farce, vocal skills (including animal impressions and funny voices, puppet theatre, shadow plays and the like), and many other different types and varieties of strange techniques and skills, like sword swallowing, fire eating, cutting people or horses into pieces, everything of that kind. For this reason, the ancients also referred to acrobatics as "Strange Theatre", the "Hundred Acts" and "Juggling Theatre".

Compared with the acrobatics of other countries, Chinese acrobatics has its own special features: we attach a lot of importance to the skills of the waist, legs and top of head, this is what the phrases "artistic acting and lively fighting" and "tumbling from Peking Opera, skills with the head from acrobatics" are referring to. Seeking stability in the midst of risk, seeking peace in the midst of movement, seeking strangeness in the midst of the ordinary to attain perfection; the special characteristics of this art are displayed most plainly in *gucai* juggling: the performer wears a simple long robe, but can produce a thousand marvellous things from it; its philosophy is creating being from nothingness, light and heavy side by side, paper-thin flowery umbrellas, coloured balls, all kicked up high to flutter, twist and float.

Chinese acrobatics is very adaptable: you can set up a stage and put on a show in squares, theatres, streets or hotel rooms, for as many as a hundred people or as few as one. All this is the unique charm of our acrobatics, and China is internationally acknowledged to be the best country in the world for acrobatics.

My specialities were the diabolo, magic tricks and light and heavy foot juggling. Heavy foot juggling is juggling with stools, light foot juggling is with umbrellas. You could say my best skill was heavy foot juggling, that's the juggling with stools; after that comes "mountain country drums and gongs", which I invented, playing music with the hands and feet, the feet beat drums and the hands beat other drums, the feet play the music while the hands keep the beat. When I was young, I was at the top of a human pyramid, and they juggled me along with the stools; as I got older and heavier I moved lower down the pyramid; in the last decade or so I was the one juggling all the people and stools!

XINRAN: How many performances have you given in your life?

YISHUJIA: I can't remember how many performances I did in how many places, but I do remember clearly that in South America alone I was in over five hundred shows.

XINRAN: Your troupe doesn't have any records?

YISHUJIA: Hardly any records have been preserved from the Cultural Revolution, and they only started keeping records on the arts in the nineties. I must say, it was tragic, the way all those cultural relics were burned; in the palaces of the Tang dynasty [AD 618–907] Chinese acrobatics was as important as music and dance, there were said to be many records in the history books. After the Song and Yuan dynasties [tenth–fourteenth centuries AD], song, dance and music were less highly regarded, acrobatics gradually became one of the humble professions, a poor man's job. In those days, who would keep records about poor people? Apparently, our troupe didn't start keeping records until after the Liberation. It's a shame they were all burned in the Cultural Revolution, a sin and a shame.

XINRAN: Before we came here we consulted many reports on you in the media. How many countries have you visited?

YISHUJIA: Well, we went to Japan for the first time in 1981; after that we were flown all over the place: Pakistan, Japan, America, Sri Lanka . . . what country's Manila?

XINRAN: It's the capital of the Philippines.

YISHUJIA: The Philippines, that's right. And then we stayed in Colombia for over a year, but we never performed in Europe.

XINRAN: What were your feelings after going abroad?

YISHUJIA: I had the strongest reactions towards Japan and America, the other countries were pretty much like us. In America, there was such a distance between their country and ours. The people there were more civilised. I'll give you a practical example: when you get on a public bus nobody pushes you, people form a queue without being told to. The cities were cleaner than ours at that time too – after two months there, the soles of your shoes would still be clean. Nowadays our cities are a lot better, some are even cleaner than theirs. In those days we knew that life in the West was better than here, but when some foreigners asked us "Does China have milk candy?" we were furious. "How could we not have milk candy?* We've got everything you have!" Behind closed doors we all admitted that they were advanced and we were poor, but we couldn't bear for anybody else to say that Chinese people were bad, or that we were deprived. How can I put it? Dogs don't hate their homes for being poor.

*

What Teacher Yishujia said was quite right. I have felt this very strongly myself: every time someone brings up China's problems or her dark side, I cannot stop myself from trying to rebut them – we need our national pride. This instinct for self-respect is as important to us as the pride of a mother who is convinced that her child is a genius before that child can even walk. In the same way, all of us feel that our home town is a special place, with a beautiful story to tell for every inch of it.

*

---

* Caramel-like sweet, high in energy and milk protein.

XINRAN: You've been to so many places, do you feel that people in other countries respect China?

YISHUJIA: Some places aren't so good. In South America people used to swear at us. I was told they were joking, but I could see they looked down on us Chinese. They liked white people. We just concentrated on our performance, we didn't have a lot to do with other people, as soon as the show was over we just went back to our dormitories or the hotel.

XINRAN: Where were the people nicest to Chinese?

YISHUJIA: The Americans were very friendly.

XINRAN: You mentioned spending a year in one country.

YISHUJIA: In Latin America, Colombia.

XINRAN: So what was your life like there every day?

YISHUJIA: We had one performance a day, and we did all our everyday things together in small groups. We went together to the supermarket to buy food, and we brought it back, cooked it and ate it together. We Chinese always stick together, wherever we are.

XINRAN: I understand that before 1995, when Chinese people went abroad on official visits, they were issued with special clothing for the purpose, is that true?

YISHUJIA: Yes, the first time we went abroad in the 1980s, we all went together to the tailors to get our clothes made, we all had the same clothes, from the skin out. We all had the same suitcases as well. After the 1990s they issued us with money instead, 700 yuan per person.

XINRAN: You started working in the 1950s, and a lot happened in Chinese history between the fifties and when you went abroad in the eighties, so what changes were there for you personally in all that chaos and upheaval?

YISHUJIA: To tell the truth, after the 1980s the country just kept improving, and things got better and better for us in every aspect of our lives. In any case, I had already experienced the humiliation of being a counter-revolutionary's daughter, so I passed over all these political movements and the rest of it in silence.

XINRAN: I've heard that you're still involved in training young people even though you're retired. Do you think there is any difference between students now and forty years ago when you were young?

YISHUJIA: Children now are cleverer than in my day. Back then we did whatever the teacher told us; with kids today, once the teacher has told them something, they'll think up a few ways to improve it on their own, and a lot of the time they improve on the teacher's own version. They're clever, but it's harder to teach them.

XINRAN: Why is clever hard to teach?

YISHUJIA: We were too obedient, we didn't dare slack off. Children nowadays can be lazier than we were, so they're harder to teach.

XINRAN: Are your teaching methods the same as the ones your masters used with you?

YISHUJIA: No, in those days teachers were just like your parents, they lectured you and beat you, but sometimes we'd spend our birthdays at the teacher's home, and get-togethers at the teacher's were a regular thing. Now relations between people have changed, all we have to do is turn up to class on time. There are rules about how to teach, we have to write lesson plans for everything. It was different then, we made it up as we went along, there was always the possibility of something new.

XINRAN: You said that they used corporal punishment on you back then?

YISHUJIA: In the past, when we Chinese studied acrobatics, it was beaten into us with a stick. By the time I was a student we'd been liberated, the teacher didn't dare beat us too much, but we all believed that corporal punishment was useful for training. The time I remember most clearly is once when I was being lazy and couldn't turn a difficult kind of somersault, then one blow high on my bottom, and over I went – the teacher had given me a taste of "dough drop soup". That's a knotted rope, a tool for corporal punishment, we called it dough drop soup, a blow from that really hurt.

XINRAN: And now?

YISHUJIA: We still give the students a taste if they're disobedient. Why? Sometimes they're just lazy – if they won't practise till they get it right, isn't that just a waste of their youth and ambition? So if somebody isn't prepared to keep practising and complains about being tired, I'll give him a taste, and up he goes.

XINRAN: So nobody objects to your corporal punishment, though it's against the law?

YISHUJIA: Corporal punishment while practising your art is against the law? So wasting life and time isn't against the law? Young people nowadays talk about "enjoying life" – how many children understand what the real enjoyment of human life is? If you have no skills for life, no success in your work, if you can't cook or do the housework, will you be able to "enjoy life"? It's enjoying other people's blood and sweat! *That's* what I call a crime!

XINRAN: I've known you for a while, but I've hardly ever heard you talk about matters of the home.

YISHUJIA: I was very young when I left home, and my family was nothing to be proud of, not like other people's, so the acrobatic troupe was like a family to me. Not only were we teachers and colleagues together for over forty years, the troupe took responsibility for everything: the flat I lived in, the children's schooling, work, medical treatment, all aspects of our lives. Even though I'm retired now, it still feels like a family to me. From the 1950s to the 1980s in China, most city dwellers were part of a work unit. Apart from the tiny minority who changed jobs or moved to another place to be with their spouse, the people in a work unit would generally stay there for the rest of their life. And since education, accommodation, medical care and even the next generation's jobs were all dealt with by the work unit, that next generation tended to stay in the same place, and work in the same professional circles. This gave rise to serious problems, as small, closed groups started to emerge, who in time came almost to form a monopoly.

XINRAN: When was your troupe established?

YISHUJIA: I can't say much for sure about our troupe's history. I know our predecessor was the acrobatic artist Guo Shaoquan's Tianjin Magical Troupe, which had started out wandering the roads and they finished up in Jinan, where they decided to stay. Guo's children trained up a batch of students, and the troupe expanded. After the Liberation it was nationalised, and a lot of dross got mixed in then – they brought in Communist Party leaders, administrators and the like, even though they didn't know anything about acrobatics. The people who didn't understand anything were put in charge of the ones who did – isn't that typical of us Chinese?

XINRAN: China's earliest acrobatics and magic tricks all had their origins in selling medicine, wouldn't you agree? In 1988 a painted brick decorated with two chariots pulled by galloping horses was unearthed in Nanyang city, in Henan province: the *Eastern Theatre Picture*. Experts say that this is the earliest picture of Chinese acrobatics, is that true?

YISHUJIA: I think it must be. They used to do acrobatics on a circular pitch by the side of the road; you'd find performers of the lesser acrobatic acts selling strengthening pills, in Shandong dialect they call them Big Strength Balls. There were also people who set broken bones and did massage during the performance, there was a lot of that, it's hard to give you a clear picture all at once.

XINRAN: Why didn't you find a husband in your work unit, the way so many Chinese people did?

YISHUJIA: At that time "introducing a partner" was all the rage, people used to introduce friends of friends to other young people in search of a partner, not like nowadays, when they take themselves off to a "party", or marriage bureaux and the like, not to mention lonely hearts ads in the papers, things we'd never even have thought of. I met my husband through my teacher; he was a soldier, studying parachute jumping in the Beijing Thirteenth Air Force School.

XINRAN: You were in different provinces, so how did you maintain a relationship?

YISHUJIA: We met once, when he came home on leave, we both agreed to the match, and after that we relied on letters. He was in the army, he could post letters for free; he used to write to me a lot – I only sent one letter for several of his, I was worried about wasting money.

XINRAN: So when were you finally reunited?

YISHUJIA: That was later on. He was in an air force unit commanded by Lin Biao's son, Lin Liguo. After the Lin family died in a plane crash on 13 September 1971, the whole unit was implicated in their crimes, they were sent away from Beijing to Bengbu in Anhui, and before long he was sent home. He felt terrible about that.

*

Lin Biao is one of the most controversial figures in Chinese history. To this day nobody has properly defined his role. Was he a loyal minister? Or was he a criminal?

The official story is that on 8 September 1971, Lin Biao, who was Deputy Chairman of the National Defence Committee, Minister of Defence and Deputy Chairman of the Central Military Commission of New China, as well as Mao Zedong's designated successor during the Cultural Revolution, personally gave the order for a counter-revolutionary armed revolt, in a vain attempt on Mao Zedong's life. The plot was exposed, and on 13 September he boarded a plane, fled the country, and died when his plane crashed in Öndörhaan in the Mongolian People's Republic. This incident became known as the Nine-Thirteen Incident. On 20 August 1973, the Central Committee of the Communist Party passed a resolution expelling him posthumously from the Party. On 25 January 1981, at a special sitting of the High Court of the People's Republic of China, he was declared the main criminal of a counter-revolutionary clique. The old feudal sense of punishment in which the criminal's entire family paid the penalty for one person's crimes, which I mentioned earlier as having permeated Chinese history to the bone, appeared once again after the Nine-Thirteen Incident in a particularly virulent form. According to those records that have been made public, over a thousand major leaders in the Chinese Army were purged or implicated, including the Chief of Staff and First Deputy Chief of Staff of the Chengdu military area, the Commissar of the Fuzhou military area, the Commissar of the Wuhan military area, the Chief of Staff of the Xinjiang military area, and the Commissar of the Jiangxi military area, to name but a few.* Some say that over three hundred thousand people were implicated in Lin Biao's crimes, and I do not believe that this is a random figure. In fact, even soldiers like Yishujia's husband who were only serving in local units under their command were exiled to poverty-stricken areas, and the families of soldiers in those units all had to bear a black mark on their record and all that this entailed because of it.

*

XINRAN: So do you still remember the scene when you got married?

YISHUJIA: At that time we didn't know anything, we just arranged with the Party to register our marriage, it wasn't a romantic wedding, not like nowadays. We got a letter from his army unit first, then we got the authorisation from my troupe, then after we'd registered, it was the custom here in the north to hold a banquet, so colleagues I was friendly with came in twos or threes on their bikes to our new flat for a wedding feast. And that was our wedding.

XINRAN: What did you wear that day?

YISHUJIA: I wore a blue Western-style suit, blue trousers and a blue top, that was very fashionable in those days.

XINRAN: After you married, did you quarrel much with your husband?

YISHUJIA: Yes.

XINRAN: Who won?

YISHUJIA: We quarrelled right up until my husband died, and neither of us could master the other, or give in to the other.

---

* To give some idea of the scale, most Chinese provinces are the size of a medium-sized European country. Some of the military areas mentioned here, such as the Chengdu military area, cover several provinces.

XINRAN: You've been outside China, you've seen the so-called English gentlemen, and men in other countries too, what do you think are the differences between Chinese men and Western men?

YISHUJIA: I haven't really had any contact with Western men. But I feel like I can see into Chinese men's hearts: no matter how well educated he is, or how smooth his tongue, we can see exactly what kind of man he is. But who can say for sure what's going on in the heads of those men who grew up eating bread?

XINRAN: Do you hope your son will become a man like those foreigners? Or retain his Chinese self?

YISHUJIA: Somewhere in between, I think, but not too Westernised. I still feel more comfortable with Chinese men.

XINRAN: In your life, have you met the perfect Chinese man, a true paragon?

YISHUJIA: Not yet, perhaps he only exists in my imagination.

XINRAN: You haven't met one yet? Not to this day? Including your husband?

YISHUJIA: When my husband got old I thought he was all right, but when he was young he wasn't any good. It was his smoking and drinking, I don't know how many times we fought over that. And then in the end he got cancer, I didn't try to talk him out of it then, but he changed anyway.

XINRAN: When you quarrelled about this, what did he say?

YISHUJIA: He knew it was wrong too. But he couldn't control himself, he just kept drinking and drinking, and then he had too much.

XINRAN: You didn't do like many wives do, running to the banquet and tipping over the tables?

YISHUJIA: I didn't, but I really wanted to! One time I made up my mind that if he was going to smoke I would smoke too, if he drank so would I. But I never managed to bring him round, so I gave up, I couldn't take any more. I even used to have dreams about making him cut down! I tried everything, nothing worked, it really hurt my feelings.

XINRAN: What do you think was the time when you were closest?

YISHUJIA: When we were courting. Once we were married and the child came along, things didn't go so well.

XINRAN: How did you fight?

YISHUJIA: I was both working and busy with the child, I was dog-tired, he didn't know how to help me with the work when he came home. So at that time I felt that there was no affinity between us, not like before we were married, I felt bitter inside.

XINRAN: Did you ever speak to your husband about this?

YISHUJIA: No, we never discussed it. Later on he retired, and so did I, and I felt everything was going swimmingly, and then before we'd had a year, he got cancer . . .

XINRAN: Have you talked to your son about these things?

YISHUJIA: Well, I've mentioned it. Sometimes he and his girlfriend quarrel and I tell him: when your father and I were courting, we never quarrelled, never fought, it was only later on when we had you that we fought; if you argue all day long while you're courting, what will your life be like when you're married?

XINRAN: When he was on his deathbed, did your husband have any last wishes?

YISHUJIA: He didn't say anything, I was the one doing the talking. He was just showing me that in the last days of his life he was prepared to listen to me.

*

Teacher Yi had once again come to a place of pain, and again she could not prevent her tears from falling. When I saw her tears, I wondered why people who are in the prime of life never have the time to connect with their feelings. Are they so busy with their craving for material things, fame and wealth and vanity that they have no time for each other? Could it really be that only death awakes a person's real self?

*

XINRAN: Before you had a child, did you want a boy or a girl?

YISHUJIA: A boy.

XINRAN: Why?

YISHUJIA: I thought a boy meant strength, a good reputation, the roots of the family. I know you'll tell me that's an old-fashioned, feudal notion.

XINRAN: So now your son is old enough to start a family of his own, do you hope he'll have a son or a daughter?

YISHUJIA: My ideas are more liberated now, either a boy or a girl would be fine.

XINRAN: Really?

YISHUJIA: Really, from the heart.

XINRAN: In our society many people say that their grandparents' generation was ignorant and foolish, and their parents' generation was fool-ishly loyal. How do you see this?

YISHUJIA: I don't see it that way. Young people take exception to the old, the old disapprove of the young, this is quite normal.

XINRAN: Back in your day, did you approve of your parents?

YISHUJIA: Not always. For example, once my mother saw that I had a new top, so she asked: Where'd you get that? I didn't dare say I'd bought it myself, at that time I handed over all my money to the family, in fact my fiancé had bought me that top. When my mother found out she was very angry, she said to me: "Silly girl, you can't go around spending other people's money! Young people these days don't care about that, they're very free with money, even the money their parents sweated and bled to earn!"

XINRAN: In your day, relations between men and women were rather traditional, now they are relatively open. Which do you personally prefer, and why?

YISHUJIA: I think the two things should come together – too traditional feels too starchy and conservative, but being too open makes people uncom-fortable. In our day, couples used to cross the road – he'd be stood on this side of the road, she'd be over there. And watching a film, couples would sit there, all prim and proper; when the film was over, one of them would leave first, then the other – they couldn't get close, they were afraid their colleagues would see! And now? It's actually a bit much, so liberated it's shameless, it's embarrassing to watch! If the feeling takes them, they just start gnawing away at each other, even on the street!

XINRAN: In your whole life, what do you think have been the three bitterest things and the three happiest things?

YISHUJIA: The three bitterest things? That would be when I was small and learning my art, and when I was very small and my father wasn't at home, and when I couldn't solve difficulties with my colleagues. The bitter-ness when I was small and at home was because my family had no money, we couldn't even afford soap, you had to wash clothes with a fistful of salt. And it used to be appallingly cold when we did our practice routines – there were no carpets in those days, just a concrete floor, so when you went down in the splits you had to stay spreadeagled there for ages without falling over, with all your weight on your legs for such a long time, and you couldn't rest, it was a bit much! Then again, people like me who are children of Reform through Labour convicts still want to better ourselves, just the same as anybody else! "Join the Communist Youth League? Who said *you* could join the Youth League?" I often found personal relationships with colleagues unspeakably bitter – they could really wear you down.

XINRAN: What were your three joys?

YISHUJIA: When my father's case was solved, it was as if a great mountain weighing down on me had disappeared; when I won a big national prize and was raised to a third-grade salary, I felt I hadn't spent all that energy for nothing; the third is when I became a National Level One Performer – at that moment I felt I'd accomplished most of my goals for this life.

XINRAN: Do you have any unfulfilled wishes?

YISHUJIA: To see my grandchild. They're all very practical things, I don't have any far-reaching ambitions.

XINRAN: What changes do you think there have been in China in the last twenty years?

YISHUJIA: That's too big a question! It's changing everywhere, everything's changing. Relationships were different when I was young. We were more innocent then, there were conflicts, but they were just small conflicts, not big ones. People these days, they're all trying to outwit each other, it's exhausting.

XINRAN: What do you think was the cause of this?

YISHUJIA: I think it was especially bad after the Cultural Revolution, it wasn't like that before! Now, people's ideas are confused, they've picked up bad habits of mind, and they don't even try to learn good habits, all they care about is money, they don't care about people. This will hold the whole country back.

XINRAN: Teacher Yishujia, do you regret your life?

YISHUJIA: I would have to say no. My father and mother gave me life, this is a part of nature; my life was hard and full of frustrations, but isn't that true for all Chinese?

XINRAN: If you had your time over again, would you follow the same path?

YISHUJIA: I wouldn't want to go over it again.

XINRAN: Why not?

YISHUJIA: I'd want to study properly, to go to school.

XINRAN: If someone were to ask you what kind of a person Teacher Yishujia is, what would you say?

YISHUJIA: I would say Yishujia is a plain, simple, diligent person. Just that.

XINRAN: Thousands and millions of Chinese sacrificed so much for the revolution, they threw themselves into it so wholeheartedly, without a thought for anything else, like when you were young, so naive. Do you think it was worth it?

YISHUJIA: In those times it was just another way of staying alive, it makes no difference whether it was worth it or not. At that time if you didn't behave like that you'd have nothing to eat, you couldn't survive. Some people say that it really wasn't worth it, but I think, what difference does it make? Everybody had to survive those years somehow.

*

I knew what Yishujia was implying by "Everybody had to survive those years somehow." This was a society that was still suffering from shock, but its life and spirit had not perished.

After the interview, Yishujia showed me some photographs of her "survival in that part of history". She chose three family photographs, saying: "My son isn't as handsome as his father. Can you see? He doesn't have his father's spirit." "The child doesn't have the spirit we did!" These words of regret are often to be heard among the elderly in China.

In order to express my thanks for Yishujia's cooperation with my interviews and her unforgettable lessons on how to read her "authentic Chinese" son, I invited her for a meal at a dumpling restaurant. During our meal, I asked Yishujia why she was pining over the son not having his father's spirit, and things being better in the old days. She replied: "Now young people think a lot, they have plenty of ideas, but they don't do that much, and succeed in even less. In my day we were very naive, we obeyed our parents at home, obeyed our leaders at work, everybody obeyed the Party and the Party obeyed Mao Zedong. Everyone had a sort of get-up-and-go about them, we were all like one big family, we might quarrel and fight, but they couldn't break us apart. At that time, it seemed that a man could do everything, mend bicycles, change light bulbs and switches, pull coal in a cart, even make some kinds of furniture." When she spoke of her son Hu, the pride in her voice was mixed with regret: "My son is a filial child, but he's too good-hearted. He's very quick at study, he learned magic, musical instruments and a few acrobatic tricks from me as a small boy; he could do anything he turned his hand to, and some he could do without being taught. He did very well in the city acrobatics troupe, but he was determined to go out and see the world, he didn't want a professional title, wages or a proper home, he was determined to go abroad to drift about, study and do manual labour, with no settled home. He's over thirty, but he still has no plans to find a proper job and start a family. I asked him why he has to live this strenuous life, and he said that he wanted to improve himself and see the real world, he really expressed himself very cleverly."

For Chinese who have barely "explored" their own country at all, it is easy to talk about seeing the real world, but very difficult to actually do it. All Chinese who can leave the country have a definite "reason", whether it is economic conditions, talent, scholarship, language ability or some other cause (often personal). Those who can go abroad simply to indulge a liking for travel are rare indeed.

To the vast majority of Chinese people who live in the countryside, the real, genuine "Chinese history and the world" takes the form of legends of the most fantastical type, whereas in the towns and cities it is found on the Internet, and also the superficial "world tour records" which reckon to cover a whole country in three days.

Whenever I came back to China I often visited bookshops of all sizes in many places, and I saw a good few "records of overseas travel". Some were written by "sea turtles" (a pun on the Chinese *haigui*, which can mean both "back from overseas" and "sea turtle") who had spent several years studying in the West. In all their wanderings, and all their years of student life, they had never managed to tear themselves away from Chinese food, or their Chinese-speaking circle of friends; they did all their research on Chinese websites, apart from their exam papers, which were written in English; they obtained their degrees while immersed in a Chinese sensory environment. Much of their descriptions of culture in these "tour records" seemed very much like the idea of Western folk culture you might find in children's stories, but this is enough to satisfy the hunger and thirst of Chinese readers for world culture, giving people who don't have the money or time a chance to get their own taste of a different world. In the same way, many children believe that their own mother's cooking is the best to be found anywhere, and almost every mother has made countless meals, but it is very rare to see a mother wearing the big white hat of a professional chef.

I too left China because I wanted to see the real world, a world that was moving out of history and towards today, a world that you could touch, a world that had not been coloured by politics.

But will we see a greater number of young Chinese like Yishujia's son, Hu, with both the courage and will to look at the real world, and who can survive and flourish on their Chinese roots? It takes more than sketching a few big characters with a calligraphy brush, or hanging a landscape painting or two on the wall, or putting up a few images of the Bodhisattva Guanyin, or eating Chinese food every day, or a few games of mah-jong a week, to make a Chinese who is still in touch with his or her roots.

On the Road,

Interlude 2:
Talking to a Chinese Colleague about Tibet, Folk Customs, Tiger Stoves and the Chinese Jews

After Qindao, we flew south to Nanjing, capital of Jiangsu. At the long-distance bus station on the way to Anhui province, I met a Han journalist called Tashi. He had spent over a decade travelling through the Tibetan areas, and had researched and published many books on Chinese folk customs, and I took this chance meeting to benefit from his advice, talent and scholarship. Because we were both journalists, there was no need for too many preliminaries, we came straight to the point, and began with the topic that I had been hoping to discuss.

*

XINRAN: What sort of people are the Tibetan groups you've met in your travels?

TASHI: I haven't seen Tibetans from every single clan, there are too many. Generally speaking, the area can be divided into three groups of people: the Amdo Tibetans, the Kangba Tibetans and the Huiba Tibetans. The Amdo people are mostly those on the high plains to the north of Tibet, around Amdo, Qula and Sangxiong, up towards the uninhabited areas.

XINRAN: So what you're calling northern Tibet is to the north of the Tanggula Mountains? Is that the source of the Yellow River?

TASHI: No, that's in the area to the south of the Tanggula Mountains, because Qinghai province is to the north, with Tibet to the south.

XINRAN: But a large part of Qinghai is in Tibetan areas?

TASHI: It's Tibet proper I'm talking about now, there are Tibetan areas in Yunnan, Sichuan, Gansu, Qinghai and even a part of Xinjiang.

*

We were discussing the complex question of the different societies that comprise Tibet. Changes of government through history, and the various branches of religion and schools of thought within Tibet itself, have resulted in many different groupings. It is simply not accurate or helpful to describe Tibet as home to a single society. In the middle of our conversation I suddenly heard a deep, resonant voice reading one of Mao Zedong's poems. For a moment I experienced a strong sense of dislocation, and I found myself wondering where I was, but soon I realised that this was somebody's mobile phone: recently, clever Chinese urbanites have taken to downloading pop songs, recordings of Mao Zedong or slogans from the Cultural Revolution to their mobile phones, to replace the mass-produced ringtones. As well as adding variety to the sounds around us, more significantly, people have discovered a form of humour that "gets close to the edge" of the political restraints that surround them. Tashi plainly had a good head for travel; as soon as he hung up he carried straight on from where we'd left off.

*

TASHI: Amdo people can be found in parts of Qinghai, like the Tongren area, part of the Inner Mongolia Autonomous Region, including south Gansu, and also Maqu in Gansu, part of the Ela Grasslands, which includes Lakes Zalinhu and Elinhu. The area we call Yushu has half Amdo people, half Kangba, and there's also a big stretch that is virtually unpopulated, with a very few Kangba people living there. They're rather different from other Tibetans, most noticeably in their funeral rites. They have different language groups as well, for example Amdo people say "*jiuduomo*" for "hello", but in places like Lhasa where they're mostly Kangba, they say "*jiusang*". There must be, give or take, seven language groups, but in each region there are variations again. Tibetans are a nomadic people, and there are considerable linguistic differences.

XINRAN: If they don't speak, can you make out where a Tibetan is from?

TASHI: Their clothes give some indication: for instance Kangba wear big red chest decorations.

XINRAN: How about hairstyles?

TASHI: You can tell Anli hairstyles at a glance, from the big pearl Anli women wear, but in another place they'll be smaller; here it's mostly turquoise, there it's mainly agates, they're all different, and their shoes are different too, usually you can tell at a glance.

XINRAN: Can you tell how many husbands the women have by looking?

TASHI: Ah, now that I can't do by looking. [He laughs.] What I respect most about Tibetan women is the way they give birth, there's nobody to help them, they do everything themselves. I actually saw it once with my own eyes: a woman, heavily pregnant, came galloping on her horse to a tent to give birth, and when she'd had her baby she walked outside, carrying the baby upside down, smearing butter on the infant's body as she walked, and when she'd finished rubbing in the butter she put the baby inside her robe, got on her horse and rode off.

XINRAN: What was the greatest number of husbands?

TASHI: I can't say for sure, for several reasons. First, many Tibetans, especially these who have yet to come into contact with outsiders, are even hostile to Tibetans from other clans; second, I couldn't communicate through language. Our daily practices were so different, that I found we had almost nothing in common.

XINRAN: What could you make out from observing their daily lives?

TASHI: I couldn't make anything out. We can't imagine that much, because our attitudes are different. There's a family over there, but how can I know if those men are her brothers or her husbands? It's hard to tell. For example, the unmarried girls live in little white tents that you can't go in; if you do you can never leave, you have to marry her. It's not like in Thailand, where the more water pots there are outside your door the more wives you have. In Tibet there are many different customs and religious teachings, so it's hard to say anything for sure.

XINRAN: Have you heard Tibetan people talk about why the Han people wanted to come to Tibet?

TASHI: I've heard lots of things about *that*, mostly that we want to steal their gods. That's people for you, they always have too many preconceived notions.

XINRAN: Has anybody mentioned the Han people going into Tibet because of the water sources?

TASHI: Water sources? What water sources?

XINRAN: Tibet is the source of 90 per cent of China's waterways. It's been this way since the Qing and Ming dynasties, hasn't it? The rulers used to say that "if the water higher up isn't clean, the water lower down may cost you your life".

TASHI: There are many different sayings about this among the Kangba Tibetans, and in the ethnic minority areas of the Yunnan-Guizhou Plateau. And throughout history there have been stories of entire villages that were poisoned by their water.

XINRAN: Did you have a local guide?

TASHI: No, I walked with the army, with the logistics brigade that supplied Lhasa. And you?

XINRAN: I was there in 1981, but not in southern Tibet, I went to northern Tibet and Qinghai, that was with the army too. It was really desolate, there were no people.

TASHI: I know. One time I walked for fifty-one days in northern Tibet. I went to Lake Zalinhu, and Lake Elinhu, the sources of the Yellow River. All that walking nearly killed me. It was completely empty, no people, barely a soul.

XINRAN: I've never walked on foot through the Tibetan areas. I have so much respect for those people who pray on the roads, walking from north to south, prostrating themselves on the ground with every three steps they walk, it's really moving.

TASHI: It's very lonely walking by yourself, but you can think; the solitude gives you your own space to muse.

XINRAN: So then you wrote down your thoughts and your feelings from the journey?

TASHI: Yes, I've brought out a few books on the minorities, such as *Horse Bucket*, and *Old Well*. But I'm even more concerned about some customs of the Han people that are on the verge of dying out all over China.

I want you to see Linhuan and the oldest tea house in Anhui, so you can see a real, unspoiled "tea culture". The water there is of the very finest quality, the locals have never used tap water for tea; every morning before daybreak they draw water from a spring, to be kept in reserve for a whole day's tea-making.

XINRAN: Is that an underground water source from a tributary of the Huai River?

TASHI: I couldn't say, but the town is built beside a river called the Huanshui – there were military storehouses in that place in ancient times. And nearby there's an old earthen town wall with over a thousand years of history, but now the wall has been almost destroyed and eroded by the wind until you can barely make out what it is. A local cadre called Chen is doing very important work there, lobbying for its preservation at all levels of society. Old Director Chen is quite a story, he's over seventy, but in the county official records they have him down as only a bit more than forty. These days there's nothing people don't dare to do in this country of ours, and nothing that can't be done: no one thinks there's anything crazy about turning an old man into a young man.

XINRAN: Why did the county government allow this cadre's file to be so illogical?

TASHI: Who knows if it's true or false? Those officials expect Old Director Chen to go to battle on their behalf, to be their shield for a few more years, don't they? If not for him standing in front of the bulldozers to obstruct the building team, over a thousand years of Linhuan's ancient tea culture would have been razed to the ground to make room for coffin-like modern blocks of flats!

*

This is a particular interest of mine. I have tried to find a way to draw foreigners' attention to the revival of our ancient culture, to curb those officials whose only goal is the appearance of Western modernisation, and to stop their destruction of these ancient sites.

I did something once, in a Jewish street in Kaifeng. There are two places in China with Jewish communities: one is Shanghai, where roughly five thousand Jews found shelter among the local Chinese people under the bloodthirsty Japanese occupation; the other is Kaifeng, which is the earliest place where Jews settled, and the place where the Jewish blood runs purest, as many of the Jews who had moved to mainland China before this had intermarried. The Jews I met in Kaifeng said that most of them had fled as refugees to China during the tsarist pogroms before the First World War, first to China's north-east, then in the next few generations they moved inwards and southwards to Kaifeng, and settled there. In the late 1980s, the Kaifeng government wanted to pull down the old Jewish streets, and a listener to my radio programme wrote asking me to enlist the help of the media. A group of us journalists looked into it and, having confirmed the story, we sent a joint letter to the Kaifeng city government, saying that the Chinese Jews were not only a precious archaeological resource for the study of the migration of world populations, but also of great historical and present-day value to China, and to the study of the development of the West's most ancient religion. The old streets of the Kaifeng Jewish quarter were precisely the right kind of material for research in these areas, we maintained: not only should we not destroy it, we should help recover the former glories of its traditional Jewish ways and culture; we Chinese had a responsibility to preserve the world's cultural heritage.

And we succeeded. The streets were saved. Tashi told me that he had heard it was a great success, and he added: "If you visit that old Jewish quarter now, it's very peaceful, incredibly peaceful. Although the people are noisy and lively, you'll feel that the place has a peculiar kind of stillness to it."

*

XINRAN: When we were choosing a location, a friend told me that tiger stoves were a part of Linhuan's ancient tea culture. Are the "tiger stoves" confined to the Yangtze Delta, or are they used elsewhere?

TASHI: Well, the ones I researched were in Shanghai, Nanjing and Anhui. And there are differences. Tiger stoves are also known as tea-water stoves, or even hot-water shops – that's a kind of small shop that mainly sells hot water, very common in the Yangtze Delta area. Because the furnace for heating water opens onto the front, it's like a tiger with its mouth wide open; there's a chimney at the back standing up tall behind, like a tiger holding up its tail. So people called them tiger stoves because of their shape. Though there's another very persuasive popular explanation: things that waste a lot of raw materials are traditionally called "oil tigers" or "electricity tigers"; it takes huge quantities of firewood (up to three hundred pounds, or a hundred and thirty kilos, a day) to heat water on tiger stoves, like a tiger eating, so that's why they were called tiger stoves.

A traditional tiger stove had three pots for heating water on top, with a hole for fuel in the centre of the three pots; and between the water-heating pots and the chimney were two more pots for storing water. In the past there were two other types of tiger stove too. The "seven-star stove" had one big vat, with seven fire holes made out of concrete and bricks inside it, and seven steel pots for heating water on top. With the "economy stove", the body of the stove was made out of sheets of tinplate, with a big pot on top to heat water; later on a thermometer and a water tap were added on top of the tinplate, to check the water temperature and let out water. Tiger stoves were usually found in the mouths of lanes or little alleys near the lanes; they were often just one room, though some had two rooms or an upper and lower storey, with the stove built in the doorway of the shop, its mouth facing the road, alley or lane in front. Woodchips, wood shavings or coal were burned in the belly of the stove.

Shanghai's tiger stoves or hot-water shops developed along with the city of Shanghai. There's a Shanghai saying: "In the morning wrap water in skin, in the evening wrap skin in water", which referred to the local people going to the tiger stove in the morning to fill Thermoses with hot water and drink tea, letting the delicate fragrance fill the stomach; in the evening, after a hard day's work, they would go to the tiger stoves for a hot bath, finding relief from toil by soaking their bodies in the water. In those years there was a strong connection between the prosperity of the tiger stoves and Shanghai's overcrowded living conditions – there was barely enough space to cook in those tiny, overcrowded kitchens, and heating large quantities of hot water on their tiny coal stoves was a real problem. There had always been a tradition of highly specialised service industries in Shanghai; at one fen a Thermos, buying hot water was cheap, and saved a lot of time and coal. Tiger stoves opened for business at six in the morning and did not close until eleven at night.

In Nanjing (or "the big turnip", as you sometimes hear it called), too, a place that many people consider relatively undeveloped, an old Nanjinger, recalling those years, told me that in districts where simple houses were tightly packed together, tiger stoves were an indispensable part of life: the inhabitants depended on them entirely for tea and hot water. These days the peasants who have flocked to the city to find work have replaced the city people in their need for tiger stoves, and now the peasants have a chance to experience tiger stoves, as they come to understand the differences between city life and the countryside. Many country people only have one bath a year, and their daily hygiene routine consists of just washing the feet before bed.

Most of the tiger stoves in the streets of Hefei, the capital of Anhui province, are businesses without a permit that haven't been checked or approved by the authorities. The majority are small, family-run affairs; the fuel is scrap wood, which sits heaped up along the dividing walls without even the most basic fire precautions, and there are residential areas all around, tightly packed rows of simple one-storey houses. It's terrifying to consider – if there's one small slip and a fire starts, these places will become a crematorium, the fire engines won't even be able to get through the narrow lanes, and the tiger stove will become a tiger that eats people.

XINRAN: So that's another reason why they are called tiger stoves! There are similar contraptions in every place, but they're called different names in China's thousands of different dialects. And I've heard yet another explanation for their name: after the Opium War the British and French armies set up communal hot-water stations, and the big chimney on the roof of the building showed people where to find these in the crowded alleys of Shanghai, so that "roof" slowly became a substitute local word for the stoves. The English pronunciation of "roof" is very close to the way the Shanghainese say "tiger", and that was how "tiger stoves" came about. But actually this explanation clearly doesn't hold water, since there are tiger stoves in places where the Anglo-French Army never set foot.

TASHI: That can't be right, I'm certain. Even as early as the Southern Song dynasty, there were two great generals in Lin'an, that's our modern-day Hangzhou: one was Yue Fei, the other was Liu Ziyu. Yue was a general in the official army and Liu was a general of the local militia. Well, both of them were driven out of office by Qin Gui, who was a traitor to the Emperor. Liu Ziyu left Lin'an and went back home to be a minor local official in Fujian, and he would order his family to cook deep-fried sticks of dough, two sticks at a time, like he was dropping Qin Gui and his wife into the boiling oil together, to vent his fury against the power of this treacherous official. And those fried dough sticks were cooked on a tiger stove.

XINRAN: But the tiger stove you're talking about isn't the kind of stove we have today, mainly for heating water, is it? The tiger stove you're talking about exists in the Zhejiang region, and Guizhou as well, but seems to be different. I think that these interconnected folk customs don't just spring from the things everyone has in common because of the instinct to survive, it may well have to do with the very earliest population movements, in particular the needs of educated people with economic power who were banished far from their old homes. Take the provinces of south China: Hunan, Hubei, Sichuan, Yunnan, Guizhou, Guangdong and Guangxi – these places were barely inhabited at all, densely forested, with bushes and weeds growing everywhere, and sweltering hot weather. In those wooded mountains it could often get as hot as the inside of a steamer, heat so intense that it produced a poison gas, so since ancient times these areas have been called the Places of Miasma. At that time, they were so unhealthy that exile there was little better than a death sentence. These areas were first used as places of exile as early as the Warring States period [403–221 BC], and after two thousand years of exile as a punishment, much of the folk culture in the southern areas had been influenced by the culture of the eastern Yangtze Delta, which could be why the accent in Guizhou and thereabouts is very close to the accent along the Yangtze River Basin. So the people who came there used their own accent and their own ideas to write down things they saw in that place, and spread them abroad. In fact, I think that after the Northern Song dynasty, the Han folk cultures could no longer be called pure Han folk culture. Do you think it's possible that the tiger stoves in history books were called that by those exiles, the people who wrote the histories – trying to make sense of things that were similar to look at but not actually the same by calling them tiger stoves?

TASHI: It might be. Many outsiders collecting local folk customs in an unfamiliar place confuse the locals' pronunciation with similar-sounding Chinese characters, and that has left the principles and definitions of Han folk customs in a very confused state. Talking of folk tales, I've heard that you once interviewed an old prostitute who had a storybook life, is that true?

XINRAN: Yes, but I found that the things she told me are not altogether the same as our popular ideas of the famous Face Powder Lane in Nanjing. Very few people know that there used to be another, more authentic Face Powder Lane, which was also to be found in the neighbourhood of Nanjing's Confucius Temple.

The prostitute with whom I talked for several years in the 1990s was an old lady who had been born into a very poor family. She was carried from Anhui in a basket when she was only a few months old. She was bought by an old prostitute who happened to notice her when she was out shopping, so from a young age she took good care of her skin and was trained up in the skills of serving tea, drinking wine and nibbling melon seeds, and before she was five years old she was sold to a brothel in Face Powder Lane. On her first day she was put to polishing the tea sets and opium pipes, and they called her the Little Pot Girl. She said that the brothel was like a battlefield, with the clients nominating their favourites among the high-class prostitutes, whose rating could be seen from whether they used gold or silver vessels for drinking, and from the shape of their beds. In the past you couldn't put just any wine in any pot, and you couldn't pour too much – if there was too much it meant the wine was poor quality. When she was a bit older, seven or eight years old, the brothel started to teach her the knowledge of sex: bed skills, the art of keeping the clients company, and nibbling melon seeds, opening melon seeds with her teeth ready to spring the kernel into the client's mouth when he opened his mouth, without touching her lipstick.

She told me a lot of things: about the prostitutes' personal hygiene, how to arouse a client's interest in sex, how to stay neat and clean afterwards, and how to keep the client after that. In those days if a man wanted to enter one of the famous brothels, he had to improvise a couplet of classical poetry based on a line supplied by the bouncer at the gate, and they wouldn't let him in until he had successfully completed the couplet. The prostitutes' name tags, the wine list and the menu in the brothel used metaphors from Tang and Song poetry too, so men who knew nothing of poetry would have no idea what those name tags, wine lists and menus were saying! She also told me about a special bed, and later I found similar beds mentioned in books of antiques. This bed had two layers of bed curtains: one was hanging gauze, with different gauzes according to the seasons, which was used for making love, then there was an opaque silken hanging that was used for sleeping; they were very particular about getting the two colours of the hangings right. When she was still very young she learned all the knowledge passed down from previous generations, about sachets of scented herbs to keep with clothes and fill quilts, and incense to burn while washing, all of which were used to prevent pregnancy. So she felt very sorry for people nowadays, who had rejected the natural techniques of cultivating the body left to us by our ancestors, and chose instead to spend huge sums of money on researching the safest contraceptive pill!

She said that often when many rich and powerful families married off a daughter they would send to the brothel to invite a "mama", an educated, elderly prostitute, to go with the matchmaker to examine the son-in-law's feet. That old lady said, "Modern people get their palms read or fortunes told, what a load of old rubbish! What do they know!" When she and her sisters were examining a man they had only to touch his foot to know everything about him, from his feet to his head. They had all learned this skill from their "mama".

During the last three generations, the brothel would choose a woman in each generation with a gift for the pen, not to do the bills, but to record the brothel's history, complete with the clients and their gifts. This was so that if they fell on hard times, these "women of dust and wind" would have funds to flee, and the record of the existence of these gifts would offer them some protection when they needed it. She said the brothel historian in her generation had hidden these things in the well of the brothel courtyard. The old lady also told me that each generation put aside a set of drinking vessels, to be kept back as a prize for the prostitute who had earned the most money for the brothel, and she remembered how her apprentice mistress had hinted to her where she had hidden them.

But when I tried to follow her directions, that place was already a mass of tall buildings and skyscrapers.

TASHI: Did you see her again after that?

XINRAN: How could I? The place where she lived has been demolished, there's nothing left! I've been looking for three to four years, the only name I had for her was what I'd heard people on her street call her, Old Lady Apple-Cheeks, but there was no such name anywhere in the household registration records.

TASHI: I'll try to help you find her. I'm sorry, I have to take a phone call . . .

*

The male voice declaiming Mao Zedong's poetry had started his recital again.

6

Tea Houses and News Singers: Three Thousand Years of Anecdotes and Wonders

The news singer reciting, Linhuan, Anhui province, 2006.

A typical traditional tea house, full of men, Linhuan, Anhui province, 2006.

MR WU, aged seventy-five, a news singer from a traditional tea house, *interviewed in Linhuan, northern Anhui province, a small town in central eastern China where tea drinking is the most popular leisure event among the locals even today. Fifty years ago in Linhuan there was no one who could read or write. Two or three men would be sent to the nearby town to get information or news; then they would come back to sing what they heard to the villagers in the tea house. Mr Wu became a news singer when he was ten. He continues to "sing his thoughts and news" in tea houses today. And* Chen Lei, seventy-four, *who has fought to preserve the ancient Linhuan and its tea houses.*

My conversation with Tashi reminded me that I first heard about tiger stoves – these hot-water shops that double as tea houses – when I was in Shanghai on business in 1995. And by that time there was only one tiger stove left in the whole Shanghai area. The older locals told me that tiger stoves had been at their height in the early 1950s, with more than two thousand in the city. After that their numbers declined over the years as the water-supply systems improved, especially after the 1980s, when almost every Shanghainese home had a bathroom with a water heater. Nobody went to the tiger stoves any more, and the scenes of people chatting as they queued for water died out along with the tiger stoves. By the time I had a chance to investigate the subject, the last tiger stove had closed down in 2005, though the old people sipping cups of hot tea under the trees nearby told me that this habit was a relic of the tiger stoves. And this in turn reminded me that many folk customs are subject to history, and also that many folk customs will one day disappear with history.

In the course of my investigation and this "unearthing" of tiger stoves, I heard a story about a customer who used to wash at one. He had been a small trader all his life, and he had his fixed place in the tiger stove where he sat every day. All his fellow bathers jokingly referred to him as "Number XX", but nobody knew his real name. A few years ago "Number XX" became ill and he wanted a wash, so his son dutifully ran him a bath in his modern imported bathtub, but the old man flatly refused to take off his clothes. When the son finally understood what his father wanted, he took his arm and supported him to the one remaining tiger stove in Shanghai. The old man was helped to his accustomed place by all his old bathing buddies, like a crowd of stars surrounding the moon. He seemed to have come to life once again, whipping out a packet of cigarettes from his breast pocket and sitting down for a smoke, beaming.

The following day, this old bathhouse customer left the world, with a smile on his face.

As we travelled northwards from Nanjing, the view outside the bus window was gradually changing from the scenery of the lower reaches of the Yangtze Delta to a landscape of "poor mountains and impoverished soil". Our driver told us that we were heading north by the side of an ancient canal running from north to south that could tell the story of three thousand years of China's transport history. The canal had been excavated in the Spring and Autumn and Warring States periods (770–221 BC), and was expanded many times in various dynasties. Up until AD 618 in the Sui dynasty it had been the main water-transport route of China's eastern region, which was the most densely populated part of China and remains so to this day. The Grand Canal went as far north as Beijing, linking it to the coastal city of Hangzhou, and sideways to connect China's three great rivers, the Yellow, Yangtze and Huai. It had a total length of over 1,700 kilometres – twenty-one times the length of the Panama Canal – making it the longest canal in the world. Together with the Great Wall, it is one of the two most important engineering projects in ancient China. Because there had once been a branch of the ancient canal in the place we were driving through, the "Tongji Channel" that cut across Anhui province north of the Huai River, the area became a place of political, economic, cultural and military importance in the Tang and Song dynasties. Later on, the Yellow River flooded in 1194 in the Southern Song dynasty, and the Tongji Channel became silted up. The surrounding regions went into decline with the end of transport on the channel, and the area to the north of the Huai River gradually moved up the list of China's poorest places. This was our destination: Linhuan.

Linhuan is not even mentioned in tourist guides, but it is well known throughout China for its antiquity. Linhuan was first built in around 200 BC, and in due course it became a rest stop for merchants and travellers heading north or south along the Grand Canal. The tea houses of the village were in high fashion for a time, and even now most of the locals are habitual tea drinkers, preferring a kind of tea with no tea leaves that is called *bangbang* tea.

When we drove into Linhuan "town" (though in fact it is no more than a village), we saw a kind of modernised poverty: a street scene covered in the dust of a thousand years. There was a dustiness to everything, from little hammered earth houses a hundred years old, through the low brick and tile buildings of the fifties and sixties, to the two-storey peasant homes of the eighties. The whole street was full of builders' rubble – it seemed that everybody in Linhuan was "hurrying in the footsteps of international development" to build a house or pave a road – but the things that were being built were the scrap material of modern China. The people were neatly dressed but not clean. It appeared that they had no requirements beyond keeping themselves warm and fed, with no aspirations for enjoyment, and their skinny dogs lacked even the strength to bark a couple of times at strangers. It seemed that only the cocks and hens scavenging for food in the street had enough energy to keep their necks stretching out tirelessly, and a little freshness and brightness to their feathers.

Here, there was none of the speed of modernised production. The small donkey carts that had been used for over a hundred years and the old wooden handcarts that had been pulled for decades had been replaced by "bong-bong cars" – motor tricycles with a small cabin for passengers built on behind the driver's seat that had long since been banned in the cities – and old-style motorbikes that made a great deal of noise even when the wheels were not going round. Your instinctive responses go into slow motion here; it takes several minutes from the first puttering sound until the vehicle actually gets going. Our driver couldn't get the people blocking our way to move aside, even with loud blasts of his horn. Occasionally you could hear a voice shout something in tones of great urgency, followed by a long pause. You would almost have forgotten what you had heard, and then another voice would yell a response.

All of this reminded me of the works of Dalí, that strange, mad artistic genius whose work I have never understood. Perhaps there had been a similar rubble of modernisation in his life? Could that have been what gave him the ability to put together those strange works of art that smashed people's old habits of mind to fragments?

I made up my mind to visit a few tea houses before my interview with Chen Lei, the man I had come to see.

Most of Linhuan's tea houses have kept the original form in which they had first been built a hundred or so years before. The dim light inside the rooms comes mainly from a series of smallish skylights; there are rows and rows of great steaming iron or aluminium kettles standing on the big seven- or eight-hole linked stoves by the doorway, and by the side of the stove there is often a long bench which acts as a table for tea-making utensils, crowded with teacups, teapots and tea leaves. The remainder of the space is the tea-drinking area, which consists of several wooden tables, long benches and little wooden chairs. Some tea houses put out rows of small, low tables and chairs on the street. No matter how long you sit in the tea house, three jiao for a pot of tea will guarantee you a place from morning till night.

According to several tea-house owners, the biggest difference between tea houses now and in the past is that in the past people drank tea and listened to the news or storytelling, while now they drink tea and play mah-jong or cards. Another difference is that women come to the tea houses. Because most of the land has been compulsorily purchased by the government, the young and strong have all gone to the big cities to earn money. The older women in the family don't have to spend their time taking care of the young children, so they have started to become a part of tea-house culture.

Originally, I had thought that "listening to the news" meant villagers sitting clustered round a little radio listening to the news or Chinese opera. But this was not the case. Because the area had been poor not just for generations but for dynasties, many of its people were illiterate and had never been to school. In every generation, however, there would be a few men who ventured outside the village to find out news and interesting things; back in the village tea house they would then say and sing the news. After a while the "News Singer" became a special job in the area.

We were lucky enough to meet a "News Singer", Old Mr Wu, who had been "singing and telling the Revolution" for the Communist Party since he was ten years old. From our casual chat I could see that he was at ease and eager to perform, so I decided then and there to hold an extra interview.

*

XINRAN: Mr Wu, while we're waiting for the cameraman to get set up, can I make a request?

WU: Just say the word.

XINRAN: We'll only say what's in our hearts, no official talk – empty words or false words – and we'll just talk, without "singing". And please look only at me, not at other people. Is that all right?

WU: I'll do as you say.

XINRAN: Have you always lived here?

WU: I'm Linhuan-born and -bred.

XINRAN: So what year were you born?

WU: I'm seventy-five years old. I'm a little deaf, but I'll tell you no lies, even though I'm seventy-five. I'm not like some people, playing up their age to cheat their way to a pension, playing up their youth to get a young wife.

XINRAN: Don't worry about your hearing, I'll shout. When did you start drinking tea?

WU: My father ran a tea house. We couldn't buy good water. When I was very small I started to fetch spring water – at eleven or twelve I could carry water with a pole on both shoulders. When did I start to drink? I can't remember.

XINRAN: How long did your father run a tea house?

WU: Many years.

XINRAN: Do you still remember what the tea house was like? How many teapots and tea tables were there? Were there many people?

WU: A fair few teapots – they were all old, there were none of the little pots you get nowadays. In those days tea houses were important places hereabouts; anything that was too big for the family or couldn't be kept in the bag, they'd take to the tea house, and they always got a result. Arranging marriages, fights between husband and wife, differences between neighbours, disciplining youngsters ... That was why women and children weren't allowed in. This was men's business. Unless, that is, one of the tea houses was short-staffed, then they'd have to let the owner's wife in to lend a hand. So I didn't see much either. What child would dare stick his nose into his own father's business back then? That would be challenging your father's authority!

XINRAN: Do you still remember what your mother did at home?

WU: She cooked. I just remember her cooking. That's what women do, isn't it? Cooking!

XINRAN: How many of you children were there?

WU: Just the one, I was the only one.

XINRAN: You were an only child? There was no one-child policy then, surely?

WU: There was just me. I didn't have any sisters, or any brothers either. Luckily I was a boy or the family line would have died out. I was the only one then, but now there are four generations of us.

XINRAN: How many sons, how many daughters?

WU: Eh?

XINRAN: HOW – MANY – SONS? HOW – MANY – DAUGHTERS?

WU: Me? Four sons and a girl.

XINRAN: How about grandchildren?

WU: Even my grandchildren's children are grown up!

XINRAN: How did you find your wife?

WU: The first one, I don't know. It was all fixed up by our parents, and after four years she had a child. It wouldn't do, so I found me another one. This one was good; she's a capable woman. I joined the Party in '54, she joined in '55; she's a capable woman.

XINRAN: So you had two wives? You were married twice?

WU: Let's not talk about that, I couldn't be doing with the first one; she didn't have any progressive thought at all, and she wasn't capable. So I got another wife. The second one, she could talk sense.

XINRAN: Is she a good cook?

WU: Pretty good – dumplings, flat pancakes on the stove, she can do the lot.

XINRAN: When your father was alive was his tea house called "the tea house", or did it have another name?

WU: It was just called the tea house. In the past there were storytellers and drum-singers in the tea houses. He sold his tea, you did your singing, he'd give you money every month, plus tips from the customers. Nowadays opera singers all sing on the stage. They turn their noses up at the tea houses – not enough space.

XINRAN: So tell me what you did all day, from when you got up in the morning to when you went to bed at night.

WU: I ran the tea house with my old man, I carried water. Every day was the same, what's to talk about? At first I went to school, until grade three. I was stupid so I stopped going. I said to my dad, "I'll do whatever you tell me to." He said, "You carry water, I'll run the tea house, and the place'll be full of the sound of slurping tea." I said, "What use is that?" He said, "What's good about running a tea house? I'm telling you, this tea house of ours is the place in the village where people talk sense. If anyone in the tea house says unreasonable things, the tea house will meet to pass judgement. The tea house is just like a court, it's like the law. And there's another good thing about a tea house: people get angry, and if they get angry at home, they fight with their sons or scold their daughters-in-law, but once they're in the tea house they don't stay angry, they chat and laugh – a trip to the tea house is a happy thing, a tea house is a good place. Besides, in the tea house you can hear about big matters from outside. Otherwise you'd be living in a dead end, wouldn't you?"

XINRAN: Then what time did you and your father start work every day, and when did you open?

WU: The tea house opened very early, six or so in winter, in summer a bit after five. We heated the water, and once the water was boiled we'd pour tea for the customers. We'd have customers as soon as it was light. As long as there was boiling water there'd be people coming to drink. People who were happy or angry would come early, and old people too. They would wake up early, while their family were still snoring away. There were no lights on at home, and no one to keep them company or talk about their dreams, so they came very early. And they drank until eight or nine in the evening. They used to come straight after supper, some from eight or ten li away. They all wanted to come and drink tea.

XINRAN: So in your opinion, now that life has changed so much for the better, and people in so many places don't want to run tea houses any more, why is it that here it seems everyone is competing to open tea houses?

WU: Who knows? In the past, before the Liberation, there were only two or three tea houses. They were quite rare and special. Now there are more tea houses, two or three with every step. A lot of people are running tea houses in Linhuan these days.

XINRAN: Are there more people drinking tea now, or before?

WU: I think there's even more than there used to be. In the past the tea drinkers were always old men, and that's the truth. Nowadays all the young people drink in the tea houses. Now it's three jiao to stay till eleven. That's three jiao a pot. It was cheaper before.

XINRAN: Did you drink tea when you were young?

WU: Yes, whenever I had time on my hands.

XINRAN: Are tea houses now the same as the one your father ran?

WU: My old man's tea house wasn't as pretty as this one.

XINRAN: Do you know how many pots the biggest tea house here has?

WU: The most? That would be two hundred or more.

XINRAN: In the biggest tea house here, what's the greatest number of people drinking tea together? A few dozen? A hundred? More?

WU: It could be 150, maybe more.

XINRAN: Can you still remember any of the words on the lucky couplets stuck to the door of the tea house?

WU: Not really. I know there are new lucky couplets for Spring Festival every year, but I can't read. I don't know, sometimes I ask people to read them out for me.

XINRAN: So what lucky couplets do you ask people to write for you at New Year?

WU: They're all to do with tea houses, places to drink tea and people who drink tea.

XINRAN: Do you know how your father got married to your mother?

WU: Someone introduced them. My dad was over fifty by the time he had me.

XINRAN: Did your father ever tell you his story?

WU: When he was telling me off he always used to say that he'd done all sorts of things, making lanterns, selling rice, keeping a tea house, but he'd never been black at heart. At any rate my old dad was a good man.

XINRAN: What did your father like to do?

WU: Make hurricane lanterns – he used to sell lanterns every year. Making lanterns, and running a tea house.

XINRAN: And what do you like to do?

WU: I do everything. I've sold rice, I've run a tea house, and sold peanuts. I've sold a lot of things.

XINRAN: Then in the Cultural Revolution was this tea house still open? Did the Red Guards drink tea too?

WU: In the Cultural Revolution they didn't let us watch opera, but tea houses could stay open. What law was there against drinking tea? The tea houses stayed open, business as usual.

XINRAN: Is the tea these days the same as before?

WU: In the past we didn't drink the kind with tea leaves. The tea now is better. In the past there weren't any proper buildings. Now there are buildings made specially for tea houses, made of bricks instead of beaten earth.

XINRAN: Do a lot of young people run tea houses now?

WU: Not many. They've gone away to make money. Most people who keep tea houses are sixty or over.

XINRAN: Do any of your children run a tea house? What do they do?

WU: Cut hair, sell rice, sell clothes, kill pigs. But none of them have a tea house.

XINRAN: And do you and your wife live by yourselves? Or do you live with your sons?

WU: By ourselves. It's the New Society now, the new family. Everybody makes their own money and spends it themselves.

XINRAN: Do your sons give you money to keep you going?

WU: They give me money, but I don't want it. My grandson's heading off to university. That's going to cost a lot of money.

XINRAN: So do your sons like drinking tea in the tea houses?

WU: Only one of them. He drinks every day. The rest of them don't like it. They say it's a waste of time.

XINRAN: You say you joined the Party in 1954. What were you doing at that time?

WU: In 1950, just after Liberation, I was a security officer. In 1951 I was made village head and then deputy head of the production brigade. I never took a penny. I joined the Party in 1954, my wife joined in 1955, and that's the truth, as I'm sitting here.

XINRAN: Have your sons joined the Party?

WU: My second son joined the Party while he was in the army.

XINRAN: You, your wife, and your son too. You must be regarded as a red family, with three Party members.

WU: That goes without saying!

XINRAN: Do you still have Party meetings?

WU: We don't now.

XINRAN: If you don't have Party meetings, do you still count as a Party member?

WU: I can't say for sure.

XINRAN: How many Party members are there in your village now?

WU: There are still a few dozen.

XINRAN: In the past we Chinese used to say that people who engaged in trade were capitalists. So, have any Party members opened a tea house?

WU: That's hard to say, there aren't that many of us.

XINRAN: You see, now we're starting to use electricity and lots of new technology. We're modernised. Are you worried that the tea houses will die out?

WU: There are people who drink tea in Hangzhou, I've seen 'em. When I went there to visit my son, I saw people sitting in tea houses drinking black tea. There's no one who can hold back tea drinkers. But people who drink tea together in the city can get AIDS, so nobody should dare to drink tea outside their house.

XINRAN: How do you know that tea can transmit AIDS?

WU: That's not what I said. To be honest, there are people like that, and diseases like that. They can spread. That's what infectious diseases are like.

XINRAN: So after you stopped running a tea house, apart from being an official, what job did you do?

WU: Well, these days I sell antiques. I go to small places to buy up old teapots. If I can get a bit for them, enough for spending money, that's all I need – the children don't want them. I'm a rough-and-ready, uneducated sort of chap. I can't read books or newspapers, but I remember everything I see and hear. If not, why would the Party have told me to "sing the Revolution"?

XINRAN: So how long have you been "singing the Revolution"?

WU: I started when I was ten. Everyone in the tea house liked to hear me sing. I could sing anything; whatever went into my ears, I could make into something to sing. I sang until the big loudspeakers came to the village. Things changed then. When the big loudspeakers from the broadcasting station started shouting, everyone could hear it. I couldn't sing the things that everybody knew, so I went looking for things the broadcasters didn't say. I kept on singing after I became a Party member and a cadre, but not as much as before.

XINRAN: How did you know what things the broadcasters never said?

WU: Need you ask? Everybody knows that they never talk about gods or fortune-telling; that's superstition. And they don't talk about the police doing bad things, right? Or about droughts or natural disasters either, or how the Yellow River drowned all those people. It was all "class struggle every day", but we were all poor here, we couldn't find a class enemy even if we wanted to. Those class enemies were all rich. Would you stay here if you were rich? That'd be like a man dying of hunger using a gold bowl for a pisspot!

XINRAN: So if you often spoke of those things, didn't anybody try to stop you?

WU: Nobody bothered about me, who comes here? If they came here to control us, what would they eat? Those officials who were so fond of class struggle wouldn't have been able to bear hunger!

XINRAN: You're seventy-five, and there are so many stories in your life, so let's narrow it down. Can you tell me about the three most painful things in your life and the three happiest?

WU: That's easy, I was happiest when I was selling rice. It was one yuan a bowl, and I could sell five hundred bowls in a day, and that's the truth. I made money from my *zhuangmo* as well – that's big hard steamed bread, the kind they eat in the north-east. That was my first happy thing. The second happy thing is that I've worked for the revolution all my life, but I've never taken a penny of public money. I want to be a decent person. I joined the Party in 1954. I went to the police station to be a public security worker, I wasn't scared. "A revolutionary must know no fear, no point in thinking of revolution if you're scared." There's no third happiest thing. Family matters like my sons and daughter don't count.

XINRAN: And the most unhappy thing?

WU: The most unhappy thing? There are people in the government who act recklessly. I don't say anything out loud, but in my heart I don't approve. The peasant cadres in the past were all better than the ones now. I've got no way to say it.

*

Judging by my experience of interviews in the countryside, I could feel that he was not being completely candid. There must have been other things that made him unhappy. But Old Mr Wu changed the subject, and his face immediately took on an actor's stage expression of "happiness".

*

WU: There's nothing to make me sad. I play, I sing. If a man's happy he'll have long life. The happier a man is the longer he lives; the more anxious a man is the quicker he'll die.

XINRAN: If you had your life over again, would you still live it this way?

WU: That's not easy to say. Me, live my life again – I would be hundreds of years old! That's not possible.

XINRAN: No, if you had your *time* over again, would you still stay here and run the tea house with your father, or would you go to live somewhere else? Do you regret your life, or do you think it was worth it?

WU: It was worth it.

XINRAN: Many foreigners say that China is very poor, and this place of yours is really very poor. You live in poverty here, is it worth it?

WU: This place doesn't count as poor. When Chairman Mao was alive, just after Liberation, it was very poor. Now? Not poor.

XINRAN: A lot of people here don't even earn three jiao a day, and you still don't think this is poor?

WU: It's not poor now, truly. Back in 1949, 1950 and 1951, we were poor. Chairman Mao was making revolution in those days. There were no buses, not many people; that was real poverty. Foreigners? I say the foreigners are poor. When I went to Hangzhou I saw the trousers the foreigners were wearing, holes all over, and their hair was all dirty. Isn't that poor? Why be like that?

XINRAN: Do you prefer Hangzhou or Linhuan?

WU: For living Hangzhou is better, of course. But it's not so bad here either. A peasant's lot has been bitter since ancient times. Who told you to be born into this life, born into a peasant family to spend all day working in the muck and mire?

XINRAN: Do you and your wife ever quarrel?

WU: I've never fought or quarrelled with her since the day we were married, not even sworn at her.

XINRAN: Comparing you and your wife, are you more successful than her, or the other way round? Who's more revolutionary, who's more successful?

WU: She's more capable than me. She's a model worker, the first female Party member in the village. She's a cut above me.

XINRAN: Can you still remember the ceremony when you two got married?

WU: It was raining that day – she came in a sedan chair.

XINRAN: Did you have a banquet?

WU: We were very poor then, we didn't have any land yet, or a house, we didn't have a thing, my family was the poorest.

XINRAN: Is there anything that you wanted to do that you haven't done yet?

WU: No, I've done it all, a man should have a conscience.

XINRAN: How old is the oldest person in the village?

WU: The oldest is over ninety.

XINRAN: Do a lot of people from outside come and see this place now?

WU: Yes, they do.

XINRAN: Do you know why they come?

WU: We've got a lot of historic sites here, but many of them have been dug up, like the temple of the Town God and the temple at the east of the walls. They've all gone. People come because they've heard about them, but actually there's not a lot for them to see.

XINRAN: If someone were to say that your tea house was too old, and wanted you to build a new one, would you be willing?

WU: If you had the choice between something old and something new, who would take the old one?

XINRAN: Do you like this kind of old-style tea house, or do you prefer the new style?

WU: Of course the old-style tea house is better than the new style. Those new ones don't look like tea houses.

XINRAN: And why did I come here? Do you know?

WU: No, I don't know.

XINRAN: Because Linhuan has preserved China's precious tea culture, tea-house culture and folk culture. Therefore, in future more and more people will come to visit your tea house. Would you like outsiders to come?

WU: I'd like that. I'd like even foreigners to come to our tea house! I'll sing a bit of history for you, and you'll believe it. I tell you no lies, they're really welcome. Listen carefully, I made this up myself.

> *Bamboo clappers, nine links in a chain,*
> *Gather round, comrades, hear what I'm saying*
> *I'll tell you about the Huaihai Campaign*
> *That's what I'll tell you today . . .*
>
> *In the first month, first day of the First*
> *An army there was under Mao Zedong,*
> *An army in Yan'an, two hundred thousand strong . . .*
>
> *In the second month, the dragon raised his head,*
> *To attack Xuzhou, Lin Bocheng his soldiers led.*
>
> *In the third month, the third of the Third,*
> *Deng Xiaoping's soldiers attacked Jinan,*
> *His soldiers surrounded the city of Jinan*
> *As his forces occupied Tianfushan.*
>
> *In the fourth month, the eighth of the Fourth,*
> *The Zaozhuang Station battle took off*
> *They didn't just take Zaozhuang for their own,*
> *But sent three regiments of foes to their final home.*
>
> . . .
>
> *In the sixth month the heat is hard to bear,*
> *Chiang Kai-shek was consumed with fear,*
> *And he took his troops and weapons out of there . . .*

XINRAN: You sing so well! Let's all of us give you a round of applause to thank you!

*

The peasants drinking tea were taken aback at my suggestion: what're we supposed to clap for? What's to thank?

It was time for my interview with Chen Lei, so I took my leave of the tea house and the excitable Old Mr Wu. Before I left, I asked him where he lived and what time he got up every day, saying that I would drop by before I left. When he heard this, disbelief was plainly written on his face, but he said politely, "There's no need to put you to so much trouble, thank you!"

I sat in the yard of the village broadcasting station with Chen Lei, the hero who had preserved the ancient village of Linhuan. We talked for a long time, until darkness fell, and all we could see was in deep shadow.

During this time, the big loudspeakers of the broadcasting station came to life at their set times and interrupted our discussion. Once it was to remind the villagers to abide by the regulations in the following day's market, and once summoning a villager to the loudspeaker station to collect something. Another was a repeat news broadcast from the radio station, and then another programme of opera, which was turned off at a shout from Chen Lei that I couldn't understand. But none of this prevented us from speaking freely.

Chen Lei was dressed in a dark green polo shirt and a pair of fawn-coloured cotton trousers. There was a capable, vigorous look to him, but his forehead bore the marks of the trials and changes of many years. He had deep, thoughtful eyes, which held the dignity accumulated over seventy or eighty years.

*

XINRAN: People have told me that the name your parents gave you wasn't Chen Lei. You changed your name, is that right?

CHEN: In 1960, when I was working on the farm, I had this notion. I wanted people to know me, to be like thunder out of a clear sky, so I changed my name to Chen Lei, which means "thunder".

XINRAN: You changed your name without consulting your parents? We Chinese say that our parents gave us life, and our names are the symbol of life that our parents gave us. Changing your name on your own whim must have got you a terrible reputation, almost as if you'd committed some terrible crime?

CHEN: Well, it didn't. My parents must have felt uneasy, but when they saw I could achieve great things . . . And in any case the thing was done, there wasn't anything to get unhappy about.

XINRAN: Can you tell us what sort of people your parents were?

CHEN: Both my parents were from poor families. They were both artisans, mending bicycles for a living. At that time there were eight of us, five boys and three girls. Things were pretty hard for my family. We all depended on my father's bicycle repairs. Later on I went to middle school; my family couldn't afford to send me to senior school so I went to work. Actually there are lots of reasons why I changed my name to Chen Lei. In 1960 I had a lot of ideas. I wanted to change life for the better, to live life at a higher level. My time in the Nanjing artillery regiment had changed my thinking: how could I change the life of our poverty-stricken countryside?

XINRAN: So how *could* you change your home town?

CHEN: I didn't know at first. I worked my heart out, and I wasn't the only one, but Linhuan didn't get any better. It was too poor here, desperately poor.

XINRAN: Did none of your superiors help?

CHEN: Before the 1980s, my superiors didn't do anything but class struggle. If you weren't leftist there was no way to survive. Besides, everybody was poor; nobody thought we were poorer than anybody else! Afterwards, just a few years after Reform and Opening, a journalist came here. He didn't take any pictures of the new-built streets, houses and shops, but concentrated on the rickety old tea houses, and it dawned on me that we had an original culture of our own that was a draw among all the decrepitude, part of a culture that was disappearing in other places.

XINRAN: This was why you stood in front of the diggers of the government engineering team, determined to block their way? But for that, the Linhuan tea houses and old city walls would have been razed to the ground long ago, isn't that so?

CHEN: We have hundreds and thousands of years of history here in Linhuan, and culture from the Shang and Zhou dynasties.* In the northwest of the town we have the remains of an old beaten earth city wall from the Spring and Autumn Period.† It's square in shape, 1,550 metres

---

* Shang dynasty: 1600–1046 BC; Zhou dynasty: 1046–256 BC.
† Spring and Autumn period: 770–476 BC.

long from east to west, 1,409 metres wide from north to south, seven to fifteen metres high, thirty-six to sixty metres wide in the base, and three to eight wide at the top, enclosing an area of 2.7 square kilometres. There are four gates in the wall and watchtowers and signal beacon towers on the top. Linhuan's earth wall is currently China's sole surviving earthen town wall. If we compare it to the Vatican in the West, it's big enough to hold six Vaticans! So Linhuan has several millennia of cultural history, but where is the living culture? How can all this history be reflected through the living culture? It's all about constant movement. It was movement up and down the Grand Canal that engendered Linhuan's tea culture. I started to wonder how to use the original tea culture we had preserved here to push Linhuan towards the culture of the rest of the world, so the Linhuan people can make a living through cultural exchange.

The old-fashioned tea houses we have here in the north of the country are completely different from southern tea houses. Northern-style tea houses serve big-bowl tea, the southern ones are for tasting tea. With us it's tea by the pot. In the past you could drink a whole day for five fen – go in as soon as it opened, and take some with you when you left. If there was a problem over land, a quarrel between wife and mother-in-law, or any other kind of dispute, they'd all say: "Come on, let's go to the tea house to talk it over!" The tea houses became news stations and cultural centres for local society.

The most important thing we do is protect the two old streets in the old town, Nail Street and Flagstone Street, and their two tea houses. The special feature of the buildings in these streets is the "single tile" roofs; the tiles are laid flush with no overlap at all. When the ancient-buildings people from the Architectural Institute saw them they said, "Don't these single-tile roofs leak?" We said, "No, they don't!" We usually start with a layer of ordinary overlapping tiles, which are then covered with another layer of single tiles. We've had single tiles here since ancient times. We told the Architectural Institute that it was vital to preserve those two streets. If we don't preserve them now they'll disappear, a bit at a time, and once they're gone there'll never be any more. We now have about 5,600 square metres of the old city left, all old houses made of small blue-green bricks baked from local clay. That in itself is a big museum of ancient architecture.

XINRAN: That's true. The city itself is a huge museum of ancient architectural culture, just like the city of Rome. Mr Chen, while you were talking I've been trying to picture it. Apart from the things that everyone knows, the ancient remains and culture that have survived here, what else is there? Is there anything else that can become a resource and a motive for opening up the daily life of the people of Linhuan? How large is the population of Linhuan?

CHEN: There are 88,500 people in the greater Linhuan district, and 21,000 in the ancient building area.

XINRAN: And what percentage of this population has been educated?

CHEN: Hard to say. There are several teachers, and there used to be an old *xiucai* scholar. We still have a hall here where the *xiucai* candidates used to take part in the national exams in the Ming and Qing dynasties.

XINRAN: Are there more young and middle-aged people in Linhuan or more old people?

CHEN: More old people.

XINRAN: So the old people are the tea houses' guarantee of survival?

CHEN: All the old people in Linhuan have something to say about history, true. That's the wealth of the tea houses.

XINRAN: Because I too once came under pressure from a different form of poverty, I know that poverty really does cause people's thinking to change. How many tea houses are there in Linhuan at present?

CHEN: Sixteen. They used to be called tiger stoves. Now we call them *tongzao* – connecting stoves. They're all linked together, for heating kettles – they used iron kettles earlier, now they use aluminium kettles. In the past someone noticed that lighting a fire in all these individual stoves was very wasteful, but if you have an iron bucket next to your heated stove, you can heat it using the excess heat from the others. You can save a lot like that. We've been poor here for a very long time. Didn't Chairman Mao say that "poverty makes people's thinking change"? That's true; if you don't come up with ideas it's impossible to survive.

XINRAN: Linhuan has four thousand years of history. Am I right in saying that it's impossible to bring back the original style of the ancient buildings along the Huai River using today's building materials?

CHEN: We've been thinking about this too. You need different materials to make different houses. In our part of the world we have a lot of fired bricks. At first they were all blue-green bricks, made in special kilns – the best kind of china comes from those kilns. Later on the quality of the clay was affected by pollution. Then there was large-scale flooding in the region along the Huai River. The river water was full of sand, and when it came washing over, it left behind a lot of sand. But if you're careful in the extraction process, it's still possible to find good-quality clay. You come and see next year, it'll be different again. It will basically all be back the way it was, and it'll be the genuine article. We're repairing the old to bring back the old.

XINRAN: In the past, did your connecting stoves include bathing, too, like the tiger stoves of Nanjing and Shanghai?

CHEN: No, it was all just drinking. They drink and chat, discussing old things and new, ordinary people talking about their own business. If you have conflicts, if you have unfilial sons or daughters, then you drag them to the tea house to mediate. Once you're at the tea house a resolution is guaranteed, and everything will be fine, and you don't have to pay lawyers' fees or bring an accusation to the court.

XINRAN: So what percentage of people in this place spend how much time in the tea house?

CHEN: I can't give you a definite figure, but at least half the middle-aged people, and most of the old men, and boys start going to the tea houses for tea from a very young age – sometimes there are even small children. I used to go to the tea house when I was small to listen to the storytellers. We didn't have a word for news, but people who'd been to market far away would head for the tea house on their return to "sing the news". It was just like storytelling. You could hear all sorts of strange things in the tea houses. Old Mr Wu, whom you interviewed, started "singing" the revolution in tea houses when he was ten years old. Our Linhuan tea houses were what our modern-day city people might call "news and media centres".

XINRAN: Did you have that sort of thing in the Cultural Revolution too?

CHEN: They sang news then too, but they didn't talk about politics – nobody dared. And every day there was someone reciting the works of Chairman Mao.

XINRAN: According to your understanding of the people who run the tea houses, what is the greatest hardship of their lives, and the greatest happiness?

CHEN: The hardship is opening at daybreak and staying open till midnight, spending all day constantly brewing tea and topping up people's pots, and slaving away all day for such a tiny income, just enough to keep body and soul together. But the joy for tea-house owners is that everybody goes there, they come into contact with people every day, they hear the news, and see a bit more of the world.

XINRAN: So do you think that there are any differences between tea houses before and after Liberation?

CHEN: They're pretty much the same. We're poor here. Nobody here wants to go messing around with these things. Almost all the old ways of doing things have been passed down from former generations.

XINRAN: Have they been influenced by all the changing governments and regimes?

CHEN: No, you reform your reform, they drink their tea. Nothing's changed.

XINRAN: Were there any cases in the Cultural Revolution of people being impeached or reported on because of things that they'd said in the tea houses?

CHEN: No, very few. At that time everybody was on their guard.

XINRAN: So are the tea-drinking utensils the same as when you were small?

CHEN: Basically they're still the same. But at that time the tables were long plank benches. Now they've started using little square tables. That has its advantages too. Small groups of people can drink tea and play cards together.

XINRAN: Do you worry that now people are surrounded by the material trappings of modern life the tea houses will be replaced by modern materialistic things too?

CHEN: Before the Cultural Revolution there were two tea houses; now there are sixteen. We can see from this change that tea culture has also changed. And there are more tea houses opening soon. Each one has two hundred teapots. Sixteen tea houses, that's over three thousand pots. It won't be easy to replace that many.

XINRAN: Might modern teapots and teacups influence the culture of the tea houses? Aren't you worried that the Chinese tea culture you've been talking about will be changed, and people will start using pretty teapots with foreign words printed on them?

CHEN: Definitely not. Foreign letters and tea just don't mix!

XINRAN: In your childhood did you use tea bowls or teacups?

CHEN: Little handleless teacups, little bowls.

XINRAN: What I was drinking just now was in a little bowl.

CHEN: There aren't any of the tiny bowls like eggcups that they once used left now – we have to order them specially. A lot of the little kilns that used to produce tea bowls and handleless cups have gone out of business. We're getting ready for a return to terracotta bowls. We want the real, earthy local culture, so earthy that you can see the mud dropping off it. We want to preserve that real, genuine, authentic tea culture.

XINRAN: Do you think the young people support your attitude? Are they calling out for this "so local it's dropping mud" tea culture?

CHEN: Some support it, others don't.

XINRAN: Are there any young people who say that these ideas of yours and the things you're doing are ignorant and foolish?

CHEN: Yes, lots! And that includes some of the local officials. They can't see that these ancient relics are our fortune. People talk about holding up a golden bowl begging for food, but we're holding up a golden bowl waiting for food. Why don't they find a way to develop our own cultural resources, and put them to good use? No, they want to run after the Westerners' rubbish culture.

XINRAN: What's your children's attitude to you risking your life to protect historic sites?

CHEN: They have their own opinions. I just think that our generation has a responsibility to preserve Linhuan's ancient things. We can't break off the family line, we must continue it. If we don't, then the line of inheritance will be cut off in this generation.

XINRAN: Have you thought that this knowledge and awareness of yours should be continued in the next generation, and not just the tea culture? That your ideas on keeping ancient monuments ought to be carried on too?

CHEN: It ought to be, but everybody's ideas are different, and everyone takes a different path.

XINRAN: Can you persuade your children?

CHEN: Before, nobody in the family supported me, old or young. Now they support me, but what it'll be like once I'm gone, I don't know.

XINRAN: Those old men drinking tea – I noticed that there is a kind of contentment on their faces that you don't see in other places. Modern people, Chinese and Westerners both, live surrounded by tension and rush, with everybody seeking a good life in the future, leaving themselves no time to "live" in their own environment as a human being. Your Linhuan old people are not rich – very poor, even – but they live very peacefully in "their own" good life. This makes me wonder: what is a good life? Our Chinese tea can settle one's feelings, isn't that right?

CHEN: Yes, Linhuan's *bangbang* tea can bring calm to people's hearts. Linhuan's old town wall can lead modern people to a dialogue with the spirits of ancient people from over a thousand years ago. And Linhuan people also want to understand the world.

XINRAN: To me, you seem to be a fulcrum for local history, and you have made a great contribution to all of this. Just talking about you personally, in your whole life, what were the happiest and the most painful things that happened to you?

CHEN: The old people say that being let down is good fortune, suffering is good fortune, but eating, drinking and idling away one's life in pleasure is not good fortune. There are many things that give me pain. For example, when I go outside the village for a meeting, and see all those people who work in architecture putting up tall buildings and skyscrapers next door to historic sites, vandalising the original scenery, I'm agitated and bitter inside. All those ancient places of culture have been pulled down, destroyed, never to be seen again!

XINRAN: What do you think is the biggest difference between children when you were young and children today?

CHEN: Will and values. Their sense of values is different from mine, my values are about changing our poor, backward state, or raising the standard of living. People these days are pretty good at their jobs, and they know how to live, but they have no work ethic. When I work, the hard part comes first, enjoyment and happiness come afterwards, I've just kept on fighting, fighting the heavens, fighting the earth and fighting people. Sometimes it's just fighting people. If I weakened I'd be finished.

XINRAN: How do you fight with the officials? I've heard a lot of interesting stories about you.

CHEN: It was all over this street. At the time there was a county road that was going to pass through here, and I was determined not to give in. I wrote our project manifesto, and I took it to the county head asking him to sign. Then I took it to the city, to the provincial capital, and asked the Office of Cultural Artefacts to support me. I went to the Construction Department too. People tried to persuade me not to make such a song and dance of it, but I persisted. To this day, this is a Historic Culture Preservation Area; you can't dig it up to build a road. Without the culture there'd be a road but no people. This is an ancient town, yet we're destroying it. We can't do this. The head of the Construction Bureau said that everything was in place for the road, it couldn't be changed, but I fought him with reason. They said this and they said that, but I said that an ancient town should have the face of an ancient town.

XINRAN: And you won!

CHEN: Yes, and it's not just that I don't like losing, I alerted the people around me too.

XINRAN: I've also heard a story that there's a difference between your real age and your age as it appears on your official record, what's that about?

CHEN: I don't know what all that's about! The people in the Construction Committee say that I'm a youthful OAP, they say the age in my records is very young, just forty-eight this year. I'm baffled. I didn't put that in there, so who did? Who told them to write it? I went to the City Construction Committee. They told me to go to the Provincial Construction Bureau, who said it was so I could work a few more years preserving these ancient ruins, so those local cadres could learn a thing or two from me. They couldn't let me walk away early.

XINRAN: So how much younger are you in the files than your real age?

CHEN: More than twenty years!

XINRAN: Just now you said that no matter how the country changes, or the government changes, no matter how the policy changes, apart from the Cultural Revolution, tea houses have always kept their folk culture, which includes discussing everything. So what do people say about Mao Zedong?

CHEN: To be honest, they very seldom discuss Mao Zedong. I believe they must have their own views, but a lot of people are sick with rage at the empty boasting, bribery and corruption we see nowadays. Compared to that, they believe that Mao Zedong did a better job.

XINRAN: So what are your views on Mao Zedong?

CHEN: I think that he was a national leader and also a human being. There's no such thing as a perfect human being, you have to be realistic. His contribution to the nation's development can never be erased: he overturned the Three Great Mountains of imperialism, feudalism and capitalism, and he built up the new China. At that time nobody but Mao Zedong could have brought stability to a chaotic country like China was then. But there were problems with him too. The Great Leap Forward in 1958 saw the beginning of a kind of empty boastfulness within the Communist Party and led to the hard years of the 1960s. And he created the Cultural Revolution, which led to ten years of chaos. Although these things were eventually put to rights, the price was too high. It's just like taking a wife – many people act on a strong impulse at the beginning and end up miserable all their lives, but they can't say that they were wrong.

XINRAN: That leads me to my next question: when did you meet your wife, and how did you get to know her?

CHEN: In 1960. I was quartermaster at the Leinongzhuang Farm, she worked in the office at the middle school. I was taken over to meet her, and we got married. In those days, marrying when you reached a certain age was as natural for people in the countryside as the sun rising in the east and setting in the west. Nobody gave much thought to "feelings" or "sympathy" or "cherishing the same ideals and following the same path".

XINRAN: Can you remember your wedding?

CHEN: I can. It was five yuan. It was simple – we just bought a big box of cigarettes, a few sweets, and that was that. It was fine.

XINRAN: With a personality like yours, did you come under attack in the Cultural Revolution?

CHEN: No. In the Cultural Revolution there were loads of factions. They always made you join this or that faction, and whether you took part or not you always ended up in the wrong. Finally three of us put together a headquarters and set up on our own.

XINRAN: Have you talked to your children about these times?

CHEN: They know some of it.

XINRAN: When they heard, how did they react?

CHEN [laughs]: None of them took it in!

XINRAN: I've heard that you have a serious stomach illness. You ought to get yourself treated as soon as possible by a proper doctor. The old tea houses of Linhuan need you to retain the health of a forty-year-old!

CHEN: Mao Zedong once said, "You can only listen to half of what the doctors say – for the other half, they have to do what I tell 'em!"

*

That night I barely slept. A feeling of oppression, of having no space to stretch out, welled up in my heart. I was both moved by "the peace and kindliness in every cup of tea" that the Linhuan people had derived from their poor life, and awed by the persistence of generations of local people like Chen Lei, looking for a future for their town, seeking the true value of their native land. I muttered a lot of these things to all the cockroaches and midges that were ceaselessly "exploring new territory" up and down my body. I think the blood racing through my veins that night must have satiated many of the mosquitoes and cockroaches that have lived side by side with Chinese peasants down the ages.

The following day at five thirty in the morning, half an hour after the time Old Mr Wu had given me, I was knocking on his front door.

Old Mr Wu was in the middle of preparing breakfast, and plainly surprised that I had kept my word, but he excitedly ushered me into his home, a converted store shed. This room was just like an antique shop or a junk shop, full of curiosities from his years of news-gathering: a magnetic Buddha, a clay statue of the Bodhisattva Guanyin, metal biscuit tins, plastic peonies, a long opium pipe of white jade, an agate snuffbox, a coarse pottery tea set and a redwood dressing table. On the wall directly opposite was a big row of portraits from Mao Zedong, Liu Shaoqi, Zhou Enlai and Deng Xiaoping to Jesus, the Virgin Mary, the God of Wealth, a laughing Buddha and his grandparents and parents. He said that all of these were "gods" in which he neither quite believed nor completely disbelieved. His wife kept off to one side, smiling but never speaking. It was hard to see her as the first female Party member of Linhuan or that frighteningly competent female brigade leader.

Old Mr Wu, his wife and I sat down on little square stools in the outer courtyard. I told them that I felt there had been words between the lines in our interview yesterday, and this was why I had made a special trip for an unofficial interview.

When Old Mr Wu heard this, he suddenly knelt down in front of me and burst into loud weeping.

"The government appropriated the 10.2 *mu* [1.7 acres/0.7 hectare] of land allocated to me. It was all agreed – I was going to get over 60,000 yuan for it, to be paid in full in ten years. That was the rule. They were going to give me six thousand every year, but it's been seven years now, and they haven't even given me six hundred. They don't give me money and they don't give me land. This is what makes me angry! I've gone to speak to the people in the township government, I've been to the county government, and I've been to see the head of the law court, but nobody would listen to me, only people with no real power, and when they'd heard me out, they just said: 'Plenty of people have this problem, your turn hasn't come yet.' To this day nobody's given me an explanation.

"Where's the money? It's in the hands of the production brigade. They say they're borrowing it. The production brigade's taken it to dig ditches and roads, and I haven't seen a fen! I'm a peasant, with no money and no land. I'm old, and I can't do much business. How are my old lady and I supposed to live? That's what hurts me most. I'd like to buy a gong and go up to Beijing to shout out my grievances! I've been treated so unfairly!

"I've had such a raw deal, fifty years a Party member, working all these years. Back in Land Reform they only allocated me three *mu* [0.5 acres/ 0.2 hectare] of land! It took another forty years, till Reform and Opening, before they gave me my ten *mu* [1.6 acres/0.7 hectare], and I lived off that land. Seven years and no money! I've been treated so unjustly. I'm wronged! Officials these days aren't like in my day. If they'd done that, Chairman Mao would have had their heads chopped off!"

Sitting opposite Old Mr Wu, the "written complaint" he had paid someone to write on his behalf clutched in my hands, my heart ached. These peasants who thought that young Westerners in fashionable "begging jeans" were poor, and that doing hard, ill-regarded labour in the city was to "enjoy life and make big money", did not even have the basic information or understanding they needed to live in the same era. But they had never made demands for a better life to the rich and powerful who requisitioned them into bankruptcy. Yet those "mother and father officials" who have survived until today only because the peasants kept to their work instead of throwing down their hoes to make revolution and class struggle apparently never paused in their daily banquets to consider the price the peasants have paid with their blood and sweat.

China's peasants have been treated as a part of the 10,000 things of nature, a group that nobody notices. People are concerned about the melting of the ice caps, they fret over the disappearance of the Asian tigers, they fume at the desert swallowing up the green lands, they even have interminable discussions over the right combination of vitamins for every dish of food. But how many people are calling out for an improvement in the living conditions of the Chinese peasants? How many people pause to consider the bowls of weak vegetable soup in China's poverty-stricken villages, with just a few grains of rice added to stave off hunger? How many people would go to read a story like "The Gourd Children" or "The Monkey King" to the children of poor farmers who don't even know which end to open a book at or where to start reading from on the page, so that those hearts, whose first awareness was of days and nights of hunger, cold and disease, can have their share of goals and beautiful memories like the rest of us? How many people realise that helping those poverty-stricken, un-educated peasants begins with wresting power from local officials who in turn have no education and simply do not understand the law?

China has become strong, China has stood up, but we cannot stand on the shoulders of the peasants for the world to admire how tall we are. We cannot let the peasants' blood and sweat water the tree of our national pride.

7

Carrying on a Craft Tradition: The Qin Huai Lantern-Makers

The Huadeng brothers in their workshop, Nanjing, 1950s.

Interviewing lantern-maker Mr Li, at his workshop, 2006.

MR HUADENG, born in 1934 of a poor lantern-making family and now owner of the Qin Huai lantern workshop, and Li Guisheng, aged ninety, master lantern-maker, and his former apprentice, Gu Yeliang, *interviewed in Nanjing, capital of Jiangsu in eastern China by the Yangtze River. It is said that the first lantern fair was held here in 1372 when Emperor Zhu Yuanzhang ordered a spring lantern festival to celebrate both the coming New Year and the prosperity of the country. This tradition was passed down from generation to generation for centuries, but declined in the early twentieth century. In 1985 the lantern festival was revived. Mr Li is the oldest proponent of lantern-making and he and Mr Huadeng want to inspire a new generation to carry on this ancient tradition.*

In the Chinese world, there are many who are hostile to the way film director Zhang Yimou has presented China to overseas audiences in films such as *Raise the Red Lantern* and *Hero*. They feel that Zhang Yimou is feeding a Western appetite for the exotic with uncouth Chinese folk customs which are a relic from the past. He is pandering to the developed world by presenting to them the humiliatingly backward face of China. In other words, he's using our warm Chinese faces to cosy up to foreigners' cold bums!

I do not know if these critics have any notion of the level of understanding of China in the rest of world.

In my ten years of wanderings outside China, I have read the English-language press every day. I have conducted impromptu surveys and asked questions about things which concerned me during visits to scores of countries. It has taught me something which I dared not believe before and am unwilling to believe now: that perceptions of China in the world today are like those of a tiny baby's first impressions – limited to mother's milk. They know this mother's milk exists but, not being capable of enlightened reflection, they cannot envisage its form. As for the sound and the way it grabs their attention, well, they have practice in distinguishing it and reacting to it, but cannot differentiate between the classic and the popular versions.

Among the world's total population of 6.6 billion, China's 1.3 billion is a huge "unknown quantity". Knowledge about China is so small, it is a decimal fraction many positions after the decimal point.

Some misconceptions about China: people in the developed world do not believe that we have had international airports for over half a century and swimming pools for more than a century; people in developing countries mistakenly feel that for us, as for them, military domination is necessary to achieve peace; undeveloped countries are grateful for the fresh milk we give them, but are not convinced that it is as fresh as it could be.

As people all over the world learn to understand China, Zhang Yimou's films have made them aware of Chinese history and displayed to them the brilliant colours of its folk traditions. These films have also given audiences a taste of a 5,000-year-old cultural tradition, albeit on a level with mother's milk.

So many foreigners with whom I have broached the subject have told me that their first impression of China was Zhang's *Raise the Red Lantern*. The majestic Qiao family compound, the refined elegance of its furnishings, the fascinating costumes of the women, the ceremonies and rules which governed the life of the family and the social class to which it belonged – everything in the film is so very different from anything else in the world. What foreigners say they find hardest to understand is the appalling jealous hatred between clan members; easiest to understand is the red lantern which symbolises their passions!

Foreigners are amazed that Chinese people still use folk art in their daily lives, and confess shamefacedly that, to them, preserving folk art and customs means sticking them in a museum so that people can go and look at them. The Chinese, on the other hand, make folk art a part of living, a tradition which is preserved through family life.

I remember, during the discussion after a lecture I had given, an Australian professor, overcome with emotion, standing up and responding to a journalist who had accused modern China of being confused about its identity and culturally reckless. He said: "I teach history in a university. National culture and folk customs will never disappear in a country which has a film director like Zhang Yimou, who can see folk culture as world culture. As people adopt an international language to interpret the world, they will see Chinese folk culture as a part of the spirit of the Chinese people, and it will also play an important part in convincing them that the world needs China, needs to respect and coexist with China."

I completely agree with him. Thank you, Zhang Yimou!

This is also why I chose Qin Huai lanterns, from among countless folk art forms, as one of the chapters for *China Witness*. Amid the ups and downs of Chinese cultural history, these lanterns stand out as a beacon of colour.

As agricultural civilisations evolve into modern civilisations, many traditional ways of life and folk art forms are neglected and disappear. People always wake up to this fact when it is painfully obvious that it should not have happened, but by then it is too late to do anything about it.

In recent years in China, calls to rescue old buildings and preserve old customs have grown louder by the day. "Worn-out old things" which survived the excited rush, in the last century, to tear down the old and replace it with the new and modern, are now respected by scholars and art experts as cultural relics of old China. Folk arts which bear witness to our past have been reclaimed from "silly old fools". Bright colours are no longer seen by the educated as peasant rubbish, and village-style flowered bedspreads have become fashion items for city people. Traditional red mandarin-style jackets are popular wedding gear, and time-honoured snacks and "big-bowl tea" for communal drinking can be seen again on the avenues and in the lanes of every city at dawn and dusk. What are generally called peasant-style lanterns once more hang decoratively in cities where their ancestors were born.

The reappearance and growth in popularity of the Qin Huai lanterns of Nanjing is one of the signs of this trend.

The Yuan Xiao Lantern Festival originated in the Southern dynasty (AD 420–589) in ancient Nanjing, capital of Jiangsu province, on the south bank of the Yangtze River. From the middle of the Tang dynasty, which succeeded it, the lantern-makers settled in the area around the Da Bridge at the north end of Pingshi Street, forming the original "Yuan Xiao lantern city". The first Ming emperor, Zhu Yuanzhang, who established his capital in Nanjing, was a huge lantern enthusiast. He gathered together rich merchants to build his new capital, and enhanced its splendour by decorating it with lanterns. At the 1372 Yuan Xiao Festival, 10,000 water lanterns were lit, at his orders, on Nanjing's Qin Huai River. He commanded that the annual lantern festival be extended to ten nights, making it the longest such festival in Chinese history. Mentions of Qin Huai and Nanjing lanterns in plays and novels can give us a glimpse of how spectacular they were then.

Lanterns have always been popular among ordinary people because they are inexpensive, make good gifts when visiting friends and are symbols of good luck. With the political turbulence which followed the end of the Qing dynasty and the establishment of the Republic in 1911, the destitution of Nanjing's population brought a decline in lantern festivals. They almost came to a complete end during the period of the Cultural Revolution, and it was only in 1985 that the annual Qin Huai Lantern Festival was revived by the city government. Even though history had blown out Qin Huai lanterns several times, they were a traditional custom which the people of Nanjing refused to give up. Like a torch passed down through the generations, they enable this part of our cultural heritage to survive to the present day.

There is a popular saying in Nanjing: "You haven't had New Year if you don't see the lanterns at the Confucian Temple; and if you don't buy one, then you haven't had a good New Year."

With the aid of my old colleagues at Jiangsu Broadcasting, I tracked down some of those people who gave Nanjing people a good New Year – a group of old Qin Huai lantern-makers. We spent a few months doing phone interviews and then settled on four people. Two of these were the Huadeng brothers, who had at first worked together to carry on the family tradition of lantern-making, although, after making a name for themselves, they had chosen to go their separate ways. The other two, Master Li and his apprentice Gu, had been introduced and paired up by "government edict", but in the course of their work became friends and today are more like father and son to each other.

The older Mr Huadeng politely but firmly said no to an interview in the end, so we could only visit the lantern workshop of the younger brother.

On 24 August 2006, early in the morning on our way to the lantern workshop, our driver treated us to a tirade about the speed at which Nanjing's roads were being rebuilt. "You can see how hard it's making life for us drivers! You wouldn't believe it, I've been driving in Nanjing for twenty years and I don't know how to get you there! I tell you, I knew the way a week ago, but now I'm not sure! I heard on the radio that a small flyover that was being repaired over there hasn't been reopened yet, and the big flyover next to it is going to be rebuilt, starting this week, so it's shut to traffic. How are drivers supposed to choose a route, tell me that? You gave me an address which any Nanjinger knows, but how am I supposed to know which roads are up for repair, and which are open to traffic? Buy a street map? You must be joking! Street maps can't keep up with road repairs! Go to the city planning office and check their road-works programme for an up-to-date transport map? That's a bit naive. You really don't know anything about China today, do you?! The city planners keep being made to change things by their bosses. Haven't you seen it on the TV and in the papers, the way the planners just hand over the drawings for the politicians, who think they know it all, to draw in what they want? If it's a politician with a bit of brains, then Nanjingers might get some city planning which preserves those features which are typical of the Jiangnan region; but if they're just some dogsbody, you might end up living in a rubbish bin!"

None of us dared argue with him, because it would have been adding fuel to the flames, and besides, what he was saying had a lot of truth in it. I thought that probably anyone who's driven a car in China would agree with him.

Strictly speaking, the younger Mr Huadeng's Jiangnan Dragon Lantern Factory was not really a factory, more of a workshop. It looked like an abandoned warehouse compound, or a car breaker's yard, with all available space filled with lanterns in the process of being brought to life. From the smallest – the rabbit lantern, about the palm width of a two-year-old child's hands in size – to the biggest dragon lanterns, they filled the compound's two hundred square metres. Half a dozen workers were absorbed in the painstaking task of making lanterns, and nodded to us by way of a greeting. Mr Huadeng led us into a cramped cubbyhole which served as his "office". Seven or eight documents which looked like report forms hung in a row from small clips at the bottom of the window above the desk. On the desk stood a telephone covered with a piece of embroidery, an electric fan noisy enough to stop us talking, and some old-fashioned photo albums with corner mounts that had been put out ready for us. Apart from these, the desk held almost no other office equipment. A display cabinet stuffed full of sample lanterns stood behind Mr Huadeng's office chair, and a dilapidated sofa, obviously intended for guests, faced the window, squeezed in next to the display cabinet. In the whole factory, this was the only place for guests to sit.

The weather that day was forecast to reach a very hot forty-one degrees – the electric fan roared as if it was on fire. Because we needed to record and film, there was no option but to turn it off. Very soon we all began to pour with sweat, and Mr Huadeng looked like he was being interviewed in a shower of rain.

*

XINRAN: Mr Huadeng, when did you start learning about lanterns?

HUADENG: I was born in 1934, and all I remember is our home being made up of lanterns. The men of the family, my father and grandfather, when they weren't out selling vegetables, made lanterns; and the women, my grandmother and mother, did the cooking and the laundry, and then made lanterns too. Every corner of the house was full of lanterns. At festivals, they were what we played with, hung up, even what we talked about when guests came. Before I was ten years old, I probably thought everybody made their living from lanterns. It was only later that I realised the lantern business was seasonal. You couldn't sell them all year round, although they were my family's main source of income. For the rest of the time, we scraped by on the money my father earned from buying vegetables wholesale and selling them in the market. But it was the money from the lanterns which paid for clothes or things for the house or things for the old folks. So every Chinese New Year, the adults in the family would take the lanterns they'd been making all year to the Confucian Temple to sell. When I was ten years old, my father began teaching me how to make them. I started from the most popular kinds, rabbit and water-lily lanterns. Between the age of ten and now, I haven't stopped once.

XINRAN: And when did your father start making them?

HUADENG: I don't know. We children weren't allowed to ask grownups questions like that. I only know my father learned from my grandfather. As they used to say, we were a lantern family, we sold lanterns for money. All arts and crafts workers were considered lower than the smallest officials, along with beggars, and other artists, singers, acrobats, martial artists and suchlike. Of course, that's the old way of speaking. When I was ten, to give the family a bit more of an income, my father took me and my older brother in hand and taught us how to make them. He told us how the skills had been passed down through the generations. I still remember him saying, if you sell vegetables, you eat gruel; if you sell lanterns, you eat rice; and if you sell good lanterns, and lots of them, you can eat pork and duck.

XINRAN: Did he tell you stories about your family and lanterns?

HUADENG: Mostly what he talked about was how to make good lanterns. What we wanted to know was how to make lots, and make good ones, so we could eat pork and duck. Eating duck was what we dreamed of in those days. It's our most delicious Nanjing speciality! People nowadays would say: "How much can a ten-year-old understand?" But at ten, I was wise for my age. Isn't there a saying: "Poor children soon learn to be head of the family"? As we were learning, my father used to tell us how strict my grandfather had been when he taught him. My father said, if you don't follow the rules, you won't be able to do something well.

XINRAN: Did he beat you?

HUADENG: All the time, really, all the time. There were very few times when he didn't beat us. When we bound together the frame of the lantern, we used bark paper, not string. You took a long, long twist of paper and pressed it around the central part which was made of bamboo, like this. There was a rule about how many times the bark strips had to go around the frame but I sometimes cheated. I went round it ten times, and it should have been twelve. Then you put on dabs of starch to glue the lantern together. When my father came to check, he would pull the starch apart and count the layers. "I told you to do twelve turns, and you did ten, you lazy little git!" he would swear as he beat me. The other children would all shout: "Little Two's eating bamboo roast pork again!" (He beat our bottoms with bamboo slats.) My father often said: "To do a handicraft well means tempering both your hand and your will." In the old man's words: "Other people may sell one for 1 yuan, but if you make a good lantern you can sell yours for 1.5 yuan. Your lanterns have got to be made in the proper way." We used to make fan lanterns before aeroplane lanterns, and he said: "If the other sellers can't spin their fans and you can, you can sell yours for five fen more." So now, I've entered lantern competitions, I've even represented Nanjing in a national paper arts championship – because kites and lanterns, and paper cuts too, all of them count as paper arts – and my commemorative lantern got onto a national special issue of postage stamps. The reason why I've had such outstanding success with my lanterns is bound up with my father's strict teachings back then. And it's also because I've tempered my skills for so many years. It's not like I just got lucky one day.

XINRAN: You've achieved unprecedented status as a great master of Chinese folk lanterns. Have you passed your skills on to anyone in your family?

HUADENG: I don't know whether to laugh or cry when you ask me that. I'm passionate about lanterns, I set up this lantern workshop six years ago, but I haven't made a cent from it. I've retired now. I get my 1,000-yuan pension every month. I just want to make sure that this factory doesn't go bust, so I struggle along. When I was trying to find someone to take over from me, I talked to my daughter and son-in-law. I said to them: "You shouldn't go and work for other people, or sit in front of computers in other people's offices. If you do that, you're not as good as me. Only folk traditions are world traditions. My lantern-making is an art which foreigners would like to do but don't know how to. It's a world-class skill. Our folk arts are so outstanding that you should get foreigners to come and learn from us, we shouldn't be running after them." My daughter listened and then she just asked me one thing: "Dad, have you got rich?

Do you live better than ordinary people?" There was nothing I could say to this. All these years, come rain or shine, through good times and bad, I've just pursued my love of folk art. It's also because I wanted to do something for my country, and to hand on the skills of my ancestors, but what have I got to show for it? Nothing at all. Even my children don't understand. Sometimes I think, times have changed – children have the right to run their own lives, life is modernised too. But traditional culture can't just be chucked into history books and forgotten. Sometimes I feel we've let down our ancestors, let down all those ancestors who've bequeathed thousands of years of folk culture to us.

XINRAN: As I understand it, the government has tried to rescue these Jiangnan folk arts which were being lost, like lantern-making. For example, in 1985, they started up the Qin Huai Lantern Festival again after a long gap. In your experience, are these just slogans, or has there been any real action?

HUADENG: What can I say? It's hard to explain. City officials have come to me and said: "Old Huadeng, we're delighted that you've set up this lantern workshop, we hope that when it's going well, you'll dig up some even older traditions and use modern techniques to make even more beautiful and artistic lanterns." I've done what they said for six years, put my whole body and soul into it, but what return have I had? My lantern design has got onto national stamps, and the Chinese Post Office sent me 500 yuan. They deducted fifteen yuan for postage, so I just got 485 yuan. When people heard my lantern had got onto a stamp, they said to me: "Huadeng, old man, you've really made good now!" But no one knows I only got 500 yuan, less money than those cadres spend on a dinner. But those stamps were sent all over the world, and I think that that's an honour that can't be bought with money. If I had 200,000 yuan, I might buy a house with it and move out of our place, which is too small to swing a cat in. I might use it to buy a car, so I don't have to queue up for buses in all weathers to get to work and back. I haven't asked the central government for money, or the local government. Why not? The lanterns I've devoted my whole life to, the Confucian Temple lanterns, have gone out to the whole world printed on our postage stamps. It's not just me that made them possible. They're the result of the years of hard craft put in by all those artists who make Nanjing lanterns. Why should I care about 20,000 yuan? My assets are not material things. They've been handed down to me by my ancestors.

XINRAN: All your life, you've sweated blood to carry on this wonderful folk art, yet your daughter asks you how much you've earned from all that work. You don't know whether to laugh or cry, and all this has caused you real pain, a pain which you can't get rid of. Do you think all Nanjing's lantern-makers, all Chinese lantern-makers, feel the same way as you?

HUADENG: I don't know about other places in China, and there are only a couple of others in Nanjing who've spent half a century making lanterns like I have. We don't have either the right or the power to make other people study this art – they've got to eat, and bring up their children, and nowadays people play mah-jong and go dancing too. There's practically no one willing to spend hours sweating away in a hole like this fiddling about with an ancient folk art. There are a few older people who are out of work, have no education and can't do any other job, who might work with us to earn a bit of money. It's a lonely business, what I do. People don't respect you, or even understand you. In 1984, for the Sino-Japanese Youth Congress, a lantern display was planned in Nanjing, and the City Cultural Department gave me the task of designing it. They wanted me to turn the traditional water-lily lanterns into more elaborate lotus lanterns. I went to Xuanwu Lake Park to see the lotus flowers because I wanted to give them a natural shape. At that time I couldn't afford a camera. It's not like now, with digital cameras you can take a few shots and bring them back to look at. We didn't have them then. I just had to go and look at the lotus ponds in the park, and once I nearly fell in the lake trying to get a good look at a flower bud. I got nabbed by the park keepers. They tried to fine me, but I said I wasn't messing around, I was designing lanterns, and where would I get the money to pay a fine? They said if the government had asked me to do the design, weren't they paying me for it? I said no, it was my patriotic duty. I just got a bit of money to buy materials at the beginning, but no fees while I was making the lanterns. And no one believed I was such a fool! Things like this have happened far too often, and I've suffered far too much grief over them, far too much. Sometimes when something like this has happened, I like to have a smoke and think about it, and sometimes I'm so deep in thought that the cigarette burns right down, and I don't realise it until it burns my hand.

XINRAN: What's brought you most hardship in life? And what's brought you most pleasure?

HUADENG: The hardest thing is dreaming up new lantern shapes. Design is the hardest thing. Making a water-lily or a lotus-flower lantern, or a dragon lantern or a lion, none of that is hard. What's hard is thinking up the shapes. If you don't design it properly, then the lantern won't work. Before we make any new lantern shape, we have to draw a simple diagram and write in the measurements. You can't start making it until you've sketched it all out. You can't eat or sleep when you're designing something new, because if you get it wrong, you've wasted all that labour and materials. Another hard thing is not being understood. People don't understand the way we work, especially the younger generation. If you've made a bit of a name for yourself, then you're even worse off. Once your family and friends get to hear of it, they ask you where you're making your money now. I tell them I'm doing this and that. They say: "But you've been doing that for years! Are you still at it? China's completely changed! How come you haven't changed at all?" It really hurts when people don't understand because then you don't get any support. The third thing I find very painful is a situation like now; I'm running a small workshop, employing ten people, and suddenly it gets busy – like the 2008 Olympics. Nanjing is planning a big dragon 2,008 metres long, and the city government wants us to find twenty or thirty craftspeople for it. Where am I going to find all these craftspeople? I told them, I can't afford to keep spare workers. If you get people in, and don't have the money to pay them, are they just expected not to eat for a couple of weeks? The government doesn't give me a subsidy to train craftspeople or to keep them on; I don't get any help at all, and that often makes me feel sad. I'm not complaining but the city officials come along and say to me: "Now then, old Huadeng, you do such-and-such, and we'll support you in such-and-such a way, we'll get the administration on to it. My goodness, your premises are too small, we'll call cadres at all levels together for a meeting to discuss it. After all, you're a 'name card' for the Qin Huai district, you've been on a Chinese postage stamp, and that hasn't happened in Nanjing for hundreds of years! So we all want to support old Huadeng!" You've seen how we work – it's like a craft workshop of a hundred years ago, isn't it? It might even be worse than a hundred years ago. And another thing – they're pulling this place down, so soon we're going to be evicted. No one has been round to take a look. You don't get any help at all. People will hold celebration parties for you but no one will help you in your work. I feel a bit lonely. In fact, I'm very lonely.

XINRAN: It's all very well for the Qin Huai district, for the city of Nanjing, for the whole country – but when your design was chosen for the postage stamp, you only got paid 500 yuan, and they made deductions from that. So if the Qin Huai local authority or Nanjing city government

Funeral for the husband, killed by the GMD in 1935, of Chen Lianshi, the "Double-Gun Woman", *centre*, dressed in a dark colour; (*inset*) Chen Lianshi with her grandson, 1948.

Fang Haijun, *far right*, first head of Mao Zedong's guard troop, with other party cadres, 1937; he later became a high-ranking Party official and founder of China's Naval Academy and submarine fleet (see p. 11).

Prospecting for oil in northern China, 1950s (Mr You, *left*).

Mr You (*centre* in raincoat) with Soviet lorry and colleagues, 1950s.

Family photos of the policeman, Mr Jingguan, *far right* and *centre*, with his wife, children and their grandmother, 1950s.

Long-distance coach with factory workers, Jiangsu, 1969: any celebration had to include a photo of Mao.

Acrobats (Yishujia, *front left*) performing during the Cultural Revolution.

Acrobat Yishujia's husband and son (now a professional magician, working in the West), at a military base, Shandong, 1970s.

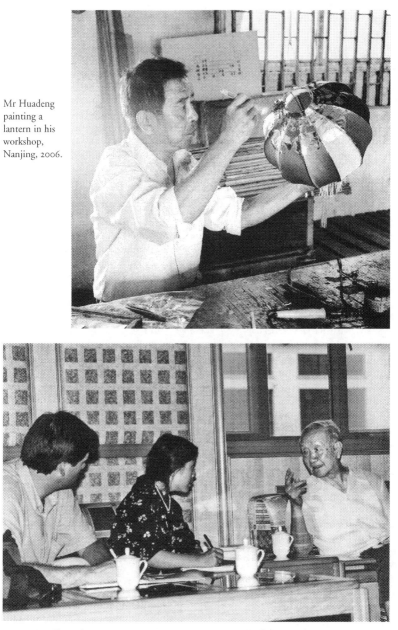

Mr Huadeng painting a lantern in his workshop, Nanjing, 2006.

Mr Changzheng, a Long March survivor, interviewed by foreign media in Beijing.

A crowd gathers, late afternoon, 2006, in People's Square, Urumqi, Xinjiang province, to watch a film on a large screen.

One of the oldest tea houses in China at Linhuan, Anhui province, 2006: one man reads aloud to the mainly elderly, all male, audience, since few of their generation learned to read.

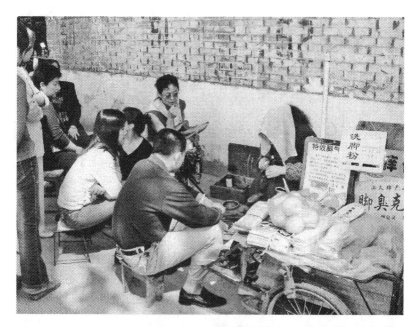

In a Zhengzhou street, 2006, interviewing the shoe-mender, who was at first too shy to be photographed; on the right of the photo are instructions on how to clean your feet.

A woman making chopsticks out of bamboo, Guizhou, 2006.

General Phoebe and her husband, surrounded by memories, at their home in Beijing, 2006.

At the monument to the 4 May Movement, Beijing, 2006.

want to use, or commission, your lanterns, or if they ask you to put on a lantern display to make the city look festive, do they pay you for it?

HUADENG: Yes, if they need props for a performance, or if they want the lanterns for a municipal event, then they pay expenses.

XINRAN: And does what they pay you cover your expenses?

HUADENG: Of course not! For instance, I sometimes make a pair of water-lily lanterns when a young couple get married. It's quite delicate work, but I only charge them fifty yuan for each, or a hundred yuan the pair. If it's the Qin Huai local authority who ask us to make lanterns, we have to drop the price a bit, because although they don't look after us directly, overall you could say that they're on the next rung up administratively, and we can't afford to put a foot wrong. All the same, they don't support us when we really need it. You have to stand on your own feet, and you're very isolated. Don't laugh at me if I say this. Sometimes I don't do any business for three months and don't earn a penny, but you've still got to pay the workers, and you can't not pay the rent, the electricity and the water, can you? Sometimes it's all so hard. I still hope, though, that one day our folk art will get proper public recognition.

XINRAN: Why don't you think you're getting public recognition? When we were doing our research and contacted Jiangsu Radio and got information on folk crafts from national organisations, the first people they recommended in Nanjing were Li Guisheng, and you and your brother, so surely this must imply public recognition? When you talked just now about feeling isolated, I could see how you felt by looking in your eyes. The art of Qin Huai lanterns has been handed down to you by your father and grandfather, so it has a vitality which has survived down the years, doesn't it? So how come, when more people than ever before have been to school, and life is more civilised and modernised, people nowadays have no respect for a tradition which goes back more than a thousand years, and have abandoned it? Why is it ignored by the public, and even by the government?

HUADENG: "Flowers grow in the garden, but you smell them outside it" – that's the kind of recognition you're talking about. Let me put it more simply: China's folk crafts are all exported. In China, the government only start to take a bit of interest if you are famous and you're someone putting your talents to good use. But it's not easy for poor craftspeople to make a difference. The Qin Huai local authority only sat up and took notice of me after my lantern won the national competition and appeared on a postage stamp.

It's not like we artists can't agree, and can't make even better lanterns. It's not like that at all. Since the 1980s, CCTV have come every year to film the lanterns, dubbing us "delightfully rustic". We weren't too happy with being called "rustic", but we laughed at the "delightfully". In the Jiangnan region, that's the kind of atmosphere at the Spring Festival among ordinary folk; they're full of delight at our local pleasures.

Lanterns are seasonal, but the craft isn't seasonal. No one supports your business needs for three seasons of the year – you have to wait till the Spring Festival, when the government has to create a festive atmosphere, and then there's too much business. So we have to get through the year, and we can't make the workers go out begging for food for nine months of it. There's another thing – the markets all had their own regulations in the past, and space for the crafts stalls was always free. But now space is like gold dust – you get a stall but you get charged for it, and we have to do a lot of business before we cover the rent and make some profit.

When we're selling lanterns in the Confucian Temple market, the high-ups from the city government and the local authority always come and see me. "How are things this year, old Huadeng?" "Fine! Thank you for your help and concern!" "How's it going this year?" "Oh, fine, fine! Thank you so much for asking!" But that's just putting a good front on it. The thing that most makes you feel warm, but also leaves you feeling desolate, is: "If you have any problems, come and see me!" Got problems? Go and see you? And where would I find you? I'm about to be evicted from these premises, and I don't have anywhere to go. I said to the local authority, if they're really going to evict me and I don't have anywhere to go, I'll have to shut this workshop. After all, I can get by on my pension. I'll stay at home and do what I want, and I won't worry any more about how Nanjing's festivities look!

XINRAN: You've got such a burning desire to do this, such a strong will, how many young people are studying lantern-making with you now?

HUADENG: None, not a single one!

XINRAN: Are you worried? Are you worried that your art, your knowledge, and your faith in it, might just disappear?

HUADENG: I'll tell you the truth. I used to worry, but since I set up the workshop, I stopped worrying. I might be wrong to say this, though.

Qin Huai lanterns have existed for thousands of years, and other people, the government, the country are not bothered, so why should I bother? You could say that the course my life takes is in my hands, but the course that Qin Huai lanterns take is not in the hands of us makers. It's down to the policymakers. Qin Huai lantern-making represents the "name card" of Nanjing's history, the "name card" of the art of the People's Republic of China. If they value that "name card", then Qin Huai lanterns can carry on going, even rise to new heights. But if they neglect it, then it means our time is up.

Years ago, I told cultural affairs officials that there were ten different series of Qin Huai lanterns. The most common ten are aeroplane lanterns, rabbit lanterns, water-lily lanterns, lion lanterns and so on, but now a lot of them are a lost tradition, and no one knows how to make them any more. The lion lantern, for instance, there's no one left in Nanjing who can make those. There were a few old artists who could, but they've died now. I still want to do my bit to keep Qin Huai lanterns going, but then I think, after I'm dead the tradition may die out, and I don't feel like bothering!

XINRAN: Doesn't that distress you?

HUADENG: There's no point in getting distressed. When I cross over to the Underworld, the King of the Underworld won't say to me, you didn't get it sorted out up there so you'd better come and make lanterns for me. He can't say that, so that's not what I get bothered about. Never mind that I'm old; I really feel I've reached my peak now. Just look at my lantern-making. I've never been as good as I am now, and if at this time I can bring a bit of happiness to ordinary people's lives with my two hands, then that's even better. As for where Qin Huai lantern-making will end up, that's not something we makers can sort out with a complaint here or a few harsh words there, do you understand what I'm saying?

XINRAN: If you had the chance, would you be willing to take on a few foreign students?

HUADENG: Of course. Anyone who wants to learn, I can teach them!

XINRAN: But wouldn't you be concerned that a traditional folk art handed down to you by your forefathers might be lost to other countries?

HUADENG: There's no reason why Chinese art shouldn't cross national boundaries. But sweet dreams and idle chat won't keep us alive! I'm on my own in this, and all I can do is run a workshop employing a dozen or so workers and keep on at people about folk art. This is a "small national business" I'm running. I pay all the taxes I'm supposed to and don't cheat my clients, and just make a living out of my art.

I don't have wild ambitions. If I can just carry on the lantern-making tradition, and help my country by taking on a few unemployed workers, then I'm well satisfied. I do my best, and that's all I can do. Of course I'd love to have a factory employing two hundred workers, divided into ten workshops, each one devoted to studying one of the ten series of lanterns, and recording them, so that the next generation can learn how to make them. I'd like to set up a training workshop so a few people could develop new designs, and bring the science and technology of ancient lantern-making up to date, and make the display period longer, which would give a clearer expression of Jiangnan art. I'd better shut up, or my workers will tell me I'm dreaming again! Anyway, as I was saying, I'd be just as happy to pass these things on to foreigners and see Chinese Qin Huai lanterns take root and flourish in other countries. Why not? No one's come to me and told me, "Old Huadeng, you're only allowed to teach Chinese people, you can't teach foreigners." No one's told me that, so I'm free to do what I want. I'm a "liberal" now, running a private enterprise. Apart from paying my taxes, I'm a "liberal", and if I want to do something, I can do it.

XINRAN: You've been through so many ups and downs in your life, I'd like to ask you, if you had your life over again, would you choose to follow the same path?

HUADENG: If I could have my life over again, I'd say to the King of the Underworld, in my last life I was a lantern-maker, can I please apply to be a lantern-maker in my next life on earth? Why? Because I think lanterns are beautiful! Just look at them, they're all the work of our own hands, the water lily standing gracefully erect, the bunny all cute and lively, the spirit of that dragon! I feel so good, looking at those lanterns . . .

XINRAN: But what about all your grievances? Your children don't want to learn from you, the government doesn't want to support you, you're not very well off. Don't you have regrets?

HUADENG: No, none. I feel I've worked hard for more than sixty years, and I've finally tamed the lotus lantern; plus I've represented the country with my stamp and told the world about Qin Huai lanterns, so I feel honoured, happy and proud.

XINRAN: How did your daughter and son-in-law react when they heard the news?

HUADENG: They were happy, very happy, though they still remind me that I haven't made any money. But I've achieved things that billions of people who are rolling in wealth haven't been able to do. You can't pay the Chinese Post Office to have your product printed on their stamps, can you? I didn't pay them money. I got there through my own efforts.

XINRAN: And what do your children say to that?

HUADENG: Nothing! I'd really like to seize the moment and shout at them to come and learn lantern-making from me, take advantage of the fact that I'm at the height of my powers and could teach them.

XINRAN: Apart from the fact that lantern-making hasn't made you any money, and has shown your children that it isn't a good way to earn a living, have you thought what other reasons they might have for not wanting to succeed you?

HUADENG: Of course it's to do with what today's young people want to do with their lives. They pursue money rather than art. That's a common problem in China. I was ten when I started to learn from my father. Nowadays, no ten-year-old, or even a twenty-year-old, will listen when you try and teach them right from wrong!

When young people come to my workshop looking for a job, I say to them: "No, my young friend, you've got it wrong. We don't do manual work here; we learn an art. If you come, you come as a pupil. I can't pay you thousands of yuan, because I haven't taken a fen out of the business myself yet, but you can learn the art of lantern-making." When they hear me say that, they turn on their heel and go.

I've had this business for six years and I still haven't bought any decent clothes or nice shoes. My mobile is someone else's cast-off, and I'm scarcely scraping a basic living in other people's eyes, but I have no regrets. I feel that what I've achieved is beyond anyone's expectations. My work's been featured on Chinese postage stamps!

XINRAN: Is there any difference between the way the Chinese cared about and appreciated the art of Qin Huai lanterns when you were young and nowadays?

HUADENG: Between when I learned lantern-making from my father and the Great Leap Forward in 1958, we went to the Confucian Temple market to sell lanterns every year. Especially after Liberation, you went and registered with the Qin Huai local chamber of commerce, and the government sent people to put up strings for you to hang the lanterns from on Jinling Road, and put up the stands for you. So my dad got Stall 1, someone else got Stall 2, and they didn't charge you a fen, do you see what I mean? The government put people and effort into supporting you.

The Confucian Temple lantern market goes right back to the Ming dynasty. It's famous all over China. Just like the way small traders in Shanghai who wanted to make money used to flock to the Town God Temple, so the Confucian Temple market was the place where people collected in Nanjing. We sold lanterns there for years and years, and the local government never charged us. Nowadays, I can't count on help from any department. They just issue an instruction that lantern-makers should be charged 1,000 yuan per stall. After the lantern festival restarted in 1985, our factory used to go and sell every year, but two tables end to end, that's 2,000 yuan in stall fees alone! Then there's the workers' wages and lunches, and you have to rent storage space and pay to get the lanterns there. It all adds up to too much, so for the last two years I haven't been.

Let me work out for you the costs for an ordinary small water-lily lantern, the sort that a new worker starts learning on and that sell for ten yuan each. If a worker starts making lanterns in August, he or she will have only made three hundred by the Spring Festival. If none are spoiled, three hundred lanterns at ten yuan each can bring in 3,000 yuan. The stall fees are 1,000 yuan, so after that's been paid, you're left with 2,000. My workshop expenses, water and electricity, business rates all have to come out of that 2,000. Each person gets at least 100 yuan a month, so that's 500 yuan over five months. Then we have to buy in all the materials from outside, rulers, paper, starch, rubber solution, et cetera. That's at the very least 50 yuan a month, and then there's at least 50 yuan for travel. That's another 250 yuan. You want lunch? The very cheapest will come to 50 yuan a month, won't it? August to December is five months of wages. That's on average only 200 yuan a month! That's not even 50 yuan for a five-day week! Ten yuan a day, less than two yuan an hour! Who's willing to work for that? I think that's an important factor in the current decline of Qin Huai lanterns. Artists have got to consider their own lives and their abilities, haven't they?

XINRAN: I remember you said that your wife supported your enterprise, is that right?

HUADENG: Yes.

XINRAN: When did you get to know her and how?

HUADENG: After Liberation, we were both working in a printer's for a time. Everything was simple then or, as young people would put it now, we were pretty dumb. We saw a lot of each other and our feelings developed.

She'd had a hard life, and people who knew her told me her mother had bled to death giving birth to her, so her father gave the baby away and ignored her after that. The people who brought her up were very poor too. They just had two pairs of thin trousers worn one over the other to keep them warm in winter. She still hates the New Year, because when she was little, on New Year's Eve when it got dark, she regularly had to go out and pick up other people's discarded rotten vegetable roots to make the New Year's dinner with. One year she got bitten by a wild dog. What she got most enjoyment from in those days was standing outside someone else's house sniffing the good smell of their dinner. And still she's trying to find out what her mother's name was.

Well, my mother had died young – both being motherless drew us together too – so there were no old people or children for me to look after at home. In those days we earned hardly anything, but as I had no family responsibilities, I could help her out a bit. We didn't get any wedding photographs done, and we didn't do a banquet. Getting married meant we each just got a new outfit, got the marriage certificate, went to the factory to distribute sweeties, and that was it, we were married.

XINRAN: So did she learn the art of lantern-making from you?

HUADENG: I did have some influence on her. Actually, she learned it from me on the quiet during the Cultural Revolution. In those days, lanterns belonged to the category of the "Four Olds" which had to be "eliminated" because they were part of a feudal way of life, but we still made lanterns in secret. At New Year, we would take a few small lanterns and sell them in the little alleyways around the Confucian Temple, and no sooner had we gone out with them than the old folks would have every single one off us.

We weren't allowed to make or sell lanterns during the Cultural Revolution, but I never stopped. Everyone knew how poor my father was and that we had a proper "red" family background, so I wasn't worried anyone was going to "make revolution" against me. When my work unit found out, they just said: "Young Huadeng, how come you're still making lanterns? They're one of the Four Olds, you know, and everyone's smashing the Four Olds and bringing in the Four News. If you're still making lanterns and selling them in the Confucian Temple market, that's dangerous, isn't it?"

In my lifetime, we've been through so many political movements. All national ones which were no concern of ours, like the 1954 Suppress the Counter-Revolutionaries, the 1957 Anti-Rightist movement, the Cultural Revolution, sending intellectual youth to remote country areas, stuff like that. But I never stopped making lanterns. I never thought that making revolution meant getting rid of festival traditions! I always thought the reason I was brave enough to carry on with my craft in secret was because I wasn't educated, and had no idea what feudalism, capitalism and revisionism meant. I didn't know about Party principles, or what the revolutionary Four News were meant to be. I wasn't the only one who didn't understand that. Most ordinary people had about as little education as I did. In fact, how many of those anti-everything revolutionaries with their movements for this and that understood what it was all about? Making revolution was just a pretext for people to settle private scores. If those movements really had been good for China, then we wouldn't have been poor for so many years. People today wouldn't be so fixated on money, and wouldn't ignore traditional arts like they do. And there wouldn't be people like me, with just my daughter-in-law learning lantern-making from me!

XINRAN: Do you often have arguments with your wife about the lanterns?

HUADENG: Yes, often.

XINRAN: Who wins these arguments?

HUADENG: She does, of course! Why? Because a man comrade has to give in a bit, otherwise you won't have a good marriage. Because when a woman comrade's temper is up, she's obstinate, she won't back down. I take charge of the technology and the design, and she's responsible for the production. We often have spats, and she sometimes says to me: "We've worked really hard for six years in this workshop, and I've never taken a fen home. If I was your employee, I'd get 500 yuan a month, that's 6,000 a year, and in six years I'd have taken 30,000 yuan home, and you haven't given me a fen!" She's right, you know. At every Dragon Boat Festival, we buy something for each of the workers, even if I'm making a loss and we're not doing any business or earning a fen. At holidays I always buy a gift for everyone, but never buy anything to take home. Why not? Because if I buy something for the workers, it's to win them over, to communicate with them . . . What I'm saying with that keg of oil or those duck eggs is they have a duty to love me! I treat every fen as if it were a yuan, and every 100 yuan as if it were 10,000, but I do spend money where it matters. We can't depend on the government for our future, or princes or court officials. Our only insurance is ourselves.

XINRAN: Can I ask you another couple of questions? You can choose whether or not to answer. Since we arrived in China, we've been from Beijing to Guiyang, then to Chengdu, Xinjiang, Gansu, Qingdao, Anhui, now we're in Nanjing, and then we're off to Henan, Beijing, Shanghai, to the area between the Yellow River and the Yangtze, from west to east, and we've heard so many different opinions about this, I'd like to know how you feel. One, are you quite confident about the way society is developing now, or do you have misgivings? And the second question is, what do you personally feel about Chairman Mao? Because we've all seen the rapid pace of urban development in China, the wonderful public buildings, the increasing glamour of China and the rise in the standard of living, but we have also seen how people are worried that our most basic cultural traditions are being neglected. How do you feel about all this?

HUADENG: We're getting into politics with questions like that, and I don't really want to say anything about it. We're popular artists – that's people's term of respect for us. In fact, we're just lantern-makers, pretty much like beggars. I just make a bit of money with my handicraft. If you're going to talk politics, I don't want to get involved. Who's good, who's bad, I don't want to comment. I feel in my heart that we must take the greatest precautions to protect the traditional art of lantern-making and keep it going. That's the only way it will blossom and produce fruit. If we don't nurture it with enough care, if we neglect it, then it might die out completely.

XINRAN: So about Chairman Mao, and what he did, what do you personally feel about that? Sometimes, you see, it seems to me that with lots of people now, some will be negative and some will be positive about him. But I feel the reason why he made the kind of mark that he did on Chinese history is that he was shaped by his times. I also feel that we are younger though not as dynamic as you are, so our impressions of him will not be as incisive as yours. What do you feel the generally accepted view of Mao is?

HUADENG: I'll just say one thing: Chairman Mao was good, and that's all I'm going to say, no more than that. Because that's politics, and we popular artists have our own views on some things. I'm an old man now, so of course there's a lot that I know, but we shouldn't express too many opinions on that sort of thing.

XINRAN: Why do you think Chairman Mao was good?

HUADENG: When he was alive, there was not so much of a gap between rich and poor, and this was the biggest advantage for ordinary people. There was poverty then, but we lived comfortably. If a worker in a Communist Party enterprise got sick, the trade union had to send them some fruit. Nowadays, there are no Party enterprises. They're all contracted out, here, there and everywhere, and everything's all topsy-turvy. Of course, there are differences in principle between state-run and private enterprises, but state-run enterprises are not the same as they were ten years ago. There are some things that have been swept under the carpet. I'm not going to say anything else about that today, just that and no more. After all, I still want to carry on working! You big reporters should pay no attention to us ignorant people, we just talk rubbish!

XINRAN: No, what you've said is really sharp and to the point. I think we all ought to start telling the truth and make the government listen. If no one tells the truth, and no one listens to it, then we Chinese will just carry on being bamboozled by lies, and our society will never improve. I believe that we, the younger generation, need elders like you to tell us where we're going wrong. We need to learn about the past from you, to understand tradition and learn about folk arts from you. That's the only way that we can walk towards the rest of the world without losing our respect for our own culture and national traditions. Don't you agree?

HUADENG: All young Chinese nowadays think that it's OK to think like you. But just thinking is useless. Soon all those who understand the old culture and arts will be gone, and then if someone wants to study, who will they learn from? Almost all the old artists learned their skills from family members – there are no books and no written records. When they die they'll take everything with them, and then all the traditional culture will go to the grave too. Who's worried about that now? Who cares about it being too late? No one!

XINRAN: Master Huadeng, I honestly believe that there are other Chinese who feel the same way as you. Otherwise there would be no hope for our national traditions, would there? Among officials, there are quite a few who love our folk culture too. Together we can help the rest get educated in these folk arts. They just need to be pointed in the right direction. They're not gods – they grew up in an era of all politics and no culture – but they're still Chinese and folk arts are an integral part of their lives, they just don't realise it. It's like older people are very sensitive to changes in the weather, the way their joints ache in response to it. But when we're young, we don't care about changes in the weather.

HUADENG: You're quite right in what you say, I'm just afraid it may be too late. Time doesn't wait for anyone, and old artists can't wait until they're a hundred! Now come and see how we make lanterns!

*

After I left Huadeng, I felt, once again, quite emotional about what I had heard and seen. After touring China's Yangtze River region, I realised that almost every single Chinese person we met was as dedicated as Mr Huadeng, fought like this, and felt this kind of sorrow. Like many Chinese, Huadeng had heard too many lies, too much boasting and empty talk to believe that there was hope for his culture. That is what hurts me most. As a Chinese person, the hardest thing to accept is that we do not believe each other.

While we were investigating Qin Huai lanterns, we also interviewed the master lantern-maker and his pupil who had been brought together by local government cadres: Li Guisheng and Gu Yeliang.

The interviews were conducted at their premises, an artisan-built court-yard in a typical period style. We made our way through a lane full of washing hung out to dry, suddenly emerging into a small courtyard of about a hundred square metres, flanked by buildings on three sides and a wall on the fourth. The buildings were of the squat and rudimentary construction traditional for craftsmen's workshops. From the main gateway it was impossible to make out anything in the darkened interiors, and it was only the roar of the electric grinder and the fan, and the chatter and laughter of women, that told us that there were people at work in there. Under a hundred-year-old tree in the centre of the courtyard a small mountain of half-finished water-lily lanterns reposed in the shade. We set up our interview equipment in front of the eaves from which hung the finished lanterns, where the blazing sunshine not only provided us with sufficient light but also proved such an effective "sweat producer" that after a few hours we were all drenched in sweat again. Even our inter-viewee, sitting before the camera's lens, was too preoccupied with constantly mopping the sweat trickling into his eyes to bother about his "media image". Li Guisheng was a very correct old man, with a very correct way of sitting and speaking, and an even more "correct" way of expressing his views. The huge generational differences in the feelings of master and pupil about lantern-making were very clear from their answers to our questions – not so much a contrast as an indication that they came from two different eras.

We were concerned that Mr Li, who was nearly ninety, would find the sweltering heat unbearable, so we limited our questions to him to checking historical facts we had turned up in our research and to oral traditions of lantern-making in the Jiangnan region. On the current state of lantern-making, the old man did not beat about the bush.

*

LI: Earlier generations, and that includes us, always treated lantern-making as a way of keeping body and soul together, a skill to be respected, and a technique which we competed to perfect and the next generation would take that forward. Not like today when lanterns have been made so ostentatious. Now, if a craft is treated as technology then it can be helped by science and won't be divorced from its time. Ostentation is a matter of "face", and craftsmanship and tradition can be destroyed by "face". Haven't we already destroyed so much? But now people without skills are using "face" to put on a pretence that they've got skills.

So many young people now look down on tradition, and regard crafts as the minnows of the business world. In my view, it would be truer to say that they just don't understand tradition. It's scary to think that a people don't understand their own cultural heritage. If someone has spent their whole life working at something they don't like, it's as if they've been living in a prison, isn't it? Even if you earn money from it, you've just been using it – in today's smart phrase – to build yourself a gilded cage.

I don't understand computers, I can't drive a car, and I've never been in a plane, but I haven't allowed the art of my forebears to be destroyed. I've carried on doing what my elders passed down to me. I've shown the age-old tradition of lantern-making to all those people who understand computers, can drive cars and are always hopping on and off planes.

I don't have the money to buy myself a gold coffin, but others can go to heaven taking with them memories of lanterns which I made for them!

*

Listening to old Mr Li's words, I reflected that as children we had all been educated by the Communist Party and "tamed" into sacrificing ourselves for our nation. Why had this education never produced the tenacity of this man's love for his country and his people? Why had the young generation, brought up to put the public good before private profit and others before themselves, turned out so selfish? Surely five thousand years of popular culture could withstand fifty years of brainwashing and a few hundred years of Western gods?

Li Guisheng's "officially arranged" pupil, Gu Yeliang, had apparently bucked the current trend for money worship. Gu, a man in his forties, told us his story.

*

GU: I started to learn lantern-making with another master at the age of eight. At the Chinese New Year, I would go with my family to set up a stall and sell the lanterns. At the beginning of the eighties, when the Confucian Temple lantern market first reopened, traders gathered on one street to sell them. The stall spaces were not fixed, so everyone arrived the night before to grab a space for their stall the next day. On New Year's Eve I took it in turns with the family to do my stint. I could see other people having family parties while I spent all night looking after the stall in the market. But that year, our family made 500 or 600 yuan from selling lanterns.

My grandfather taught me a nursery rhyme that was popular then: "*Come out and play with a lantern, kid. Never mind your red and green party clothes, just come with a red candle!*" My father also used to say that when he was little, children got just as much pleasure out of lanterns as they did from firecrackers, new clothes and new hats. Every year, the excitement of those dazzling lanterns made them happy for ages. But nowadays, old Nanjingers sigh sadly: "Every year the different varieties of lanterns get fewer!"

People don't realise that there are twenty-one different steps in making even a simple water-lily lantern. You work for a whole year, and you don't earn much from it. I come from a lantern-making family, and I started to learn at a very young age, but now it's got to my son's generation, and they don't want to learn! A few years ago, most of the paper lantern-makers lived in the area to the east and west of the Confucian Temple main gate. There were about 260 of us. We all worked together, and were friends, and met up socially. We were moved on because of redevelopment, and now we're all scattered. Who's going to spend thirty or forty minutes on a bus carrying their bags and packages to meet up? In the whole of Nanjing there are still 110 or so people who can make lanterns, most of them in their forties, but there are fewer and fewer lanterns made with traditional bamboo strips and paper and paste. The market is full of blown plastic, factory-made lanterns.

There used to be more than three hundred kinds of lanterns, but now there are only around twenty or so left. Only artists in their eighties and nineties know how to make lion, aeroplane and unicorn lanterns. We've known for a long time that the skills might die out. I only employ twenty or so lantern-makers here.

*

But Mr Gu, who is also a People's Congress representative, is like millions of Chinese of his generation in that he doesn't spend his time complaining that things are not what they used to be. He thinks anything is possible, and he doesn't believe it's too late. He wants to set up a museum to showcase the whole range of Qin Huai lantern art and to have a big lantern festival to nurture the tradition of folk lanterns. He also wants to provide training in lantern-making. "If there are people out of work, they just need to be willing to learn, and we would be happy to teach them the secrets of making lanterns."

I wanted to find out more about the generational differences between master and pupil lantern-maker.

*

XINRAN: Mr Gu, how well do you understand your teacher, Master Li Guisheng?

GU: How should I put this? When I became his pupil, I was not related to him, and I didn't go cap in hand asking to study under him. Instead, government officials were kind enough to bring us together. After the Gang of Four were smashed in 1976, the city government permitted some of us artists to make and sell lanterns for ourselves at the Confucian Temple market. In 1984, a lantern-makers association was set up in Nanjing, and Mr Li was its head. There were twenty-four members, and I was the only young one. That year we had no idea whether there would be a second or a third festival for Qin Huai or Jin Ling lanterns. I designed and made up some new lanterns and when the head of the Cultural Office saw them, he asked: "Who made those lanterns?" He was told: "Young Gu made them." "Call him here." Then he said to me: "You're an able young man, go and present yourself to Master Li Guisheng as his pupil and learn everything you can from him."

XINRAN: Did he first ask Master Li if this was agreeable to him?

GU: No, he didn't. A cadre's word was law – we all knew that! Besides, my teacher was worried about not having a successor. I could tell he was really pleased at this sort of "government interference".

226

XINRAN: So I suppose you know a lot more about Li Guisheng's life story than anyone else?

GU: Well, yes – a bit more than most people anyway. Actually he's always been very reluctant to talk about it, because he says people always put a modern interpretation on things which happened in the past, and that's miles from the truth. He's always said that the only reason he learned lantern-making was because his family was poor, and it was just a way of keeping body and soul together. When he was learning, no one talked about it as an art form or anything. Learning the craft the old folks in his family passed on to him was just as natural to him as the sun rising in the east and setting in the west. In those days, he says, no one thought about it. It was just a matter of having some craftsmanship and some skill, and using them to earn a bit of money. As for "folk culture" and "folk art", carrying forward and developing cultural traditions and all that, he was clueless. He only read about it later in articles written on him. Yet I know he takes such pains with the artistic side of lantern-making, and he's such a good guide that when we make something new, we run it past him.

XINRAN: So what made you take up lantern-making?

GU: It was because my father made lanterns too. Our house used to be piled high inside and out with lanterns we had made during the year, waiting to be sold at the New Year festival. We had all kinds of lanterns, but I never got excited about them until one day when I heard that the city government of Nanjing had taken a Li Guisheng unicorn lantern with them on a visit to Japan and received two colour televisions in exchange for that one lantern! I thought that certainly had more of a future than peddling lanterns in the market! I may have been little but I had big ideas.

XINRAN: Just now your teacher told me how worried he was about the art of lantern-making dying out. What do you feel about that?

GU: He's right to an extent. Very few people are taking it up these days. The way I look at it is this: to ensure the continuation of Qin Huai lanterns, we first have to preserve the craftsmanship used in their manufacture, and record the way the old people did it. I've already proposed that the government should set up a lantern museum, to display the craftsmanship and allow an exchange of academic knowledge. We could attract public attention and engage people's interest by means of hands-on workshops and other things. We could divide up the 1,700 years of lantern-making history into separate chunks – from the Western Han dynasty through the Tang dynasty, the Mongols, the Ming and the Qing, to the Republic of 1911, and finally our People's Republic – and display to everyone examples of work from each period, as well as the lantern-making tools. Second, there should be a training school attached, providing a sort of patriotic education, and giving children the chance to understand this folk craft. International academic exchanges could be organised to link up lantern-making with folk customs overseas. We've been to Germany to teach classes, and we're off to England soon. Then we'll be going to other European countries to link up with folk artists there. In Nanjing we ought to develop the lantern festivals more, so as to attract Chinese and overseas visitors to the home of lantern-making.

XINRAN: I believe that the art of lantern-making is extremely precious – to Nanjing, to China, indeed to the entire world. But how do you envisage the transition from the primitive workshops in which they are currently made to the scenario you've just described to me? Who do you think will pave the way to the future? Is this something you lantern-makers will fight for on your own? Or do you need the government's help? Or international support?

GU: Ordinary artists don't have the financial resources to fight this battle on their own. A museum like this would need 3,000 square metres of space, and would cost at the very least 2 to 3 million yuan. Who's going to stump up that amount? It needs to be the government, or it could be a joint investment by businesses. The government could own the building, investors could fit it all out, and we artists could contribute the materials we have collected down the years and our techniques. We could share the profits, as we would share the risks. The thing is we mustn't lose sight of the popular characteristics and traditional style of lantern-making. Otherwise it would be meaningless.

And if we could publish some books describing exactly how lanterns are made, with illustrations, introducing each separate technique – for instance the twenty-one steps needed to make a water-lily lantern – then when we're dead and gone, at least we can give these books to the next generation as a permanent record, as a way of handing on the Qin Huai folk culture. That's the way I see it.

XINRAN: You spoke just now about your hopes of building on the techniques and craftsmanship of the older generation as you develop the art of lantern-making. Can you tell us what you feel are the main differences between you and them?

GU: I would say there are a few differences. Back then, they made lanterns in order to keep body and soul together, whereas we do it more out of interest in and enjoyment of a cultural tradition.

Qin Huai lanterns are a form of festival folk art. Festival folk art can be divided into the static and the dynamic, and Qin Huai lanterns are a static form.

If we compare the materials used now with thirty years ago, there have been major changes and innovations: wire has replaced bamboo strips, and silk has replaced coloured paper. In the old days, all lanterns were made of paper. If you hang a paper lantern outside, it's useless as soon as it rains. We use modern materials and modern techniques – what we're making are the same as traditional Qin Huai lanterns, but you can hang them outside for four or five years and they're still fine. Old-style lantern shapes like aeroplane and lion lanterns play a less important role, and recently dip-dyeing has become popular, so that lanterns in new water-lily and lotus shapes, and pineapples and so on, have gradually become the main decorative lanterns at festivals and on holidays.

There are administrative changes as well. With the older generation it was usually the head of the family who ran the business. Lantern-making has always been run as a single-family craft, and working methods are still very primitive. But now we're experimenting with cooperative production methods, with a production line. This should increase our output and improve the quality of the lanterns too.

And now I have a few questions, but I don't know if I can ask them.

XINRAN: For the future of lanterns, ask away!

GU: You live and work abroad. In your view, do foreigners like Qin Huai lanterns? Are young overseas Chinese interested in learning this folk art?

XINRAN: At the moment, I don't know what answer they would give to those questions. But I believe that many foreigners really like Chinese folk culture. Just like you said, folk culture belongs to the world. My book will take your questions to my readers, my listeners and my friends. I hope that more and more visitors to Nanjing will provide the answers to your questions through their interest in Qin Huai lanterns.

8

Across Mountain and Grassland: A Witness to the Long March

Mr and Mrs Changzheng, in PLA uniform, in their wedding photo, 1947.

Renewal of their wedding vows, 1997.

MR CHANGZHENG, born in 1916, a witness to the Long March, *interviewed in Beijing, capital of China. Mr Changzheng joined the Red Army when he was a teenager, set off on the Long March in 1934 and lost many of his comrades along the way. He describes the hunger and hardship, and how they crossed the Snow Mountains and walked through the "marshes of death". He cannot understand the new generation questioning the Long March. He and his wife have been married for almost sixty years and have five children; one of their grandchildren is in England.*

2006 was the seventieth anniversary of the Long March of the Chinese Peasants and Workers Red Army, and once again the question of whether the Long March really happened became a matter of fierce debate.

I was born into a military family – both my parents spent their lives in the army. Stories about the Long March surrounded me, from the family histories of the senior officers on my father's side, to the stories of my childhood schoolfriends' parents and grandparents, to the history books in my classroom. Then there was the obligatory Long March Memorial Day every five years. It never occurred to me to doubt the existence of the Long March just as I never doubted records of my own life's milestones. However, when, in my early twenties, I began to search for my own identity and to trace our national identity through history, I got differing accounts of the same events – even the people involved, and the places and dates on which they occurred. Faced with these confusing "re-recordings" of history, I began to investigate the truth or falsehood of what I had believed.

The most interesting doubts I have heard concern the following three questions:

1. Was the Long March really 25,000 li* long?
2. What was Mao Zedong's involvement in the Long March?
3. Was the "Long March to resist Japan in north China" a policy of the Chinese Communist Party at that time?

1. *Was the Long March really 25,000 li long?*

Having visited a number of Red Army fighters and Party historians of the

---

* 12,500 kilometres/8,000 miles.

older generation, and the new generation of researchers into Chinese history, I heard differing views expressed.

Most of the witnesses I interviewed believed that it was 25,000 li long, or even more. Old army chiefs said that they had marched back and forth, and made a number of long detours. After leaving the Central Soviet Area* in Jiangxi, no one knew where to go. It was not like the way things are currently presented, with leaders, plans and directions. In October 1933, the Guomindang (GMD) mobilised nearly a million troops to attack each of the rural base areas held by the Chinese Communist Party (CCP), and another half-million to carry out a key attack against the Central Soviet Area. CCP chief Bo Gu (real name Qin Bangxian) decided to adopt the proposal of Li De (the German Otto Braun, a military advisor sent by the Comintern)† and make this into a decisive struggle between the GMD and the CCP. They decided on a pre-emptive strike against the GMD and committed the entire Red Army to a full onslaught. But there were only around 100,000 regulars in the Central Soviet Area together with a few tens of thousands of guerrilla troops, and these were comprehensively routed soon after the attack began. On 10 October 1934, as the Long March was about to begin, the Central Red Army was by no means clear about its destination, and even after they had left, most of the troops were none the wiser. They simply set off in blind flight.

Soldiers who had participated told me: "We zigzagged back and forth along many different routes and constantly backtracked. We did this to confuse the enemy, so that they would not guess our route, especially in January 1935, after the Red Army had captured Zunyi [in the south] and the CCP Central Committee had called the Enlarged Politburo Conference." The Zunyi Conference stripped Bo Gu and Li De of their leadership powers

---

* The Central Soviet Area, also known as the Jiangxi Soviet, was an independent government established by the Chinese Communist Party in Jiangxi province in southeastern China, 1931–34.

† Li De was the Chinese name given to Otto Braun, the German advisor sent by the Communist International to advise the Chinese Communist Party in 1934. Later that year, Braun, Zhou Enlai and Bo Gu became the leaders of the early First Front Army and made all decisions, despite opposition to them and their tactics from revolutionary leaders Mao Zedong and Peng Dehuai. Much of the Communist Army was destroyed due to Braun's doctrine of direct attacks on the far larger and better-equipped GMD Army.

and resolved that Zhang Wentian would take over from Bo Gu his responsibility for Party and political affairs, and Zhou Enlai would become military commander, with Mao Zedong as second in command. (Shortly thereafter, the military triumvirate of Zhou Enlai, Mao Zedong and Wang Jiaxiang was formed.) From then on, Red Army troops used outflanking tactics on their march westward, many of them crossing the Chishui River four times and the Daxue Mountains two or three times. In October 1935, the Central Red Army, making its way north alone, arrived at the town of Wuqi Zhen, now called Wuqi county, in Shaanxi province. It was the first to complete the Long March. The Second Front Army, formed at a later stage of the Long March in 1935, made a journey of nearly 20,000 li, joining up in 1936 with the First and Fourth Front Armies at Jiangtai Fort in Jingning county, Gansu (now Ningxia) province. Subsequently, Zhang Guotao, who opposed the Central Committee's "Northward Route", led the Fourth Front Army southward at the end of 1936, renaming it the West Route Army. Zhang Guotao imagined he could break through to the Soviet Union but in the course of a long and arduous trek suffered disastrous losses at the hands of local warlord Ma Bufang's Hui Muslim troops. They dared not stop to rest, and many died of exhaustion. Eventually the entire army was annihilated, and there were only 436 survivors.

Long March scholars say that it is entirely possible that the total distance was 25,000 li. Their reasons include the fact that the People's Liberation Army was not simply formed of the Red Army, the Eighth Route Army and the new Fourth Army, but was formed out of an amalgamation of diverse local and national minority armies and remnants of the GMD who surrendered and came over to the other side. So, they argue, the concept of the Long March should not be taken as limited to the route taken by the three main Red Army forces: the Central Red Army, that is the First Front Army; the Second Front Army, formed of the Second and Sixth Red Army Corps combined; and the Fourth Red Army on its own (there was at that time no Third Army). Instead, the concept and the distance of the Long March should also cover all subsidiary marches made, by the 25th Army and the Fifth and Sixth Red Army Corps and other troops.

2. *What was Mao Zedong's involvement in the Long March?*

I was very young at the time of the Cultural Revolution, but I remember seeing an old academic standing on a platform being "struggled against" and nearly beaten to death by Red Guards for spreading the "vile rumour" that the Long March had not been led by Mao Zedong. I don't know if the professor escaped with his life, but his "crime" often recurred in my thoughts. Why would he dare to say that the glorious achievement of the Long March had not been led by Mao Zedong? During my years as a reporter in search of the real China, this question came into ever sharper focus as I discovered more. Academics and others had been denounced by Red Guards for questioning what were almost accepted as "unalterable" historical facts, for example that Mao Zedong had led the Long March. However, if what that professor said was true, then what was Mao Zedong's involvement in the Long March? In recent years, memoirs, released by China's "opening up" reforms, have appeared which shed fresh light.

Mao Zedong's bodyguard at that time was Wu Jiqing. In 1983, Jiangxi People's Press published his memoirs, *At Mao Zedong's Side*, in which he recalls not being able to commandeer supplies when the Long March set off because Mao Zedong's name did not appear on the Central Committee's list of columns or formations. Wu Xiuquan, Li De's Russian interpreter, in his *Story of My Life*, published by PLA Press in 1984, writes: "At the beginning, they planned to leave Mao Zedong behind, and had actually expelled him from the core leadership of the Central Committee and sent him off to do investigative work."

Another bodyguard, Chen Changfeng, in his *With Chairman Mao on the Long March* (PLA Literature and Arts Press, 1986), records: "From the Gannan Conference of 1931 to the start of the Long March in October 1934, Mao Zedong was in a very difficult position. Even though he was Chair of the Central Government of the Chinese Soviet Republic, he was in very adverse circumstances, subject to continuous criticism and unjust treatment. He made many proposals which proved correct and effective, but which were condemned as 'ultra-empiricist', 'taking the rich peasant line', 'conservative retreating' and 'right-wing opportunism'. Within a short time, he was even stripped of his job."

However, from the 1993 *Memoirs of Kang Keqing* comes the following extract: "He [Zhu De] paced the room, and then came over to say to me in a low voice: 'They've now decided to let Mao Zedong come. Our only hope is to have him with us.' I asked about Chen Yi, and he shook his head: 'It's already been decided that he should stay in the Soviet Area to carry on the struggle, and that decision can't be changed.'"

Finally, while conducting these interviews in China, I heard this report:

"Xinhua Network, Nanchang, 8 August 2006. Chinese Communist Party historians have now publicly confirmed the following: the first list of Long March participants did not include Mao Zedong's name. When key decisions were taken in September 1934 about which cadres should go and which should stay, Bo Gu and Li De, who were the decision-makers, were at first against allowing Mao Zedong to set off with the Central Committee and the main forces of the Red Army, and in the middle of September dispatched Mao to do investigative work. On the eve of the Long March, whether Mao should stay or go was not merely a matter of his individual safety, but was also connected to the fate of the CCP and the Red Army. Mao Zedong only joined the Long March after Zhou Enlai had argued strongly in his favour, and succeeded in persuading Bo Gu and Li De."

3. Was the "Long March to resist Japan in north China" a policy of the Chinese Communist Party at that time?

That the "Long March to resist Japan in north China" was a Chinese Communist Party policy became an immutable tenet both of my school books and of media propaganda, and in fact was a source of national pride to generations of young Communist Party members. However, I later realised that where "north China" was concerned there was a difference between north-east and north-west, and the Japanese came south from the north-east, while the Long March of 1934–6 went to Shaanxi province in the north-west.

On the night of 7 July 1937, the Marco Polo Bridge (Lugouqiao) incident occurred just south-west of Beijing. All-out war broke out as Japan launched a full-scale invasion of China. On 17 July, Chiang Kai-shek, the head of the Guomindang's military committee, issued the Lushan Declaration: "Once war breaks out, every person, young or old, in the north or in the south, must take up the responsibility of resisting Japan and defending our homeland." On 12 December 1937, 50,000 Japanese troops entered Nanjing, capital of the eastern province of Jiangsu, the then headquarters of GMD resistance against Japan, and began the week-long Great Massacre in which around 300,000 Nanjing troops and civilians were killed. It took until the spring of 1938 for the Japanese Army to advance to the western part of Shanxi province, and by the end of that year they had reached the riverbank opposite northern Shaanxi, the neighbouring province, although they could not muster the strength to cross the Yellow River.

Looked at from another angle, the aim of the "Long March to resist Japan in north China" was to allow CCP members to rest and recoup their strength, and provided a reliably safe and self-sufficient base area in the north-west for the armed resistance against Japan which came later. This, I believe, was one of the reasons why, in the years after 1940, the CCP was able gradually to become the main force in China resisting Japan.

In 1940, the Eighth Route Army under General Peng Dehuai launched the Hundred Regiments Offensive against 40,000 Japanese and their puppet troops, resulting in losses for the Japanese of over 20,000; in 1941, the GMD's General Xue Yue, who had already inflicted heavy losses on the Red Army, annihilated 50,000 Japanese in the Third Changsha Campaign. These victories boosted the morale of the Chinese in their struggle against the Japanese invaders, and there was a gradual increase in strength of other forces not under direct control of either the CCP or the GMD, for instance the Mongolian Anti-Japanese Guerrilla Forces.

Nonetheless, Mao Zedong was most unhappy with Peng Dehuai's Hundred Regiments Offensive because, as a result, the Japanese invaders turned their attentions to the rear, where hitherto they had been militarily weak – that part of north China controlled by the CCP. The Japanese countered the CCP forces' guerrilla tactics, cutting the latter off from local militia, by means of the old imperial Neighbourhood Administrative System, tightening local government controls over the population. In order to restrict Eighth Route Army activity, they established areas of no-man's-land and adopted a triple scorched-earth policy of "Kill All, Burn All and Loot All". The result was a massacre of soldiers and civilians alike in north China. The Eighth Route Army suffered severe losses; the commander of its HQ, Zuo Quan, lost his life, while Deputy Chief of Staff Peng Dehuai made a daring breakout of the encirclement and the Eighth Route Army was forced to withdraw from north China.

Different factions may rehash the motives for the Long March for their own political ends, but its results are not in dispute: in the process of the Long March and all the benefits which resulted from it, the CCP acquired a newly formed self-confidence, put its organisation on a firm footing and had the time to train up regular army units. All the People's Republic of China's main leaders, like Mao Zedong, Zhou Enlai, Liu Shaoqi, Zhu De, Chen Yun and Deng Xiaoping, were on the Long March, as were nine of the army's ten field marshals, the exception being Chen Yi.

During the two years of the Long March, various forces that make up the Red Army fought their way through fourteen provinces, and covered a total distance of around 25,000 li. They crossed a number of remote regions inhabited by national minorities as well as Han Chinese, and faced natural hazards such as great rivers, snow-capped mountains and grasslands, they also evaded encirclement by hundreds of thousands of GMD and local armies, and succeeded in avoiding splits caused by the struggles between the Mao and Bo Gu factions, and between the First Front Army and Zhang Guotao. Out of it a new nucleus of CCP leaders, with Mao Zedong at their head, was gradually formed.

In August 1980, Deng Xiaoping said in an interview with the Italian reporter Oriana Fallaci: "The Zunyi Conference of 1935, called during the famous Long March, established the leadership position of Comrade Mao Zedong within the Party and the army. This marked the formation of the first real leadership of the CCP. Previous leadership structures had been both immature and unstable."

And when Deng Xiaoping's daughter, Maomao, asked her father what the Long March had been like, he replied: "We kept marching!" I believe that this is the instinctive, most truthful and commonest view of the Long March.

One of my ambitions was to find a Red Army survivor of the Long March who had "gone the distance". I was looking for someone who had done it on foot, not a general who had ridden the route on horseback. This was no easy task – of the tens of thousands who had taken part, few were still alive, while even fewer had done the whole march.

I was very lucky. Yan, a Chinese girl studying in the UK, came to see me asking for my help in drawing up a bibliography on Chinese history and culture for her dissertation. When she heard me talk about *China Witness*, and say that I was looking for an old soldier who had done the entire Long March, she asked, quite forcefully, that I go and interview her ninety-year-old maternal grandfather, who had done just that. "I want people to know what my grandfather contributed and what he went through," she said. "Some people think he's just a political stooge, who gives patriotic lectures for the Party, but I know that he does it because he really believes in it. At the beginning, so many Long Marchers deserted from the Red Army, but he wasn't like that, he marched on to the end." Not wanting to let this young woman down, we pencilled him in as a possible interviewee.

On 2 September 2006, we visited Yan's grandfather in Beijing. I chatted to the old man and his wife, and then their two daughters, the eldest one Yan's mother. Mr Changzheng was an imposing figure, with a round face and rosy cheeks. He talked volubly and punctured our interview with bursts of laughter and occasional renderings of snatches of revolutionary songs from his youth. No wonder people say that music is one of the repositories of memory.

I had not had enough time to do background research on the old soldier, and so I started by putting the safest and commonest Chinese question.

*

XINRAN: Have you eaten?

CHANGZHENG: Yes, I have.

XINRAN: What did you have to eat today?

CHANGZHENG: I had noodles – Beijing noodles with minced pork and bean sauce.

XINRAN: What is your favourite food?

CHANGZHENG: I eat anything.

XINRAN: So what was your favourite food as a child?

CHANGZHENG: As a child? I am from the north of Sichuan province. When I was a child, we were poor, and I didn't get a lot to eat.

XINRAN: Could you tell me how old you are, sir?

CHANGZHENG: On 10 November this year, I'll be ninety-one years old. I was born in 1916, in the mountains of northern Sichuan.

XINRAN: Did you go to school?

CHANGZHENG: When I was in Sichuan I did. I got a year and a half of primary school. My school was far from my home and the teacher was very strict. If you didn't have your satchel on straight, he hit you on the back of the hand. If you didn't know your characters, he hit you on the back of the hand. If you were disruptive, you had to go up to the teacher, stick out your backside and he would give you a hiding. I was terrified, and after a year and a half of this, I ran away from home and never went back. At home, I used to cut the grass and collect firewood. When I was thirteen, the Red Army came to my village. The head of a Red Army Propaganda Unit, from Henan, came to the house and tried to recruit me. But I didn't know anything about the Red Army. I knew that the GMD swore at you and knocked you about, but I didn't know what the Red Army was like, so I couldn't make up my mind. He came three times, and after the third time, he took me to the local town to have a look. The Red Army had a company of machine-gunners, they showed me the machine guns, and then they gave me a bowl of rice, with meat too. In the north of Sichuan, we only ate meat at the Chinese New Year.

I went home and told my mother, "They're not bad, the Red Army, I saw their machine guns, they have rice to eat, and meat too, I'd like to join up." My mother didn't stop me so at the age of thirteen, I joined the Red Army, and went away with them.

XINRAN: How many were there in your family then?

CHANGZHENG: My older sister, my younger brother, my younger sister and me, that made four.

XINRAN: You said your family was poor. Just how poor were they?

CHANGZHENG: We didn't have enough food. All we thought about every day was eating, and it was because we could never eat our fill that I told my mother I wanted to join the Red Army. They had food, and so my mother agreed.

When I first joined up – that was 1929 – they didn't make me fight, and so I didn't. When I was fifteen, I started fighting. The head of the Propaganda Unit had said: "Your schoolmates and the friends you play with, you can get them to join up too." So I started talking to them about it, and in the end a new company was set up from our village. When I first started fighting, I didn't have a gun, or any real weapon at all. So we made sticks into martial arts spears, by tying big knives onto the end. When we went into battle that time, we were two Red Army companies, and the GMD had one battalion. In we charged, killed and killed, and wiped out the whole battalion. That was my first battle.

XINRAN: Were you afraid? Afraid of the blood, getting wounded, of death?

CHANGZHENG: No, I wasn't afraid. I was a brave lad, and besides, there were lots of us, not just one or two, so I wasn't afraid. After that battle, they issued us with a gun each. Then we started fighting all over the place. We criss-crossed Sichuan, back and forth, slaughtering the enemy at our gates. Then we went to Jiuzhaigou. We were billeted with the local peasants, and I began to run a high fever. Then the GMD bombers came, and the cottage I was in took a direct hit. It gave me such a fright that the malaria left me, and I was well again!

XINRAN: When did you join the Long March?

CHANGZHENG: In 1934, I set off from my home.

XINRAN: Did you cross the Ludian Bridge [about 15 km south-west of Beijing] while you were on the Long March?

CHANGZHENG: Of course I did. I was carrying a big trunk on my shoulder as we marched, so crossing the bridge was really difficult. It had no guard rails, so I found walking across it really hard. I could see some of the people in front were going to fall, and I wanted to go and help them, but my chief wouldn't let me. He told us on no account to start running or it would be chaos and many more people would fall in. Some of my mates fell in, it was really sad.

We couldn't travel by day, only by night. Once we heard that two generals and their troops had dropped behind. The two generals were the only survivors of an attack. They went up a mountain, and found a temple, and one knelt on the ground by the temple wall and supported the other on his shoulders. Then the one on the top pulled the bottom one up, and the two generals hid behind the big Bodhisattva on the temple wall. When the worshippers had finished burning their incense and gone, they used the incense fire to keep warm. They were smart, they caught up with the rest of the unit after that.

XINRAN: Did you know that, in the West, some people say that a lot of the Red Army didn't do the Long March?

CHANGZHENG: That's rubbish. All of the Red Army regular troops joined the Long March. Some got separated from the rest along the route, or got lost, or died or just disappeared.*

XINRAN: How many lost their lives during the Long March?

CHANGZHENG: The First, Second and Fourth Front Armies were involved, and each one lost many soldiers, but I don't know exactly how many. After it was over, people said that out of hundreds of thousands only 30,000 were left. I can't be more precise on the numbers than that, I don't think anyone can be.

XINRAN: Did any close comrades of yours die on the Long March, and if so, did you see it with your own eyes?

CHANGZHENG: Of course I did. Every survivor of the Long March lost comrades. A young cousin of mine, he carried arms and ammunition, he was always in the front line when we charged. He didn't die in battle, no, he

---

* In fact, some units did not participate in the Long March, but of course a single soldier could not know what was happening in detail to the whole army.

died on the march. When I went back home, his wife asked, where is he? He died ages ago, I said, and she cried . . .

XINRAN: Some people also believe that the distance wasn't as great as the 25,000 li that we all say nowadays. You participated, so you must know the truth.

CHANGZHENG: If you add up how much everyone did, it definitely was. In some places, we retraced our steps several times, we even crossed the mountains and the grasslands three times. The amount we actually walked really was that far, and the proof of it is the damage I suffered to my feet. Lots of those who survived were left with injured legs and feet like this. Here, look.

*

And I saw a pair of feet which it's hard to find words to describe: the misshapen soles were a mass of scars, and his feet looked as if they were made up of odd bits of skin of different ages.

*

CHANGZHENG: Why did we do the mountains and the grasslands three times? Well, Zhang Guotao didn't go along with the Central Committee leaders, he took the Fourth Front Army away on their own. The GMD chased us, we ran, and that was why we ended up crossing the mountains and grasslands three times. It was a terrible experience, dreadful, something you could never forget in your whole life!

We went through Lazi Kou Pass and got to Jiajing Mountain. It was sunny down below, but the higher we climbed, the more fiercely the wind blew. It was raining too, and the rain was mixed with hail, and as soon as we reached the mountain top, it started to get unbearably cold. We had our hats on – if those big hailstones smashed onto your head, they really hurt. Climbing was hard work for all of us, and then we had to go down again, and that was harder than going up. Some of our comrades didn't take enough care going down, and they rolled over the edge and died! When I think back to all that, it makes me really, really sad. We never knew who would be next. There was an old folk song about Jiajing Mountain, which went:

> *Mount Jiajing, Mount Jiajing,*
> *Where no birds fly,*
> *No monkeys can climb it,*
> *Only Immortals come down to the world from it.*

Jiajing Mountain is four thousand metres above sea level, so we had to be fiercer than the Immortals to climb it. A lot of people died then, because there were no paths on the mountain. We followed animal tracks.

When we crossed the grasslands, we had nothing to eat. Our dried food was all gone, and we had to pull up grass and eat that. When there really was nothing to eat, we ate leather. It was awful, awful, very hard. When it got to night-time, we slept out in the open. Some of our comrades found a mud hole and slept there. They wouldn't wake up in the morning, so they were tied to horses' tails and pulled along. They looked like they were sleepwalking, I saw it with my own eyes.

After the mountains and the grasslands, we started to fight. We hadn't eaten, we hadn't slept properly, and we had to fight, can you believe it? We won that battle too.

So we'd fought well, we got something to eat, and had a sleep, then after that we arrived in Gansu. There we faced another battle on Wuliang Mountain. The GMD had a cavalry division, and on the first day of the battle, my political instructor said to me: "You head up a group and go and reconnoitre." So at night I went to check out the lay of the land. On the second night we took rope ladders and went into the area. The GMD cavalry division were camped up there and we finished them off! After that we went off to Guilin [in the south] and joined up with the First Front Army. That was in 1936, and by then I couldn't tell you how many of us were in a bad way, and a lot of the officers too, it was pitiful. No one looking at us nowadays would have believed that those troops could take the whole of China!

XINRAN: Did you believe it then?

CHANGZHENG: I didn't know a lot about the bigger picture then. Our chiefs treated me well, and wherever we went the poor people treated us well too. I thought that was proof of their common decency. Once we had joined up with the First Front Army, we moved straight off to Yan'an.

XINRAN: Do you know why the Red Army went to Yan'an? Why was Yan'an chosen as a base area?

CHANGZHENG: No one lived in the Great North-West, and the enemy wasn't there either so we could rest and reorganise ourselves. So many had died on the Long March that we had to do that. We had a song:

The struggle is tough,
But we're doing it

> *To build the North-West Base Area.*
> *We'll overcome all difficulties,*
> *We'll beat the enemy,*
> *We'll wipe out the enemy.*

After we moved up to Yan'an, we didn't get support from ordinary people, so we had to shift for ourselves. Yan'an was so poor that not even Chiang Kai-shek [and the GMD] wanted to go and fight there. We started to produce our own food and clothing. Every morning, the troops went off up into the mountains with their hoes to clear the land for planting. The ground was very hard, and some of the vegetation needed two people to dig it out. By day we prepared the ground, and by night we spun and wove cotton. We had a song which went:

> *Till the wastelands, till the wastelands,*
> *The front-line soldiers need food.*
> *Weave cloth, weave cloth,*
> *The front-line soldiers need clothing.*

No one nowadays would believe the hardships we suffered then.

I got an anal boil in Yan'an, which didn't heal properly, so I went to see the Canadian doctor Norman Bethune.* I said I didn't want a general anaesthetic because I would be out for too long. "Not to worry," he said, "I'll operate at eight, and by nine you'll have come round." I was just a soldier but he was very sympathetic: he cured my illness, and reduced the awful pain so I wasn't suffering like before. Many of my comrades were cured by Dr Bethune. He was a good man.

XINRAN: Did you see Mao Zedong in Yan'an?

CHANGZHENG: Back then, the troops saw a lot of the chiefs, so I don't remember exact dates and places. But Mao Zedong came to give a speech to the guards training course, and I can still remember that today. He said: "Your guard duties are extremely important. Now you're guarding the Party Central Committee, and the people of Shaanxi and Gansu, but in the future you'll be guarding the whole of China." At the end of the course, Zhou Enlai came to talk to us too. Once during the course, there was an

---

* Canadian surgeon, b. 1890, Ontario. He joined the Communist Party, after a visit to the Soviet Union, and went to China in 1938 where he became a hero for his dedicated work, and died in 1939.

air raid by thirty or more enemy planes. There were three or four hundred of us and we helped each other into the caves. After we came out, Yan'an had been flattened, and all those poor old people and children had been left without homes.

XINRAN: Can you tell me who you were guarding in Yan'an?

CHANGZHENG: Kang Shien.

XINRAN: Kang Shien? The man who was Deputy Chairman of the State Council in the 1980s and died on 21 April 1995?

CHANGZHENG: Uh-huh.

XINRAN: And when did you leave Yan'an?

CHANGZHENG: There was a call to demobilise, but I thought to myself, what will I do if I go back to the poverty of my home? So I didn't demobilise. I left Yan'an with the rest of the troops and we crossed the Yellow River, fought through the Zhangjiakou Pass, then to the Rehe River, and then we arrived in the north-east, and went to Chengde. Me and my old woman, we married in Jilin, in the north-east, and after we got married we set off with the troops to Tianjin, where our eldest daughter was born.

I remember a huge building in Tianjin which housed a department store and the residence of a big GMD official. Our bombs had destroyed this building. The ordinary people said to us: "Your bombs must have eyes!" After we had taken Tianjin, we went to Shijiazhuang, and then came to Beijing.

XINRAN: Mr Changzheng, can I interrupt you a moment? You say you fought through the Zhangjiakou Pass. What army were you in then?

CHANGZHENG: I was in the PLA, which started off as the Eighth Route Army, but afterwards everything got called the PLA: the Eighth Route Army, the New Fourth Army, and other troops too.

XINRAN: Were you with the Fourth Field Army then? From the places where you fought battles, it sounds like you must have been in Lin Biao's Fourth Field Army.

CHANGZHENG: That's right – the Fourth Field Army.

XINRAN: May I ask you who its chiefs were then?

CHANGZHENG: Generals Wang Ming and Wang Zhen. In Yan'an, it was also General Wang Ming. He was chief when we were clearing new land for cultivation, and he led us to the north-east too.

When the People's Republic of China was established, I attended the founding ceremony in Beijing. There were no trees and paths in front of

Tiananmen Gate then, and I watched from an earth embankment on the west side. After the ceremony was over, I went to the suburb of Dongbeiwang. After that, I got a train to Hankou, then Guangxi, then Vietnam. Then I went to Shanghai, Tianjin, Qiqihar and Manchuria. We had an old army friend who was working there as an official. He asked me if I'd like a trip to the Soviet Union. I said I couldn't possibly go, I was still in army uniform. But then I was sent there anyway. When people found out I'd been in the PLA, they were very nice to me. When their chiefs talked, I couldn't understand a thing, but there was one who spoke Chinese, so I could understand him.

I've been on the move for most of my life, going here and there. I went back with the army to Beijing, then Nanjing, then Zhenjiang. Then I got a civilian job and moved to Tianjin.

XINRAN: When did you leave the army?

CHANGZHENG: In 1956. I got transferred from Tianjin to be a researcher at an oil depot, for what is now Great Wall Lubricants, part of Sinopec. I worked there until I retired. The first time I went to the Daqing oilfield, the first oil well, I said to my boss I'd never seen an oil rig, I'd like to go and look. He said, go ahead. So in the evening, off I went. I was at the base of the oil rig and they gave me a quilt, and I spent all night there, carefully watching the drilling. The Daqing oilfield really pulled out all the stops for China. If it hadn't been for Daqing, we couldn't have run our vehicles, or developed our industries. The Americans, the British, even the Soviets had wanted to get a stranglehold on us then. Times were really hard, but we broke through. Just as in the grasslands, we never thought how rosy life would be now, so in the fifties, who would have imagined we would have televisions and fridges? At that time, our idea of a good Western meal was potatoes and roast beef from the Soviet Union!

XINRAN: How did you get to know your wife?

CHANGZHENG: We met in the north-east. After we got there, almost all my army mates found themselves partners and married, and so they introduced me to her. That was 1947. The day we were married, I had just arrived at her parents' house when someone shouted: "The planes, the planes are coming!"* They pulled me into the house and we dashed for the cellar, and that was where we got married, with planes flying overhead,

---

* Guomindang planes.

dropping bombs on us. My wife had no wedding dress, we had absolutely nothing. But we've never been parted.

XINRAN: How many children have you got?

CHANGZHENG: Five. Our eldest daughter, then a second daughter, then a son, then a third daughter, then our youngest son.

XINRAN: How do your children's lives compare to yours when you were young?

CHANGZHENG: I don't know. I'm just an army man. It's mainly been my wife who's done all the work. She brought all our kids up.

XINRAN: Do you argue? Are there things you fight about?

CHANGZHENG: We don't fight about anything. She knows how I suffered on the Long March, and the health problems it left me with, and she's very good to me. Now that I'm old, she does everything for me. She gets the food, she's the buyer, the phone-answerer, the messenger, the nurse, the cook, and so on and so on. She has a lot to cope with.

XINRAN: From what I hear, you haven't been idle since you retired, you still give patriotic education classes. Isn't that right?

CHANGZHENG: Yes, that's right. I've taught in primary, secondary, right up to university level – I've lectured at Qinghua University, for instance. I've given more than 430 talks. More than 130,000 people have been at my classes, and I can still remember which schools I've taught at.

XINRAN: Why do you enjoy going to talk to them about your experience?

CHANGZHENG: I'm very concerned about whether or not the next generation understand us. We suffered so much hardship and so many people died. As the new generation grows up, I want them to remember those fallen comrades. They died for us today and they cannot be forgotten.

XINRAN: If your children asked you what were the worst and the happiest things which have happened to you in your life, what would you tell them?

CHANGZHENG: The time when I'm happiest is when I look at my children and grandchildren. That's what makes me happiest. My second daughter has a grandson too, that's my great-grandchild, so the fourth generation has arrived. My childhood may have been hard, but now I'm very fortunate. That's made me think of a song I know. [He begins to sing at the top of his voice]:

> *Our childhood was steeped in the waters of bitterness,*
> *We follow the Red Army to fight all over China. Hey!*

We rush into the forest of guns. Hey!
We run through the rain of bullets. Hey!
We cross the mountains and the grasslands. Hey!
We weave cloth and make clothing. Hey!
We pass our days amid flames and gunpowder smoke. Hey! . . .
Our spirit remains undimmed. Hey!
Our guns will never get old and die. Hey!
New China is springing up.
We're on the road to the Four Modernisations.
Love is everywhere in China
And we will never forget the goodness of the Communist Party. Hey!

XINRAN: You sing well! Do you remember any other songs?

CHANGZHENG: There's "Yellow River":

> *The wind is moaning,*
> *The horses are neighing,*
> *The Yellow River is thundering . . .*
> *The Yellow River is thundering,*
> *Troops laden with weapons charge forward,*
> *So many heroes fighting the Japanese . . .*
> *We're protecting China, protecting the Yellow River,*
> *Protecting China's mountains, protecting China.*

XINRAN: Can your children sing them?

CHANGZHENG: No, they never learned them properly.

XINRAN: You say that things were hard in the past. Your generation suffered so much. What was the worst thing you suffered? And what have you enjoyed most?

CHANGZHENG: It *was* very hard, but it was for our country. The Party and China have looked after us well. You see, when the People's Republic was established, I went to the ceremony. At the Spring Festival every year, I go to the Great Hall of the People. I've been interviewed by reporters from other countries, and by people from the Army Museum. Canadian reporters were here doing an interview. They said to me: "You can't go to Canada, but your photo can go."

XINRAN: Your songs will go to lots of places in the world too, and everyone will read the words of the songs you have just sung.

CHANGZHENG: What a pity they can't hear me sing.

XINRAN: If you could live your life again, how would you live it? Would you choose the same life as before?

CHANGZHENG: Of course I would.

XINRAN: Would you still follow the Communist Party, and suffer all those hardships?

CHANGZHENG: Ha! If I'd known in advance, of course I wouldn't have. But if we hadn't been through all that, would we have peace today? We were fighting every day, so of course everyone suffered. But because of us, China stopped fighting, so it was well worth suffering for. Otherwise our children and grandchildren would go through what we went through as children. China has developed and changed enormously; this sort of development never happened before.

XINRAN: How do you know China has changed so much?

CHANGZHENG: I like to follow the news, I watch the TV news, I read the Party magazine *Qiushi*, and the newspapers – the *Workers News, People's Daily, Beijing News, Beijing Times* and *World of the Elderly*. My eyesight is good, I can read the small print perfectly. The one I like most is *Qiushi*.

XINRAN: Why?

CHANGZHENG: Because it's put out by the Central Committee, and there are a lot of study topics.

XINRAN: Have you told your children and grandchildren stories of when you were young?

CHANGZHENG: Yes, I have. They know most of it. My children and grandchildren come and see me on Saturdays and Sundays. These children of mine all understand how to behave properly.

XINRAN: What kind of people would you like your grandchildren to turn into in the future?

CHANGZHENG: Well, that depends on their abilities.

XINRAN: You're ninety years old now. Do you have any unfulfilled wishes?

CHANGZHENG: Ninety years old . . . No I haven't. My health is quite good, and I go out every day to do morning exercises or to do other things, and everyone says I'll easily live to be over a hundred.

XINRAN: What would you like to do most now? If you had the time and energy?

CHANGZHENG: Keep myself fit. When I go out every day I take my dragon-head walking stick given to me at the Great Hall of the People. I do at least 5,000 paces daily, that's 50,000 paces every ten days. I'm not boasting. To get really fit, live a bit longer, see China change. Those are the things that will make me even happier. I go to bed at nine thirty at night, get up at six and eat breakfast. Once I've eaten I go out and do my exercises and my paces. I told the reporter from the China-Japan Friendship Association: "I did the 25,000 li Long March, and now I've walked a new Long March of 25,000 li."

XINRAN: Do you know where your granddaughter Yanyan is now?

CHANGZHENG: I'm not exactly sure where she is. Sometimes she writes to me.

XINRAN: She's in England.

CHANGZHENG: I had heard but I don't know anything about it. Her granny keeps in touch with what she's doing, I don't.

XINRAN: You say that you saw Chairman Mao. Did you know that many people are saying that Mao made mistakes? Do you agree?

CHANGZHENG: I can tell you that Chairman Mao was a very open-minded man. When we were clearing land for cultivation, he planted vegetables too. When we were tending our vegetables, we saw Chairman Mao in the vegetable garden too. Think of that . . . a chairman, tending his vegetables just like a peasant. He did neglect some things though. He didn't even keep an eye on his wife, Jiang Qing. He used to say: "Women are like the weather – they can't be controlled." But he was a terrific man.

XINRAN: Are the cadres nowadays the same as they were before?

CHANGZHENG: Of course not, they're nothing like they were before. You can see it on the news every day. Cadres nowadays do nothing but "eat, take, extort and demand". In the past, whether they were senior cadres or ordinary cadres, they would be disciplined if they did wrong.

XINRAN: Were cadres in the past as corrupt as they are now?

CHANGZHENG: Very few of them were. I think it's because now they don't have much to worry about, and they have a good standard of living. Some cadres develop the wrong attitude to their work – they do a bit and they think they're great. They guzzle huge dinners and gulp down the liquor – that's something I can't get used to. I was asked to give a lecture at Shanghai University, and they invited me to dinner afterwards. I said, "I'm not eating your food. Thank you for inviting me to speak today. When I was on the Long March, we ate roots and leather, and those hardships and those struggles were what I was talking about today. If I come and eat your banquet, then none of my stories would mean anything, would they?!"

XINRAN: How many survivors of the Long March of your age are there in the world?

CHANGZHENG: If you add together those in Chinese cities and villages, there are reported to be only around two thousand of us in total.

*

I accompanied him to the next-door room where he would take a rest. Changzheng's wife watched his hands gripping the dragon-head walking stick, and said to me: "That walking stick has a radio and an alarm – it has everything. He was given it at the ceremony at the Great Hall of the People. His life has not been easy. I suppose you've seen his feet. So many scars – all of them from the Long March. His life has not been easy, not easy at all." She then sat down for a chat with me.

*

XINRAN: He's just told me how well you look after him. You do the main jobs at home, right?

CHANGZHENG'S WIFE: That's right, I do everything at home myself, I do all the tidying up, I don't need anyone's help.

XINRAN: May I ask how old you are?

CHANGZHENG'S WIFE: I'm seventy-seven. Thirteen years younger than him. We married in the army. I was a soldier too. We married in 1947.

XINRAN: I'd like to ask you, if I may, how you met your husband.

CHANGZHENG'S WIFE: Times were hard back then. Women comrades who had no education, we couldn't think about things like that, so our chiefs did the matchmaking for us! Think of it – a difference of thirteen years between us.

XINRAN: And what did you feel when you first set eyes on him?

CHANGZHENG'S WIFE: It didn't matter what I thought, we had to do what we were told by our chiefs.

XINRAN: Did you have a boyfriend back then?

CHANGZHENG'S WIFE: No.

XINRAN: No?

CHANGZHENG'S WIFE: Well, discipline in the army was very strict, so there was none of that sort of thing. We were in the vehicle unit, we were always on the move so we were always busy.

XINRAN: Where did you join the army?

CHANGZHENG'S WIFE: In Jilin, where my family were.

XINRAN: You joined in 1947?

CHANGZHENG'S WIFE: We were a very poor family. My father, his sister-in-law and his older sister all joined up. After they had joined, my father said to me: "Guiying, you join up too. The good thing is they'll give you your meals." My grandmother disagreed. She said: "You must have seen how hard it is being a soldier. It's no life for a girl! If you're all soldiers and the GMD come, they'll kill our whole family!" My mother didn't want me to go either. But I joined up anyway. I hadn't been in the army long, when my chief introduced me to him. At first I wasn't keen, because when he talked I couldn't understand him.

XINRAN: How many of your age group joined up in that way?

CHANGZHENG'S WIFE: Quite a few. But they checked you very carefully back then. They wouldn't let you in if you were from a rich family. I'd done six years of primary school in the north-east, but then the Japanese devils came, and you couldn't go on at school. Being a soldier was another way of leaving home, wasn't it? So that was how I left my home village.

XINRAN: Your five children, what do they do?

CHANGZHENG'S WIFE: My oldest daughter worked for Great Wall Lubricants, but she's retired now. The second daughter has been in the army for twenty-one years; she's still a doctor in Sichuan. The third was also in Great Wall Lubricants, and is also retired now. The fourth works in Capital Hospital in Beijing, after being in a commune during the Cultural Revolution. The youngest also became a commune member. None of them were wild, like children in some families, they're all very decent. When they were small, I didn't worry about them. I went out to work, and I brought them up too. I was in the army then, and in my position as a cadre, I could get a nanny. Later on, you could take them to work with you. In 1955, there were too many people in the army, and there were economic problems in the country too. There were cuts, and I was made redundant. I couldn't afford the nanny any more, so after that I took care of the children.

XINRAN: What benefits do you get now?

CHANGZHENG'S WIFE: I get money from the National Civil Administration Department, but it's a bit of a problem. After I left my job, I did "army dependents support work" for twenty-five years, but I never got a fen for it, except the last two years, when they paid me a little, twenty yuan a month. I've dedicated myself to the army for my whole life and I've hardly got a thing. The government ought to fix up jobs for ex-army people like me. The National Civil Administration Department has regulations for demobbed soldiers, they pay them a few hundred yuan a month, but no one's said straight out what I should get, so I have no income now. But in any case, we've got my husband's house to live in and the children are very good. Everything's fine and I've nothing to complain about.

I'm an impatient sort of person, and if I want to do something, I'm not worried about it being hard work. The grandchildren phone me and say: "Granny, get yourself someone to help, I'll pay for it." But I can still do it on my own, I don't want a maid. I do all the buying, cooking and cleaning myself and getting someone in won't spare me any worries.

XINRAN: What kind of upbringing did you give your children?

CHANGZHENG'S WIFE: When I was a child we were poor and we had no needle and thread so I had never done needlework. But after I had the children, I did all my own sewing. I got the kids ready for bed and I started work. That meant making everything clean as a whistle, wiping the floor, washing the clothes . . . then I made their clothes. Every winter, the whole family needed two outfits each. I lined the cotton with kapok and slowly stitched it together. When it was done, and nice and clean, then I went to bed. The next evening I did the same again. I didn't take a siesta like everyone else. When we first got a sewing machine, I didn't know how to use it, but I knew I could learn. I practised by sewing bits of rag, old bits of clothes, and kept on going at it, practising on scraps, and that way I taught myself.

XINRAN: There's another question I'd like to ask you. I've visited many couples, but very few husbands have expressed such a high opinion of their wives as yours has. So I'd like to hear what you think about things, since there's a thirteen-year age difference between you. When people get old, they probably think more about what happened in the past, and the further back in the past, the easier it is for them to remember. What part of your life do you think most about? Your childhood, your parents, or the difficulties you had bringing up your children?

CHANGZHENG'S WIFE: I don't have anything I think about, I don't have any views on that.

XINRAN: Do you never think about your mother when you look at other people, and when you look at your children? Don't you think about when you were little?

CHANGZHENG'S WIFE: Oh yes, I do. I was the only girl in the family, and I had two elder brothers and one younger. When I joined the army, girls could earn a bit doing cleaning work. I saved it and bought things for them when I went home. The thing I most regret is that my mother didn't live long enough to enjoy our good fortune. We live well now, but she's not here. I often think of her.

XINRAN: When did you last see her?

CHANGZHENG'S WIFE: I last saw her when she was eighty-three. She died soon after that. I can't bear to think about it. My husband was in the army, and we were a bit better off. I wanted her to come and live with us, but she wouldn't come. She said she was too old-fashioned: since she had a son, it wasn't right to go and live in her daughter's house. My mother had her principles, and she didn't want to be a nuisance. My father worked on the railways and could travel free, so he always used to come and see us, and my mother came several times to fetch him and take him home. But every time she arrived, she'd go straight home with him. Eventually he got too old and retired, and they didn't come any more.

XINRAN: Did you ever hear how they met each other, your mum and dad?

CHANGZHENG'S WIFE: In those days it was all done by the parents. The old folks paired them up – they'd never met before they married. When my mother talked about it sometimes, she was very against that way of doing things.

XINRAN: How did you help your mother when you were a child?

CHANGZHENG'S WIFE: Cooking, putting the cotton wadding into quilts, washing, making quilt covers, that kind of thing. I was always tired when I worked, I was always yawning. My dad said to me: "If you're so tired when you work, you'll never finish such a big quilt. If you don't finish it, what are we going to put on the bed at night?" I didn't pay attention, I carried on very slowly with the wadding. I had so little to eat when I was a kid, I was always hungry, and then I was too tired to work. So my mum gave in, and said I could go and be a soldier and save my life. That was how it was at home.

XINRAN: Have you ever talked to your children about how things were then?

CHANGZHENG'S WIFE: No, I haven't.

XINRAN: Why not?

CHANGZHENG'S WIFE: Because it makes me too sad. Besides, my children have never wasted money or food like other people's children do. They're good kids, they've never given me any cause for worry.

XINRAN: If anyone asked you what was the hardest time of your life, what would you say?

CHANGZHENG'S WIFE: When I was at home, before I joined up, that was the hardest. In order to get that bit of schooling, I had to go out weeding in the heat of the day in the summer. I didn't want to go. My mother said: "You're doing it to go to school, aren't you?" So then I went. In those days, boys got sent to school, but no one bothered about the girls. My mother was a capable woman, she reared pigs and sold them, and kept chickens. I remember when I was a kid, before Liberation, there were bandits, they were terrible, scared us to death. We lived in a small house and the bandits tried to get inside. The door was shut and they were banging away on it, which was frightening in the middle of the night. We were so poor then that we didn't even eat dumplings at New Year. I remember when I was a kid, the Japanese devils came and killed the cattle. They hung their hides up outside, and they got covered in flies, but some people still ate the scraps of meat left on them. If pigs and chickens died, no one cared, you ate them because, if you didn't, you starved.

XINRAN: Your husband told us earlier what a hard time he'd had. Has he ever talked to you about it?

CHANGZHENG'S WIFE: Sometimes about the Long March. Actually, he doesn't need to say anything – you saw his feet, his toenails. The veins are all black and the toes are thickened, all from walking. I was a soldier too, so I know what he went through, and it was all for China.

XINRAN: Was it worth giving all those years of his life, do you think?

CHANGZHENG'S WIFE: Oh yes. If that generation hadn't made the sacrifice, and we still had what Chairman Mao called the "three mountains" of feudalism, imperialism and the GMD on our backs, then where would we be today? I think it was definitely worth it.

XINRAN: Do you think that young people today understand what your generation went through and what you did?

CHANGZHENG'S WIFE: Some do, but some don't.

XINRAN: Is there anything else you'd like to tell me? If you had your life again, would you still set up a family with Mr Changzheng?

CHANGZHENG'S WIFE: My old man's OK, he's a good man. We've never fought about things, we get on really well. We only fought once. It was in Guangxi, and his office was in our house. Our eldest daughter was squabbling with a friend and he wanted to shout at them, but I wouldn't let him. We only fought that once, and it never happened again. I must have been twenty-two then. In 1997 we had our fiftieth wedding anniversary, and next year it's our diamond anniversary. It's hard to believe we'll have been together sixty years.

XINRAN: You can see his rosy cheeks, and he's in good voice and good heart. He's a credit to you.

*

I was not able to find here the answers to the questions I had been asking about the Long March. If we were lucky and these old people lasted until there was real freedom of speech in China, then we might really be able to prove or disprove some of the stories of the past. But perhaps it was already too late, the old had taken the "real yesterdays" away with them, and that was another loss to the Chinese people.

But the "marital Long March" of these old Red Army soldiers was a success which led me onward.

9

Savouring Her Blessings after Trials and Tribulations: The Woman General Born in America

日本年 拍了美国芝加哥,
吶唷郅多年

Chicago, 1933.

With General Phoebe and her husband, Louis, Beijing, 2006.

GENERAL PHOEBE, female general, born in 1930, and her husband, Louis, former Secretary to the Mayor of Shanghai, *interviewed in Beijing, capital of China. General Phoebe was born in Columbus, Ohio, and moved back to China with her parents, both academics, before the war with the Japanese. She joined the PLA in 1949 as an instructor at the Foreign Languages Institute, and was part of a secret unit for "foreign relations". She was head of the Institute before she retired. Her second marriage with Louis, whom she had known years before, came about after they had exchanged more than 200 love letters, which were later published as examples of a model relationship. They see themselves as being part of "the most fortunate of generations".*

In the twentieth century, China experienced the chaos of war and political dissension, and after nearly one hundred years of this, the country and its people were exhausted, with all infrastructure near paralysis. In 1981, a group of world economists predicted in a Chinese government journal that it would take China at least a century to climb out of poverty. Their prediction attracted a great deal of attention: it piqued Chinese self-esteem and provoked a deep-seated popular indignation, stirring a capacity for serious reflection and for hard work long numbed by government policies. I say this because it took less than thirty years from that moment for China to soar to the position of an up-and-coming superpower, arresting the attention of the world in so doing.

Where did that energy come from? Some people say that it was the peasants, hitherto ceaselessly engaged in primitive cultivation, who nurtured China's political dreams. Bound to the soil for generations, Deng Xiaoping's reforms allowed them to migrate to the cities. Their cheap labour helped to break down the rigid constraints of the planned economy. In the process, they "re-educated" a leadership who were feeding on "pie in the sky".

Other people say that the army and academics have risen up and redeemed a Chinese society immobilised by deadly internecine power struggles. Some claim it marks the rise of a new, historically determined, period in China, and is a necessary part of the dynastic cycle. Others view it as a new budding growth from the rootstock of China's great civilisation. And still others say that it is because China is on the rebound from years of extreme misery.

But in my view, this energy is the product of the accumulated self-esteem, wisdom and sheer grit which has been nurtured by five thousand years of civilisation, coming from a people who have learned the meaning of happiness and how to achieve it.

While I was growing up, I knew a woman who had turned tribulations into fields of endeavour, grievances into sport, dedication into responsibility and the vicissitudes of life into the brilliantly coloured fragments of a kaleidoscope.

A year ago, we were chatting on the phone about how each of us felt about China today, and I mentioned the *China Witness* project, and that I was reaching the final stage of interviews. "Come and see us," she said cheerfully. "Come and listen to the stories of a pair of old folks from the most fortunate of generations."

The "most fortunate of generations"?

From what I knew of her, and judging by any normal standards, she had been fortunate in many ways, but had suffered pain and injustice as well, which hardly made her one of the "fortunate generation".

During the interviews I made on my travels around China, people told me of their pride, I saw their confidence and felt their self-esteem, but so far had heard nothing of "the most fortunate generation". Indeed, few of my interviewees had used the word "fortunate" about themselves.

My friend holds an important position, so I needed to avoid any suspicion that I was digging for classified information. The following is her story, which is an edited version of articles published by Chinese military reporter Mr Tu Xueneng in the *Keji Ribao* newspaper (online) in July 2002.

Spring 1996, USA.

A saloon car sped along the freeway from Maryland to Columbus, Ohio, USA. In the car sat the woman general; her daughter Lan was at the wheel. Their destination: the place where the general had been born sixty-six years ago.

As the car drew to a halt, the general climbed nimbly out and stood at the steps of the maternity hospital entrance. A breeze touched her face and ruffled a few strands of hair. She did not look like a woman in her sixties, with her erect bearing and agile movements. "Was it really sixty-six years ago?!" The duty officer's face betrayed intense emotion. When she heard that they had travelled halfway across the world to visit the older woman's birthplace, her astonishment knew no bounds.

"Yes, it was sixty-six years ago," smiled the general, in a pure American drawl, gazing at the hospital before her.

A detailed folder of material was placed before her. On the first page, a small red footprint impressed itself on her gaze. "Well, that is incredible!" Now it was her turn to be astonished, a feeling accompanied by deep gratitude.

The file on the little Chinese girl born here sixty-six years ago was astonishingly comprehensive. The duty officer took them to the ward where it was recorded that she had first drawn breath – the room was still a maternity ward, and still held the sweet smell of milk.

The date was 28 December 1930. When the future general came into this foreign corner of the world, her father gave her the beautiful name Phoebe, the Greek moon goddess, "the shining one", with the wish that his daughter, like moonlight, would bathe everyone around her in warmth and happiness.

One autumn day three years later, the future general returned to China with her illustrious parents. Her father, with his American PhD in psychology, was made professor at the Nanjing Central School of Politics by the government. Her mother sent her to an American-run primary school where she did exceptionally well. After completing the first grade, she was told by the teacher: "Next term, go straight to the third grade."

Then came the Marco Polo Bridge incident on 7 July 1937, marking Japan's invasion of China proper, and from one day to the next everything changed. With the occupation of Nanjing, Phoebe's family took to the road along with the millions of other Chinese families, forming a wretched, endless stream of refugees constantly on the move in search of sanctuary. First they went to Changsha, but had scarcely had time to get to know their new home before they had to flee to the small county town of Zhijiang Xian in western Hunan province. Not long after, they took a boat to Chongqing. During their flight, no matter where they were, nor how hard life was, Phoebe never dropped out of school. She attended seven of them during six years of primary education.

Six years of middle school followed, and Phoebe was again tossed between schools in five different places. First grade (lower middle school) in Chongqing, followed by a spell in Fujian province; second grade in Nanping; third grade in Jianyang; and first grade of upper middle school in Jian'ou. With the successes of the resistance against Japan, the family made the longed-for return to Shanghai, where Phoebe continued with the third grade.

In the spring of 1947, the future general entered the Foreign Languages Department of Shanghai's Fudan University. An assiduous student known for her political zeal, she joined the Chinese Communist Party at the age of eighteen, and threw herself heart and soul into the struggle for Liberation which faced the city of Shanghai . . .

Before the PLA Ranking exercise of 1955, almost all women soldiers were given non-combatant roles, had their battle dress replaced by plain uniforms, and were not ranked. Phoebe was moved to non-combatant duties but, in recognition of her professional ability and excellent work record, was permitted to remain in her teaching post at the PLA-run Foreign Languages Institute. Five years later, she became the youngest woman to head the teaching and research section of a military college.

In 1983, Phoebe was promoted to the position of deputy head of the Institute's training department. Her reaction, when told by the head of the Institute prior to the public announcement, was to object. "You must be joking!" she blurted out. Four years later, another unexpected "happy event" befell her, when she was told that her superiors wanted to promote her to deputy head of the Institute. She laughed, and out came the same catchphrase: "You must be joking!" General Phoebe has been raised to this level of seniority by the Chinese military's push to modernise. Her belief is that the key to language learning is the linguistic environment: if foreign-language teaching does not open itself up to cultural exchanges, then it will perish. She has called for increasing and strengthening international exchange programmes, advocates an increase in the numbers of officially sponsored Chinese students sent to study abroad, and more investment in teachers and teaching materials.

General Phoebe is an educationalist of the first rank, and has edited ten sets of textbooks, including *The English Language Reading Course*, which has become a core work for advanced English teaching nationally and was awarded the PLA Institute's First Prize for Educational Excellence.

General Phoebe has devoted her life wholeheartedly to teaching for almost half a century. She has dedicated herself to her students and, in so doing, has won their love and esteem in return. At the end of each year, three days of celebration follow one after another – Christmas on 25 December, her birthday on the 28th and New Year's Day on 1 January. Beautifully designed congratulatory cards rain down on her like confetti, and as General Phoebe peruses each familiar name and reads their warm messages, she is often moved to tears.

In September 1988, Military Commission Chairman Deng Xiaoping promoted General Phoebe to the rank of major general.

On 27 July 1984, General Phoebe's first husband passed away. Bereaved after twenty-eight years of a loving relationship, her grief was almost unspeakable. On her way back to Luoyang from Beijing, she exhorted herself, I must be strong, I must be strong. When I see our chiefs and comrades, I must not cry, I absolutely must not cry. And when they came to visit her, she really did bite her lip and remained dry-eyed. But when everyone had gone, and only she was left, when she looked at the empty room, and remembered the laughter and chatter she had shared in it with Mei Xiaoda, now a thing of the past, then she wept bitter tears.

After nearly ten years of respectable widowhood, General Phoebe happened to be at a Soldiers' Reunion meeting where she bumped into Louis [Lu Yi], an old school friend. Forty years previously, she had headed a study group at the North China People's Revolutionary University, whose other members included her late husband and Louis, to whom she is now married. Louis had been discharged for medical reasons in 1952, and allocated a job in Shanghai. By the time they met again, they were both widowed.

15 February 1992 was a day to remember both for Louis and General Phoebe. It marked the blossoming of a friendship in which for two years letters between the pair of old comrades flew back and forth between Luoyang and Shanghai.

A year has 52 weeks, and a weekly letter makes 52 letters per person per year. That's over 100 a year, or over 200 for two people for two years. General Phoebe and Louis exchanged over 200 such letters . . . "If a couple is lucky enough to have this kind of chance meeting, and true intimacy grows, then they begin to miss each other when they are apart." Every one of those letters was full of noble ideals and aspirations, every word an expression of true and sincere feelings. The upshot of around 200 of them, combined with a number of face-to-face meetings, was that General Phoebe and Louis married. At the end of 1993, the 63-year-old woman general became a new bride again in Beijing.

Life since their marriage has been good. We can tell how happy they are from the joint name card which they use: "We seek perfection of character, Our hearts are ever youthful, Our bodies still healthy, Light of heart, we face old age."

In September 2006, I visited the Beijing Officers' Village to hear the stories of this "old woman from the most fortunate generation". We had not met for a very long time, but the emotions we shared about the state of China today soon replaced conventional pleasantries. Afterwards, we were both surprised at the way we had so unreservedly immersed ourselves in deep discussion. She said with a smile that this too came from a yearning for happiness.

*

XINRAN: Auntie, over twenty years, of all the people whom I have interviewed, you are the one who knows me best. For years I have looked to you to teach me about life and about China. Every conversation we have had has stimulated me, and under your tactful guidance, I have acquired a kind of faith, one which resonates with that of your generation, to sacrifice oneself for love. I also believe that you understand what I am doing and why I am doing it. I'm convinced that it will be we who have to answer to the next generation, if the years bring a rupture of communication between the generations. I feel I have a personal responsibility here, one which others may regard as naive and laughable. When today's young people grow old, they may feel they are a lost generation. They may blame us, although they may not understand why they are blaming us. In the course of recent history, this has already happened: many young Chinese do not believe that their parents had a glorious past, do not recognise the values which former generations held dear, and may even have no way of confirming what happened to their own parents in the past.

For example, for the last few years, I have bought all the new editions of Chinese history books, and I have discovered that pre-1949 history accounts for 80 per cent of the material, and only 20 per cent is devoted to the period after 1949. The ten years of the Cultural Revolution receive scarcely any space at all, and are covered in just a few vaguely worded lines. I realise that some historical truths can evoke painful feelings for some people, but we are talking here about facts. We should not rush to hasty judgements about whether the past was right or wrong, but we do need to link it to the present.

I believe that history is formed and continues inseparably from social and family education. The education given in school is very limited and is just the beginning of the process. What I am trying to do is introduce into a Chinese society which has been frozen solid for thousands of years discussion of new issues, "fresh streams of water", to provide counter-currents for those generations who have seen such dramatic changes over the last hundred years; counter-currents in history, in the existence of truth, in the values and beliefs of a different era.

I have spent many years conversing with the elderly in different parts of China. I have been in the sitting rooms of families of three who have eight cars between them; I have been in country toilets where the floors crawled with so many maggots that there was nowhere to put one's feet; I have nibbled salted pickles at the tables of families living on a few jiao per head a day; and I have drunk champagne on the patios of private seaside villas. This is how the Chinese live today, coexisting in a multilayered society.

How can one be objective about China, explain it, analyse its causes and effects? I'd like to hear your opinions. And I'd also like to interview your husband, because you come from such different social backgrounds, although both were equally cultured – one of you comes from a family of Western-influenced intelligentsia, the other from a Confucian-style merchant clan. You both grew up in the same era of dramatic changes, and I would love to know what you have in common and how you differ.

GENERAL PHOEBE: I don't think there will be any problem with that. He won't object, I know him.

XINRAN: Auntie, the first thing I would like to ask you is about your mother.

GENERAL PHOEBE: My mother is the person I remember most. My father provided the family's only source of income, and ratified the policy decisions, but my mother was at the heart of the family and devised the plans. There are many stories about my mother's family. Her father came from the Hangzhou scholar-gentry. If you look at my mother's family tree, my great-grandfather and his forebears were all noted scholars and teachers, so there was a family tradition of study. As for my grandfather, he was very unfortunate because his father died at an early age. The family fortunes declined, and while he was still a small child he had to go and pawn their belongings to keep them alive.

He and his younger sister had to support themselves. My grandfather got a government grant to train as a PE teacher, which is what he became, while my great-aunt learned embroidery and supported herself that way. My great-aunt led a rather amusing life. When she was sixteen, it was still the Qing dynasty, before the Republic was established, and she went to be housekeeper for the family of an important official – his rank would be equivalent to the head of Zheijiang province nowadays. My great-aunt was a beauty, and became a junior wife of the official. She was a clever woman, and she bore him children too. Then the empire fell and the Republic was set up, but she was still a grand lady – the revolution did not affect her, and even after the Republic, the property of the Qing dynasty nobility was protected. Not only did her social status not suffer, but she also gained more freedom. She was able to use her contacts and went to Shanghai to set up a girls' middle school, called Kunfan Girls' Middle School. She became an educator like the rest of the family too.

My maternal grandfather, apart from being a teacher, became a devout Christian, but he married a woman who was a devout Buddhist. In our family the two religions coexisted quite peacefully. When my mother was small, her father took them to church on Sundays, after which their mother would take them to worship and burn incense in a Buddhist temple. So the children grew up under the influence of both religions. This kind of situation in the family was really a product of the way China changed between the Qing dynasty and the Republic. Christianity in those days in Shanghai was a "foreign" fashion – my mother and her siblings were young and easily influenced by new trends and she became a Christian. So her family was very westernised.

My grandfather had three daughters in a row, then the fourth baby was a boy, and the fifth another girl. He decided that all his daughters should go to university – at least to do an undergraduate degree. The elder three girls studied economics, and all got their degrees. The family sitting room looked like this: big photographs of four of them in mortar boards hung in a row – my eldest aunt, my mother, my third aunt and my uncle. My eldest aunt was born in 1905, and in those days very few people took degrees. They were among the earliest graduates. My youngest aunt did an English course but not to undergraduate level. My grandfather wanted her to get her degree, and to go and study, but there wasn't enough money, and she never got it. It was my grandparents' lifelong regret. They really should have had all five in mortar boards.

XINRAN: Tell me about your father's family.

GENERAL PHOEBE: My paternal grandfather was very westernised. My great-grandfather was in Anhui province in the Taiping Rebellion, I'm not sure where he was before that. During the rebellion he left Anhui and found work in Shanghai, but he suffered from ill health and died relatively young.

My great-grandmother was from Suzhou and was a skilled embroidress. Suzhou in those days was economically developed. When she arrived in Shanghai, her one aim was to have her sons study English. So this woman with her bound feet hired a pushcart to take her all over the city, as she looked for a school which taught English. My great-uncle became an important official at the Shanghai Tax Office, and my grandfather, whose English wasn't so good, ran an accountancy firm in Shanghai.

Because of all this, my family was a bit different from those of my schoolmates. There were very few feudal remnants in our family, and besides, after the Opium War, Shanghai became very westernised, not only in terms of religion but also, because it was a port, in its culture, food and so on. My grandparents enjoyed eating Western food, and from an early age I always felt that eating Western food was fun. At that time, I saw many feudal families, wealthy ones too, which were much more backward than ours. My father was a graduate of Fudan University, and an excellent student. He took the entrance examinations for many students, and helped them get university places . . .

XINRAN: Was that regarded as cheating?

GENERAL PHOEBE: You always get that kind of thing with some people, it's human nature. It's a by-product of kindness and a desire to help.

XINRAN: How did your parents meet?

GENERAL PHOEBE: My father's sister and my mother were good friends, and my aunt introduced them. They started courting, my mother got her degree, and just then my father won a scholarship to study in the USA. So first they got married, then they went off as overseas students.

XINRAN: My uncle on my father's side did the same thing – got a GMD government grant to study in the USA.

GENERAL PHOEBE: Yes, he got a government grant. The family was delighted, and topped up the grant, so that they travelled first class, and had a month's honeymoon on board ship. I was born not long after they arrived in America. My mother wasn't able to carry on studying economics. My father was doing a master's at Harvard, and then went to Utah to do a PhD. My mother took a course in child education in the school my father was in, and I was her first subject of study, so I got the best possible education.

I really can't say enough about her influence on me. She was a very unusual mother, so all of us children were very carefree and optimistic. We got a lot of respect, we weren't repressed children.

XINRAN: What did your mother do after that?

GENERAL PHOEBE: She went on being a wife, having children and being a mother. My parents had a very good relationship, very harmonious and affectionate, a bit westernised really. We had so much fun, but my mother didn't really. She was an educated woman, and she felt that her talents were constrained by her family responsibilities.

Actually, as far as running the family went, and feeding and caring for the children, she went to a lot of trouble. Our house was always nicely decorated, even when we were fleeing as refugees to Sichuan and we lived in a mud hut with lime-washed walls – there was no wallpaper in that region in those days – she still found a way to decorate the house. She bought that shiny green-coloured paper, cut out circles and stuck flower patterns on the wall by the table where we ate. Some were flower patterns and some were other designs, and the whole house looked very "Western". Sometimes we found it hard to believe we were in an adobe hut! I loved making these pretty walls with her. She made all my clothes too. When I was a child, I adored Shirley Temple. Whatever she wore, my mother would make it for me, so we girls had lots of Shirley Temple outfits.

She used to tell us stories – she was good at storytelling – tales from Balzac, Tarzan stories, she could make us cry with her stories. She sang in English and Chinese, really movingly. She was such a clever woman, but she could actually only display her intelligence and talents within the confines of her home. Later on, when I thought back on it, I realised that she can't have been very happy at home.

XINRAN: Do you think she was unhappy all her life?

GENERAL PHOEBE: She enjoyed herself more after Liberation. Immediately after Liberation she shot off on her own. She and my father loved each other a great deal, and he understood and supported her. The three eldest of the five children were beginning to leave home to work or study; my mother, who was very well educated, became a professional and did her job extremely well. She worked in a cooperative nursery, quite far from our home, and could only come back once a week. So my father looked after my younger sister and brother.

This father was almost a complete stranger to me. When I was small, my father had never so much as brushed my hair for me, but with the youngest two, he looked after them and did everything for them! When he talked of how he had done nothing to look after us older ones, he felt very "*sorry*" [in English].

XINRAN: He must have understood, from looking after your younger brother and sister, what a wonderful woman your mother was.

GENERAL PHOEBE: That's right. My mother *was* a wonderful woman. Her biggest success was in educating us. She behaved very rationally towards us. When I was about to leave home, I didn't realise that she was like that, but when I came back to visit, she cried. She hadn't wanted me to go away knowing how desolate she felt. But she never interfered in our lives. Even as small children, we did things for ourselves. She was very well organised, and believed in proper behaviour. When we returned to China, we brought back a very interesting custom with us: I used to drink a glass of cold water with every meal, that was a habit I had picked up in America. Years later, my younger brother and sisters would say before we started eating: "Pour us a glass of cold water, Phoebe," and I would pour them a glass each, and everyone would say thank you.

My mother would set me up as an example which she wanted my younger siblings to follow. She brought us up to overcome difficulties by ourselves, she wouldn't do it for us. Nowadays, if a little girl falls over, her mother will say "Naughty floor!" and tell the child to hit the floor. I think that's daft, it's like saying it's never the child's own fault. With a small child, you have to get her to understand why she fell down. In 1935, my mother published a book called *Your Bonny Baby*.

XINRAN: In Chinese or in English?

GENERAL PHOEBE: In Chinese. My father did lots of illustrations for it.

XINRAN: What did your mother do after she retired?

GENERAL PHOEBE: After Liberation, she went to work in the nursery, and my father taught psychology at East China Normal University. Then the Beijing Educational Research Institute transferred my father and the whole family to Beijing. My mother was forced to give up her work at the nursery; and soon afterwards she died. She was sixty-four.

XINRAN: So young! What did she die from?

GENERAL PHOEBE: A cerebral haemorrhage. She was under too much pressure. That was the time of the Cultural Revolution. The university professors were treated like animals, they bore the brunt of the attacks. The Red Guards drove all the professors and academics onto the sports ground and made them all kneel down. It was all too much for my mother.

XINRAN: What about your father?

GENERAL PHOEBE: My father lived to the age of eighty-four.

XINRAN: He got through the Cultural Revolution.

GENERAL PHOEBE: Yes he did. He was a psychologist, and psychologists in China went through hard times. He had come back to China to help fight the Japanese, but during the Anti-Japanese War, it was hard enough just to survive, so who cared about your psychology? From an academic point of view, he was under enormous constraints. After Liberation, China was under the influence of the Soviets and they ignored psychology, so he had no alternative but to do Pavlovian experiments, that is, to concentrate on the physiological aspects. But it was only fifty years after his return, during the reforms which opened up China, when he was over seventy and already retired, that he finally achieved academic recognition for the discipline of psychology and became very famous as a psychologist. In spite of his age, he then threw all of his energies into training up researchers, master and PhD students. So his later years were very enjoyable. He also trained some students in sexual psychology, an area previously taboo in China.

XINRAN: Forgive me for interrupting you, but I am a self-taught student of broadcasting psychology, and my many years of working in the media have made me aware of the thirst for psychology in Chinese society. It's very difficult for many Western theories in psychology to find acceptance in China because of distortions in our society which have developed over a long period. But China badly needs psychology to help smooth out the frictions between different elements in our society. Sexual psychology, especially, is urgently needed to deal with huge problems.

GENERAL PHOEBE: My father's very last student was a researcher in sexual psychology, and my father said to him: "Whatever level you achieve in your studies, that represents the highest level in China!"

XINRAN: Did your father ever discuss with you the future of psychology in China?

GENERAL PHOEBE: Yes he did. He felt that although China has developed quite fast since the reforms, and psychology was now quite well recognised, and there were far more people registering for psychology courses, nevertheless it would still take a long time for China to catch up with psychology in developed countries.

XINRAN: As the daughter of a psychologist, did you find that his work persuaded you of the value of psychology to Chinese society?

GENERAL PHOEBE: Undoubtedly! He did psychology, and we five children all went through higher education. I taught English; my younger brother studied mechanical engineering, and then did rehabilitation engineering; my next sister is a film actress; my youngest sister is a doctor; my youngest brother works in computing. In each of our areas of professional expertise, my father could hold his own in a discussion, and we often discovered that he was more knowledgeable than any of us.

I did languages, but I had to admit that he knew more about it than I did. He had been to a primary school in Shanghai run by English people, so his English was extremely good. When he was young he read lots of foreign-language books, so his knowledge of English was much more profound than mine. I was at school during the war, so obviously I didn't have the solid foundation that he had.

My brother then started to do rehabilitation engineering, and an idea of my father's had a great influence on him: he said the psychological process was transformed into the physiological process and the physiological process was transformed into the physical process, so that when my brother made artificial limbs and electronic and mechanical devices, he could use the same principle. I should add that by that time my brother was China's foremost rehabilitation engineer, but my father still outstripped him.

XINRAN: What are the strongest impressions you retain from your childhood?

GENERAL PHOEBE: My childhood was very unusual, because I was born in America, and I lived there until the outbreak of the Anti-Japanese War. My Chinese wasn't very good then, but when I first returned to China, and heard people say that they wanted to hear me speak English, I was scared to death, and didn't dare utter a word. I said to my mother, did our family and friends think I was a doll? That was when I was very small.

Until I was six, I was an only child. Even though my mother was a child educationist and tried her best to ensure I was not lonely, I had no companion at home, so when my girl cousin came to visit, I was absolutely delighted. Of course, this had a lot to do with my character, I've always enjoyed lively company because I was so alone as a child: even though I had plenty of friends at school, at home there was just me.

When my younger siblings were born, every two or three years, they formed a group. I wasn't in their group because I was six years older, and my mother deliberately made me their role model, so they looked up to me more than ever. It got quite ridiculous – when the little ones cried, they didn't cry for their mummy or daddy, they cried for their elder sister. That was how it was in our house, I was Big Sister.

When I was little, my father was a university professor, and before the Anti-Japanese War, university professors lived pretty well. When he came back, we had a small detached, Western-style house in Hangzhou and one in Nanjing, and my father was taken to work in a special rickshaw, of the type that used to go "clank, clank" as they went along.

But once the war had begun, we became refugees on the run. Our education suffered a great setback. I was first at the American School, and continued there when we arrived at Lu Shan, but then we left and fled to Hunan, first to one place then to another. I've worked it out: my primary school was six years, and I went to seven schools in that time, and never had one fixed school. And it got more and more difficult just to survive as we headed into the hinterland. We went as far as Chongqing, and in those days you couldn't just hop on an aeroplane like now. Fleeing for safety involved an arduous journey.

When I think back on it now, the hardships of our childhood have served me well in later life. After the outbreak of war, our whole standard of living fell dramatically, so we got to know what rural life meant. We lived on the outskirts of Chongqing, we were on the edge of the countryside, and we could see the extreme poverty of Chinese villages. I had never felt anything like it, not in America or in the big cities. I was greatly affected by my feelings – in some way I suppose I felt a kind of responsibility. I felt that our country was bad, backward, poor, and allowed foreigners to beat us. So I did lots of war-relief work, like making collections of padded clothing in the autumn and things like that.

Our lives changed so much, and those changes affected the whole nation. That's why old people in China today still burn with anger against the crimes committed by the Japanese seventy years ago. I still feel that hatred. The Japanese people did such great wrong to the Chinese.

My father was teaching in Nanjing at the time, and when we fled, we gave our house to a rickshaw puller to look after. During the Nanjing Massacre of December 1937, they cut off his arm. When we heard about it, we felt so bad. He was completely innocent, he was just a manual worker, who had he offended?

If you listen to our generation talk about the Anti-Japanese War, all of us, not to mention the wretchedly poor, have personal experience of the horror of it. When I see the Japanese flag now, it still makes me feel bad; my head is full of blood-soaked images, and I simply can't forget them, because they are so deeply imprinted on my consciousness.

When the war ended, I was fifteen years old. We finally made it back to Shanghai. Our standard of living was a lot worse than when we had been in Shanghai before. Even though my father was a professor, we were very poor. There was terrible inflation and we were like beggars, our daily lives just wretched. I was at middle school, and I had no shoes to wear to school. I just went in straw sandals – having cloth shoes to wear was a luxury.

We always made a fuss of everyone's birthdays in my family, and one year when it was my birthday, my mother wanted to give me a present, but she couldn't afford to buy anything. So she cut out a piece of ordinary blue cotton from the pocket of an old garment, frayed the edges, added a few little red flowers around the edge, and embroidered the flower petals onto it with red thread. Her clever fingers turned that bit of pocket into a pretty handkerchief in no time at all, and made me a birthday present which I have always remembered.

The truth is that we were still considered quite well off in those days. Many, many people lived in far worse conditions than us, not to mention those who starved to death.

Our poverty made a profound impact on me. I felt inferior, even though I went to a middle school which was very well known in Shanghai – it was called the Xiangwen Middle School, and was attached to the Catholic Institute. My cousins also went there and were in the same year as me, only I felt inferior to them in every way – in the clothes I wore, in the food I took to school for lunch. But I got better grades than them, which gave me a few crumbs of comfort, and a reason to be proud.

When I was in upper middle school, our home was at Fudan University in the Jiangwan part of Shanghai and my school was quite far away, in the city centre, so I moved in with my maternal grandmother. An aunt of mine also lived there, a very progressive woman, who often talked to us about progressive topics. I had seen poverty at first hand, and had seen how unfair society was, so I was very receptive to being indoctrinated by her ideas. But they kept us under tight control at my school and we had very little opportunity to go out and do our own thing.

After I started at Fudan University, I found the atmosphere there very good, and the students were active. It was just like my father's descriptions of his time at Qinghua University, when he and his fellow students were militant and felt that the GMD were terribly corrupt. By contrast, after we had defeated the Japanese, we university students felt that Chinese society had been destroyed by the Japanese devils, because the government was so riddled with corruption. First, carpet-bagging officials sent by the GMD to take over from the Japanese had arrived from Chongqing, and appropriated all the wealth for themselves, and then they used galloping inflation to fleece ordinary people. When I was at university, every time my father got paid, he had to hurry to do the shopping, before the prices of food and household goods rose again beyond his means. After the victory against Japan, large amounts of food aid was distributed, like US Army tinned food, those big green tins of luncheon meat. We really liked eating such stuff, and you could store the tins. So my mother bought lots, and when prices went up and other people had nothing to eat, we still had meat. We rushed to convert our savings into silver dollars, either the Yuan-head coins with Yuan Shikai's head on them, or the Sun-head silver dollars with Sun Yat-sen's head on them, because silver dollars kept their value. When my brother and I helped my father with the shopping, we had to carry a lot, because you needed big bags of money. It was common to see people going shopping carrying their money on shoulder poles.

In Shanghai I saw with my own eyes people who had died of starvation or frozen to death – it was a common sight. How could I carry on with my studies? I just couldn't. Some of my fellow students at Fudan University were from very poor families, and many of us took to the streets to demonstrate against hunger. The Communist Party was very strong by now, and everyone read Chairman Mao's books on the quiet. We were looking for a way to save China because many people had begun to realise that Chiang Kai-shek was useless and was not governing our country properly. When I was eighteen years old, I joined the underground Party branch at the university.

XINRAN: What did you study at Fudan?

GENERAL PHOEBE: English. But times were so turbulent that I hardly got any studying done. The students were constantly on strike, and we were involved in activities both on and off campus. All of us were in a high state of anxiety. What were we to do with our country? By that time, the CCP-liberated areas were expanding, and many students just hoped that we would be liberated soon and, whichever government took power, that the fighting would stop and the economy would start working again.

Our generation had very little opportunity to pursue our studies. I mean, what could I learn at primary school while we were on the run? And schools were so poorly equipped that I have never lost the habit of saving paper. There was no paper as white as we have today, it was all grass paper, browny-black in colour, we called it "horse-dung paper". When you used a pencil to write on it, it tore, and when you used a pen, the ink soaked through and went everywhere. If you could get hold of a good pencil, you were very happy. When I see paper swooshing through the photocopier now, with just a few words on one side, and nothing printed on the reverse, it hurts me. I've still kept the habit of using the edge of the paper to make notes or jot things down. It's a habit I would find difficult to change, because I lived through those times. Materially, we were incredibly hard up, plus it all happened at the time when I was beginning to be aware of these things – twelve or thirteen years old, right up to when I was seventeen or eighteen.

XINRAN: I know what you mean by "habits". I never used to understand at all, not until the first time I went to do an interview in a small village in Yuanyang, in Henan province, in 1989. The village was very poor, and I saw children with absolutely no toys. So I took some pages from my notebook and made them some origami rabbits out of the paper as a present. Some years later I went back –

GENERAL PHOEBE: And the rabbits were still there.

XINRAN: Yes, they were, alongside the portraits of Chairman Mao and the Goddess of Mercy. I was just putting my hand out to take a rabbit down and tell them about my first visit years before, when a small child stopped me and said: "Don't touch it. My dad told me that a visitor from far away came and gave it to us." I felt moved to tears: as far as I was concerned, these were just paper toys I'd casually made them, but to a generation of peasants who had never had visitors from the outside world, and had never seen the world outside their village either, it meant so much because they were living in a forgotten corner of China. Many rural children have never seen clean white paper, so after that, I acquired a new habit: I would collect together scraps of paper and make them up into little notebooks of all shapes and sizes, and when I went into the countryside I would take them to give to the children. I completely agree that unless you've experienced poverty and seen it with your own eyes, you can't understand what it's like to be poor, and you won't know how to help.

GENERAL PHOEBE: That was true all over China then – so we know why it was called the old society – and we weren't at the bottom of the heap.

XINRAN: And what do your son and daughter think about your habit of saving paper?

GENERAL PHOEBE: Our standards as parents, in bringing up our children, were very much army standards. When they were in primary and middle school, we made two round trips to work every day, so we saw them at breakfast, lunch and dinner, rattled off a few things we needed to say, and then we had to go back to work after dinner. We had no time to spend with our children, we really had no time at all in those days, everyone was so busy working, it seemed like the only way to do right by our country. We only had Sunday off, and only for half a day. We bathed once a week – that took two hours – then I had to hold a meeting with core cadres within the department and organise the next week's work. These memories hurt me deeply, but one can't turn the clock back. I understand the way society works today. People are so busy with their work that they have no time to spend on the family. They have a higher standard of living than we did, so they simply hand their children over to the school or get other people to look after them. That's even worse for the children, who sometimes don't see their parents at all during the week. I do worry for them when I see that happening. Those children are growing up, they need their family and their parents in a way that they never will again. Many people are working to get a better life for themselves but if, when you've got it all, you discover that in the process you've lost out on enjoying your children and family, that mindless rushing around is a tragedy. And the pain of that loss can never be compensated for.

XINRAN: During the interviews we've done, almost all the parents have shared that pain – that is, they didn't give their children the family and the love that they should have done, or fulfilled their needs, and it's the biggest regret of their lives. It's something that many of our generation are still searching for. Some of us even look for that parental love and warmth at work or among our friends. How many times have I dreamed that I was small again and my parents were making a fuss of their little girl . . . ?

*

General Phoebe's hitherto unclouded expression faded and, with it, her air of self-confidence and acuity. Her eyes reddened, and filled, and she gulped hard, as if to choke back the rising tide of pain. I also felt anguish – the reminder of this family and mother love which I was still looking for bubbling up to the surface – and we were both silent for a few moments, letting time ease the intensity of our memories.

*

XINRAN: Auntie, I'm sorry.

GENERAL PHOEBE: It's OK, this is excellent, it shows we're not completely numbed, that we haven't lost our ability to feel. The way we lived before, we had little opportunity to express our real selves. Don't worry, this is fine, please carry on asking me questions.

XINRAN: Did you see Shanghai being liberated? Do you still remember scenes from then?

GENERAL PHOEBE: Those were interesting times. On 27 May 1949, the city of Shanghai was liberated.* By 25 May, troops had already occupied some of the outskirts so the city was not completely liberated, but where we lived, it was basically liberated.

Before this, on 25 April, in the middle of the night, the GMD military police surrounded every major Shanghai university, to arrest so-called Communist elements. First, they drove all the students who were boarders into the dining hall, and then got spies who were standing around to identify CCP members. These were then dragged away and thrown into prison. Those were the mass arrests prior to Liberation. At the more famous universities, like Fudan, Tongzhi and Shanghai Jiaotong, large numbers of students were seized and imprisoned. I lived at home, so nothing happened to me, I probably wasn't on their blacklist. But our area was also surrounded, and I climbed up to the roof with a neighbour to hide. My brothers went outside to see if the army and police were making arrests, and whether we ought to make plans to escape.

After these mass arrests, there were no more classes at college, and the underground Party branch was extremely active. Party members kept in close contact and our task was to fight for liberation and be there to meet it when it came. The underground CCP in Shanghai mobilised all sectors of society – workers, peasants and traders – with the workers in the lead. Students were a force to be reckoned with too. We didn't have phones then, but we used the Shanghai Park Hotel which was the tallest building in the city; now, it's scarcely visible, because it's dwarfed by crowds of other skyscrapers. We arranged that when we hung a great length of white material from the top of the building, everyone would immediately go and gather in a prearranged spot. Our job was to do the propaganda work, and some

---

*Post-war liberation from Guomindang control by the People's Liberation Army, the troops of the Chinese Communist Party.

of us would do guard duties too, watching over key cultural sites and national archives.

On 24 May, the scenes on the streets in Shanghai had been quite farcical, because the GMD had organised demonstrations to celebrate the victory of their armed forces, and the streets had been full of their troops. We found it very funny, and we shouted at them: "It's almost over for you, what are you doing celebrating victory?!" Actually, they were covering their retreat.

XINRAN: I've heard about GMD victory parades in Shanghai on the eve of Liberation, but I've never been given an eyewitness account. I interviewed an old man in Shanghai who told me about it, but he said things were very confused – everyone was saying that the CCP were about to take the city, and yet the streets were full of GMD. I said that couldn't be true: if he insisted they were GMD in the streets, not CCP, how could he say it was the CCP who liberated Shanghai? He admitted that he had been very confused about what was happening at that time. But you've confirmed the truth of what he said.

GENERAL PHOEBE: Yes, on the 24th the streets were full of GMD troops, but by daybreak on the 25th they were full of PLA troops, every one of them with a gun on his shoulder. But no one went into anyone's house. All this made a very good impression on the city's inhabitants.

XINRAN: Was there a big contrast?

GENERAL PHOEBE: There was a joke going round then: the PLA didn't know what a flush toilet was, but they didn't want to bother any of the city's inhabitants, so they thought they must be for washing rice in. They put their rice in and poured water on top, swooshed the rice around and rinsed it clean. I don't know if that was true or just an urban myth, but the point of the joke was that the PLA were completely different from the GMD soldiers. Lots of GMD soldiers would come and ask to borrow something and never give it back; but if a PLA soldier came to our house to borrow something, we'd get it back immediately.

XINRAN: Were you someone who thought that the PLA were "hicks"?

GENERAL PHOEBE: No, I didn't.

XINRAN: So you didn't feel that since their uniforms were in tatters, and they were dirty, they were uneducated peasants?

GENERAL PHOEBE: No, on the contrary – we found them very educated. The GMD soldiers were pretty dumb. Their officers beat them, we all saw it happen, we saw them beating soldiers on the street with their truncheons, and the soldiers on their knees begging for mercy. I saw it when I was a kid, but nothing like that ever happened with the PLA soldiers.

XINRAN: That must have been a dramatic change for the Shanghainese. One day it was all GMD troops, and the next, it was all PLA troops and the CCP. So, how long did it take for the whole city to change from one system to the other?

GENERAL PHOEBE: At daybreak on the 25th, my aunt phoned my mother and told her that Shanghai had been "liberated". (My aunt's family were considered rather wealthy – my aunt ran a private bank.) She deliberately used the word "liberated" and I knew that this word was not in the GMD vocabulary, so it showed how many people accepted this huge change straight away. Of course we all ran to the front gate, and people ran out of the lanes, and saw how orderly they all were. The PLA didn't beat anyone, didn't take stuff and behaved properly. The CCP had done some propaganda work beforehand, but the best proof was ordinary people seeing it with their own eyes.

Well, then I worked for many, many years in the PLA Institute. The army belongs to the people – that's a principle which permeates it from top to bottom.

XINRAN: Before we began this interview, we talked about how China was a country formed by very particular circumstances. We don't have a national religion; we've taken in Buddhism, Christianity or Islam, we accept them all, though in fact these arrived more than a thousand years after Chinese indigenous philosophies and faiths. The result, when a country has no national religion, may easily be a confused medley of beliefs, a confusion produced by the lack of a guiding principle. By this I mean an accepted vertical analysis of history, in other words, an understanding which is the product of generally accepted immutable moral rules and common articles of faith. In China "each Son of Heaven brings his own retinue" and this moral framework changes with each new emperor on the throne, so that people's understanding of good and bad shifts accordingly. This could be one of the reasons why Chinese is so extremely rich in adjectives, but also why its language and culture are so closed to outside influences, and why we as a nation can be suspicious of religious belief.

I have been thinking about the fact that China has experienced a hundred years of dynastic and regime changes. After the end of the feudal Qing dynasty, China never stopped changing – from Empire to Republic took just a few years, and the change from GMD to CCP also happened quickly. Especially in the cities, regime change was really rapid. It's like you said, in Shanghai people's political outlook changed in twenty-four hours. How is it possible, in your view, for ordinary people to cope with such rapid change?

GENERAL PHOEBE: Ordinary people don't care. You change the dynasty or the emperor, it's all the same to us. We'll follow any emperor, so long as you don't stop us going about our business.

XINRAN: So people "got used to" these transformations just as previous generations had.

GENERAL PHOEBE: I think they got used to things, and didn't care. It's "I'll obey anyone, and any authority, who's good to me".

XINRAN: Political authority is like a god for an awful lot of ordinary Chinese.

GENERAL PHOEBE: Authority is very important, not just for a nation, but also within the family. The patriarch of the great Chinese family is an authority who cannot be disobeyed by family members. A family without an authority figure will quickly disintegrate; the children and grand-children may scatter, and some will begin to fight between themselves. Within the family, the main head of the family is basically a ruler. If he or she is an enlightened and wise one, then they can deal with all family relationship problems, and guarantee that future generations have family rules that they can follow – rules which can make those family ties indissoluble and keep the generations together. When that authority weakens, then other family members may involuntarily gravitate towards a new authority, and this may bring conflict in its wake. Interestingly enough, we can see the reappearance in national history of the traditional cultural consciousness of the great Chinese family, as the "cells" of family life penetrate the bone marrow of the nation.

XINRAN: So when Shanghai was liberated, how was the new government's power imposed on Fudan University, where you were, and how was it received by staff and students?

GENERAL PHOEBE: When the CCP took over, our underground Party was not yet out in the open, but the organisation was very strong, and very active. Everyone knew who was a Party member, and who had links with the Party. In those days, CCP members were usually models of behaviour in that particular environment. Then, to become a Party member, you had to be an exceptionally good person. You had to have real warmth and care for ordinary people, and if you were a student you had to be a better student than the rest. And only people with exceptional technical skills could join the Party. It's different nowadays – mediocre people with no real ability can join too. So every Party member had the power to bind people to them. If one of them spoke, we listened – of course we listened, we knew that what they said included instructions from higher levels of the CCP, and was integral to the interests of ordinary people. The Shanghainese very soon began to feel that life was an awful lot easier under the new leadership.

XINRAN: By Liberation, roughly how many members did the underground Party at Fudan University have?

GENERAL PHOEBE: I don't really know, the figures had to be kept secret, but it's true to say that a sizeable proportion of the students were members.

XINRAN: And then, after Shanghai was liberated, society became quite calm. It was even a natural transition.

GENERAL PHOEBE: That's right.

XINRAN: Did any of the students harbour any doubts about the new government?

GENERAL PHOEBE: It never occurred to us to doubt the new government, because the Youth League of the Three Principles of the People were the only opponents of the CCP members. They were bad people, who did despicable things and had a very bad social influence. We, in Shanghai, were liberated later than Beijing so, for us, all the news coming out of Beijing was good news, and very encouraging. No one wanted to stay still; we all told ourselves we should go and join in the reconstruction, and get to work to make China strong again. That really was what we felt, we didn't want to study.

XINRAN: What about the teachers?

GENERAL PHOEBE: My father was a professor so when he came home he told us how they were reacting. Of course, the Party did its work well, and just a few days after Liberation, the CCP Mayor of Shanghai, Mr Chen Yi, spoke to the intelligentsia in the Grand Cinema. Many professors attended and were extremely pleased, quite reassured. Mayor Chen was very clear on his hopes for the future and what he was inviting them to do at that moment. No one had any complaints, in fact they were falling over themselves to back him! I think that was why my family supported me joining the army.

XINRAN: When you decided to join the army, did you find it hard to leave your family? Did you think of the worry it would cause your parents?

GENERAL PHOEBE: To be honest, no. Everyone had made it their personal task to reconstruct the country, and that was the reason why my mother and father had come back from America to fight the Japanese.

XINRAN: What about your brothers and sisters?

GENERAL PHOEBE: My next brother was six years younger than me, and when he saw me join the army, he falsified his age and joined up too. Later, he left because of poor health, and became an academic. My other brother and sisters were too young at that time. I joined in July 1949. We were instructors first, and then I was sent by the Party organisation to take a written exam. It was only afterwards that I discovered that it was for the Foreign Ministry, who were recruiting . . . All of us had been chosen by people who had already been recruited, for our all-round excellence and because we were high-achievers. They wanted to use us to set up the China Military Diplomatic Academy.

XINRAN: The whole system for training military diplomats was set up by your cohort, wasn't it?

GENERAL PHOEBE: Not entirely by us. The precursor of the PLA Foreign Languages Institute was the CCP Military Committee Foreign Languages Training Unit set up in 1938 in Yan'an. In August 1949, this was formally established as an institute in Beijing, and we were its first cohort of instructors. There were about four hundred of us, about a hundred or so from Shanghai, and then some from Beijing, Nanjing and other places, but the Shanghainese were in the majority. Our institute was called the Revolutionary University then, part of the North China People's Revolutionary University. Section One was the Party School, Section Two was for diplomats, and there was another section, and ours was Section Four. There was a huge sports ground, where we gathered for reports and briefings, starting with learning what the sickle was.

XINRAN: Was it at that time that you met your first husband?

GENERAL PHOEBE: I and both my husbands were in the same section. Of course, at the time, I only knew that they were very nice to me, but I didn't realise that both of them loved me. Louis had been at St John's College, Shanghai, and had a diploma from there when he joined up. Most of us were sent to the Foreign Ministry. As I said, they recruited us specially, and then told us our unit was directly under the control of the ministry. We didn't know this at the time but our unit was to deal with "foreign relations". . .

XINRAN: Did your birth and your family's foreign background count against you in your work and your career?

GENERAL PHOEBE: Everyone knew I was born in America, I had made that clear from the start, and there wasn't anything illegal about it.

XINRAN: In the thirty years from the 1950s to the 80s, there were so many political movements in China which stifled the intelligentsia, and meted out punishments to many Chinese who had returned from overseas and were suspected of allegiance to US and British imperialism. Were you not subject to any unjust accusations?

GENERAL PHOEBE: Not really. We were protected to a certain extent. The Cultural Revolution was simply ridiculous: they said I was a powerful, reactionary academic, which was glorifying me. I never regarded myself as an academic, still less as someone with power. When they made me wear the "reactionary's hat", I found it funny.

XINRAN: So you were attacked?

GENERAL PHOEBE: At that time, we were living in the Hongxingyuan compound at Zhangjiakou, and the Red Guards put up big character posters attacking the "Four Big Diamonds". My late husband and I were two of those under fire, and the posters stuck on our house were mainly an attack on me, a fierce onslaught on my "criminal record" and my political views. After that, we were taken under armed guard to do Reform through Labour in the Hubei Cadre School. I didn't know how to do anything, so they gave me kitchen duties, and I cooked! I just learned and made the best of things, and I didn't endure any great suffering. Eventually, I even learned to kill pigs – I killed lots of pigs!

XINRAN: But how did you feel about what was going on? Did you feel wronged? Or indignant? I've discovered that many old people who went through hell then and survived into happier times talk very amusingly about that period, but are actually explaining what happened from the perspective of now, not then. What I really want to know is what you felt then, at that time.

GENERAL PHOEBE: What were my inner feelings then? It was just like when a revolution breaks out. First, there was the question of one's political attitude. What Chairman Mao said was very effective: "You should believe in the Party and the masses," so I believed in the Party and the masses. I don't think it was anything very frightening, because historically, when there were "rectification movements" in China, cadres' personal histories were investigated, we all knew that. When a period of time is past, and the storm is over, things eventually become clear, so I take a moderate view of history.

XINRAN: You were in military education for forty years, weren't you?

GENERAL PHOEBE: Yes, from 1949 right up to 1993.

XINRAN: If someone were to ask whether you could explain the ups and downs of Chinese history, how would you answer a question like that?

GENERAL PHOEBE: I feel that the Liberation of China in 1949 really was a fantastic event. And I include Mao Zedong in that. Even though Chairman Mao did a lot wrong, and even committed crimes – I do acknowledge that. But we have to recognise Mao Zedong's contribution to the revival of the Chinese nation as a whole. He was actually a great historical figure and his name will go down in the annals of history. He's like the Emperor Qin Shi Huang Di, who burned books, buried Confucian scholars alive and tyrannised the people, but this can't obscure his achievements in uniting China, setting up the legal code, developing commerce, and even building the Great Wall, one of the wonders of the world. Mao Zedong gave the Chinese back their self-respect as a people after the Opium War, and that achievement can never be wiped out.

What does Liberation mean? The greatest liberation has been for the working people. Previously in China, workers and peasants had absolutely no status; now, they may still be poor, but it's not the same. At last now, society and the media and officials have to show respect for them, whether they mean it or not, and they're supposed to be the masters! Before Liberation, the expression "Chinese people" didn't include them. The difference between then and now is really huge. That's why I tell you we are the most fortunate generation, because we have seen with our own eyes the difference between before and after Liberation. We have seen the whole process – from war, starvation, poverty and unrest, to the imposition of order, our growing strength and the development of a humane society.

The liberation of women in China has been more thorough than elsewhere, in a certain sense and within defined limits. The emancipation of urban professional women has been marvellous, and my mother was a witness to that change.

Of course, we lag behind in some things. Culturally, we are rather backward and haven't caught up. New China has been built by workers, peasants and the Red Army, and their influence should not be underestimated. Plus, for a long period after 1949, the majority of those who held power were worker and peasant cadres. Even though we knew that they had many shortcomings, we had to recognise that they had many good points. It's the same kind of liberation as the Paris Commune; even though afterwards many people suffered greatly in all sorts of ways, it was a very good thing that it happened. When the Gang of Four were crushed, we were so poor we didn't have any meat to eat, but each family somehow bought a chicken, and we had a hundred-chicken celebratory banquet. Educated people were beside themselves, to have seen this day come at last.

XINRAN: I'd like to hear you compare Chinese society today with how it was just after Liberation.

GENERAL PHOEBE: Nowadays, there are still many good Party members and leaders. It's not just a few individuals, you find them all over the place, really good people. Of course, they may bear the imprint of society today, and that includes wrongdoing and self-interest, but when it comes to disaster relief, you'll find that there are lots of good people, and that's the absolute truth. Every time there's a famine, China is so big that many, many people die, but you find that people help and give to each other. It's as we say, in a disaster, you really know who your friends are.

XINRAN: People of your generation really believe in the Communist Party, don't you? Do you know the story of my father and my younger brother? Did he ever tell you?

GENERAL PHOEBE: I don't think he ever did, no.

XINRAN: After my younger brother had joined the army, he went home on a visit, and my father asked: "How come you haven't joined the Party?" My brother said: "In my unit, the bad things are all done by Party members. I'm not joining." My father trembled with fury when he heard this. "Get out!" he shouted. So my brother took his bags and left. It was nearly three years before they spoke again.

GENERAL PHOEBE: It's because before Liberation we all saw so many bad things, and we firmly believed the CCP could resolve all those undesirable things. We pinned all our hopes on the CCP, so I can understand your father's feelings. But if you take a broad view of the development of the whole of human society, it's not that simple, it can't be explained in black and white terms. Human beings are always in search of truth, goodness and beauty, that's a universal trait, but it's not so easy to find. Human nature has so many contradictions. No political system is without its faults, and that's because we have many problems: people are weak, opportunistic, corrupt, selfish, everyone's got their failings. It's really worthwhile looking into how people come to a common understanding on how to solve these problems. In my view, war, religion and culture are all avenues through which people seek to resolve these contradictions and weaknesses. The expectation has been that we can deal with evil by using goodness, but many studies of human nature show we still have a long way to go; we have still not solved fundamental issues like poverty and war, let alone other problems.

XINRAN: War and poverty are precisely the factors which have torn apart modern China, and in my view it is only people like you, who have had both a Chinese and a Western education, and are of a generation who have experienced these dramatic changes, who can see things clearly and make comparisons. Many of the worker and peasant cadres, who benefited from these changes, just keep saying: "You don't know what it was like in the past." But they don't have any idea how to resolve past problems which persist today. They believe that it's easy to exchange one faith for another.

Apart from the kind of face-to-face interview which we are doing now, I have also conducted a series of telephone interviews, where I called people from London. One of them was a violin-maker called Wu, who was in his second year at university fifty years ago when he said something wrong and was clapped in prison right up until the Cultural Revolution. Two days before he was due to be released, he was in a group reciting the quotations of Chairman Mao and he made another mistake, and instead of saying "We should support those who oppose our enemy", he turned it into the opposite, "We should oppose those who oppose our enemy", so he was condemned to another fifteen years and didn't get out until 1985. He had completely and absolutely lost his entire youth. He went to Hong Kong in the end.

I met him in London, and I asked him one question: "Do you have regrets?" He said: "No, none." I asked him why not, and he said: "For an era to become an era, people have to endure it." And he went on to say that he had become a witness to a part of a particular era. "Through me, people will see one aspect of this era." I found Wu's self-evaluation very moving.

GENERAL PHOEBE: A man of noble spirit.

XINRAN: I did another telephone interview with a senior cadre who had never had any setbacks because he was a worker-peasant cadre, son of a Red Army soldier. I asked him: "Do you have any regrets about your life?" and he said: "I regret the fact that my father achieved nothing of value in his life, apart from his good name; not a thing in a whole lifetime, and I was a loyal and filial son to him." I really didn't understand that at all. I thought his answer was going to be the opposite because he had profited from his father's status, his house, his work and everyone's admiration of his family. Don't you think? I would have thought that Mr Wu might have said his life had not been worthwhile, but actually he thought it turned out fine!

GENERAL PHOEBE: In the past, the dominant things in our lives were controlled within society, but now we can't have complete control over things. Because changes have happened so fast, society fragments into many different viewpoints. It's all so complex and quite out of the ordinary, and that's a product of our age.

We old people see things a little more clearly because we are on the margins of society, not at its centre at all. We have been through a lot and have thought about it a lot. Many uneducated cadres have been through a lot too, but haven't been enlightened by education, so they can't think it through rationally.

We should take a calm look at things and put everyone back in that time, because Chairman Mao was not a god, he was an ordinary human being, and people allowed him to assume great powers. He put terrible pressure on people then, and that wasn't good, but all of that developed completely naturally. Power has always been tyranny over enemies and opponents, because it is born out of the struggle to subdue enemies and opponents, and the greater the power, the greater the number of people subdued. It's always been like this from ancient times. One can't see Mao Zedong as an unnatural phenomenon.

XINRAN: There are Westerners who think that Mao was the biggest murderer of the last century, a worse tyrant than Stalin and Hitler. Personally, I hate Mao Zedong. I was only a child during the Cultural Revolution, but I suffered a lot because my mother and father were attacked. If you accept that this was the work of Mao, then I was also one of his victims.

But if you go to Chinese villages and ask many ordinary people, peasants who have lived on the lowest rung of society, for their opinion, then you get a completely different point of view. At the very least, they feel that Mao Zedong did something for the peasants and the poor that no emperor had ever done, which was to burn the landlords' title deeds, redistribute the land and give everyone a livelihood. And he made housing, education and medical treatment free in the cities.

So we still see Mao's portrait hanging on the walls of peasant homes, and they still do their devotions to his statue as if he were a god. Some of them wept and shouted at us: "When Chairman Mao was here, there were never land snatches by the government or the kind of cadre corruption that there is now!" If 78 per cent of Chinese still make a living from the land, and they still have this kind of faith in Mao Zedong, then should we consider and respect the people's aspirations when we pass judgement on figures from our past, or not? Historically speaking, it isn't a simple issue of love and hate, it's about how we, the younger generation, define our forebears, and how we understand today's society. Why did families like yours return to China during the war?

GENERAL PHOEBE: In my generation, the intelligentsia looked at China and felt hope. That was the strength that knowledge brought them. Knowledge can make people love their country, and educated people can feel their country's pain, they're not at all bothered about their standard of living, they understand life but they're not living just in order to live. Many intellectuals say: "If my life's not that great, it doesn't matter, but to see China becoming powerful, that makes me happy, it's worth almost any degree of hardship." Many intellectuals, if they're real intellectuals, have this kind of response.

Millions of Chinese are educated now, but they're not intellectuals by my definition; their enjoyment doesn't come from seeking knowledge, it comes from the number of houses or fine clothes they have. Real intellectuals' greatest enjoyment comes from having an environment conducive to their studies, by means of which their country can make progress.

In fact, a prosperous lifestyle is appropriate for today's China, because China has just stepped over the threshold of the reforms which are opening up the economy, and needs a settled period of transition. This will provide those intellectuals who have the ability to make adjustments in the mechanism of Chinese society with an environment in which they can reflect and study. Prosperity means having a simple and easy spiritual and cultural life, and no fights and worries about great wealth or great poverty, still less painful entanglement in human affairs.

China today is witnessing an explosion of materialism, and consumerism is rife. When you open the newspaper, it's frightening how there are more and more ads for luxury homes, and anyone who doesn't have one is seemingly a non-person. If everyone wanted to live in a luxury home, where would we find the space? If our entire population of 1.3 billion people all wanted a luxury home, would there be enough? Of course not. In which case we'd have to move to the moon, and then that wouldn't be enough either. And after you've moved into your luxury home, you will inevitably have a whole lot of new desires, and it's never-ending . . .

XINRAN: What do you feel about the reforms in education which followed the economic reforms of the 1980s?

GENERAL PHOEBE: Education is the biggest failure of the economic reforms! I absolutely detest modern methods of English teaching, they're destroying people, and young people will never learn to love the English language. Whenever they get to year six in primary school, they have to cover the topics for the middle-school entrance exams, so the way they teach foreign languages is just to teach them a few idioms and tips. It's not teaching them to understand, speak, read and write, it's just spending time on memorising grammatical structure in order to get through the exams. It's the reason why our English teaching is so poor. When our English majors go abroad, they can't speak enough to get around. This is a "*sorry situation*". [And here she drops into English.] We didn't use to teach like this, and we didn't study like this before Liberation. After Liberation, we followed Soviet methods, and learned nothing at all. Have you seen what kind of students we turn out? It's such a waste of people, materials and lives!

XINRAN: Is it because the whole educational system was destroyed during the Cultural Revolution, and the educational level of the first cohort of teachers in 1977 was inadequate, and classroom education after that suffered from the economic upsurge of the 1980s, which had a serious impact on people's respect for academic study?

GENERAL PHOEBE: Chinese worker and peasant cadres have a popular saying which goes: the lowly are the cleverest, posh people are the daftest. The more you know, the stupider you are, and the greater your knowledge, the more reactionary it is. By the end of the Cultural Revolution, intellectuals were one of the Stinking Nine categories of society – they had really hit rock bottom.

The reforms of the 1980s came, created new respect for knowledge and talent again. So how did they show you this respect? Well, you got fantastic treatment, both in terms of material goods and your reputation. Then there was a reaction against this, but after that, there was another reaction against the reaction. Things change so rapidly. Now we're overwhelmed with a respect for material things, and knowledge has once again been devalued. How senior does a PhD make you nowadays? There are so many of them, doctorates aren't worth anything. Worse than that, there are lots of people with heaven knows what kind of doctorate, plagiarised or bought, and the academic world and society has absolutely no respect for that kind of thing. Only real study and real talent brings you real, unshakeable respect. Writing superficial work to get that PhD certificate makes people lose faith and then doctorates lose all credibility!

XINRAN: What do you think can be done to put that right?

GENERAL PHOEBE: The pendulum needs to swing back.

XINRAN: Isn't that like letting the market rule?

GENERAL PHOEBE: It's not the market. It's the country that needs to consider if it should be training people in this manner.

XINRAN: Why is this happening in China? In a lot of other countries, for instance developed countries in Europe and America, it has taken them nearly 250 years to go from control by religion to democratic republican systems. China has spent the last hundred years struggling towards the same goal, don't you think?

GENERAL PHOEBE: We've gone too fast. We were afraid of not catching up, and we really haven't caught up. Our thinking has lagged behind reality.

XINRAN: Do you think this is related to beliefs and culture?

GENERAL PHOEBE: Where do human beliefs come from? Why do humans create gods? All of us believe in a higher authority. But now the higher authority is the American dollar, and the dollar empire uses the dollar to realise its supremacy. And why is it so arrogant? Because it has plenty of money, it's perfectly natural. Humanity has not yet advanced past money worship to a spiritual civilisation.

XINRAN: Do you think China will emerge from dollar worship?

GENERAL PHOEBE: Yes, because more and more Chinese people are looking into very profound matters like the ones we are talking about now. Where is our society going? Our priority must be to allow personal enmities to fade so that we can believe in China's future.

XINRAN: Are there many others in this Officers' Village who are as reflective as you are? Is the government aware of your wealth of experience, and does it make use of it?

GENERAL PHOEBE: This care organisation is very big. We are all high-ranking, and it's hard for the management services department, they are all overworked. You see, our average age here is seventy-nine, there's a lot of dementia, and many of us can hardly walk, and are in wheelchairs. Everyone's going deaf, and when we gather together no one can hear anyone else. All these are problems specific to old age. The management's main duty is to keep us safe, and to do their best to take care of us in a general way. There's hardly any of that sending of retired people into different domains to change people's thinking and consciousness, like in American institutions.

However, society seems to be increasingly aware of our worth, and a lot of old cadres act as consultants, which of course also fills a need for social contact.

This place offers everything you could need. It's like a small country. There's a hospital, a bank, shops, a cinema, an activities hall with card-playing, ball games, music and entertainment. There's everything. The dining hall is not like a restaurant, the food is all home-cooked. All the old ladies and gents have their main meals with their friends, and getting snacks is very convenient too. You can pop downstairs to eat or, upstairs, there are small private dining rooms where you can order special meals. Our dining hall can seat a thousand. At the weekend, people take their children and grandchildren there for a meal, and then they don't need to cook. To be quite honest, when we lived in a cowshed during the Cultural Revolution, I never dreamed that we would enjoy the degree of comfort and respect that I do today.

XINRAN: What's your view of the current Chinese leadership?

GENERAL PHOEBE: Hu Jintao and Wen Jiabao? They're better than the old ones. They're new people, and they're hands-on. There's no personality cult.

XINRAN: I am very interested in their policies on giving aid to the west of China, developing rural education and tax relief for peasants in poor areas. These are the first leaders in a hundred years, with the exception of Mao Zedong, who have really thought about the peasants. They suffer great hardships and the tax burden on them is appalling.

GENERAL PHOEBE: And it's been like that since ancient times.

XINRAN: When we visited Anhui to do interviews, the peasants north of the Huai River told us that they had never dared to dream of tax relief. They said that there had never been a time when you tilled the land without paying the Emperor's Grain Tax. Never, since earliest time. Then there's the funds to develop education in the west. I see that as incredibly important. You can't develop the west of China and let education there lag behind.

GENERAL PHOEBE: Yes, we've begun a strategic opening-up of the west. In some areas, the infrastructure is quite good, like the Qinghai-Tibet railway, and the new Xinjiang-Gansu highway. I think that the leadership are investigating the situation. China is so big, the population so unevenly distributed. There's a great disparity between east and west, between town and country, and it's very hard to administer.

XINRAN: I have another question, I don't know if I can ask it, and that is about your second marriage. I know that it's the Chinese custom that one shouldn't ask questions about, one, changes within a family, and, two, about the private lives of the elderly. But I have heard that you had a very romantic courtship in your old age. Can you tell me about it?

GENERAL PHOEBE: I've known you since you were a child, you can ask me anything you like, and I'll answer anything that I can, and if I can't, I'll tell you. It's true, ours is an extraordinary story of love and marriage. We put our letters together in a book, called *160 Roses*. But I suggest you listen to my husband tell the story.

*

General Phoebe's husband looked like a scholar who had walked straight out of the pages of traditional Chinese literature – a very cultured man, still glowing with the vitality of the elderly academic. I had only heard of him through friends and family, and had not met him before. During this visit, I was observing his role in this marriage. Was he a realist who depended on her? Many marriages among those of advanced years were born of convenience. Was he just attracted by her reputation? General Phoebe's abilities combined with her moral integrity had been a magnet to many men. Or was he a romantic who had happened on her by chance? A lot of elderly Chinese were only liberated from political marriages and their parents' matchmaking in their later years . . .

Our interview would fulfil a long-held desire: I had always wanted very much to talk to a couple whose lives had harmoniously encompassed the culture of both China and the West.

*

XINRAN: You say you came from a traditional Chinese family. What kind of family was it?

LOUIS: I was born in Shaoxing in 1925. Our forebears were all salt merchants, who moved from Anhui province to Shaoxing in Zhejiang province during the Qianlong period, towards the end of the eighteenth century. Before the Anti-Japanese War we were well off, an extended family with four generations under one roof. As a boy, my first schooling was in the *Three Character Classic*. I received my primary education from a private tutor at home, then I went to a lower middle school in Shaoxing.

The salt market collapsed when the Anti-Japanese War broke out. Our family fell on hard times because our livelihood had gone. Then my father became a bank manager and in 1941 the whole family moved to Shanghai. I had gone from being the child of wealthy salt merchants to being the son of a bank employee. It changed our lives dramatically. I had been the "Little Master", now I was just an ordinary kid. In Shaoxing we had had a large house and courtyard, and everyone had their own room, but when we got to Shanghai, the seven of us were squeezed into two rooms, so our standard of living had plummeted.

XINRAN: Do you have any memories of his work in the bank?

LOUIS: He was in a merchant bank, a very small bank. I only went there once, and it didn't make much impression on me.

XINRAN: What happened to the bank's employees after Liberation?

LOUIS: In 1952, many small banks collapsed, and my father's later years were quite hard. I've always had a guilty conscience about that. After Liberation the Party wanted us to "make a clean break" with any capitalists we knew. In principle, my father's class origin was top-level white-collar, but I didn't understand the political categories, and I told them he was a big landlord. Top-level white-collar workers were at most "petit bourgeois", but a big landlord wasn't the same thing at all, and as a result my family got put into the "black" categories. After Liberation, my parents lived on their own in Shanghai, and my brothers and sisters and I didn't see much of them. We just gave them a bit of money to live on every month. I hardly ever saw him, especially after the Cultural Revolution began. Firstly, because I had been sent to do labour in the countryside for six years, and secondly, because of something very painful which happened.

When the Cultural Revolution began, my father was still a bank manager, and he helped the son of my wet nurse by getting him a job as an office boy in the bank. When the bank closed down, the boy went back to Shaoxing and joined the Red Guards, then he came back to Shanghai along with other rebels. He said that when the bank closed, the guards had given a firearm to my father. Keeping a private firearm was very serious indeed. He went to my father's house and said: "Will you confess, or shall I report it to the Shanghai Red Guards?" When I heard this, I said: "We'll deal with it. I and my rebel brothers and sisters will confront my father." This must have been the end of 1966 or the beginning of 1967. My father knew nothing about the whole business, so he said he really didn't have a handgun.

I took my politics pretty seriously in those days, and I wanted to "make a clean break" with him. It was like the public struggle sessions but in the family. This hurt my father deeply, and it's one of the things that has caused me the most sorrow in my whole life.

My mother died in 1969, and none of her children were with her. Only my sister-in-law and my first wife went to the funeral home. I put in a request to go to the funeral, and my chief said, sure, I could go, but I had to remain firm politically, she was the wife of a landlord. So I took my son and daughter, and we went with my first wife and my sister-in-law to the funeral. My father was standing there alone, crying and making his bows, and we just stood there expressionless. We had "made a clean break" so we couldn't cry. That's something I feel ashamed of too.

After the smashing of the Gang of Four, my father and I talked it over, and I said that we had been too extreme then.

XINRAN: Did he understand?

LOUIS: Probably he did. He still loved us as a father. Though at that time, we really had made a clean break between him and us.

XINRAN: But you can't really make a complete break, can you, with all the upbringing you received from your family?

LOUIS: That's true. No matter what, we were brought up with Confucian standards. There was an order of seniority between young and old, and even walking down the street, you couldn't walk however you wanted. My mother, especially, took our upbringing very seriously. What made the greatest impression on me was the three things that she asked of us. She said that to be a person, you must first: Impress people with your appearance. And by "appearance", she didn't mean looking good, but that you carried yourself with dignity. The second thing was: Impress people with your language. When you spoke you had to use appropriate language. And the third was: Impress people with your pen – you had to write well. My father taught us the Analects of Confucius, and that made a big impression on me too. We children played around, it's true, but we couldn't be too mischievous, and I never did anything really improper.

I went to upper middle school in Shanghai, and in 1945 I started at Sui'an University. Sui'an was pretty strong in foreign languages. It was an American Church college. During my four years there, I began to believe in the Communist Party and in socialism, and became a CCP member. But I think that Christianity had a very big influence on me all the same. When I first arrived at the university, I discovered that my classmates helped each other in a Christian spirit, and helped me too. Students had to register for courses when they started, and it was a credits system. You chose your own classes and how many credits to build up. I was building up economics credits, and the college had four or five classrooms I could choose from, but I didn't know how to choose. My classmates were in the University Christian Fellowship and explained the differences between the five classrooms. They were extremely patient. This spirit of mutual support made a big impression on me. Our university had a college-wide organisation called the University of Christianity, with lots of sub-groups which included other religions and political views. The underground Communist Party wanted me to rally my fellow students, and the best way of doing this was by organising the groups. So I got together a hundred or so students into a larger group, with me as its chairman. The aim was to provide student support services, including holding lots of parties, and what drew people in mainly was this ethos of service.

XINRAN: And did you retain this Christian spirit alongside your faith in the CCP?

LOUIS: I never was a Christian, I've always been a very free spirit. But I've followed the spirit of Christianity. I joined the CCP because I was critical of Chiang Kai-shek. He was advocating a civil war, and imposing a dictatorship, but our college was very strong on democracy, and democracy and freedom was an aspiration for many of our students. When I joined the Party I didn't at that point have a very clear idea of what Communism was.

XINRAN: If I were to ask you about the three happiest and the three most painful experiences you have had, what would you say?

LOUIS: I'm not sure I can give you three of each, but I can talk to you about happiness and sorrow.

Before I retired, I was head of the secretariat at the Shanghai municipal offices. I was employed by the municipality continuously after I left the armed forces. Before the Cultural Revolution, I worked in the secretariat of its Standing Committee, in Archives, Meetings and Reports. I was in charge of handling documents for the archives, organising the municipal meetings and conferences, and writing up reports. It wasn't that I wanted to do this sort of work, I was just following orders.

I feel quite gratified that, one, I have never made a serious error during my whole career; two, I have never been infected by the bad habits which some officials have, I feel quite proud of that; and, three, friends have been very important in my life, and I have a lot of them. My wife says I've been in the dung heap without getting dirty, but I say Chinese officialdom isn't absolutely and completely corrupt, is it?

There are several things which have caused me great sorrow in my life! The worst was being imprisoned for a year during the Cultural Revolution and doing six years of hard labour in Nanjing, because of a couple of things I said.

The first thing I said was in 1968, when I was leader of the study group at work. No one understood what the Cultural Revolution was about and, as group leader, I had to explain it to them, but I didn't understand it either. So I said that according to Lin Biao the achievements of the Cultural Revolution were huge, and its failures were minute. But, I said, I saw it as exactly the opposite: all I'd seen were failures, and its failures were huge, and I hadn't seen any successes yet. Afterwards, it was put to me that I could have got shot for saying that, because it was not only an attack on the Cultural Revolution, it was a smear on the reputation of the deputy commander-in-chief of the revolution.

The second thing I said was that if Zhang Chunqiao, one of the Gang of Four, had not had the backing of Jiang Qing, Mao's wife, he would not have come to prominence. This was interpreted as an assault on the headquarters of the proletariat and I was immediately attacked as an active counter-revolutionary, and locked up in the basement of our offices for a year!

Luckily I'm a philosophical sort of person. After a year, I was transferred to Nanjing to do hard labour and there I stayed until the Gang of Four were smashed. Only then did I get my job back. That was the worst thing that ever happened to me. Working in the underground Party against the GMD was nothing compared to being condemned to hard labour as a criminal, by the very government and Party that I believed in. Then there was the death of my first wife, the premature death of my son, my daughter's illness. If it wasn't for my son and my daughter, now that I have Phoebe as my partner I would be absolutely 100 per cent happy.

XINRAN: Do you feel that the lives of your generation have been worthwhile?

LOUIS: I think so. We've suffered so many trials and tribulations, but I believe that the progress of human society is never straightforward, and that's true of society and a country and of each individual.

XINRAN: Don't you think people like you have paid too heavy a price? For instance, your father was from a great salt merchant family, but his family fortunes collapsed because of the war. And in the 1960s, the Party that you believed in inflicted such injustice on you. Don't you think that was too great a price to pay?

LOUIS: No, quite the opposite. As far as I am concerned personally, my contribution has not been enough. Because everyone who's born into this world, into society, should make their contribution, irrespective of their ability; the main thing is that they should offer it, it should not be demanded of them.

I never thought about the contribution that my family had made in the past as salt merchants. After all, the salt trade was rather feudal, and was built up on the basis of exploitation of many people. I've been to see the salt fields on Taishan Island in Zhejiang province. That's where the seawater comes in and labourers dry out the salt crystals in the sun. It basically requires no investment or technology, just physical labour. It occurred to me that my ancestors had made their wealth by exploiting countless numbers of people down the generations. And the salt merchants had to be on good terms with the salt officials, the so-called salt officials–salt merchants arrangement. As a salt merchant you had to have an official licence without which you couldn't trade; everything else was called "illegal salt".

We were a very large family, and owned maybe 2,000 *mu** of land. We were self-sufficient in grain, and rented out land on which, each winter, we collected rent. We sent boats to collect it. Until I was sixteen, I'd never even washed a handkerchief, let alone cooked, I was completely dependent on other people to look after me. If our society had carried on in this way, how would the labouring people and the poorest in our country ever have made a better living?

XINRAN: So do you think that people of your generation feel the same way as you do?

LOUIS: I think the majority do. As for China's development after Liberation, whether you're talking about inside the Party or my old comrades, there are differing views.

First, on Mao Zedong. I don't hate him, I admire him actually, but I

---

* 330 acres/133 hectares.

don't accept everything he said and did. When he launched the Anti-Rightist movement, I didn't know then, we none of us knew ... traditional "absolute loyalty" was the measure of a good cadre, and we certainly never assumed individual responsibility as we do in modern politics. It was only when Mao died that I began to feel that he had made serious mistakes. I have forgiven him, because from the upbringing he received, after he had achieved power and status, he might well have felt he wanted to be emperor and to live in the emperor's palace. When he stood on top of Tiananmen Gate at the proclamation of the People's Republic, there were so many people cheering him on, and everyone was shouting, "We wish you ten thousand years of life!" The worst thing that happened was the appearance of all those sycophants around him, with their foolish "loyalty", and I include us in that. When Liu Shaoqi was declared a traitor and expelled from the Party, everyone in the Central Committee had to raise their hands and vote. One person pretended to be asleep – her name was Shuai Mengqi – but we all knew she wasn't asleep: it was because she didn't agree. It made me think – what kind of high-ranking cadres are you? Are you responsible for a country or are you just courtiers to the emperor? Why did they all stick their hands up? So China's stagnation in the last hundred years is not the sole responsibility of some imperial minister. We all have a responsibility for it, it isn't just a problem of Mao Zedong as an individual. I sometimes wonder, if I'd been in his shoes, might I have become complacent too? We can't escape our human instincts, that's why we need democracy and a political system to suppress the despotism and dictatorship which can be a product of such instinct.

XINRAN: So you're saying that not only was Mao Zedong destroyed by blindly loyal flatterers, but also, while we Chinese were spending the last hundred years searching for a "saviour", we were on a slippery slope, like the "blindly loyal" saddled with old monarchist feelings when the dynasty has come to an end.

LOUIS: That's just how it was. We were only too happy to put our leader on a pedestal, and gave very little thought to the need for personal responsibility. In our recent history, no leader has had the courage to face up to this and state it clearly. When Mao Zedong launched the Cultural Revolution, he ended up passing responsibility for it to the Gang of Four. Some people say that the Gang of Four was really a Gang of Five. Everything bad was done by the Gang of Four but Mao agreed to it. I am critical of Mao for this, but my main feeling is that we didn't have the proper mechanisms in place within the Communist Party. If China doesn't have proper political mechanisms, then it will be possible for a second Mao to appear. Our generation has been enlightened about this, we haven't condemned Mao Zedong. I am a victim of the Cultural Revolution, but I don't brood on it. As we say nowadays, "no recriminations, no regrets". This was not something one person did – we were all responsible, and maybe it was something Chinese society had to go through.

XINRAN: Do you think the young generation understand this? Do they know what you went through?

LOUIS: Hard to say. They haven't had the intense experiences or suffered the hardship that their parents' generation did. This generation have grown up, mostly, in comfort, so we'll have to see whether they arrive at a proper understanding of that period of history.

Nowadays, we greatly admire the Hu Jintao and Wen Jiabao model. Their slogan, "put people first", is admirable. When we watch the televised proceedings of the People's Congress, we see them bow to the delegates before they speak, and then bow to the podium. We feel that in the past, they were only giving the people a casual wave, but now they're making a bow to the lower ranks. Surely that's a good beginning. It should always have been like that. In the past, Communist Party doctrine held that everyone was equal, no matter what their status. Actually everyone had different jobs, so they couldn't be equal. As educated people, the most exasperating thing was we were not treated equally, but we didn't dare say anything. Back then, we intellectuals couldn't support egalitarianism, liberalism or democracy in any way at all, because our kind of democracy was condemned as capitalist democracy. Of course, democracy for me probably *was* capitalist democracy. I got it from school and from the Church. Our democracy was the French Revolution kind. But we *were* a bit democratic, we always had that tendency.

XINRAN: Does democracy have a class nature in itself?

LOUIS: That's really hard to say. Before the smashing of the Gang of Four, I didn't say what I felt, but I was democratically minded. My position as an individual was different, not the same as the accepted political view. But nowadays everything's a bit more democratic than it was.

XINRAN: Tell me about your first meeting with the General, and your feelings for her then.

LOUIS: As you know, we both joined the army at the same time from Shanghai. The hundred or so Shanghai recruits were divided into three units, and she was the head of one unit, and I was the head of another. We had a lot to do with each other in those days – we met at all the meetings of unit heads. I was very struck by her, and I once said to her: "You are so youthful, and beautiful too." I so wanted to marry her, that would have made me very happy, but I also felt she was beyond my reach. She had a sort of high-minded purity, much more than I did. I joked with her that she was like the Maid of Orléans. Later we started studying and training, and we were in the same group again, with her as the leader, so we saw even more of each other. I felt she liked me too. But in those days, leaders were not allowed to get into romantic relationships, so I just went on loving her in silence.

XINRAN: Did you feel she was keen on you then?

LOUIS: I felt she was. But she was warm to everyone around her. Although she was in the Party, she was still gentle and kind, not brusque and aggressive like a lot of the Party members. Why was I so sure? Well, after all, we were both from Shanghai and had both been underground Party members. We were from similar backgrounds, so I thought then that she was probably keener on me than on other people.

XINRAN: When you left after a year, did you write to her?

LOUIS: No, she was in a secret unit, you couldn't just write letters – when we met again, forty-two years had gone by, and in the intervening time we'd had absolutely no news of each other. In 1988, articles about China's five women generals appeared in the newspapers, and her name was there. That was the first time I knew what had happened to her. But by then, I felt even less able to bother her. She had a top job, Deputy Head of the PLA Foreign Languages Institute, and besides, the PLA Foreign Languages Institute was still a secret unit. Although all this brought back memories of our youth, I thought she must have married, and I had a wife too, so that was another reason why I couldn't think about her in that way.

XINRAN: What chance encounter brought you together again?

LOUIS: My wife died in 1990, and the head of my work unit and my colleagues soon began introducing me to eligible women. But I was over sixty, and it's difficult to start a new relationship at that age.

In the spring of 1992, Phoebe and I met at the house of some mutual friends, and the next day I arranged to meet her for lunch. I asked her: "Old friend, how do you want to spend the rest of your life?" She said that marriages late in life rarely worked out well! She gave me many reasons:

when two people had led such different former lives, it was very hard to find things in common. Problems with children, social relationships and so on, all were potential sources of conflict. Besides, an older person on their own is not necessarily lonely: one can read books and have friends. That day I felt that she had turned me down flat. We agreed that we would just be friends, and wouldn't marry. Even though I was introduced to more women, her image was so strong in my heart that no one else could hold a candle to her.

XINRAN: You began to write letters to her?

LOUIS: At the start I was very impetuous, but slowly, I became wiser. I wasn't sure I was a match for someone of such elegance. Then I discovered through her letters that her feelings for me were growing stronger all the time. She wrote that sometimes she would go out for a stroll in the evenings, and she would look at the stars, and it was like talking to me. She felt that she was getting emotionally involved, in fact that she was falling in love. We began to open our hearts to each other. Other people's love letters talk about their love, but ours were not like that; we talked of how we felt about life. It was through our letters that our true feelings for each other were born.*

XINRAN: So your letters were like angels, bringing you lovers together. Then after you got married, did you feel there were any problems, any major differences, you hadn't foreseen?

LOUIS: To be honest, the differences between us in our daily routine are very obvious. Then there's the fact that she is a general, and I'm an ordinary government official – that's a very big difference. In terms of administrative rank, I am four or five grades below her. Then again, our family backgrounds have very little in common – she's from the intellectual elite, I'm from a feudal family of provincial officials. The kind of "salt merchant" upbringing that I had and her upbringing among the westernised intellectual elite were completely different. So on the surface, it's like the gap between the West and China, not an easy one to bridge. But in fact, "*we are very [well] matched!*" [he drops into English]. Everyone thinks it's strange, and even we're surprised that it's happened.

On our tenth wedding anniversary, I wrote her a poem called "Ten Years – On our tenth wedding anniversary, to my beloved".

---

* See the following chapter, p.307, for a selection of these remarkable letters.

Ten years, a mere flicker in the evening of the river of our years.
Ten years, an instant in your life and mine.
Hand in hand, we know life's brilliance; shoulders hunched, we face life's
*   storms; all is exquisite and beautiful.*
First knowing your heart was like pure heaven.
Without you, I, Louis, do not exist.
All is like a heartfelt whisper,
All is heart-born poetry, my ten-year enjoyment.

I dedicated this poem to her, and it came from the bottom of my heart.

We had only been married six months, when my son suddenly fell ill and died. This was a very heavy blow to me, but General Phoebe comforted me by saying: "You must not feel that it is only *your* son who has died. I would drop everything to go and help if it were just an army friend's family this had happened to, let alone you! Let's weather this storm together." So we went to Shanghai and she helped arrange my son's funeral. She steeled me. She said: "You still have me!" She knew I couldn't stop worrying about my seven-year-old grandson and she told me that we would take on supporting my daughter-in-law and grandson together, like we would take on the future together. All this was a huge support to me, and gave me great strength.

After that, I transferred my retirement pension from Shanghai to Beijing. A year or two after that, in 1996, my daughter got cerebellar ataxia. Her cerebellum atrophied, and walking and activity became very difficult for her. The doctor told me, this is like a terminal illness, there's no cure. Again General Phoebe comforted and supported me. "Your daughter is my daughter too," she said. So we go back to Shanghai frequently, to see my daughter. Once, when she was in hospital, I went out to look for a nurse, and she stayed with my daughter. When I came back, I saw she had been washing my daughter's feet for her. All the other patients and their families said to my daughter, what a good mother you have! I was very moved.

She doesn't just hold my hand and watch the sunset, she weathers the storms with me, and that's so important. And for me, losing a son and having a seriously ill daughter were bad storms! Without her I might have collapsed. So from then on our feelings for each other kept growing deeper and more ardent.

I really feel in my heart that I am very fortunate, she really is a very good woman.

XINRAN: Auntie and I talked a bit about how she felt after you married. She said that she gained from you another chance to be a woman, you gave her the chance of tenderness, gave her a man's protection. Don't you feel that this marriage of yours is actually one between equals?

LOUIS: I feel this relationship is of value to both of us. I'm a deeply emotional person, in the old days I'd be criticised for being "petit-bourgeois sentimental". Actually she's that kind of person too, she's given me real love. I can only answer in terms of our love.

XINRAN: If you disagree over something, who gives way, General Phoebe or you?

LOUIS: In principle we always talk things through. I tend to be more hasty, and she is more circumspect. She is usually very tolerant of me, but now that I realise I go too far sometimes, I try to catch myself straight away. There are no rifts between us, and really no secrets either.

*

As the *China Witness* trip was coming to an end, we went one Friday afternoon to sit in on an English class taught by General Phoebe in a University of the Third Age which she had set up at the retirement village. Thirty-odd retired generals came to the class, and after each one had handed in their homework, they sat down, straight-backed, at ordinary school desks. They started by singing three songs in English, "to remind them of their English", and then listened attentively as General Phoebe read them a short story about a family; after that, they broke up into small groups for earnest conversation practice. Finally, a number of them told the whole class stories in English about their families. According to these white-haired students, the story they most liked reading aloud was one they had written themselves called "We are the Fortunate Generation".

I asked them why they worked so hard at their English, and they gave me all sorts of different answers.

An artillery instructor: "If I learn a bit of English, then when I go abroad to visit my children, I can get around on my own."

An army doctor: "So many of our home appliances nowadays have instructions in English, so if I learn some English, I don't need to bother other people so much."

A hero of the Korean War air battles: "During the war, we were fighting in the air. Now it's peacetime and we should make friends on the ground. If you can't speak English, you can't make your own foreign friends."

A quartermaster: "All those foreigners who are coming to China for the 2008 Olympics, if they stop us in the street and ask the way, and we can't understand English, how can we help them out?"

I don't know any other people on this earth who are as concerned about others as the Chinese are.

Interlude 3

Love Letters

In the West there is a long history of love letters. But in Chinese culture, especially in recent times, we are not used to seeing this kind of "emotional life" in writing, particularly as most marriages were arranged. Many young Chinese still don't believe there was romance between their "politically uniformed" parents and grandparents, and Westerners will hardly have read love stories from Communist-period China before the 1980s. I was so amazed reading the love letters between General Phoebe and her husband, Louis, not only by their writing about love in such a "revolutionary voice" for China, but also by their sacrifice, by how much love and emotion had been kept controlled in the deep ocean of their daily lives. I have, therefore, selected some of their love letters from *160 Roses*, in the hope that readers can, like me, be moved and encouraged that the feelings of these two people have not been worn away by political storms. Let not the love that surrounds us be lost; let not the heart that adores you suffer pain.

I.

15 February 1992

Dear Comrade Phoebe,

As the poet Wang Bo said, "*While there exists on Earth one who knows me for my true self, / Though separated from me by the expanse of Heaven, / She seems close at hand.*" When we said goodbye, on the evening of the 12th, at the entrance to East China Normal University, as I walked home under the waning moon, I felt immersed in those ancient lines of poetry. It has been a New Year of such unforgettable happiness. I shall always remember the 1992 Spring Festival.

Before the Spring Festival, when our former colleague told me that you always spent the festival in Shanghai, and gave me your address, I very much wanted to meet up with my old army friend after so many years apart. I cannot conceal the fact that you made a deep impression on me during our short time together at the Beijing Labour University Foreign Languages Training Course in 1949, and I thought we were both fond of each other. The thought even occurred to me once (although certainly not now) that, if I hadn't left the university, you might not have chosen to marry our old friend who died so prematurely. Since my wife died a year or so ago, I have been introduced to half a dozen potential matches, but I have not been able to make up my mind. I've often thought, and said to other people too: how is one to find that one good woman to partner up with from among that immense sea of humanity, of strangers? If I am to marry again, then I'm going to maintain my high standards, and I would especially hope our relationship would be founded on real familiarity. So when I heard the news of your sad loss, and learned where you were, I came to what you called my "great" decision, and resolved to set off in pursuit. Meeting you, in the restaurant on the fourteenth floor of the Hengshan Hotel, was a further spur: I jumped in at the deep end and asked *that* question, to find out how the land lay with you. Firstly, because you were still you, the same you as four decades ago. That was the most fundamental thing. And also you remembered so many details of the things we did together back then. You hadn't even forgotten that we bumped into each other at the Spring Festival in 1956 in front of the Shanghai Park Hotel. Added to that, when we talked I discovered that we saw eye to eye on so many things and shared a common outlook, which secretly delighted me. I wasn't deliberately playing up to you, it was a true meeting of minds, as if we happened to have been practising t'ai chi in the same place.

At the restaurant table that day, when I laid bare my true feelings to you with that probing question, and you gave me your counter-arguments, I was deeply impressed by your sincerity and wisdom; indeed I was inspired to model myself on you. I said then: I'm disappointed but not lost. And that was the truth too. For a brief moment, in that elegant dining room, I was disconsolate. That was the moment when we fell silent and sipped our drinks. But I very quickly shook that feeling off, because even if you had rejected my probing, I had not only not lost your friendship, my feelings of tenderness were deeper than ever. I not only had absolutely no reason to mope, I had found new life beliefs to adopt, the "triple action, triple happiness" you talked about – adequate work, exercise and social activity, and the joy of helping people, being content with one's lot and getting enjoyment out of life. I wanted to put your formula for happiness into practice, and I talked about it in our senior cadres' branch office and to friends, and they also found it inspiring.

You said that my probing "was very natural" and I realised that you understood my feelings and would forgive my presumptuousness. I am so grateful to you! It's true – when I came to think about it more calmly afterwards, I really had overstepped the mark. At the very least, I was naive. The differences between us exist objectively, and I have to acknowledge that. How could I have had those foolish thoughts, on the slender basis solely of my feeling that there was "a definite basis" for the relationship and of the honesty and goodness in my own heart? Of course your negative answer was nothing to do with dislike for me, but arose from reasons at a much deeper level, which indeed I should have considered myself. Well, it's over now, and luckily there was no one nearby to make fun of or criticise us. So let's regard it as just a minor episode in the course of our new friendship! However, I still have to apologise most humbly to you. In this, my first letter to you, I have blabbered on and repeated much of what I said to you then, but it is only to get it off my chest, and we won't mention it again, all right?

I will put down my pen now; allow me to wish you every happiness. At the same time, I hope that we may be able to fulfil our heart's desire – to become truly good friends, and to exchange many, many letters. I'm also looking forward to us inviting two or three close friends to accompany us on a trip around China soon. I particularly hope that we can go to my home town and have a look at the Dayu Palace, King Yue's Burial Mound, the Orchid Pavilion, Lu Xun's birthplace, and enjoy the shady mountain paths and the black-awning boats . . .

With best wishes,
Louis

2.

15 February 1992

My dear old army friend,

I hope you are well. I was delighted to have the opportunity to celebrate the Spring Festival with you and have such a good talk about everything, after an interval of forty years. I arrived home this afternoon at 2 p.m., after a smooth journey.

We all find that memories come flooding back at the Spring Festival. Our joining the army together then is still, today, so vivid in my mind. The boys and girls of that time have become old men and women, but our hearts haven't changed, we've still kept our revolutionary spirit. That part of our lives will always bring back beautiful memories for us, don't you think?

I'm sending you some photos of me in military uniform, as a memento. I'll close now.

Best wishes,
Phoebe

5.

5 March 1992

Dear Phoebe,

Your letter of the 27th and the article about "the common people's general" gave me another reason to be happy! The fact that in two short weeks we have exchanged letters twice – the pair of us are well capable of being "activists" – is sufficient proof that we're going to make a go of rebuilding our friendship. How happy I am!

I found the article, "A good Party member in our midst", both intimate and moving. It is actually written with great simplicity; when the writer calls you "the common people's general", she is saying something quite profound, but does not conceal your brilliance either. I appreciate the way you behave as an official, and admire still more your high-minded determination to avoid self-seeking and greed with regard to the standard of living the government offers you (even in the broadest sense). Reading the article has given me a deeper knowledge of you: your ideology is even loftier than before, you are even more you! Really, I have so much to learn from you. If all Party cadres – especially high-ranking cadres – were like you, then the Party, our country, our socialist endeavour, would be so much stronger.

In this letter, I mainly want to tell you briefly what happened to me after I left the Foreign Languages Training Course, to reciprocate the account you gave me that day in Hengshan Park of the last few decades of your life. I left the army in May 1952 and was allocated a job back in Shanghai by the Jing'an Party Branch Committee, in the Jing'an District Educational Course for Unemployed Workers, first as education section leader and then as director of the course. The Five Antis movement had just finished, and there were a lot of unemployed workers, most of whom had been activists. The government had guaranteed them jobs and, in the meantime, they received political and general education. We had around a thousand students and a score of cadres and instructors on the course. So the Foreign Languages Training Unit's classes in current politics, social development and basic philosophy became the "capital" which I put to immediate use – and the teaching also made me miss the war years. At the beginning of 1954, I transferred to the Shanghai Municipal Labour Office to do workers' education; and in the autumn of 1965, I was transferred again, this time to the Office Party Committee of the Shanghai People's Committee (in the Municipal Government). I was first made Theoretical Instructor in the Officer Cadres' School, and then my job was changed to secretarial work: handling documentation, organising meetings and drafting reports (leaders' speeches, work summaries, short reports and so on). From then on, I earned my daily bread in Archives, Meetings and Reports, apart from the ten years between 1968 and 1978 when I was expelled by the Gang of Four and sent to 7 May Cadre School and to work in a factory. This carried on being my job (from 1978 onwards I was in the Shanghai Municipal Office) until I retired at the end of 1987.

I had my ups and downs during a thirty-odd-year career in office work, but basically I wanted to make myself into a good "tool" for the job. I have to say that I succeeded, that is, after I had undergone a difficult process of personal transformation, I achieved it. You know, in those days, I minded the fact that army life was "not free"; and government organisations did not permit "personal freedom" either. So gradually, I moved from a lack of awareness to being very aware, and consequently had to give up my "personal freedom". I sometimes think that since I was willing to make myself into a good "tool", why did I need to leave the army in the first place? But there's another side to me. In my heart of hearts, I always regarded myself as a student, but always found it difficult to act the "government official". At the same time, in the presence of VIPs like the mayor and deputy mayor, I showed them respect but would never bow and scrape to them. I have another secret in my heart, and that's the feelings about "democracy" which I revealed to you at dinner that day. Even though I very rarely bring it up in front of people, it's something which deep inside me doesn't let me rest . . . Well, that's a brief introduction to me. I'll tell you in more detail when I get the chance.

The spring rain has been pattering down in Shanghai since the day before yesterday, and a lot of people have caught colds. The weather on the central plains must be pretty much the same, so please do take care of yourself. Will write more later.

With very best wishes,
Louis

6.

1 March 1992

My dear friend,

I hope you are well. I assume you will have received my last week's letter to you and the *PLA News* article which I enclosed. I got a letter today from our friend, saying how happy he was to hear that we had met at the Spring Festival, and how impressed he was by you.

I heard recently that my three problems about moving to accommodation at the Beijing Cadre Retirement Institute where I live have been resolved, so I really can step down this year. Mentally, I've already made a number of preparations to retire: apart from the physical living arrangements, the most important thing is creating a sort of "microclimate" which will bring happiness to one's soul, and that includes friendship, music and many other spiritual aspirations. I feel I just need to put my mind to it, and I should be able to do it.

With very best wishes,
Phoebe

21.

29/30 April 1992

My dearest friend,

This morning I headed back to my office after three happy classes with my research students, and I spotted a thick letter from you on my writing desk. This added a further warm glow of happiness to my already good mood. It's that head-over-heels-in-love feeling that you described! I never thought that as an old woman I would get back those feelings of my youth – and what beautiful feelings! And if my true feelings for you enable you to shake off the misery of loneliness, then that is wonderful. I sometimes think that it would really be worth a psychologist doing some in-depth research into this new-style relationship which we have created between us! (You call it love, but I feel that it seems to go beyond the common concept of love, because it is purer, more lofty, richer in poetic feeling.) We could joke that we've unwittingly created a new and original way of loving, don't you think?

I savoured your so-loving letter over and over again, and it gave me much food for thought. I recalled our feelings for each other right from beginning to end. I think the affection between us dates back to 1949, when we had just joined the army, but from my point of view this was just a "diffuse" sort of affection, because I was only eighteen years old. My mother had instilled into me the need to be extremely prudent where love and marriage was concerned, and not to get involved too soon. I did what she said, and pushed love right to the back of my mind. Of course that didn't stop me being attracted to friends of the opposite sex, so I knew the difference between those whom I liked, and the rest, but it never went beyond that. Then we went through ideological reform at the Foreign Languages Training Unit, and I thought even less about things like that. Even so, there were some students from among so many whom I was especially fond of, and wanted to be closer to, and you were one of them. Then, later on, a number of chance meetings brought Comrade Xiaoda into my life. Marrying him was a natural outcome to that, and we had a happy and fulfilling life together. After Xiaoda died, I buried the love he had given me deep within myself – it is hard to forget a love like that. But he had, after all, passed away, and I was still a woman with what Buddhists call feelings and appetites. I longed for my feelings of love to be reciprocated, and this was especially true because I was living completely on my own. But I never realised that I had this longing, because I had a very fulfilled emotional life: I had my job, I am very close to my brothers and sisters, and have a wonderful relationship with my children and the deep and enduring friendship of comrades, both old army friends and my students. So I felt I needed nothing more emotionally – until I bumped into you again this Spring Festival and was bowled over by the depth of your feelings for me. It all seems rather different to what I talked about above. It's more refined, more moving, more constantly present, very like the ardour of youthful passion. And yet not like that (which is why I think I can't describe these feelings as ordinary love) because youthful love brings with it sexual love and longings for happiness in one's future life together. But we're old now, and have had abundant experience of life, so our feelings are more rational, more mature. We don't want the feelings between us to have any kind of outcome, we just hope we will always be able to feel the communication between our hearts. It's even hard to find the language to describe this, but it makes us feel both happy and very fortunate. These feelings are so pure that they do not allow us to be troubled by the least unhappiness, which is why I described them as "diffuse". Even more essential is that our feelings have been nurtured through our correspondence, because letters can express the most beautiful, most heartfelt feelings. Our feelings are beautiful so the language we use is beautiful, and we can read the letters over and over, and constantly savour the words. Do you think I'm right?

I also think that it's not just anyone who can achieve this level of emotional communication. Firstly, it needs to be based in mutual love; secondly, the couple have to be relatively well matched intellectually, educationally and culturally; and thirdly, and this is even more important, both have to share the same sublime aspirations, constantly exploring aspects of human life and constantly rising, through study, to ever higher realms of the soul. It is, I believe, only under such conditions that this kind of love can be firmly grounded and can gradually evolve towards a degree of perfection.

Perhaps because of my career as a teacher, I have always been willing to look for the answers to many questions in books. Since I became aware of these special emotions between us, I've been exploring and researching it a great deal, and have even read *On Love* by Vasilyev. This is a rather serious book, which I bought because many of my young friends were reading it, and I wanted to know what it was about so that I could set them some ideological tasks. I brought my own questions to it and read through the relevant chapters; but although I found the book inspiring, it didn't quite accord with our own reality. That's why I wrote above that somehow our feelings seemed in some way "original", still to be researched! I hope you're not going to laugh at me for being too bookish!

You asked me if I could go to Shanghai after I retired. In theory, yes, but it's a bit late now, as I have already been fixed up with a place at the Cadres' Retirement Institute. Actually I really do prefer Beijing. Wherever I am, it won't make any difference to us. The main thing is that we should be able to write unlimited letters to each other. I'll definitely come to Shanghai every year, so we can always see each other, and after I've moved to Beijing, you are welcome to take a trip up here whenever you have a chance. You can stay here, and I can take you to see other old army friends or we can go sightseeing in Beijing. I've rambled terribly in this letter, so I'll stop now. I hope you won't fret any more about not getting letters from me. Believe me, I will write to you sooner or later, so don't worry.

With best wishes,
Phoebe

24.

10 May 1992

Dearest Phoebe,

Let me throw restraint to the winds, and shout out my feelings vehemently! I got your letter of the 6th yesterday, and having my dear distant one's letter to read at the weekend was a great stroke of good luck for me. At dinner I like to drink a glass (about three fluid ounces) of locally brewed liquor, and so I warmed up my tipple, quickly sat down and gently tore open my love letter. As I read, I sipped the wine; only you can share these tender feelings! In the evening there was the weekend dance at my old workplace, and so I went out. I generally go dancing two or three times a month – it's free of charge. Too bad I'm such a country bumpkin from a foreign school that I don't dance very well. If only my valiant and gentle Phoebe were in Shanghai, my dancing prowess would no doubt soon attain postdoctoral level.

After the dance I came back home, and got your letter out to read it for the second time. I marked in red pen such memorable phrases as "Dear Lou" [in English], "In any case, you are already at the centre of my affections". I read and read, and marked and marked. My eyes were wet with tears, and my heart trembled. Such true joy! To be able to receive so much true, fervent and constant affection from you fills me both with excitement and contentment, and is even rather flattering, because I'm really a rather mediocre and superficial person, even though my love does run true and deep. But here too you have infected and inspired me. I rejoice that I can have your deep love for myself, I must do my best to reciprocate and, just as you do, irradiate and deepen life and everything around me!

Now it's eight o'clock on Sunday morning and I've finished my various chores. I have "shut myself up away upstairs to become one with you", as Lu Xun put it, and to perform my sacred task – writing a letter, to you. My daughter-in-law has taken my six-year-old grandson, whose name is Erjia (his baby name is "Jimmy") to see her parents, and my son is sleeping late. In such an atmosphere of warmth and gentleness, I open my heart to my dear, faraway one and make a reading of its rhythms. First I take out of the drawer all those much-treasured letters you have written to me, and read them again. In the forties, I saw the Hollywood film *Review of Lovers' Dreams** and, although I've long forgotten what it was about, I remembered its name while I was doing this because, just as if I was watching the film, I replayed in my mind our love, from that early spring day in February to the fiery heat of May. How amazingly quickly time has passed, and how very logically things have progressed. Let me quickly sketch in how things have developed: the happiness of our deepening feelings as we met again – I, far below you, probing; you,

---

* Its English title was *Random Harvest*.

from your high position, enlightening me; then re-establishing relations on the basis of "good friends" – "letters between the two of us" linking us together, bringing us the closeness and happiness of intimate friends – further reminiscences and further exchanges, filling the voids in each other's souls, and "feeling abundantly enriched by life" – having the pleasure of reading each other's letters, and "getting boundless satisfaction from our love" – quantitative changes bring with them qualitative changes, leading to "deep, deep love", which "is pure because it reveals trueness of heart; noble because it rises above this vulgar world; beautiful because it can excite the most beautiful feelings in the reader" – now we are increasingly "in love", a new form of love, full of originality, pure, noble, filled with poetry, we have become lovers, in a "diffuse" yet real sense. Let us sing of the spring of our love, of this rush of longing, we are each at the centre of each other's love, "we want to clear away all obstacles" – and make the future all roses! Let vulgar people mock at our passion – some great writer may one day immortalise this rarest of feelings in a work which will amaze the world!

Let me now revisit an old dream: just as you were fond of me in the past, so your loving image never once faded from my mind in forty years. Although you weren't constantly present, you were with me almost every night and morning. This is not something which I've just made up – I can prove it. Every time I thought back to when we joined the army together, your beautiful image came naturally to mind. When I looked at photos of that time, especially, I thought of you; there was that photo of me in an army helmet with a chin strap, taken when I got a new army uniform, and you laughed at it and said I didn't look anything like a PLA soldier, I looked more like an English one! So whenever I turned up that picture I thought of you, and seemed to hear your tinkling laugh again. Then, in the summer of 1956, I bumped into you and Xiaoda at the entrance to the Shanghai Park Hotel when I took my niece for a drink in their fourteenth-floor restaurant. I was not yet married, and seeing you brought so many feelings back, as if a multi-flavoured bottle of seasoning had upended and the flavours gushed out, predominantly unbearably bitter. I wrote recently to you that if I had not left the Foreign Languages Training Unit, then perhaps it would not have been our departed friend who had the good fortune to marry you. The instant I bumped into you both at the Park Hotel, that was the thought that occurred to me. Another example: on 26 December 1989 (I now know it was two days before your birthday) about a dozen of us from the office took a trip to Nantong, and stayed at the Youfei Hotel. The manager told us the hotel's name commemorated a group of eminent scholars of old, but – as if I had had an electric shock – I thought of you because the "Fei" was the same character as in your name. That night, what with thinking of you and being in a strange place, I hardly slept. In the autumn of 1978, I met our Director again in Shanghai, and in the following three or four years, until he retired and went back to Beijing, I paid frequent visits to his house. Every time he mentioned old friends from the Foreign Languages Training Unit, I would think especially of you, but I dared not ask him how you were because I harboured ulterior motives. Then a month before the Spring Festival this year, he came on a trip to Shanghai and I went to see him at the Yun Feng Hotel. He told me that you came to visit your brother in Shanghai every Spring Festival, and gave me his address, and that was what first sparked the beginning of our romance.

When you were good enough to advise me to look for a life companion to care for me, I couldn't be angry or take it the wrong way, because you really meant well. But I won't accept it. I'm sure it's easy to find someone to look after one, but a true lover is hard to find. I *will not* be so foolish as to desert my soulmate – my true lover! You say "We can dissociate ourselves from our feelings", and I respect your opinion. It wouldn't be the first time this has happened, especially outside China. But if we dissociate ourselves from our feelings, all that's left is carnal desire; I'm afraid even sexual love is not enough. I am also still me, my darling, so let our future be all roses . . .

I will stop now. I grasp your hand!

Louis

25.

13 May 1992

Dear Louis [in English],

The photo of you holding your grandson is lovely. I can see that you've completely recovered, you look about the same weight as when I saw you at the Spring Festival, and you look younger in spirit. Being in love keeps you young, that's true! Who would believe from that picture that you will soon be an old man of seventy! Your grandson looks adorable, what a good-looking boy! Those great big eyes are so appealing, and he's a sturdy little boy. I hope you'll give him a good upbringing; his parents' generation want to make life easy for their children because of the hardships they suffered as children themselves. But then, because they're the only child in the family, today's children end up spoilt rotten and that's actually harmful to their health. As a grandfather, you need to spend a bit of time on scientific child-rearing, which will turn him into the ideal, able young person, don't you think?

The depth of the love and affection in your letter made me read it over and over again, as if nothing less than this would enable me to assimilate your true love in its entirety. I didn't stop there – in spare moments, I read all the letters you have sent, from beginning to end, savouring them as I do so. Feelings of immense happiness wash over me – that's what's called being "madly in love". I always used to laugh at the "madness" of young people in love, and I certainly never imagined that I'd be "madly" in love myself in my old age. I think that we are really very fortunate to be able to enjoy being madly in love at our age. As soon as I've retired, as long as nothing bad happens, then we can really make this into a topic. We can write about it and the effects may be sensational! Of course, I just can't put things into words the way you can.

When you told me candidly in your letter how you had thought and felt about me during all those years, I felt very honoured to have made such a profound impression on you. I really had no idea; if it had not been for our chance meeting, all this would have been buried forever, which would have been a terrible pity. I find your love very pure and precious. As for me, Xiaoda and I were so very happy together that I didn't think about you much, even though I had been fond of you. But after Xiaoda had passed on, that fondness was the basis on which you kindled the flames of feelings which had been hidden deep in my heart, and new and intense emotions were born, miraculously, out of our feelings all those years ago. You never can tell how life will turn out. Maybe we're destined to be together! I think that staying "madly in love" as we are now is probably the best way to deal with things, as it's the only way to keep the flames of our love alive forever.

I think you are one male comrade who is really capable. I've always felt that the more capable one is, the better, and the less one depends on others, the happier one will be. I always make a point of impressing this on the younger generation, especially the girls. It's fashionable nowadays for young girls to think that if you're "helpless", you can "use men" and so "manage men". That's a complete lie! If I were a man, I would find it unbearable to spend my life with a girl who couldn't do anything for herself, depended on me for everything, and just chattered away, no matter how pretty she was. Beauty on the outside diminishes for everyone as the years roll by. But inner beauty is much more important. It's what really fascinates, and it's *everlasting* [in English]. Of course, I still approve of people dressing themselves up in suitable outfits when they're middle-aged or elderly. At the moment I wear a uniform every day and I've got a bit sloppy about my other clothes. When I've retired, I'm planning to come to Shanghai to get a tailor to run me up a few things that fit nicely. The last time we met at Zhu Nan's, from the way that everyone joked about you being just a municipal cadre but you couldn't tell by the way you dress, I realise you're a bit of a dandy!

The story you told me about your name was really interesting, typical of the feudal society of the old days. My name was different from yours, because it reflected Western influence in the old society. You know I was born in Columbus, Ohio, and was given the English name Phoebe (pronounced fee-bee). Phoebe was the goddess of the sun, so my parents wanted me to spread joy and warmth like the sun. Perhaps the name achieved something of this, as my philosophy of life has always been to give people warmth and happiness. If you turn Phoebe into Chinese characters and pronounce it in Shanghai dialect, it sounds very like the English. Either way, both your name and mine bear the stigma of the old, semi-feudal, semi-colonial society. People are creatures of society, so people's names most clearly reflect social changes.

I'm glad to hear that you have a busy life. Dancing is a great social activity, and I think you should keep it up. I do like dancing – we have weekend dances here too, and I sometimes go and dance – but I watch more television. When people get older, quick dance steps are just too hard, and I prefer slow dancing so that I can enjoy the music and chat at the same time. That's what I enjoy most.

I've thought and written a lot to this point, and maybe I haven't expressed myself clearly, but I really don't care, just so long as our hearts have communicated. I know you will understand, and will forgive the deficiencies in my letter.

With best wishes,

Phoebe

31.

30 May 1992

Dear Phoebe [in English],

I hope you are well. Your letter from Shanghai arrived in due course and I have read it. You have sent me another deeply loving and wonderfully philosophical love letter.

I accept and respect your analysis and reasoning. When I commented on the previous period of your letters to me, that is, on your attitude to the love between us, I used the word "appropriate", as heartfelt praise. Actually, after our conversation at dinner in the Hengshan Hotel, I passed beyond disappointment, became more aware and completely accepted your choice. I also broadly settled on the path my own life was to take, even if there was really no other way! Our letters flew back and forth, and elaborated more fervently our feelings, and these rapidly underwent a most gratifying development from their original basis in friendship. Nevertheless, I never forgot, and never tried to defy, your simple injunction, even though there were times when I cast restraint aside and showered you with tender regards. I believe that what exists between us is a real, yet also "diffuse" love, different from but surpassing a husband-and-wife relationship. I have suddenly remembered a line inscribed at the mountain gate of a monastery on top of Jade Emperor Mountain in Hangzhou: "Not in heaven, yet not of this world" – a realm which is not easy, yet not so very hard, to understand! I understand it like this: especially deep love is love which is deeper than normal love and also completely original, and I value and treasure it all the more for that. I feel and understand at the deepest level your very deep love for me, and offer you my deepest gratitude. To obtain one bosom friend in one's life is surely sufficient! To obtain a bosom friend who loves one so deeply is more than sufficient! I hope, I believe and I will strive to ensure that the especially deep love between us will continue to grow and will have the most wonderful outcome. It is also best to keep it a secret between us. Incidentally, the only person I have told of our special love, in sketchy terms, is my younger brother. He was delighted for me, and thinks this is a very good thing. I will obey your wishes and not let anyone else in on the secret – this I swear. Let me adapt, albeit inappropriately, a line of poetry: *In a vow are the words of two hearts, our love will last forever*!

About *first love* [in English]. I have never actually enjoyed real first love. The first time I was in love dates back to the spring of 1947, at St John's. She was a fellow student, her name was Chen, and she was very keen on me, and we spent time together for a while, but it was limited to talking and walking around the campus, and we seemed closer than I was with other students. But soon I was told by another student, an underground Party member, that Chen was "essentially not a very good person" (I clearly remember that phrase) and it was hinted that I should see less of her. So I didn't take it any further. Then in the autumn of 1951, after I had left the Foreign Languages Training Unit, and was recuperating from a lung infection in a convalescent unit in Pudong, Shanghai, I became the Party Secretary of the unit, and the Deputy Party Secretary was a young woman, also convalescing. She had been an underground Party member in Shanghai's Sanzhong area. We were eating, living and convalescing together, and working together too, and gradually we grew close, although we never got to the stage of being open about it. In early spring the next year, I left the convalescent unit and in the beginning we kept in contact, but we gradually stopped because of a certain amount of "pride and prejudice". To be strictly truthful, these were no "sweet first love" experiences, they were brief and painful. Then in 1954, while I was in the Labour Office, I met Ren Dacheng, my late wife, and love was kindled again. However, our courtship did not go smoothly, mainly because her family and fellow workers were putting a lot of negative pressure on her and she didn't want to risk giving rein to her feelings. We married in June 1958, just as the Leftist movement was in full swing, and we didn't dare have a warm and loving home life in case we got labelled "petit-bourgeois lovey-doveys". At the same time, her family was just as short of cash as ever, and she and her older sister were the sole support for her five school-age brothers and the parents, so she had to carry on looking after them. In April 1959, when we hadn't been married a year and my wife was about six months pregnant with our son, I was ordered to go and "toughen up" with a year of labour in the countryside, so when the baby came, I wasn't with her. From 1962, she had to do two stints of farm labour and socialist education, one after the other. That was followed by the Cultural Revolution, and I was imprisoned for a year and then "exiled" to Nanjing for six years, which meant that our family life was even more fragmented. Things got much better after the 3rd Plenary Session of the CCP 11th National Congress, and we could get a bit of time to be a family together at home, but from 1979 onwards, she was suffering from cerebellar ataxia, which got progressively worse, and the whole family went around with long faces. We were powerless to help her and she died prematurely in middle age. All that took up more than half my life, so I never really got to enjoy a happy family time. My memories are mostly of pain in the midst of happiness, and affection which was beyond my reach. Luckily I'm quite a strong character. Although physically puny, I'm strong in spirit! I never let it get me down, or put the blame on anyone else, least of all my sick wife. After all, she suffered more than me, and never had a good life after she married me. Sometimes I found it difficult, especially when she wet and soiled herself, it was really unbearable to deal with, I felt like swearing at her, even hitting her, but I could never bring myself to be that cruel. Sometimes I thought how she could have been a wife to me, and I never got any of that love and affection; but then it wasn't her fault, and besides, I didn't give her anything more or better. So I pulled myself together and faced reality, and didn't let myself get downhearted. Anyway, that's enough of all that . . . you may take it or leave it!

Again, thank you so much for the birthday greetings you sent me. I am deeply moved by all the efforts you made for me, I am such a lucky man, so lucky, so very, very lucky!

I got back here, as arranged, from the Shengsi Islands, on the 28th. I wasn't terribly impressed with them, except for eating twenty different kinds of seafood, which were very tasty.

Well, I'd better stop now, though there's never an end to lovers' talk, but anyway, let it remain unfinished!

With best wishes,

Louis

32.

Evening of 2 June 1992

Dear Louis,

I hope you are well. The first thing I did on my return from Nanjing on the afternoon of the 31st was to read your letter, several times over. I've found lots of advantages in writing love letters. Apart from the ardour you feel when writing them, which unlocks the floodgates of love, allowing it to pour over the loved one, and confers enormous happiness, there's also the fact that you can read them again and again and thus savour their mysteries. This is true delight for the soul. I am so glad that you had a very happy birthday this year!

The article you enclosed in your letter of 23 May was really good . . . full of fervour, and charmingly written. May I also say that the way our love has developed is a credit, in large part, to your skill with your pen. You are so good at cutting to the chase. And your General can only admit defeat, and become your prisoner of war, don't you think?

Your example of the line "Not in heaven, yet not of this world", is really very clever. At the Spring Festival I felt so very fortunate to be receiving your pure, deep love – perhaps only such a love as an immortal spirit can enjoy! – so incredibly fortunate. Because, for the immortal, there is absolutely none of the murkiness of human relationships, so two hearts can collide without needing to analyse the reasons why. It is only because this love can draw them together at the highest level that this attraction has nothing in common with the naivety of youth, but is mature and wise. Anyway, the way we are imprinted on each other's hearts can't adequately be described in words. Reading your letter of 30 May gave me an even better understanding of your goodness and fortitude. I do so admire you! You have really had a hard time of it for the first part of your life. The problems you faced were considerable, and yet you managed to deal with them very well, and endured. I also admire your unsullied integrity in your job as a bureaucrat. The beauty of such inner qualities is absolutely at one with your handsome and spirited exterior! So I hope you will consign what you regard as your "Treatise on Mediocrity" to the waters of the East Sea – only a mediocre person would regard you as mediocre.

I was in Nanjing to attend the Annual Meeting of the Chinese Universities Foreign Languages Publications at the International Relations Institute, and I saw your old college friend from St John's. He used to work at the institute and is now retired. He remembers you very well.

As I write, I remember what you said about your emotional problems. From what you said in your letter, you missed out on love in the past. This, of course, had a lot to do with the political climate back then, but also perhaps something to do with differences in your and your wife's backgrounds and temperament. I feel that we should let bygones be bygones; we don't have much longer to live, but at least while we are still alive, we should make up for what you missed. And I intend to put all my efforts into that!

As far as our relationship goes, I went to Beijing in April to see my youngest sister, and confided in her about it. She endorsed my own views, and thought it was a sensible course of action. Of course, outsiders can't necessarily fully understand the warmth of the love between us. Only our two hearts can know each other, and let us enjoy that to the full!

With best wishes,
Phoebe

91.

18 December 1992

Dear Louis,

I hope you are well. Today I received another love letter from you. I read it many times, savouring every bit of your news, and it set off ripple after ripple in my heart. It gave me much cause for thought.

To tell you truthfully, since our feelings have become so deep, I have begun to feel rather confused and bewildered. Not long ago, I got letters from my Shanghai sister-in-law and the wife of a cousin in Guangzhou, both saying that I seemed to be bothered about something. I always felt I was someone who could handle conflicts in my life. The word "bother" just wasn't in my vocabulary. But facts are facts. If I think about it carefully, I have to admit I am "bothered", and it's about what to do about us.

I have to admit that in the past, I've been too naive and simplistic, especially about feelings between men and women. I always thought that my original idea was very good, that is, that we could be "lovers", could have a relationship much deeper than friendship, and also be rid of all the hassles that come with marriage. But as our love developed, quite apart from your insistence all along that we could create the loving warmth of a new family, this whole process made even me begin to feel the same need. Especially now that I am about to retire completely and embark on a totally different life, one which is no longer work-centred, where I am on my own too. In my subconscious, how I was going to live in the future was really a big question mark. And I never really thought it through, so that question mark always lurked under the surface. Your latest love letter, by stating that question so clearly, has forced me to face reality, and give the whole thing serious consideration.

First, I think that love between us has brought us extremely close. In your letter you call me the "madly in-love young girl inside the Spring Festival General", and I think you're right, because our love has very deep foundations. Its foundations go back to our youth, when we were fond of each other. Those feelings were based on mutual attraction and affection and, even more, on a similar outlook: we were both from the non-labouring classes, and both had had a regular university education. And we were both progressive thinkers, and had enthusiastically joined the struggle. So when we met again forty years later, and those feelings were rekindled, we could recall all our youthful passion. If you just go by external appearances, we're old, and anyone giving us a glance would just see an old man and an old woman; but I never stop seeing you as the handsome young man that you were, even though if you look carefully, your hair is frosted with white and your face is lined with wrinkles. But I don't see this, because in my eyes, you're still the fine-looking young man that I remember. As our letters have brought our hearts closer, I have come to understand you better, and many such emotional "encounters", including the disasters that have befallen us in our personal lives, have resonated strongly in our hearts and minds. That's why I say I may be falling into love's snare!

And when a man and a woman are in love like this, then they're going to demand something: they will want to spend more time, or even all the time, together. I never realised this before, but what's bothering me now is that I so much want really to be with you completely! But I also have very many misgivings, and I keep having a mental block, which I feel is stopping me from taking that step. I realise from your letter how badly you need a new family, but I'm holding myself back and I don't feel I can answer that need, and this has been both bewildering and difficult for you. I understand that, so I have encouraged you to find someone else suitable. But now that you've actually started looking for a new partner, it's given me a real feeling of uneasiness which is hard to put into words, mainly because I feel I might really lose you, which I couldn't bear. Previously, when you told me about the woman with five children who got university degrees, I didn't feel like that, because we didn't have such deep feelings for each other then. But I can't see any way out, so of course I feel very distressed. I said to you that my love for you has never altered, and you said to me: "I believe that those are your true feelings." But if you really married again, I would of course take a conscious step back, not because I loved you less, but out of consideration for your happiness. I would rather bury our love deep in my heart, and turn our romance into a beautiful feeling, a memory which will be precious to me forever.

What I have written above is what I truly think. Until you find a new partner, we can still carry on this beautiful love that we share. And I've had another thought: if you still can't find anyone suitable, I'm willing to discuss getting married with you. I feel I ought to try and change these inhibitions of mine. It's not that love has taken me over and I'm regretting it because I've made a mess of it – I'm not that kind of person. When I make up my mind to do something, I always do it calmly, and once I've decided, I don't have regrets.

I've always had space for manoeuvre in our relationship, so why am I encouraging you to find another partner? I'm mainly thinking of your happiness; I'm worried that you might miss out because of me, and that I might be doing you a real wrong. That would make me feel bad, but that's my problem, and it would be better than both of us feeling bad, don't you think?

I've thought very hard about every word of this letter, and it's taken me a long time to write. I don't know if I've managed to explain clearly what's in my heart. Nor do I know if it will create many more contradictions after you've read it. But I like to tell the truth, to tell things as they are. During the last eleven months, we've exchanged nearly a hundred letters – on that basis, I do hope you won't find fault with me!

Maybe because recently I've been busier than usual, together with the changes in the weather, I caught a cold yesterday, and ran a bit of a temperature. I took "emergency measures" straight away – took a lot of medicine, drank boiled water, and was very good and went to bed for most of the day. By this morning I had fought it off and was completely well again, so was happy to go off and teach my two classes as planned.

It will soon be New Year and I have sent you a card – you could say the message on it tells you how I feel. Before the New Year, we'll have the chance for one more exchange of letters. When the time comes, I'll send you another card, with my very best wishes to you for the New Year. I'll stop now.

All the best,

Phoebe

157.

Afternoon of 29 August 1993

Dear Phoebe,

I received your letter of the 25th today, and you've confirmed the date for my trip up to Beijing on 15 September, so that's it then! In the nearly two years that we have been friends, I have been the recipient of your inestimable love in all parts of my life. Shall I give you an example? I could give you so many of them. Soon, I will be able to tell you in person: when we are chatting together, when we stroll out in the morning and evening, in that special enjoyment when two people are dancing and talking together, amid the extraordinary autumnal hues of the Western Hills . . . What I want to tell you is that the one who has been really fortunate is me. I am so very grateful for everything you have given to me! Even if it was me who "sought out" this "love", or rather who got you into "trouble", I have never regretted it for a moment, and I have felt incredibly fortunate. There was a time when I fretted about the "distance" between us two, to the extent that I could not help hesitating about getting involved with you. This had something to do both with the obvious difference in our rank, and the geographical distance between us. But now it doesn't seem that this has ever been or ever will be an obstacle to us having regular contact with each other. This is mainly thanks to you! And that truly comes from the bottom of my heart. May I be allowed to suggest that surely, out of the two of us, the person who ought to feel most fortunate, and express the deepest gratitude, is me?

My situation hasn't changed recently, but the man you will be meeting in a couple of weeks' time is a just a poor, skinny old scholar – only his heart remains constant! I could say more, but let's wait until we meet!

With very best wishes,

Louis

158.

1 September 1993

Dear Louis,

I received your letter of the 29th the day before yesterday.

I think we can do all the things you have described once we are together, and may even think up some new ones. How lucky we are, that we can still have such beautiful longings at our age! When we meet, we can decide what to do, day by day, and after we've had a good time out and about, we can sit down and savour all the details, so that the lovely time we have together will imprint itself indelibly in our minds. I have made the necessary arrangements for your arrival, mainly to do with practicalities. I remembered that you said that before you do your relaxation exercises every morning, you drink a glass of soy milk, so I've bought soy milk powder. And don't you like your favourite tipple every evening? I've got some in, and I can join you in a glass too.

It sounds like you're giving me advance warning that I'll mind you being "old and skinny". Honestly, you don't need to worry. Everyone gets old, that's a law of nature. If you go by appearances, the signs of ageing can only increase. These biological changes are natural. You can see through them, and they don't matter. Take me, for example: my hair's going whiter all the time and I'm getting more wrinkles and liver spots. Of course, I can make myself look nice when I want, but really, I'm not that interested. I believe the most important thing is inner youthfulness – we're both good at that, and we should keep it up. If we're psychologically youthful, we'll never feel old. And once past the aged exterior, the you which is in me is ever-youthful, and always irresistible, really! I await the arrival of the man of my heart.

With best wishes,

Phoebe

159.

Afternoon of 5 September 1993

Dear Phoebe,

I hope you are well. You and I may have created a phenomenon with our exchange of letters which, at least in terms of numbers, has outdone Lu Xun's famous love letters. It is so interesting to think back over the scores we have sent each other, which have united two once lonely and shattered hearts, brought a new glow of youth to them and planted in them constant tenderness. There is one thing which marks our letters out particularly, and that is clarity. I remember the first letter I wrote to you last year, how I racked my brains and struggled with it . . . But later, writing felt much more natural, and we wrote more and more just as we liked. The words on the page flowed as freely as if we were having a conversation. The content of our letters has always been completely real, with sometimes a bit of description, a bit of embellishment, but always revealing our true feelings. And right here in these letters is the proof of how we value and put into practice your tenet that "the truth must be told"!

Your going fishing reminded me of fishing for shrimps near my home when I was small. We were fleeing from the Japanese bombardment, and at one point had taken refuge in a village. When we had nothing to do, my brothers and I used to go out fishing for shrimps. We would attach an earthworm to the line at the end of a bamboo pole, and throw it into the river. In a little while, the shrimps would come and nibble the worm. I would gently lift the bamboo rod while with the other hand I slowly slid a net under the shrimps, and then quickly caught them in the net. It was certainly easy, but always seemed a lot duller than real fishing.

I've booked my ticket for the 15th on the number 14 train, and would love it if you came to meet me. We've already agreed the guiding principles for this trip, so I won't say any more about that. But I'd like to make three practical points: one, I don't want my presence to change or get in the way of your daily routine in any way at all. Just stick to the way you've always done things. Two, we'll eat just the sort of meals that you do now, or as the local expression in my home town went, "just add more chopsticks, but not more dishes". Be sure not to go adding anything extra. Third, don't buy anything especially for me, just do everything as usual. OK?

This morning I went to say goodbye to my two brothers, and they were very happy for me. And thanks to your summons to "come a bit sooner" and "stay a little longer", my heart has already flown to Beijing. It's incredible to think that two people nearly in their seventies can be fired up like a pair of teenagers, and such fun! The rest can wait until we meet.

With very best wishes,

Louis

PS I've just been to post this and found your letter of the 1st in my mailbox, so had to open the envelope and add a sentence or two: I was moved to tears at the trouble you have gone to, even down to the soy milk powder and my "tipple". How did I come to be so lucky? I am greatly moved.

I always feel how lucky I am as a Chinese person to live in this historic moment of change, as China moves forwards what sometimes feels like five hundred years. I have seen how the old China lived through those "ancient lives" in the poor countryside, and how the future China lives in our modern cities. People are between such different life styles and capabilities. Before the 1990s, 90 per cent of the Chinese population was made up of peasants and farmers who had very little education. Life for them means food in your stomach, warm clothes in the cold winter and a simple place to sleep; reading and writing must seem like a myth. When you move on from these romantic love letters to Chapter 10, you will see the huge difference between Chinese people of the same age and at the same point in this nation's history. If there is a wall between different cultures and beliefs, then they might so easily have had war between the classes over the last one hundred years in China.

On the Road,
Interlude 4:
Reflections Between the Lines

Having got this far with my second draft of this book, I awoke with a start early on the morning of 30 December 2006. Outside the window, there was driving wind and rain, and the previous night the BBC had warned of storms to usher in the New Year. Switching on the light, I saw it was ten past three. I remembered the words of General Phoebe, that amid the disasters of Mao Zedong's regime, they were "a fortunate generation, because they had witnessed war and peace", and my head was suddenly flooded with a strange idea: this was the good fortune that only survivors of war could have, and only they could truly comprehend what peace meant.

Do people who have grown up watching American action movies really know what the reek of blood is like? I don't know. Nor can I imagine whether children brought up on a diet of killer games understand the results of war. Are wars and killings necessary for the creation of heroes amid the peace of contemporary life? In what way is this different from the class struggle which Mao Zedong needed? How is struggle possible when there is no enemy? We surely cannot use antagonisms between social classes to bring us together in bonds of friendship?

As I turned this over and over in my mind, I felt, though I didn't know why, that I should watch BBC News 24. But first I wanted to begin the day's writing. I needed to write down as quickly as possible the thoughts that had been surging through me since the last interview. Ugo Betti says: "Memories are like stones; time and distance erode them like acid." I did not want time and distance to wear away the emotions of love and hate which filled me.

At about 6.30 a.m. the urge to watch the news flooded over me again. I thought I might as well brew myself a cup of Biluochun, a Chinese green tea, and sit down in front of the TV. No sooner was I settled than big red news headlines made me jump up again: Saddam Hussein had been executed four hours previously.

On the BBC, a debate raged between two contending sides: on the one hand, there was satisfaction that justice had been done; on the other, condemnation of an unfair sentence. Everyone was concerned, too, about the chaos caused by fighting among the peoples and religions of Iraq. I could not help engaging in a dialogue with those being interviewed in the TV studio: do those developed nations who bestowed freedom and democracy onto Iraq by force of arms really understand the stage that Iraqi religious cultures and national beliefs have reached? How can there be such different interpretations of war and death carried out in the names of Bush and Saddam? Can human society really progress to democratic republicanism from religious commandments? Can humankind share the same definition of civilisation if its members do not perceive things in the same way?

In just the same way as the century which China had just passed through, here we have the saviours of the world "fighting for the truth", and liberating others by forcing a "just freedom" on them. There is reckless "planned development", people are punished and honoured as a unity of moral values is imposed on everyone, and all this has even become a "one size fits all" sort of fashion. And this is what we acclaim as "a fortunate era", this is what we unquestioningly call "correct leadership", this is the passion into which we have thrown ourselves without regard for personal safety. Our passion is doubtless ignorant and foolish, but it certainly won't be military might which awakes us from this fanaticism.

IO

The Policeman: A Cop Who Entered the Police Force As the People's Republic Was Founded

Family photo, Zhengzhou, 1960s: Mr Jingguan, *second from right*, and his wife, *back, third from right*.

In 2001, Mr Jingguan, *centre front*, with his wife (in wheelchair), their children and grandchildren.

MR JINGGUAN, aged seventy-five, a policeman with the same length career as the PRC, *interviewed in Zhengzhou, capital of Henan province in central China, near the Yellow River. He became a policeman in 1948 and was a sergeant at seventeen. He is the Henan police history's voice recorder and has an amazing memory; he remembers most cases since 1948. But he quit the police in the 1980s, aged fifty-eight, because he couldn't bear the ignorance and corruption that surrounded him. He lives in a two-room flat with his sick wife, whom he cares for with the help of two daughters.*

On 6 September, we arrived in Zhengzhou, the capital of Henan, a central province. At the last census, Henan had 97 million people, making it China's most populous province. Up until 1990, Zhengzhou was Asia's biggest rail transport hub, while Henan was one of China's poorest provinces. In terms of public security, it set records too – for modern China's biggest bank robbery, the earliest case of a foreign contract killer, the most brutal murder . . .

I began my career as a journalist here, although before 2003 I could not be as candid about it as I am now, for fear of incurring suspicions that I was "betraying my country".

Soon after the founding of the People's Republic of China in 1949, a 150kW "United Front Jamming Station" was set up in Zhengzhou. This transmitted meaningless radio interference to prevent people in mainland China and neighbouring areas from listening to "enemy stations" such as Voice of America, the BBC, and Hong Kong and Taiwan radio.

In 1988, the reforms which opened up China reached the national media, or rather the interfering signals no longer had the power to prevent people, aided by modern technology, from accessing information freely. The decision was taken to turn the Jamming Station into a cultural and economic channel, and create a new model for the Chinese media. The first radio station to begin direct broadcasting for its main programming blocks was Pearl River Radio in south China, but it was small and covered only a limited area. The Zhengzhou one would be a major channel, and to ensure that, post-reforms, it would continue to be the mouthpiece of the CCP, as all the other strictly controlled provincial radio stations were, Henan People's Radio Station had the job of recruiting programme anchors from all over China to conduct an "experiment in direct broadcasting" under the "instruction and guidance" of old radio hands. From the thirty or forty thousand applicants, the Central Broadcasting selection committee chose seven men and seven women under thirty to be the reform team.

Before this, there were radio stations only at provincial and city level, and these were under the management of the Central Government Propaganda Department. Television did not become part of the mass media until the end of the eighties, when most people had a TV set.

A radio programme went through at least four processes: it had to be read and approved in draft, after which not a single word could be added or changed; then the tape had to be approved again, and the background music added, before final approval was given. In addition, no one's broadcasting voice was permitted the slightest trace of individuality. As we said in the business, there were only two broadcasting voices – one male and one female. This meant that Chinese radio broadcasting was one giant media machine, almost military in its management.

I was one of the fourteen chosen to form the Direct Broadcast Reform Team, and the exception, in that I was over thirty. I still remember how swiftly our initial excitement was replaced by dread induced by the "news discipline" and the "list of rules" which hit us in the face. When we learned that all our direct-broadcast programmes would be monitored and assessed, in order to prevent them from "going down the wrong road" and misleading public opinion, we felt as if we were on the high wire of media reforms with politics the abyss beneath our feet.

We tended to play it safe in the setting up and structure of our broadcasts, since none of us had experience of or training in the "free media", in fact none of us knew how to broadcast without reading from a script. Also, none of us wanted to tackle the explosive issue of "freedom of speech" head on.

Probably because I was the oldest, and also because of all the fourteen "guinea pigs", only I had worked for twelve years in a military academy, and was therefore supposed to have a better awareness of "discipline" than the rest, I was assigned an unscripted night-time chat programme, called *Words on the Night Breeze*. What were we to talk about? How? What was safe talk? No one told me, but I very soon realised from the large numbers of readers' letters that the resources for my programme lay in the highways and byways outside the office, in the villages where I had never been, in life as it did not appear in the books I read, in the stories told by those women who reared their children and transmitted the Chinese way of life to future generations.

It was the Henan police who helped me to reach these true media sources in safety. They not only gave me police support, they even taught me how to open the minds of these unschooled peasants, in ways which they could understand, so that they could improve their lives and protect the rights which were properly theirs.

One incident I shall never forget. In 1990, someone wrote to me asking why people in certain places on the banks of the Yellow River in Henan had for generations suffered from eye disease. On investigation, we discovered that the cottages of the inhabitants, with their wood-burning stoves, had no chimneys, so that the women who worked indoors every day and the babies they carried on their backs spent their time in a smoke-laden atmosphere. As a result, the locals developed eye disease from an early age, and many were blind by forty.*

A group of us set out to try to resolve this age-old problem. With me were a doctor, a civil engineer and two policemen, one local to the area and one sent from the provincial capital. We set off down the Yellow River to mobilise the peasants to fit some kind of chimney to their houses, but two days and four villages later, not only was no one accepting the truth of our arguments, they were coming back with their own question: if they opened up the roof, and the souls of those who lived there were sucked away during the night, who would look after them?

On the way to the fifth village, the doctor, the engineer and I were alarmed and angry. We had reached an impasse. Then the local policeman, a taciturn man who hitherto had just been our driver, put a cautious question: could he try something for us? "Of course, of course!" we cried. "What are you going to do?" we asked, but he said diffidently: "Just let me try first. You bosses watch what happens, and then I'll say more. OK?"

As we got to the fifth village, the policeman saw a village cadre coming towards him, slammed on the brakes, stuck his head out and said: "A new instruction from Chairman Mao!"

"Chairman Mao? But surely he's passed away?" responded the cadre in surprise.

"They've just discovered it. He left an instruction that 'The Yellow River waters, and the eye disease of the villagers, must both be brought

---

* This phenomenon is also recounted in Cao Jinqing's *China Along the Yellow River: Reflections on Rural Society.*

under control'." The policeman was so earnest that we stared at him open-mouthed.

"Control it how?" The village cadre was obviously taking this seriously.

"Put 'heavenly eyes' on your houses. All Chairman Mao's top cadres live in houses with 'heavenly eyes'!" The policeman continued confidently: "You call a meeting and pass on Chairman Mao's instructions, and in two days, we'll be back to check up."

And with this, he put his foot on the accelerator, and we drove off.

"What are you playing at?" the civil engineer couldn't help asking.

"Wait and see," the Zhengzhou policeman answered on behalf of his colleague, and then added: "Haven't you heard the expression, 'the mighty dragon can't keep a ground snake down'? Local people have local ways!"

Hearing this, there was nothing we "civilised" city folk could say, except follow the policemen and "spread Mao Zedong's instruction". But none of us believed that it would work. Privately, we even thought: "It's us city folk they're making fun of!"

We were dumbfounded, however, when two days later we went back to the village where the policeman had left word. To our amazement, there were chimneys on the rooftops! Chimneys of all shapes and sizes, to be sure, and most of them fixed on in a very unscientific way, but the people had listened to Chairman Mao! They had obeyed someone who had been a god to them, but who had long been dismissed by city folk as a tyrant now dead and gone.

I asked the local policeman how he knew to use Chairman Mao to "civilise" these peasants. He answered quietly: "They're peasants. They only believe in the gods that work for them."

The peasants only believe in the gods that work for them? They certainly did not believe us. From this point on, the Henan police became my teachers. They taught me the difference between town and countryside, opened my eyes to aspects of human culture which had passed me by, and made it possible for me to understand the peasants.

Now, some years later, on my return to Henan, I wanted to interview an old policeman, Mr Jingguan, who had been with the People's Republic of China Public Security Bureau (PSB) from its inception to the present day. I'd heard he had an amazing memory, so was one of the people who were writing the history of the PSB in Henan.

When we were on our way to his house in the Central Plains Region

Law Enforcement Agencies family housing complex, a policewoman who had done some prior investigation for us said: "He wants to be called 'policeman', not 'judge', even though he worked for years in the courts and even rose to be chief justice. When you mention the courts, he gets indignant. And he hasn't been out of the house for years, because his wife went into a coma, and has become a 'vegetable', and he doesn't want her to wake up one day and find him gone."

I was moved by this man's loyalty and sense of responsibility to his wife – it was a million miles away from men who "keep a mistress", "have a love nest" or "play away"!

At the same time, I became anxious. Could someone who hadn't been out of doors for years cope with questioning by strangers? If he'd had no contact with the outside world for so long, would he identify with our values and understand the significance of this interview? How were we to win his understanding, and get down to the kind of topics which I wanted to know about, in a natural way? I thought it would probably be best to start with recent events which he was most familiar with and which he most wanted people to know about – his family situation.

What we were confronted with when we were taken into his home was, once again, almost unbelievable: this man, noted for his outstanding contribution to the establishment and development of Henan's public security system, lived almost on the poverty line, in a tiny housing unit in a low-cost, five-storey block, one of those hurriedly thrown up after the reforms at the beginning of the eighties. His flat consisted of just two rooms with no entrance hall; the ceiling was not even the regulation 2.3 metres high and the whole area no more than a cramped 25 square metres. Facilities such as kitchen and toilet were squeezed in somehow, and there was no communal area or washroom. The light was so poor that it was almost impossible to read during the day without electric light. The paint on doors and windows was faded, and the walls were flaking. The floor was of rough concrete. The only furniture to be seen was a bed, a dining table and chairs, and two battered old wardrobes, each in one corner of the room. There was a small bedroom which doubled as the food-preparation area, with a shelf which held a chopping board, a vegetable knife, two spring onions and a piece of ginger root. A rusty, old-fashioned washing machine was squeezed into the space by the doorway; there was no fridge, nor was there even the sort of air-conditioning unit that most people had, just a decrepit, noisy, vibrating old electric fan doing battle against the stifling heat. But the flat was very clean and there was none of that smell which often hangs around the bedridden elderly.

Looking at all this, I even began to doubt whether this really was the honoured old official. Had no one enquired why his living conditions were so poor? After all, he was one of the first cohort of PRC police in 1948! From what I knew of national policy to support the elderly, special care was given to senior cadres who had worked for the revolution in the Communist Party before 1949: the army had Retirement Institutes, regional governments had Retired Cadre Villages. Unless he had committed a serious offence at some point . . . but then someone who had committed such an offence would not have been permitted to write the history of the Public Security Bureau.

Once more, I was nonplussed.

Still astonished at this scene of poverty, I first went to greet Jingguan's wife, who lay in a comatose state in a reclining chair. I put my hand gently on her forehead, and said, "Hello, Auntie."

*

JINGGUAN: It's no use talking to her. She's not conscious, and can't do anything.

XINRAN: Yes, I can see that, but I believe it's right to say hello to her, and maybe, somehow, my respect for her will get through. [As a Chinese person, I know I must ask first about her condition, to show that I care in a Chinese way – though Western readers may think my questions intrusive.] Does she seem to react to light? Is it possible she may gradually wake up?

JINGGUAN: She can't do anything, even if you wave your hand across her open eyes she doesn't react.

XINRAN: You look after her very well.

JINGGUAN: Thirty years ago she had high blood pressure, and twenty years ago she got a cerebral thrombosis. Ten years ago she became paralysed, and eight years ago she became doubly incontinent and lost the power of speech . . . the children help me look after their mother.

*

I can see from his body language that he is worried about what my reaction will be to his circumstances and the surroundings.

*

XINRAN: What a good thing you've got children to help. You're lucky in that respect. Your house is so clean, and there's absolutely none of that smell that so many old people's houses have.

336

JINGGUAN: That's the most difficult thing to deal with. Sometimes in the night, I get up at two or three o'clock to relieve myself, and she's wet through and groaning to herself. When I've changed her and cleaned her up, she stops groaning.

XINRAN: So she has a certain amount of feeling?

JINGGUAN: I think she does, but of course she can't say anything.

XINRAN: So she has no feeling in her arms and legs?

JINGGUAN: Absolutely none at all. When the doctors give her an injection, she doesn't react at all.

XINRAN: And she doesn't have any bedsores?

JINGGUAN: No, her skin is fine.

XINRAN: That's a tough thing to achieve. Coma victims often get bedsores, don't they, since they're not moving or turning over. Can she swallow when she has food?

JINGGUAN: No, she can't, so we use a stomach tube, and a masher to liquidise the food, and get it directly into her stomach with the tube.

XINRAN: That's hard work, I really admire you all.

JINGGUAN: Any family would do the same.

XINRAN: Not necessarily. It's true that our custom is to care for our elderly, but reports of the old being neglected are common too, aren't they? Does she get work insurance and medical insurance now?

JINGGUAN: She gets 850 yuan a month.

XINRAN: Well, that's a good thing. Otherwise someone as sick as this can drag the whole family down with them.

JINGGUAN: Yes, that's true.

XINRAN: Is that a photograph of the whole family?

JINGGUAN: That was at the Spring Festival in 1959. That's our eldest daughter, that's the second, that's the elder son, he's retired now. The fourth, the youngest boy, hadn't been born yet.

XINRAN: And that photo must have been taken during the Cultural Revolution. You're all wearing Chairman Mao badges.

JINGGUAN: It was at the end of 1970, taken just before the eldest became a soldier.

XINRAN: And that one looks like a group of cadres.

JINGGUAN: They're the senior cadres of the Public Security Bureau in 1986; we were at a senior cadres symposium.

XINRAN: Is that your wife? How old is she now?

JINGGUAN: Seventy-two. That was our fiftieth wedding anniversary. She couldn't hold her head up, or eat, she couldn't understand anything, but we had our picture taken together, on 28 October 2002.

XINRAN: You said you were born in 1931, sir. May I ask you if you still remember your parents and grandparents, and what memories you have of your childhood?

JINGGUAN: My family moved to Zhengzhou in the twenty-first year of the reign of the Emperor Qianlong, over two hundred years ago. Before Liberation, I went with my grandfather to visit the original family grave, and it was all written on the gravestone, right down to my generation, the tenth. Our forebears were rich. It was the last generations that fell on hard times. If you want to live, you need money, at least enough for food and clothing, and my father and grandfather both had this failing – they had a bellyful of knowledge, but couldn't earn a living, and in the end they starved to death.

I think my grandfather was born in 1886, when the family still had about a hundred *mu** of land. They lived well. Zhengzhou had no foreign schools in those days, so he went to an old-style private school, and graduated from Kaifeng Normal University. And my grandfather was a dreamer, the couplet pasted on either side of his gate read: "All pursuits are lowly. Only studying is exalted." He had no idea how to earn money – he only knew how to study – so if someone was ill, he sold land; if someone got married, he sold land, until finally, when I was at an age to remember things, there was only forty *mu* left.

XINRAN: How did he meet his wife?

JINGGUAN: In those days, the parents arranged it, and whatever they decreed, you obeyed. Before Liberation, almost 100 per cent of marriages in Zhengzhou were arranged.

XINRAN: And when it got to your parents?

JINGGUAN: The same. The matchmaker knew the girl's and the boy's families, and spoke to both sides. The adults came to an agreement, then the young people were married. When my grandparents got married, my paternal grandfather's family probably still had seventy or eighty *mu* of land left. My maternal grandfather didn't have as much, but he was good at making money, and in disaster years they had enough to eat and drink.

---

* 16 acres / 7 hectares.

My other grandfather just had his bellyful of learning, and that couldn't feed them. When my father had finished lower middle school, he milled grain in the slack season, and tilled the fields in the busy season. In a disaster year, they starved.

XINRAN: Have you ever told your children about this?

JINGGUAN: No.

XINRAN: Why not?

JINGGUAN: What would be the point? It's all about hard work and dire poverty, and my children have grown up in ease and comfort. The flavour of their lives has just been different.

XINRAN: Well, are you willing to tell me about it?

JINGGUAN: Yes, I'll waffle on a bit, if you're happy to listen to me rehashing that stale old business.

As I said, I was born in 1931. The first things I remember are from about 1938, when I was six or seven. After the Spring Festival, I began at an old-style private school. Do you know what that is? One teacher takes on three or four pupils and, to start with, you just studied the *Three Character Classic* every day: "People at birth are naturally good." Then we went on to study the *Book of One Hundred Surnames*: "Zhao, Qian, Sun, Li". After two years of that, I went to "foreign school", what today would be the first grade of primary school. By then, we were poor. I struggled on for four years, and then left without completing primary school.

In 1942, there was a great drought in Henan and we didn't harvest a single grain from our crops. By autumn, all the wheat had been consumed and there was nothing to eat at the Mid-Autumn Festival. People ate up all the grass, roots, shoots and leaves and when it came to the Spring Festival, there really was nothing left to eat. My grandfather proposed that the family split up, and each branch of the family go their own way. My uncle's family (there were four of them) made one new household, and my grandparents another. My grandfather said: "I don't want any of you to bother about me. Leave me here, and make your own way in life." My father, who was thirty-eight, died of hunger that year and after that my mother took us children back to her family. Her father sold bean curd, so they had a bit of money and could squeeze us in. Even if we didn't get much, at least it kept body and soul together.

In 1944, the Japanese attacked Zhengzhou and my grandfather had no money left to support us any more, so my sister was married off at fifteen, to keep her alive. But she starved to death when she was fleeing the famine. I started doing labouring jobs for the Japanese before I was thirteen, and earned three pounds of coarse, mixed-grain flour per day. It wasn't enough but it kept the whole family from starvation for the time being. We ate one meal a day, in the evening. We had no oil or salt or vegetables, we just steamed pancakes and that was what we ate every day. After a year, the Japanese surrendered. Our fatherless family – mother, my younger brother and I – were stranded once more. For six months I could only get odd jobs, and it was a major problem to feed ourselves every day. At the Spring Festival in 1946, a neighbour who lived opposite gave me an introduction to the Guomindang Yellow River Henan River Affairs Bureau. There I wiped tables and swept floors, served food and drink and generally waited on people.

Then on 22 April 1948, Zhengzhou was liberated, the Communist Party arrived, the People's Liberation Army arrived, and the GMD government offices shut down. To stay alive, I couldn't let the grass grow under my feet, so that same day I was out finding out where people were wanted. It was night-time before I found that the Zhengzhou Public Security Bureau was recruiting household registration officers. I went, but I just stood in the door. I didn't dare go in. What was the use? They wanted people who had done lower middle school and I'd only been to primary. But I needed the work! So I forced myself to go in. "Have you got your school certificate?" "It's at home, I can't find it." "Well, take the test, then!" I took the test and came third. So in November 1948, I was one of the Zhengzhou PSB's first bunch of recruits. First we started with three months of training, and then I was made a sergeant. I was seventeen years old.

XINRAN: You were running things at seventeen . . . ? This is the first time I've heard that China had sergeants that young. Could you tell me a couple of stories from each post you held? I've heard you have a remarkable memory.

JINGGUAN: Well, 1948 was a time of great upheaval, good and bad people, and people with different "historical backgrounds" were all mixed in together. At that time, the Zhengzhou PSB chief was thirty-two, the Henan county PSB chiefs were generally twenty-five years old, substation chiefs were twenty-one or twenty-two, and I was a sergeant at seventeen, and in charge of a dozen or so people. I watched over a number of streets, checking household registrations and keeping an eye on bad elements. I didn't know anything about anything. I ate my fill and did my work, and if something came up, I did my best to sort it out by following the rules.

XINRAN: Who was good and who was bad then?

JINGGUAN: We were told to ignore people like petty thieves, vagrants and prostitutes for the time being, just leave them be. We had to concentrate our efforts on counter-revolutionaries. Things were chaotic in those days, and counter-revolutionaries were being arrested almost every day. There were two thousand privately owned firearms in Zhengzhou city, and these would have been a time bomb in the hands of counter-revolutionaries.

XINRAN: And how did you define counter-revolutionary?

JINGGUAN: We were given five criteria by our chiefs: the first were bandits who held control in local areas; the second were tyrants who had guns and armed forces in the countryside; the third were counter-revolutionary core GMD members – anyone from the heads of the Youth League of the Three Principles of the People regional forces upwards counted as "core" people; the fourth were followers of reactionary religious beliefs, who wanted to restore the old regime; the fifth category were spies – GMD spies, national spies and armed spies.

XINRAN: Did you have arrest warrants then? How did you know if someone was a spy or a tyrant?

JINGGUAN: Firstly, some of them turned themselves in, and then they would be treated leniently. Secondly, we regularly went around checking households and asked in each family what each person had been doing, and noted it all down in their file. Thirdly, through ordinary people reporting offences. The local police who made the records then were uneducated people. If they didn't understand something, they wrote it down in language they understood and in characters they knew and sometimes it came out quite different. Or the person reporting it wasn't clear – they just thought once it was recorded that would be an end of it. It never occurred to them that those records could cause trouble for the rest of their lives, let alone that it might implicate their relatives and friends too.

No one understood politics in those days, not even our leaders, I think. Otherwise, why would they have got involved in all those political movements?

Checking and recording went on until 1956, then there was a new policy: Hit "army, officials, police and the law" hard.

XINRAN: And what did that mean?

JINGGUAN: "Army" – this was after 1946 and the beginning of the Third Chinese Revolutionary War – meant any GMD officers of brigadier or company commander rank and above. Quartermasters, army surgeons, majors and above weren't important – the key people were those who had committed crimes and aroused popular anger. "Officials" meant any GMD who had been leaders of township or county government and above, again depending whether they had committed crimes, were hated and had killed people. "Police" meant GMD police of patrol officer rank or above. "The law" meant GMD military police of company officer rank or above. At that time, the key criterion was whether they had committed crimes and were hated by the people, but after 1956, the policy started to become more "leftist", until it got to the Cultural Revolution and became nonsensical.

XINRAN: How did you catch counter-revolutionaries when you were a sergeant?

JINGGUAN: The first time was in February 1949, I was working in what was then Changchun Road, now called 7 February Road. People were saying that a head of a street committee was dealing in drugs. I ate my lunch but didn't take my siesta, I just ran to his house, pushed open the door a crack and looked, and there he was selling drugs. I kicked the door right open, and hauled him off to the station and banged him up. Afterwards we found out that he had been a local leader under the GMD and when the Communist Party arrived, he changed sides and became head of the street committee.

Then a month or so later, we heard someone say that another street committee head was a counter-revolutionary and had been a senior official in the GMD, but I didn't arrest him. I'll tell you why – it really didn't matter then if you'd been an official, even a senior one, even after 1946, the crucial thing was whether you had aroused popular anger or you'd committed crimes. I was young and I didn't know how to investigate properly, but then I heard that he had, so I reported back to my chief and he sent someone to the man's home town to investigate. It turned out he had committed murder, and so he was arrested. So I personally got two arrested, the first for drug-dealing – I didn't know if there were any political problems as well – the second because he was a counter-revolutionary and had murdered someone.

XINRAN: And then?

JINGGUAN: In 1950 came the CCP Central Committee 10 October instructions on cracking down on counter-revolutionaries. In November, I was station sergeant at a small-town police station. One evening, I was suddenly told that all of us station sergeants had to attend a meeting at the PSB sub-bureau at 9 p.m. to discuss the leadership's new onslaught on counter-revolutionaries. At the door of the sub-bureau, they got hold of us and made us go in, then wouldn't let us out. Midnight passed and we saw that PLA soldiers from the Guards HQ were waiting at the entrance. Our chief told us: "Station sergeants, these platoons of thirty or forty soldiers are under your orders. Here are your lists with twenty-four counter-revolutionaries on each. Go and pick them up." I went back and shouted for my household registration constables: "Each man take a list and ten soldiers, and go and make the arrests." That night five or six hundred were arrested in Zhengzhou!

XINRAN: Do you still think now that they were counter-revolutionaries?

JINGGUAN: If you go by the policies in force then, maybe they were. But some people went so far "left" that they weren't sticking to the policies and they started to make bogus arrests, and the more the campaign went on, the fiercer it got, until even Liu Shaoqi, the State Chairman, and other old revolutionaries became "counter-revolutionary". How did that happen? Because the information against them was all false.

XINRAN: So is it possible that the information you had was false too?

JINGGUAN: It may well have been. Things were chaotic then, and it wasn't easy to tell true from false.

XINRAN: Who verified the information against the detainees?

JINGGUAN: We were only in charge of making the arrests, then the detainees were handed over to a higher level, and our local station had nothing more to do with them. When I was twenty-nine, and went to the interrogation section of the PSB, then I started to deal with offenders. It was in 1964, once I was working in the courts, that I realised how many miscarriages of justices there were in China. The Supreme Court issued a communiqué about anyone appealing: once they had been sentenced and the second appeal heard, then they couldn't appeal again. At that time, there were over a hundred appeals going through the regional courts. When I audited them, I found many miscarriages of justices. For example, there was a man called Han Guangxiang, and I remember this case very clearly. He was a demobilised soldier, allocated a job in a film factory. His boss said to him: "Comrade Han, you're needed in Supplies."

"Yes, sir, whatever you say." And he went. People were under a lot of pressure in those days and one day he was going on a business trip and was sixty fen short. Factory funds were low so he made it up out of his own pocket and got the factory finance department to write him an IOU, for five yuan. When it got to the end of the year, they owed him a lot of IOUs, and the head of finance says: "How about if we write you one big IOU to cover the whole sum, Han? Is that OK?" "Fine!" says Han Guangxiang. And so they wrote him an IOU for 290 yuan. In February 1958, there was an investigation into bribery and corruption, and Han was accused of embezzling public funds. This was such nonsense. He had gone to the trouble of digging into his own pocket for the factory, and now he'd got fined for corruption – a hundred yuan a year for three years. When the three years was up, Han put in appeals everywhere he could. His wife divorced him and his daughter and her husband got divorced too. He ended up begging on the streets. In the depths of an icy winter, he took his lawsuit to Beijing, and begged on the streets there. No one paid any attention to him, but at the end of 1964, I became a court chief justice, and I looked into his case. I discovered it was all rubbish, so I cleared him of any wrongdoing. But he was nowhere to be found. His original work unit had been restructured, and no one had responsibility for him any more. In those days, people like him with "black backgrounds" could never be completely cleared. I still feel bad whenever I think of that man.

XINRAN: Why do you think these miscarriages of justice happened? Was it because the police weren't well enough trained? Or the calibre of the people handling the cases was poor? Or was the system at fault?

JINGGUAN: I think – this is not what the papers say, it's just the way I see it – it was the calibre of the Party Central Committee that was the problem. It was always said that, at the lower levels of government, we went too ferociously left, but the fact is it wasn't the lower ranks. Let's just take 1958: a production team leader who reported low yields to the brigade got punished. The same with the brigades reporting low yields to the commune. And the communes to the counties, the counties to the provincial government, and up to central government. So every level told lies. You could only play up the figures, you couldn't tell the truth. The truth was "rightist".

During the 1957 Anti-Rightist movement, I was working in the municipal PSB, and all the staff came from poor or lower-middle peasant backgrounds. They were all Party members, and the poorer they were, the more "red". The atmosphere was very tense, and if you wanted to say something, no matter what, if it wasn't in line with what your bosses said, then you were a rightist attacking the leaders and the Party. The Anti-Rightist movement meant that no one dared tell the truth.

In 1958, the Henan provincial party committee secretary was honest and conscientious, while the provincial leader was just a bigmouth, but central government favoured the provincial leader, and not only removed the secretary from his job but put the leader in his place, and then called on everyone in the province, including the peasants, to criticise him. Back then, it wasn't that people didn't think, it was that they had no education, they didn't know how to think things through. You know, at the 1959 Lushan Conference, Peng Dehuai spoke the truth, and they condemned him as a rightist.

In 1969, out of the approximately 1,200 people who worked in the Zhengzhou PSB, 110 in the courts, and 80 in the procuratorate* – a total of around 1,400 – 360 were detained as counter-revolutionaries! I was one of them. I was asked why I had done labouring jobs for the Japanese. They called me a traitor, and no one listened when I said it was just labouring work. Why did you work for the GMD River Affairs Bureau? No one believed me when I said I wiped tables and swept the floor for them. They just mindlessly arrested anyone, and said they were going to finish the task of "arresting class enemies", but then those making the arrests wanted to stop, because they could see that they were going to end up being arrested themselves! Investigators were sent down, and the result was that all 360 of us were cleared. Not a single one was a real counter-revolutionary, it was all trumped up. The leadership said that all the evidence should be burned immediately, and we should all be cleared, so we were.

That was how bad "arresting counter-revolutionaries" was back then.

XINRAN: What were your daily duties at the police station?

JINGGUAN: By day, the household registration officers went around checking, but in reality this was just a formality. The main thing they did was to find out how many people there were in each local family, who had relatives who visited regularly. But many of those from pre-Liberation days had worked for the GMD, and carried on trading things to stay alive. And

---

* Part of the Chinese court system, formed of a hierarchy of prosecuting offices called People's Procuratorates, the highest being the Supreme People's Procuratorate.

there were probably GMD spies lurking around there too! After dark, we patrolled with guns. If bad people saw the PSB on patrol, they might stay clean. We patrolled in shifts all night, but we didn't catch many thieves.

XINRAN: Did you keep an eye on temporary residents?

JINGGUAN: Of course. The rules said they had to register at the police station, and they were ticked off if they didn't: "It's wrong not to register. Just do it next time." If they didn't register next time, they got a warning. And if they still didn't? Before March 1949, they got taken to a PSB sub-bureau and were kept in an underground cell overnight, had to sign a statement and then it was, off you go, and that was that.

XINRAN: What about after?

JINGGUAN: After March 1949, generally if they were caught, they just got a talking-to. From 1953, I was transferred to the public order committee in a PSB sub-bureau. There were two main parts of public order work: the transient population, and special businesses. Special businesses meant checking places like hotels – a lot of shady types hung around there. We also had to keep an eye on all kinds of shops, because counter-revolutionaries were in and out of shops all the time. We were in charge of monitoring "key elements" of the population as well, which meant those who had done bad things, or had been locked up. We could check and verify any cases which came within the remit of local police stations, but anything major had to be passed up to a higher level. I was in charge of the community police branch, the public order offences branch and the traffic branch. Traffic was the responsibility of the municipal PSB, but they were short-staffed and got people from the sub-bureaux to do the work. Zhengzhou municipality was quite small then, and there were only forty or fifty people in the traffic branch. So each sub-bureau was allocated responsibility for certain points. For instance, we got the railway station, and did three-hour shifts from morning to evening. The rest of the time the municipal PSB took charge. There were only four or five people in the traffic branch in each sub-bureau, not like now. There are over a thousand in the traffic police branch now.

XINRAN: How good were PSB cadres then? What about your bosses, for instance?

JINGGUAN: Cadres in those days? They weren't greedy and money-grubbing, everyone got allocated supplies, ordinary clothes and ordinary food. Not like nowadays. Ordinary cadres got twenty or thirty yuan a month, not enough to buy cigarettes, it would get you a pair of shoes at most, not good quality, just ordinary ones. Our PSB head, who was head of the organisational department of the provincial committee, and the deputy head of the PSB and the intermediate courts chief justice, whom I knew too, they worked in the evenings, and sometimes did an overnight shift at the PSB, and if they got up in the night for a pee, they'd check out this and that, like parents keeping an eye on their children, and pull the quilt covers over the young officers in the station dormitory. That was what leaders were like then. We took it for granted.

XINRAN: In your résumé, you said that in 1956, you became deputy head of the PSB. What were your wages then?

JINGGUAN: Seventy-four yuan.

XINRAN: In 1957, you were transferred to the municipal PSB Section 8. What were your main duties there?

JINGGUAN: Anyone arrested by Criminal Investigation, including suspects, was sent to Section 8. Section 8 was divided up into a number of subsections. The detention centre looked after the prisoners' food and drink, hygiene, even down to the toilet paper issued every day; it also looked after them if they got ill, and provided baths, haircuts and everything. Then there was preliminary examination, interrogation and investigation. After the detainees had arrived in prison, they were passed to a prison examiner whose job was, first, to look into the detainee's circumstances and, second, to clarify the family's circumstances. If it was a counter-revolutionary charge, they had to look at the detainee's friends too.

XINRAN: And were corporal punishment and torture part of this?

JINGGUAN: They were not permitted in the rules, but in fact to a certain degree the police did connive with prisoners punishing prisoners. Some of the prisoners really were lying, but the police were not allowed to beat them, so they would drop hints to the head prisoner: so-and-so's not telling the truth, give him a helping hand! At the beginning, we really would interrogate them in a civilised way but because prisoners would reckon it didn't matter what they said, the police would still say they were lying, they simply messed around. Sometimes, the police did extort confessions. One day, I was on duty, and I heard that a prisoner had broken a pile of bowls. That sounded strange, so I got him out and asked him: "How did those bowls get broken?" He said: "They fell off my head and broke." I said: "Why did you put them on your head?" He said nothing, so I told him I was in charge of the detention centre, and if he didn't say anything then he would be punished! So he said the police examining him had said he was lying and made him stand there with a pile of bowls on his head. His neck began to ache, he felt dizzy and the bowls fell on the floor. At this, the police got the senior prisoners to beat him up. It looked like he'd taken a heavy beating, and when they'd finished with him, they made him say he'd deliberately broken the bowls.

XINRAN: So in reality there was corporal punishment and forced confession.

JINGGUAN: Oh yes. The people running the section would rely on the chief prisoners or long-term prisoners to beat up the new ones. Another way was for four or five of the older men to form a group which tyrannised the detention centre, and mostly this mafia would be chosen by the prisoners themselves. We indicated who should be godfather, and who should be in for a bad time, and then we left it to them to choose. But these godfathers became prison bullies, and everyone knew that. When there was proof, they would be punished. But the prisoners were afraid of them and protected them.

XINRAN: But the cadres in charge needed this mafia, didn't they?

JINGGUAN: That's right. Without them, the prison would be even more unmanageable. I think it's the same in all prisons.

XINRAN: How did you feel when China began to move towards the extreme left?

JINGGUAN: The move to the left began in 1956, it was ridiculously "left", frighteningly so. There were newspaper reports every day, saying that the slogan for agriculture was 1,000 pounds of grain and 10,000 pounds of vegetables per *mu* of land, but in fact this was impossible. Yet if you told the truth, you became a "rightist", so you couldn't, and I didn't. The leaders made their speeches and no one wanted to be a rightist. Rightism was wrong, but wasn't leftism wrong too? There were people taking care of rightism, but no one was taking care of leftism. If you were honest and conscientious, then that equalled being a rightist.

In the counties on the outskirts of Zhengzhou, 1,000 pounds of grain per *mu* of land was quite impossible! And 10,000 pounds of vegetables was impossible too. But especially after the Anti-Rightist movement of 1957, that was the mood. The *Henan Daily* published the first explosive news report in 1958: the per *mu* yield for wheat in Henan was 7,320 pounds. By the time of the 1958 winter wheat harvest, the papers reported that the per *mu* yield was 200,000 pounds! In 1959, I was sent down to a village on the northern outskirts of Zhengzhou where they had an experimental field. When they reported the yield, they had to have the signature of the inspector. I was the inspector. They were getting 470 pounds per *mu*. I could see that the scales were accurate, but the production team leader wanted me to report 1,000 pounds per *mu*. I wouldn't. In the end, the commune reported that his per *mu* yield was 520 pounds. If you didn't make such reports, you weren't revolutionary! There was a woman production team leader who talked such a lot of rubbish. She was eighteen or nineteen and unmarried, and she challenged them to get 200,000 pounds per *mu* on the experimental field, or she wouldn't get married! The old men and women in the village laughed and said: "You're going to be left on the shelf then!"

XINRAN: Generally speaking, in the counties on the outskirts of Zhengzhou, what is the per *mu* yield now?

JINGGUAN: Six or seven hundred pounds is normal for a wheat field. Because seeds and fertiliser are better now than they were then, that's why it's increased. Back then a lot of nonsense was talked. There was a production team leader who said he wanted to haul the 300,000 pounds of sweet potatoes grown on one *mu* of land to Moscow to present to Stalin. That was just rubbish, quite impossible. But no one dared contradict him.

XINRAN: The prisoners you had at the end of the fifties, what kind of people were they? Were there more criminals or more political prisoners?

JINGGUAN: In 1958, most were counter-revolutionaries, too many for the detention centre to hold. We had to commandeer warehouses and store-rooms for the prisoners, not like now when there aren't any counter-revolutionaries.

XINRAN: Do you remember what kind of prisoners you interrogated?

JINGGUAN: I didn't do much interrogation because I was section head. I attended meetings with my seniors, and I managed those under me. When other officers had finished the interrogations, they reported to you, you checked everything, signed it off and passed the report up. It should have been the PSB chief who put his signature and seal on the reports, but he was busy with meetings, so he delegated it to his deputy, and when he got too busy, it got delegated to the section head, who signed it. Then it received the seal of the municipal PSB, who referred it to the procuratorate, who examined it, and referred it to the courts, who passed sentence. In fact, referring it to the judiciary was a formality; the real power was with the PSB and, in the PSB, with the policemen who did the work. The courts only knew how to deal with the big cases, like murder, arson and hold-ups. Everyone was so poor then that there was nothing to steal. Most of the work was arresting vagrants, and illegal squatting by the transient population.

Before 1980, the police had to go and interrogate a man and a woman if they'd been sitting together. And sleeping together before marriage put you in prison. If you could get someone to vouch for you, you wouldn't get a big punishment and they'd let you go. But if it was homicide, you'd get decent food, but no one would dare let you out. Not like now – if you've got support from someone senior, they get you to write a false confession, change your file and before it's sent to the procuratorate, the killing's been changed into "self-defence". So daring of them!

XINRAN: You have said a number of times that the police were poorly educated. To your knowledge, how many of the police in those days really had any legal or professional training?

JINGGUAN: None of them, not one! In the municipal PSB, only one or two of the section heads had finished lower middle school, most had just done primary. The PSB had a regulation, by the way, that the police had to have good political backgrounds, so many of them were from poor families, poor workers and the lowest peasants.

XINRAN: So their professional skills were very limited. Was their outlook as individuals influenced by their class background?

JINGGUAN: In those days, the political ethos, right from central government to the regions, was that in the countryside you relied on the peasants, and in the cities you relied on the working class. It could be summed up simply: rely on the poor. Particularly in the law enforcement agencies, people with learning or from a high-class background were not permitted.

XINRAN: Were there a lot of people with learning or from a high-class background in prison?

JINGGUAN: Yes, especially among the counter-revolutionary prisoners.

XINRAN: So how were cases investigated and decided if law enforcement officers were so uneducated?

JINGGUAN: Our leaders divided it up into several different stages, didn't they?

The first stage was the 1950 consolidation period, when the focus was on bandits, tyrants, key GMD counter-revolutionaries and Chiang Kai-shek's spy network.

The second stage was 1956, defined as the "army, officials, police and the law" stage. In the GMD Army there was no criminal activity: most of the senior officers hadn't committed any crime.

Here's an example of a serious crime: someone came to Anyang to arrest a suspect on the run from his village. The suspect had killed the chairman of the village council, disembowelled him, dug his heart out and eaten it. Then he had killed the Women's Federation leader, then a dozen other people, and then he had fled. The person from Anyang contacted our local police station and our household registration officers went to the home of a relative of the suspect and were told that he was at the Dongguan Airport construction site. Anyang county PSB rushed off there, but another family member had tipped the suspect off and he'd gone again. But a dozen of us surrounded the relative's house and hid out for a few days, and eventually caught him.

XINRAN: What do you think was the most "leftist" period in China?

JINGGUAN: Most "leftist"? That was the Cultural Revolution!

XINRAN: Where were you during the Cultural Revolution?

JINGGUAN: I was Chief Justice at the Central Plains Regional Courts. There were just eight of us, and I was the only one who was "struggled against".

XINRAN: How long did that go on for?

JINGGUAN: Altogether, two months and twenty-nine days. Twice I had to stand up for more than four hours. I had no enemies – whenever people saw me they just said, "Take a bit of a rest," and no one was really brutal to me. The Cultural Revolution was a complete nonsense.

XINRAN: Why do you say that?

JINGGUAN: Haven't you heard? Liu Shaoqi's Party file describes how he was arrested in Shenyang in 1931. You didn't know, I didn't know, only Mao Zedong and Lin Biao's Special Cases Group saw the file and sent investigators to Shenyang. They swore they would prove he was a traitor.* There was a Mr Yang in the Shenyang GMD branch which had arrested Liu Shaoqi and after Liberation this man was given a commuted death sentence. He was in a Reform through Labour camp, and the Special Cases

---

* Liu Shaoqi (1898–1969) was Chairman of the People's Republic of China from 27 April 1959 to 31 October 1968 but during the Cultural Revolution he was labelled a "traitor". In July 1966 he was displaced as Party Deputy Chairman by Lin Biao. By 1967 Liu Shaoqi and his wife, Wang Guangmei, were under house arrest in Beijing.

Group went and asked him about the Liu Shaoqi business. He couldn't remember it at first, but after a week he said they had arrested a Liu Weihuang for selling salt without a permit but there was no case to answer and they let him go. He didn't know if that was Liu Shaoqi. Liu's file recorded that name; it was one his grandfather had given him. The Special Cases Group person said to him: "How come you haven't confessed that you only released him after he had turned traitor. Liu Shaoqi's admitted it, so why are you still shielding him? I can see you don't want to go on living. If you carry on lying, tomorrow we'll take you out and shoot you." Yang cried all night, and thought to himself: I'm not happy about lying, but if they shoot me, I'll be dead. That was the first idea that occurred to him, and so he made his "confession" accordingly, and he was released. But then he reconsidered: It doesn't matter if they shoot me, but I can't frame the State Chairman! So he withdrew his statement and wrote numerous documents telling the truth, but no one dared take any notice of it.

XINRAN: I suppose you know that China's first State Chairman died in custody in Henan?

JINGGUAN: I didn't know it then.

XINRAN: When did you find out?

JINGGUAN: In 1979. A plane came from Beijing to pick up his ashes because the government was organising a memorial service for him. Before that, the Special Cases Group people came to Henan and looked everywhere for them but couldn't find them. Finally, they were found in Kaifeng – they got hold of a Mr Niu who used to be in charge of the crematorium. He said, oh yes, definitely, they had the ashes of a Liu Weihuang. He had had the feeling this man had been a top cadre, but no old army comrades or family had turned up for the cremation. The army had sent the body for cremation, but no one came to pick up the ashes. It was only ten years later that they found out that this was Liu Shaoqi.

XINRAN: So you also didn't hear about Liu's sad end in Henan?

JINGGUAN: At that time, all we heard was that Liu Shaoqi had been using the war to make a name for himself. Plus a lot of old cadres were transferred away from Beijing in disgrace. Liu Shaoqi became a "class enemy". He fell ill and they refused him medical treatment. He was in very low spirits. It was cold in Henan and there was no heating. I heard that the Special Cases Group were very cruel to him.

XINRAN: When he died, was it from illness, or starvation, or ill-treatment, do you know?

JINGGUAN: I reckon it must have been illness, because he was seventy-one then, and if he didn't die from illness then it must have been from the ill-treatment and humiliation.

XINRAN: You didn't know the details even in the PSB?

JINGGUAN: Right from the start, we were told he had died of illness.

XINRAN: Were there rumours going around within your organisation?

JINGGUAN: Yes there were, but we didn't believe them. Things like Tao Zhu* dying in Anhui on 22 November 1969, and we were also told that General Xu Haidong† had died from an illness. I saw a film which was among some classified material of the struggle sessions against Liu Shaoqi and his wife, Wang Guangmei, in Zhongnanhai in 1968. They were dragged into the assembly room, by strapping great toughs, and they were beating him up, forcing him into the "flying aeroplane" position, grabbing him by his wisps of white hair and forcing his head up to face the camera. Then the pair of them were taken to a corner of the room, had their heads forced down and were made to kowtow to a couple of cartoons of Red Guards. Finally, Liu Shaoqi hobbled away, his face badly battered. He had obviously taken quite a beating.

XINRAN: I heard a story about Liu Shaoqi's last days, from someone who had worked in 301 Military Hospital in Henan. Liu Shaoqi had diabetes, and had a feeding tube in his nose. Before he was sent to Henan in October 1969, his nurse wanted to warn Liu Shaoqi, so she dipped a cotton bud in gentian violet and wrote in big characters on a piece of newspaper: "The Central Committee has decided to transfer you to somewhere else."

When he was being transferred, he was dirty and smelly, because he

---

* Tao Zhu (1908–1969) was Secretary of the Guangdong Provincial Committee and Commander of the Guangzhou Military Region. He later became First Secretary of the Central-South region, and in 1965 was moved to Beijing as Director of the Central Propaganda Department. He was a Vice Premier of the State Council and Secretary of the Central Secretariat of the CCP, as well as an advisor to the Central Cultural Revolution Group. In May 1966, he was promoted to No. 4 in the Party, behind Mao Zedong, Zhou Enlai and Lin Biao, but was purged during the Cultural Revolution in early 1967 and died under house arrest in 1969.

† Xu Haidong (1900–1970) was born into poverty and was made Grand General in the People's Liberation Army of China in 1955. Mao Zedong praised him as "a banner of the working class". He died in Zhengzhou in March 1970.

couldn't look after himself any more. The nurses gingerly stripped off his clothes, and wrapped him in a pink satin quilt which they covered with a white sheet. About seven in the evening, under the supervision of the Special Cases Group, and accompanied by the nurses and Liu's bodyguard, Liu Shaoqi was put on a stretcher, placed in the rear cabin of the plane and flown to Kaifeng.

Apparently, martial law was suddenly imposed on Kaifeng Airport and the staff had no idea what was happening. Everyone was very tense. A military aircraft touched down on the runway, and two nurses in white uniforms carried a stretcher out. The person on the stretcher was stick-thin, and all that showed was a bony face buried in an unkempt mass of hair and beard. A blanket covered the white-sheeted figure, and the stench coming from under it was enough to make you retch . . .

Liu Shaoqi's naked body was too frail to withstand the freezing conditions on the flight and he caught acute pneumonia when he arrived in Kaifeng. Soon afterwards, on 13 November, his bodyguard came to his bedside in the underground cell in the early morning and found he'd stopped breathing.

At dead of night on 14 November 1969, Liu's remains, tightly bound in cotton cloth, were loaded into a Model 69 jeep. The back of the jeep was too short, and Liu Shaoqi's feet were visible, sticking out at the back.

On the cremation certificate was written: "Names: LIU Weihuang; Profession: none; Cause of death: illness." It was signed by Liu's son, Liu Yuan. His ashes remained in the crematorium for ten years without anyone knowing.

JINGGUAN: So the State Chairman, so proclaimed in black and white in the 4 January 1965 *People's Daily*, became a "jobless vagrant" without ordinary people being told anything about it! When eventually his widow, Wang Guangmei, and children received his ashes in Number 1 Conference Room of the Henan Province People's Congress Hall in Zhengzhou, the staff on duty said that the grief-stricken woman clutched the bag of ashes and buried her face in them for a long time – it was enough to make the onlookers weep!*

XINRAN: Your information mostly came from files kept by the law enforcement agencies, is that right? Was this information kept afterwards?

JINGGUAN: No, it was a real mess. First of all, the people in charge

---

* After Deng Xiaoping came to power in 1978, Liu Shaoqi was politically rehabilitated (in February 1980) with a state funeral.

of it were uneducated, and they had the files stacked up like so many discarded bits of equipment. Those with any education looked after crime data, and they never had enough time, so how could we send them off to be archivists? Document storage was given to people who couldn't do anything else. Secondly, when officials left, retired or whatever, they cleared out all the files. Those who were well meaning but ignorant did it to clear things out for the next person in the post; those with something to hide simply burned stuff, to avoid leaving the proof in other people's hands. Besides, so many of the political movements relied on old information to punish people. Who dared to leave anything written down? Who knew if the next official might be a relative of someone you'd arrested? Anything written down was proof, and so many people had lost their lives because of characters on paper that we were all afraid. So anything that could be destroyed was destroyed, and the only things that were left were broad statements of principle and other documents that had nothing to do with one's own work. That's why, if people wanted to redress miscarriages of justice, they couldn't find the original material. If you were a good man, you had to go and prove you didn't kill someone, that's all there was to it.

*

The lack of original material is a disaster for modern Chinese historical records. As Mr Jingguan put it, it is not only a clearing-out when there is a regime change, it is also a by-product of the fear of taking responsibility because no one wants to assume lifelong responsibility for everything they did while in office. In the Chinese system of government and administration there is no such legal concept as "official actions entail lifelong responsibility". As a result, no matter how corrupt you are as an official, so long as you're not caught while in office, after leaving it you can rest easy and enjoy the privileges you have won for yourself.

*

XINRAN: After the Cultural Revolution, you were transferred to be manager of the Sanguanmiao office. Why were you sent there?

JINGGUAN: I'd done forty years of law enforcement work, and I felt very low and didn't want to do it any more. The more I did, the worse I felt and the more fearful too. Well, that's life. At the beginning of the year, I didn't want to go on, and the next month I went out into the streets and saw a new lot of big character posters. It was the anti-crime and anti-reactionaries campaign. Most of my cadre colleagues had been sent to work in communes, and the constables had been sent to work in factories. That left just ten cadres and ten constables. I thought of the cases I was handling and [holding up the thumb of his right hand] I was this one, and the other nine were no good, and I thought if I don't go back to work, there'll be even more miscarriages of justice in this district, so I went back and dealt with 174 cases that year. I relied on facts and proof. Basically I stopped at that point; the sentence was determined by my seniors in uniform, I didn't have anything to do with that.

I left the PSB after more than forty years. If I'd gone on any longer, my life would have been a few years shorter. Why? Because the work was too hard. I left the courts after more than twenty years, and if I'd stayed there longer, my life would also have been a few years shorter. Why? Because there were too many cock-ups, and these cases all involved human lives and required the greatest care.

When I gave in my notice, I was disciplined for it. You want to leave? Then you'll be demoted! I said, OK, that's fine by me. I'll leave this place that gives me sleepless nights, and have a bit of a rest, why shouldn't I?

XINRAN: Why did forty-odd years of law enforcement work give you so much pain?

JINGGUAN: No one believes you. There's a stream of political movements that punish people in law enforcement first. Every day you want to arrest bad people but you're worried about being arrested as a bad person yourself. You don't know what political wind will blow tomorrow. Tell me where else it's like this to be a policeman. People like you don't know, all you see is either the police swaggering around or the bad people we've caught, but the police in China don't have an easy life!

XINRAN: Do you think China has a healthy legal system?

JINGGUAN: What legal system? The law hardly exists. The law is the expression on your chief's face. The law is what your bosses say. Even in 1958, at the first Chinese conference on law and politics, the head of the PSB, a man called Luo Ruiqing, said on behalf of the Central Committee that Chairman Mao had said from then on there would be no amending the law or the constitution, the law was what the Party Central Committee maintained and what the *People's Daily* wrote. That was what he said.

I'm an old man now, and as far as crime is concerned, I say what I know, and what I've told you is the truth about all those people's lives.

XINRAN: Do you have regrets about the life you've led?

JINGGUAN: ... [He looks up at the ceiling, the corners of his mouth working in a great effort, exhaling a long breath through his nostrils. His body language clearly expresses the pain in his heart.] None at all! Wouldn't regret mean I'd done something wrong? I haven't done anything wrong. I couldn't determine the time when I was going to come into this world.

XINRAN: If you were born again, would you work in law enforcement in China?

JINGGUAN: Never! In every dynasty, working in law enforcement in China has always been like living in the eye of the storm, and that's hard. And it doesn't matter which dynasty, see? Everyone knows in China that when the dynasty changes, all the ministers change too. What does that mean? Well, where do the ministers from the previous regime go? If they're not demoted, they retire or they're killed! Who kills them? The emperor! "The emperor kills wrongdoers, but the ministers get the blame."

XINRAN: There's been a big increase in students studying law and law enforcement at university level, sir. So is law enforcement in a better position than it was before the reforms of the 1980s?

JINGGUAN: There's more awareness of the law and regulations than there used to be, but now that people know more, there are new problems. Central government makes policy, but the grass roots carries it out. Every time the policy is improved, it comes up against an ignorant, reckless response at the grass roots, and that's the end of it. The law is enforced by people. Take, for example, people who used to run the courts, basically us senior cadres. In 1982, at the 12th Congress of the CCP, Deng Xiaoping instigated the policy of appointing younger cadres. This policy began to work its way through the layers of government: generally speaking, the age of departmental heads in central government was not to exceed sixty-five, for deputy heads it was sixty, and central government committee members should not in principle be older than seventy. By the first half of 1983, the policy had reached provincial governments, and by the end of that year, municipal governments. By 1984, the policy had reached the regions, and affected cadres of fifty and over, and without diplomas. Most of them were demoted. Back then, most didn't have diplomas, as they hadn't completed lower or upper middle school, let alone university. Also, they had no specialist training. Court officers nowadays are basically all university graduates, starting from the 5,000 constables recruited by the

PSB, all with university diplomas – and 40,000 applied, all with these diplomas, but even a university diploma doesn't necessarily get you the job – people don't exist in a vacuum, though, they come in all shapes and sizes, so how does it work? Today's courts may look on the surface as if they're run according to the law, but actually it's according to who's got power, and even more, according to who's got money. Young cadres today are pretty daring, one of them stashed away up to 200,000 yuan in bribes in a year or so, and was sentenced to eighteen years.

XINRAN: Do you think there's any hope for the law enforcement agencies in this province?

JINGGUAN: There are still problems in public security, and the calibre of the officers is very uneven. Court officers at all levels are university graduates, so they should be higher calibre.

XINRAN: So there should be some hope, then.

JINGGUAN: That depends on what you mean! At the Spring Festival 2007, I saw a film on TV about the last Qing dynasty emperor. From the first emperor, Nurhaci, to the last, Aisin-Gioro Pu Yi, there were constant violent revolts. Now China's changed too rapidly, it's too extreme.

XINRAN: You've experienced life both before and after Liberation, you were in Zhengzhou's first cohort of police officers, and you've seen how public security in China has changed. What has made you happy or sad in all those years in public security? Can you tell me three of the happiest and saddest things?

JINGGUAN: The saddest? I've cried three times in my life, and shed a tear or two another three times. The first time I cried was in November 1942. It was so many days until the Spring Festival, and there was not a grain to eat. The family had split up and there was no one to look after us. We had nothing to eat or drink and I was young, and I cried. The second time I cried was when my father died before the New Year, at only thirty-eight. We had no adult male in my family, and I cried for the whole night! Another time was when the Japanese reached Zhengzhou in 1944, and we had nothing to eat for days. Then I went to be a coolie for the Japanese, and worked from first light until dark. Those Japanese were bad people and I'm a good person, but I had no money to keep us alive, all I could do was work for the Japanese. When I thought about this, I cried, I really cried . . . then when my mother died, I didn't cry so hard.

I shed a tear or two, you can't call it crying, just a tear or two, in 1952, when I had been a sergeant for three years, and the Three Antis and the Five Antis campaigns had begun. I was investigated. They said: "Your employees are corrupt, you must be corrupt too. You're not honest and conscientious." It was awful. I didn't cry, just shed a tear or two.

Another time was when the Cultural Revolution created chaos in the PSB and the courts in 1969. I couldn't see, I just couldn't see why they were getting at three of us. One of us was an old cadre who had fought against the Japanese, he was the head of the Zhengzhou PSB, he had worked as a grade-one secretary in the Soviet Union, and had carried on writing letters to people he knew there after his return. So they made him out to be a Soviet spy. The second was the chief procurator; he'd been a cadre since 1938, and in 1942 was on the run from the Japanese when he arrived in a village. He thought he was going to die, so what was he to do? He found the head of the puppet village administration, held a gun at his head and said: "If you save my life, then you save your whole family. If you don't save me, then I'll kill them all right now." The village head saved him. But the Red Guards said: "Why did you go for the puppet village head? Why not go to the peasants and Communist poor?" The third one was me. I'd worked in the police or the courts from 1948 right up until then, and hadn't done anything wrong, but hunger had forced me to be a coolie for the Japanese, and that made me a traitor. I shed a tear or two about that, but I didn't cry.

XINRAN: How many good memories do you have?

JINGGUAN: Lots of ordinary things, but not many particularly special ones.

XINRAN: How did you get to know your wife?

JINGGUAN: The first time the person who introduced us brought her to my police station, I just asked about her family background. Class background was very important then. Then we got to know each other. Sometimes she came to the police station, and if I had time, I came out to see her.

XINRAN: How did you propose to her? Do you remember?

JINGGUAN: Ha! I didn't really propose! It was understood. If someone introduced a couple, then that was what it was about, wasn't it? It wasn't like the fun and games you see on TV and in films.

XINRAN: So did you have a wedding?

JINGGUAN: Good heavens, what's the point in talking about that?

XINRAN: Oh, please. Young people today never hear about it. Teach them something about traditional customs.

JINGGUAN: There was a troupe of waist-drummers in our sector, and the police station got them in and fixed a time and a place with them. That day, I took five yuan, and got, maybe, two yuans' worth of sweets, two of melon seeds and one of cigarettes, and that was all my five yuan spent! That was a lot of money in those days. In general, a junior police officer only got eight to ten yuan per month. Everyone came and got everything ready, and then the drums rolled, bong bong bong. Back then the young men used to have a bit of fun – you had to bow to the woman, because of equality between the sexes and all that – so I made my bow, and after that, the drummers on either side beat their drums, bong bong bong. Then one of the chiefs just said: "Right, everyone eat the sweets and have a smoke and chat." It was all over in about an hour. Accommodation was tight at the police station in those days, and we had nowhere to live, so we went off for a walk for a couple of hours and then went back to my mother's house in Nandajie Street. You got three days off when you got married, but they were short-staffed and the next morning I went back to work in the police station.

XINRAN: After you got married, did you and your wife have any major fights?

JINGGUAN: Not really. We had a few minor set-tos, but not in the first ten years of marriage, we didn't have any fights.

XINRAN: What kind of person was your wife?

JINGGUAN: There were three things about her. One was that she was a good woman, and a tough one. The second thing was that she worked incredibly hard – in the factory and at home. When she got out of work, she cooked our food and sewed our clothes, and never took a minute's rest. The third thing was that she was sure of herself. It was best to do what she said – she had a bit of a temper, and she meant what she said. But she was usually right anyway.

XINRAN: When did her health problems start?

JINGGUAN: On National Day in 1975, she was in the Workers' Propaganda Team of the Zhengzhou Number 15 Middle School, and went to hospital. When they took her blood pressure, it was very high, 190 over 110, and the doctor told her to take sick leave. After six months, she gave up work and got sick pay, and in 1977, she formally retired from her job. She was only forty-three, and had to retire. It was the Cultural Revolution and our eldest girl was working in the countryside. The rules were that they could only come back to work in the city if they were needed to take a parent's place, and only for that reason. My wife was retired, so she spent her time looking after me. In 1986, she was cooking the dinner when she dropped the food. She went to hospital for a check-up and they discovered she had a minor blood clot on the brain. In 1991, she tripped and fell over in the house. When she came to, she couldn't stand – she would fall again if she tried to stand on her own. They took her to hospital, but then later she became doubly incontinent, and couldn't even sit. On 23 June 2004, after she had gone into a coma, the hospital confirmed their diagnosis that she had become a vegetable.

XINRAN: Do you live like this every day?

JINGGUAN: To start with we hired a nurse. The nurse slept on a cot in here, I slept in there and my wife slept on the outside of the double bed. If I woke up in the night and I felt her and she had wet herself, then I turned on the light and called the nurse to come and change her nappies. It's uncomfortable for her being wet down there, and we can't afford stuff like proper incontinence pads. Every day there's a huge line of washing hanging up to dry like the flag pennants on a paddle steamer that you see on TV.

XINRAN: Have you talked to your children about your life and how you feel about it?

JINGGUAN: To my children? I'd be afraid of them blabbing to the grand-children. And they wouldn't believe that things like that had really happened to me.

XINRAN: You don't think they would understand what hardships you went through as a child?

JINGGUAN: To hell with "understanding"! They'd say, what's the point of talking about stuff like that? Can I go back to the old society? Can I relive starving to death? If I told them their grandfather died of hunger, they'd ask why he didn't eat bread. Eat bread? If he'd had a bit of corn cake, he wouldn't have starved. All they learn about nowadays is how to make money, they don't know how poor people get by. What's the use of someone who's studied if they haven't got skills? It's just the same as my grandfather and father – a bellyful of learning and they starved to death!

XINRAN: So do you think young people should study, or should learn a skill?

JINGGUAN: Studying is the foundation. All things being equal, if you haven't got an education, then you'll lose out. See how city folk are always complaining: "It's terrible, this job's too hard, that job's too hard." Zhengzhou has a migrant population of 600,000. They live in shacks, and survive on dry steamed bread and pickled vegetables, but not one of them has starved to death. Migrant workers are prepared to do dirty, hard and tiring work that city folk won't necessarily do. When it comes to the end of the year, city folk get into fights about money, but people from the countryside go back home for the holiday with their pockets bulging with money.

XINRAN: Have you talked to your children and grandchildren about your views, and does it do any good?

JINGGUAN: Sometimes it does and sometimes it doesn't. I've got a granddaughter of twenty-three; she graduated from the Arts Institute in Chengdu last year and came home, and after a year she's still looking for work. A good job is hard to find, and she doesn't want to do one which is a bit worse. Every day she frets that no one realises how talented she is. But this world isn't made just for you. You need to go and work at something, and then look out for opportunities to do something better.

XINRAN: And have you said that to her?

JINGGUAN [looking at me as if I'm a bit strange]: Me, talk to her? She would just tell me I was completely wrong! All they study nowadays is moonshine.

XINRAN: What do they think your life has been like? [He gives a look as if to say: There's no point in asking that.] Do they know what your job is about?

JINGGUAN: They think the uniform is impressive, but they don't think we're as intelligent or know as much they do.

XINRAN: Do they think you have that "blind loyalty" of the old society, or that you're ignorant?

JINGGUAN: That's just what they think but they don't dare say it to my face. Luckily I'm still the grandfather! But they still complain about me being demoted. My youngest grandson said: "Granddad, there aren't many cadres as senior as you in Zhengzhou, why aren't you living in one of those hundred-square-metre, two-storey houses built for cadres like you?" And my old friends say: "You should count as a big cadre. How come you're still living in that dark hole of a room? How do you feel knowing there are people who haven't as many years' service as you and aren't as senior who live in apartment blocks and detached houses? Isn't that corrupt?" I say I don't feel bad, I'm not nearly as good as Eighth Route Army veterans.

During the Red Army's Long March, during the fight against the Japanese, living off corn cakes, they went up to the front line in the middle of the night, and they never knew who would live and who would die. Tough times for me meant kipping down on the floor at three in the morning, but I did get three meals a day, and at least I could eat my fill. Those veterans never got enough to eat.

XINRAN: If you had enough time left, and energy and money, what would you most like to do?

JINGGUAN: Have a nice meal with my wife. After all, she might wake up at any time, no one can tell for sure. I don't want not to be at her side the day she wakes up, or she'd never stop telling me off. I've said to my two daughters, I can look after myself now, I can make my own breakfast when I get up. If you make the midday meal that's fine, but if you don't, that's fine too, I can make my own dinner, I can do simple things for myself, and it's good that I can.

XINRAN: What would you wish for your children?

JINGGUAN: They're grown up. The youngest is nearly fifty, so there's nothing more in prospect for them. They haven't benefited from me being a policeman. I've always been upright, and I have a clear conscience, but they've suffered for that. If I'd followed the crowd and used my power and influence, they wouldn't still be factory workers. Sometimes when I think about that, I feel bad . . .

Well, I must go and feed my wife, she has to have her meals on time, otherwise she might get stomach problems.

*

While Mr Jingguan and his youngest daughter prepared his wife's "tube food", I interviewed their elder daughter.

XINRAN: What is the strongest impression you have of your mother?

ELDER DAUGHTER: That she could not be disobeyed. There was always so much to do in the house, and she did an eight-hour shift in the factory too, and got us to school. It seemed like Mum never slept, she was always out buying food, cooking, washing, making clothes. She did the night shift, then in the morning came home and cooked and did the housework. She just slept a bit after lunch when she was doing that shift. Just an hour or two, and she'd get up and get busy looking after us and the house. Then every evening, she'd be off to work. It was really tough.

XINRAN: If your mum could hear, what would you like to say to her?

ELDER DAUGHTER: What I want to say is: "Thank you, Mum, for working so hard for us all those years. When you should have been able to put your feet up and enjoy life, you weren't able to. Your children are grown up now, but you've had no opportunity to enjoy life . . ."

*

At this, she started sobbing. Her younger sister came into the room for something, and seeing her tears, gave the things to her and indicated that she should go and help her father with feeding her mother. Then she turned to me.

*

YOUNGER DAUGHTER: I'll answer your questions, shall I? We all have to share the burden, otherwise we wouldn't be able to bear what's happened to our mum.

XINRAN: Thank you for your understanding and your courage. Tell me, where do you work?

YOUNGER DAUGHTER: I had a job in Zhengzhou Recycling, but I was laid off. I'm at home all day, and I come here to look after my mother. I was laid off twelve years ago, and I haven't worked in all that time.

XINRAN: Do you know about your father's and grandparents' early lives?

YOUNGER DAUGHTER: I don't have any memories of my grandparents. I was only three years old when my grandmother died.

XINRAN: Do you know about the sad times in your father's youth?

YOUNGER DAUGHTER: They were so poor then. I've heard my father talk about how the family was very poor and it was all down to him to support them, because my grandfather died young.

XINRAN: Do you sometimes wish you knew more about your grandparents?

YOUNGER DAUGHTER: I don't really know, I've never thought about it.

XINRAN: How old is your child?

YOUNGER DAUGHTER: Twenty-three.

XINRAN: Do you think your child understands what your father's life has been like?

YOUNGER DAUGHTER: They don't understand anything. Our generation are better than they are. They just spend their time knocking back good food and drink, and they don't have a care in the world.

XINRAN: Do you think your father's life has been worthwhile?

YOUNGER DAUGHTER: I haven't thought about it. Sometimes it's unbearable.

XINRAN: What do you mean by "unbearable"?

YOUNGER DAUGHTER: . . . I can't explain it . . . Dad looks on the bright side – he always says it's much better now than in the old society, what did we get to eat back then? There's plenty to eat and drink now, so we should count ourselves lucky!

XINRAN: Do you agree with him?

YOUNGER DAUGHTER: My generation has been unlucky too, but our lives are much better than my mum and dad's were.

XINRAN: Why has your generation been unfortunate?

YOUNGER DAUGHTER: We were born during the Great Leap Forward, 1958 to 1962, the years of natural disasters and there was nothing to eat. When we went to school, it was the Cultural Revolution and education stopped. We had to work and we were sent off to the countryside. When we married and had children, they came up with the "single child" policy. My child had just started school, and we lost our jobs, across the board, everyone without a diploma or qualifications was laid off. Now we're old, and there's been a reform of pensions and medical insurance, and we don't qualify. It seems as if the whole of government policy is against our generation.

XINRAN: I'm from the generation that "got on the wrong bus" too, so I know about the misfortunes you've mentioned and understand your feelings, but I think we still have some of that "relative happiness" that your father talked about, don't you? At least we haven't come up against war and starvation.

YOUNGER DAUGHTER: That's why we've never blamed my father, even though he's been so just and honourable in his work that we never got any of the advantages in life and work that the children of most senior cadres do. We also sympathise with him. He's old and my mother's become a vegetable, and he's afraid to leave the flat because he thinks she might wake up at any time, and would be angry if he wasn't there. So he never goes out. The most he'll do is sit in the doorway sometimes. And he hasn't even got anyone to talk to!

XINRAN: All these years, he's never been out?

YOUNGER DAUGHTER: Never. He's very good to my mum. He says he didn't look after us as children, or take any interest in the housework, she handled everything. She never wanted him bothered by all that, and it wasn't easy bringing us up. Mum never got to enjoy life for a single day, she just became a vegetable. My father feels terribly sorry about that.

*

The flat was so cramped that, with the cameras we'd set up, there was only enough room for the person who was looking after the patient, the person who was being interviewed and me. Everyone else had to wait outside. So when I had finished interviewing Mr Jingguan's younger daughter, I went out to look for him, to say thank you and goodbye.

I went down the stairs, which were so dimly lit you could see nothing at all, and as I emerged into the brightness outside, I saw the old man seated on a rickety old chair, reading a newspaper in the sunlight. With the darkness behind him and the bright light in front, he appeared perfectly posed, a glowing figure in a monochrome tableau. Here was the retired policeman, an old man no longer valued by Chinese society today, but a witness to history who would surely be remembered and revered by China in the future.

The policewoman who had acted as go-between and set up our meeting was clearly also moved by the openness and courage of the old officer. She had said she would do everything in her power to help us in our survey of the real China of today, to help the future understand the uncertainties of today and the price paid in the past. In fact, without her help, how would I ever have found this outstanding PSB officer, since he had already been consigned to limbo?

As we said farewell to Henan, the policewoman presented me with her personal case notebook and the newspaper clippings she had put together for our survey, as a memento. I only realised after reading them that she had made me another gift too. There was a sheet of paper tucked into the back of her notebook:

Ten very sad stories: From this mountain, I cannot see our present era clearly.*

1. *I want to go home, I want my wages!*
This was the last thing Yue Fuguo, a worker, said before he died. After these words, he suffered a cerebral haemorrhage and lost consciousness. Thirty-six hours later, the hospital reported that he had died. Yue Fuguo had still not received the wages that were due to him. The grief-stricken widow, Yao Yufang, asked indignantly: "How could they not pay him?" (Reported in *Chengdu Commercial News*)

---

* Date is 2005. This text as been reproduced a number of times on blogs and even university websites.

People say: When his parents named him "wealthy nation" [fu-guo], little did they imagine that he would not succeed in making even himself wealthy.

2. *I will never abandon my dream of going to Beijing University.*

Because her university entrance exam results had not given her the number of points required to get into university, Xiao Qian (not her real name), a seventeen-year-old from Shaanxi, threw herself from the balcony of her fifth-floor home. A week later she died, and after her death, reporters found a note in her room which read: *I will never abandon my dream of going to Beijing University.* Her leap, however, put paid forever to her dream. (Reported by Xinhuanet)

People ask: Are you happy, children of China?

3. *What are you actually doing?*

It was the small hours of 18 May 2004, and Chang Xia was still asleep, when five police officers and an informer erected a ladder and broke in through the window of her flat. A stunned Chang Xia plucked up the courage to ask them who they were. "They" wanted Chang Xia to "hand over that man who did it with you". Eventually they discovered that, apart from the uninvited guests – themselves – there was no one else there, whereupon they said, somewhat sheepishly, that they "might have got the wrong person". Still thunderstruck, Chang Xia asked again: "Who are you, and what are you actually doing?" but "they" simply swaggered out. Looking through the window, Chang Xia saw their car number plate. The fright they had given her unbalanced her mind. She mutters over and over to herself: "The car number plate, I remember it, those people, the middle of the night, they climbed in through the window, they were looking for someone, they searched my flat . . ." (Reported in *Shenyang Today*)

People ask: West of the Taishan Mountains, there's a saying which goes: "Wind and rain may get in, but the King of China cannot get into my house." But now there's no one to ensure people's privacy.

4. *He went to the Great Wall but was drowned by the waters.*

The "he" here refers to Zheng Jinshou, a young labourer from Fujian province working in Beijing. He and his girlfriend Xu Zhenjie were interrogated by the Civil Defence while meeting in the park, and were beaten up for not having their documents with them and for refusing to pay a fine for not having them. Zheng Jinshou staggered blindly off in panic and, as he was injured, ended up falling into the river and drowning. After his death, his girlfriend said: "He used to quote the saying that 'to be a real man you have to get to the Great Wall', but he went there and the waters took his life." His elder brother, Zheng Jinzi, said: "My brother was a strong swimmer, he was an athlete at school. If he hadn't been beaten almost unconscious, he definitely wouldn't have drowned." (Reported by Digital Media)

People say: To misquote Confucius: to think that the Civil Defence may take more lives than venomous snakes do!

5. *I wanted that child.*

When being interviewed, Ma Weihua said quietly: "I wanted that child." Ma Weihua had been arrested as a drug dealer. She was pregnant at the time and, according to the law, the death sentence could not be carried out on a pregnant woman so, without her permission, the police authorities anaesthetised her and carried out an abortion. Afterwards the police spokesman said that they suspected that Ma Weihua had become pregnant deliberately, in order to avoid the death sentence. (Reported by *South Weekend Review*)

People say: No comment.

6. *You go to school now, Mum's got to be off . . .*

When Huihui was born a girl, her father abandoned the family. For seven years, her mother endured all kinds of hardships to bring up her daughter. However, she was not a very capable worker, and life was indescribably hard. For seven years, she had not had any new clothes, for seven years, she had lived off pickled vegetables. If she did happen to buy a fish, she gave it to her daughter to eat. Even so, on Huihui's birthday every year, her mother would always buy her a birthday cake. But this year, Huihui's mother just couldn't get together the 100 yuan, so when Huihui had gone to school, her mother hanged herself. (Reported by *Anhui Market News*)

People say: A harmonious society, huh!

7. *If you didn't force me, would I volunteer to go out and sweep snow in the streets?*

Sun Fengmei is a blind girl. After a snowfall, the local area committee asked Sun Fengmei to "volunteer for snow-sweeping" under threat of removing her minimum living standard benefit from her. When news of this got out, they changed their tune and said that even if she didn't, they still couldn't take away her benefit. At the same time, they absolutely deny that they ever said she had to sweep snow or they would remove her benefit. But Sun Fengmei asks: "If you didn't force me, would I volunteer to go out and sweep snow in the streets?" (Reported by *Shengyang Daily*)

People say: It seems as if "volunteering" is often used as the opposite to its real meaning.

8. *I'm wearing my best clothes.*
Putting on his convict's uniform, Ma Jiajue said: "I'm wearing the best clothes I've ever had." Police officers who heard him say this could not help shedding a tear. Ma Jiajue was a murderer, but the law could not take into account how he had grown up. When his school grant was not approved, Ma was so poor that he did not dare go to school because he had no shoes to wear. His schoolmates remembered that, after this, his character completely changed, and he stopped talking to anyone. (Reported by *Sohu Cultural News*)

People ask: Don't the poor also have their dignity?

9. *By the time you read this, son, I won't be alive any more . . .*
"Son, when you read my letter, I won't be alive any more, because I'm not capable of getting you into school, and I can't face you. Only with my death can I truly apologise to you . . ." When the son of Sun Shoujun, a Liaoning peasant, received his school placement letter, his father had no money to send him. So he left a suicide note to him and killed himself. (Reported by Xinhuanet)

People say: Don't say stuff like if you don't go to university, you can still make a good life for yourself. Even comedian Stephen Chow's screen characters know everyone's desire to go to school gives you a way of deceiving people.

10. *I could have put up with it for three more days.*
Guan Chuanzhi is a miner. He was trapped in a mine shaft during a mining accident, where he survived for seven terrible days. The first thing he said when his rescuers brought him out into daylight was: "I could have put up with it for three more days." (Reported by *Nanjing Morning News*)

People ask: Brother miners, good brothers, how long will you have to put up with this?

Will Chinese law become the sticking point in China's progress to a democratic future? I know a lot of Chinese people are asking, and waiting, but we need many more Chinese people who will work hard for the law, like old Mr Jingguan.

On 30 December 2006, I had just edited the second draft of *China Witness* to this point, when I got a phone call from the BBC World Service *World Today* programme, asking me to join a discussion on some news from the Xinhua News Agency in China:

On 1 January 2007, the Supreme People's Court is to implement a policy requiring ratification by the Supreme People's Court of all death sentences handed down by lower courts. This is a historically significant step in the development of Chinese criminal law, not only for China's criminal justice work, but also for the progress and development of the Chinese legal system.

With regard to criminal cases, China operates a system of the Court of Second Instance being the Court of Last Instance. Judicial review of death sentences falls outside the First and Second Instance system, and there are special procedures set up which are targeted at death penalty cases. After New China was established, the policy of retaining and strictly controlling the death sentence was implemented and the ratification system for death sentences was set up. In 1954, regulations on the organisation of the People's Courts were issued and these decreed that death penalty cases must be ratified by the Supreme People's Court and the Higher People's Courts. In a decision made at the fourth session of the First People's Congress in 1957, all death-penalty cases were thenceforth to be decided or ratified by the Supreme People's Court. Between 1957 and 1966, all death penalties were ratified by the Supreme People's Court.

During the Cultural Revolution, the People's Courts came under heavy attack, and the system of ratifying death sentences ceased to operate except in name. In July 1979, the second session of the Fifth National People's Congress passed the Chinese Criminal Code and Criminal Procedure Law, revising the organisation of the People's Courts. It was decreed that all death sentences other than those passed by the Supreme People's Court, must be approved by the latter. However, in February 1980, not long after the Chinese Criminal Code and Criminal Procedure Law had been passed, another decision was passed by the Standing Committee of the National People's Congress, with the aim of meting out swift and severe punishment to criminal elements who had seriously jeopardised the social order: the Supreme People's Court thereby authorised Higher People's Courts to handle some death-sentence cases for a limited period. Following further reforms of the organisation of the People's Courts, and repeated delegation of authority, this system has persisted up to the present day.

My first reaction was to telephone Mr Jingguan. I hoped I would hear him say: Finally the Supreme Court has reclaimed the right to confirm the death sentence, and removed it from the hands of muddled and incompetent judges who indiscriminately execute the innocent! But when I called him, just before the Spring Festival in 2007, to send him and his family season's greetings, and we talked about the new legislation, the old policeman said: "These are just words on paper, miles away from the heads of the people who deal with the cases. It's only when everyone is capable of understanding the significance of those words that people will understand the law, and the law enforcers will no longer dare persist in their reckless ignorance. How many people has China tortured? How many 'Clear Sky Baos' are there?"

From the first Qin emperor of China, and the first law to operate on the principle that "the nine clans bore responsibility for the misdemeanours of their members", to a China, two thousand years later, which has just emerged from political adversity, the ghostly wails of the countless wrongly accused, victims of corrupt local officials who use their power to trifle with human lives, echo down the centuries. In two thousand years of Chinese history, for all our boasting about our ancient political and judicial system, there has only been one great judge, the Song dynasty's Justice "Clear Sky Bao", known to every Chinese for his uncompromising honesty. Just one.

II

The Shoe-Mender Mother:
28 Years Spent out in All Weathers

The shoe-mender woman, Mrs Xie, was at first
shy of our camera . . .

. . . but later invited us home for lunch.

Mrs Xie, a shoe-mender, *interviewed in Zhengzhou, capital of Henan province in central China, near the Yellow River. She has worked on the same street for twenty-eight years in all weathers, repairing the shoes of passers-by. At the end of the day she returns with her husband, a bicycle repairman, to the same place they have lived since she came to the city from the Hubei countryside almost thirty years ago: underneath some factory stairs. Yet, with their hard-earned savings they have sent both their children to two of China's best universities. Their son is starting his PhD and their daughter is studying for an MA.*

The way I saw it in 2006, there are five kinds of roads in China.

The first kind is what are called the national roads – fast highways planned and built at the national level and maintained by local government. I could clearly "feel" the difference between those built after 2000 and those built before; on the newer ones, you didn't get the stomach-churning effects of their appallingly fissured and bumpy surfaces. Nor did you need to hire a local guide to alert you to traffic hazards along the road, although not even the newest map could steer you accurately through the ever-changing road system. The toilets on the national highways are "national-grade toilets" and are, most of them, much better than the houses the local peasants live in. No wonder a lot of drivers say that these highways are not only good for driving on – you get "national-grade" treatment while you're at it.

The second kind are city trunk roads built by the municipal government and generally very wide: six to ten lanes in big cities, two to four in smaller ones. The roadsides reflect a government image and vary little in their "local touches". They are uniformly lined with tower blocks and smaller buildings, flowers or sculptures. The wealthier municipalities have real flowers, the ones that have no money use plastic ones. In most cases, there are pavement studs for blind pedestrians. The traffic lights show a standing person on red, and a scuttling one on green. The most enjoyable thing about them for ordinary Chinese who can't afford cars is the wide green verges, squares and benches on which you can sit and chat and get a breath of fresh air. They are unlike the city roads of ten years ago. Then, scooters, mopeds, bicycles and pedestrians were all jumbled together. The narrow pavements were too packed to move during peak times, and all you could hear were car horns tooting in competition with each other, the endless cursing of drivers as they jockeyed for position, and the shouted admonishments of the traffic cops.

The third kind are streets in working-class districts. There are more bicycles than people and cars, the streets are narrow, and there is only a single lane for scooters, into which vehicles going in both directions are squeezed by traffic jams on the main carriageway. The sides of the roads are crammed with daily necessities and everyday life, businesses and things. There you can see people who yesterday ran stalls, and today have opened shops. The space where goods are piled high during the day is converted at night into the place where the family eats and sleeps. These city streets are more or less equivalent to the high streets of a small country town, although with fewer agricultural items and cheap plastic goods.

The fourth kind are the back streets and alleys which link the homes of the teeming populace. These are chiefly inhabited by small traders and craftspeople who have come in from the villages to "make their fortune" in the big city, and make a start by setting up stalls and kiosks. There are a few cars who don't believe that the streets are impassable to traffic until, half an hour later, they have proudly made it fifty metres through the people and goods only to discover that their triumphant vehicles are a mass of scrapes and scratches and bespattered in grime. These back streets are one big "breakfast bar" in the morning, a street market by day and a kind of leisure market in the evening, providing profits all day. The beneficiaries of all this activity are the residents' committees. In order to ensure that "no manure should escape onto someone else's land", the levels of administration are the most regulated in China; there are toilet attendants, security guards, overseers of regulations, administrators of local commerce, guardians of public order and of household registration. Then there are the "bound-feet vigilante aunties" with their "keep order" armbands, who focus on things that "don't look nice". These range from serious matters, such as accusations that city folk are treating peasant labourers unfairly, and the rights and wrongs of a fight between husband and wife, to the more trivial – a man with inappropriately long hair, or a woman with an indecently short skirt. City folk say that the red-armbanded aunties look after stuff that the government and people's families ignore. No matter what rank the administrators are, so long as they have a sleeve badge, wear a uniform and can show their certificate, they are all "supported" by the local stallholders who keep the local government or street committee going. Those who scrape along at the bottom of society are fleeced on a daily basis by one or other of these numerous administrative charges. But they still feel that they are living better than in the countryside. I sometimes think that their past lives must have been unimaginably hard.

The fifth kind are the dirt roads of the countryside, and the "construction roads" of the cities. Twenty years of frenzied urban construction in China have given rise to many original ideas in the heads of those whose inspiration has been stifled for a century: why not install a "zipper" in the ground so that you don't have to dig down to make repairs? Why not set up a crane so that new-builds which have been "programmed out" can be lifted out of the ground and shifted to the countryside for the peasants to live in? Why not get an advance picture of what's in the minds of people who are going to be important officials in ten years, so that today's policymakers don't have to start all over again? So many ideas! And most of those who thought them up have trodden these "construction roads", quite a few of which are made from metal grids. These are fine in dry weather – apart from being wobbly – but when it drizzles, they turn very greasy underfoot, just the thing to send you flying head over heels! The worst sort are made of a dozen or so planks of scrap wood, and before you walk on them you have to check there's no one at the other end. There is? In that case, make sure you know who's the heaviest, or you may be "see-sawed" into the mud on either side. And then there are roads made of bricks and stones, forcing you to "skip". Some of them simply take you over building rubble.

While our group was on the road doing interviews, we became thoroughly familiar with the five kinds of roads of modern China. Not only that, but these roads somehow came to embody in a very real way the *China Witness* experience. Once off the plane, we would be on a state highway, the sort used by upper-class Chinese in their daily lives. When we interviewed famous people, we would take the city trunk roads to go and call on them – famous Chinese people invariably move into the cities, and always have done. Town streets were what we used most – breakfast, night markets, nosing around and making purchases, all were successfully accomplished there – and we had experience of construction roads in Gansu and Anhui. Finally, the back alleys "developed" by migrant workers gave us a story to add to our interview plan.

On 10 September, we took a taxi to a chaotic and jam-packed back street in the Zhongyang area of Zhengzhou city, to interview an intriguing woman who had turned her back on her village to come to this back street and make her living as a shoe-mender. By dint of twenty-eight years spent repairing shoes in all kinds of weather, Mrs Xie had managed to put her son and her daughter through the best universities in China.

As we drove, the female taxi driver said to us: "I can hear you speaking a foreign language. Which kind of English are you speaking? Which English-speaking country are you from? What have you come to do in this dirty old street?"

We wanted to make sure she was not one of those Chinese taxi drivers whose "alertness and vigilance" might lead to trouble from the local police, so we earnestly told her about educational charity work we were involved with. She was so moved by our description that she refused to charge us. We wrangled for some time before we could get her to accept the fare.

We went into the side street, past a store selling cigarettes and other sundries, a stall selling home-cooked flatbreads from a cooker, two carts with general household items, a fruit stall, and a cart selling cold dishes from a glass box mounted on it, before arriving at the shoe-mender's stall. This consisted of a crudely made cart topped with an old oil-paper umbrella. On the cart lay a collection of insoles, and an assortment of creams and folk remedies for foot problems, together with bits and pieces for repairing shoes, such as soles, heels, heel tips and so on. Her stock, while not large, was neatly arranged. A few customers waited by her stall, apparently queuing to have their shoes repaired. A man in his early forties sat opposite, and there was a middle-aged woman, and a girl in her teens.

Mrs Xie did not look much more than fifty. Her dry, wispy hair was tied into a ponytail and she wore a Western-style, mixed-fibre purple top over a pair of very cheap denims. On her feet were a pair of ill-fitting leather shoes – which I guessed were someone's cast-offs – and her arms were covered by a pair of flower-patterned oversleeves. Nothing she wore appeared to match, city-style, but she was clean and neat.

The friend who had set up the meeting for me went over to greet her: "Big sister," – country folk respectfully call women in the towns, big sister, and men, big brother, sometimes even when they are younger than them – "I often come and get you to mend my shoes. But you have so many customers, do you remember me?"

✳

MRS XIE: Of course I remember you. You never try and bargain my prices down. Your husband is in the army. You're a good person.

FRIEND: This is my friend Xinran, whom I've known for nearly thirty years.

XINRAN: Hello. I'm delighted to meet you.

MRS XIE: Hello. I've got a job in hand. Why don't you sit down?

XINRAN: Can you mend my shoes? They've come unglued inside at the bottom.

MRS XIE: I'll have a look. [Gives a quick glance.] Yes, I can, it's very simple. Wait till I've finished this pair, and I'll do them for you.

*

But the middle-aged woman customer sitting on a stool objected that she had been there first. And I quickly agreed.

*

MRS XIE [to the woman customer]: Don't worry, her shoes just need gluing. They'll only take a second to stick. Yours need new heel tips. She'll have to wait half an hour or more, and everyone's busy . . .

XINRAN: No, really, I'm happy to wait my turn. It gives me a chance to learn your craft and chat to you. My friend told me that you've scrimped and saved your shoe-mending money to send your children to university. You're amazing!

MRS XIE: Aren't all Chinese mothers like that?

XINRAN: When I came here looking for a shoe-mender, everyone said you were the best. They all sing your praises.

MRS XIE: They look after me. They look after poor people like us.

XINRAN: When did you start mending shoes here?

MRS XIE: In 1978.

XINRAN: Nearly thirty years! Where do you come from? Did you come alone or with your family?

MRS XIE: From Hubei. I came with my husband.

XINRAN: And your children?

MRS XIE: It was only my son then. He was just born. We left him at home, for the grandparents to bring up. We left to earn money.

XINRAN: Why did you leave?

MRS XIE: We were so hard up there. The land was truly poor and barren.

XINRAN: You have one son and one daughter?

MRS XIE: Yes.

XINRAN: Where are they at university?

MRS XIE: My son works, my daughter is at university.

XINRAN: Where does your son work?

MRS XIE [maternal pride in her voice]: He's doing his doctorate at Xi'an

Communications University [one of the top science and engineering universities], and he has some teaching work there.

XINRAN: And your girl?

MRS XIE: She's doing a master's at Beijing University.

XINRAN: Do they come and see you?

MRS XIE: Of course! My daughter comes more often than my son. She's good at getting jobs to pay for her fare. My son has a girlfriend, so he's busy with her family too!

XINRAN: Why did you decide to come to Zhengzhou to earn money?

MRS XIE: In 1978, you weren't allowed to leave your home, and if you just left, you would be arrested. It's not like now, when you can go wherever you want. But where we were was poor and there was no education, so when my son was born, we discussed it and decided we definitely wanted to leave so that my son could go to school.

XINRAN: Was there no school in your village?

MRS XIE: There was, but it was a disgusting place! A primary school needs a schoolhouse and a teacher, but this one had neither. A relative of the village accountant just took it on for a bit of money. For middle school you had to go to the county town. Hang on a minute and I'll tell you a story about the county middle school!

MRS XIE [to the middle-aged man]: These shoes are ready. Thank you.

MIDDLE-AGED MAN: We agreed on the price, four yuan, isn't it? Here, four yuan.

MRS XIE: Thank you for giving me your business. [The middle-aged man does not respond and leaves. She turns to the middle-aged woman.] Your shoes?

MIDDLE-AGED WOMAN: Last time you put a new heel on. I've worn them six months, and the heel tip has worn through again. Can you put a better one on this time?

MRS XIE: What I used last time was the best. You walk on the outside of your foot, so you wear away the outside of your heel. You've had those shoes at least two years now, and the leather has stretched and the shoes have lost their shape. Now when you walk, your foot moves in the shoe and wears it down even faster. I can put in an insole so the shoe and your foot fit better, and that should improve it.

MIDDLE-AGED WOMAN: How much will the insole cost?

MRS XIE: One yuan each.

MIDDLE-AGED WOMAN: So expensive! Other people charge one yuan the pair!

MRS XIE: That's the price. Go and ask someone else if you don't believe me. I pay eighty fen per insole, so if I let you have one for fifty fen, I lose thirty fen on each insole, and I'm not doing that! Otherwise I can just reheel them for you, and you go to a cheaper place for an insole.

MIDDLE-AGED WOMAN: OK, just reheel them for me.

*

I watched as Mrs Xie rifled through heel tips of all sorts in an old shoebox and found a couple of metal ones which matched the old pair in size and colour. She rubbed them clean with a cloth, and put them on a wooden box beside her. Then she dexterously pulled off the heel tip with the hammer claw and carefully filed the bottom of the worn-down heel until it was quite flat. Finally she used her apron to give the surface a good rub and get rid of the flecks.

Then she applied a layer of viscous rubber solution and put the shoe down on the tip. She repeated this procedure with the other shoe, and when she had completed the repair work on both shoes, she reinforced the heels with a kind of square-headed shoe tack.

She was eager to tell me the story of the county middle school as she worked on the shoes.

*

MRS XIE: Wasn't I going to tell you about the county middle school?

XINRAN: Yes, if it doesn't interfere with your shoe repairs, please tell me.

MRS XIE: Not at all. When I talk about it, it gives me more energy and more *qi*. Did you know that the more *qi* you have, the more energetic you are?

XINRAN: OK, tell me then!

MRS XIE: When I was at the county middle school, I was an excellent student. I came top in the county results. But when it came to university, they wouldn't let me apply. In those days, the middle school put your name forward, and they said I had a bad class background, that I was from a rich peasant family and so I couldn't go to university.

That was a muddle my mother had made in 1951 – it was nothing to do with me. Just after Liberation, when property was registered and people were put into class categories, the recorder didn't do the figures properly and they came out wrong. My mother had just got married. She was illiterate, and also didn't hear what was said. It was only when the class categories were announced that she found out that the family had been put into the "rich peasant" category. How could that be? If we'd been rich peasants, why would my father have gone to make revolution? He'd have been making revolution against himself!

My father worked in the county government offices, and the cadres told him the mistake had been corrected, but they were bad guys and they deceived him. During the Cultural Revolution, someone made it known that my father had misrepresented his rich peasant background, and said they'd found the original testimony. The original cadres hadn't written an explanation of the mistake on his documents, they'd just put a line through his name and left it at that! So my father, after working for the revolution for twenty-something years, was turned into a "counter-revolutionary covertly working within the ranks of the revolutionaries". Just like that, it was over for my family, and I couldn't go to university. I was furious! Ever since I knew about it, I had been absolutely desperate to go to university. I liked literature, I liked history, I loved anything in books; I was the best in the county but they wouldn't let me go to university. When I sit here every day mending shoes, I think about that, and it still makes me angry!

You couldn't go to university somewhere else and get on in life, like you can nowadays. You couldn't do that then. Once my father had "become" a counter-revolutionary, the family had no means of earning a living, and very soon we were packed off back to the village to work on the land. All my studying had been a waste, hadn't it? I wouldn't ever be able to go to university, would I? I wasn't reconciled to this, I really wasn't! Every evening as I watched the sky grow dark, I would think to myself, I should just wait, the sky will get light again. Even if I can't go to university, my children will definitely be able to go, and to the best ones!

XINRAN: And the sky did grow light. Your son went to the best university, your wish came true.

MRS XIE: Well, it didn't all come true. Xi'an Communications University isn't as good as Qinghua or Beijing University, and Qinghua and Beijing University aren't as good as Oxford and Cambridge. If it were me, I would definitely want to go to the best university, to show those people who wouldn't let me go. I've told my daughter, when she's finished her master's, she should go on studying. Mum'll support you, I said. We don't want the government's money. People say we're poor, but that poverty's given us ambition, and out of poverty has come university learning. That'll show those people who look down on us! Neither of our children applied for a grant. I told them: "You're not allowed to borrow money or ask the government for money. If you've got talent, you'll fight your own battles! Don't compare how you eat and dress to other people. Don't worry that people will laugh at you if you look less smart or work harder than they do. The only thing you should compare is how educated you are!" I sit here repairing shoes and lots of people look down on me, but I think to myself: Have you sent your son to do his PhD? I'm not talented, but my children are talented. And I've earned every penny of their fees and their living expenses!

*

Once more I was left speechless, struck dumb by the indomitable spirit of the mothers of China, by their soaring aspirations. As a race, we really are like the wild grasses in the poem by Bai Juyi: "Wild fires cannot consume them, they grow again in the spring breeze." In fact, I was not the only one to be quite overwhelmed by the shoe-mender woman's straight-talking. I could sense a silent surge of feeling from everyone around her, and I believe it was because of our mothers that we felt that way.

I realised that the middle-aged woman had been listening as she quietly chose two pairs of appropriate insoles from the pile on Mrs Xie's cart. She put down five yuan and was about to leave with her reheeled shoes when the shoe-mender stopped her: "I told you, the insoles are one yuan each, two yuan the pair, you've given me too much!" "Take it, buy your daughter a pen," said the customer. "No, no, I can't take it," said Mrs Xie. "You're helping them just by bringing me your shoes to mend. I can't charge anything else!"

Back and forth went the argument, just as I had so often seen women in Chinese restaurants fighting for the right to pay the bill. The shoe-mender woman won, and only accepted four yuan. The customer left, and I saw that she really was bandy-legged. I turned to the girl and said: "It's your turn." She was embarrassed and told me to go first, she wasn't in any hurry.

*

MRS XIE: Let the girl sit here a bit longer, and I'll glue your shoes. She comes with a pair of shoes every weekend. She says it gives her something to do.

XINRAN: Is this true?

GIRL: Yup. My mum and dad are divorced and neither wanted me, so I'm with my grandparents. They only have two rooms, and they use my room to play mah-jong every day, so it gets very smoky. When I'm out at school it doesn't bother me, but at weekends there's nowhere to go, so I come here and watch people.

XINRAN: Watch people?

GIRL: That's right, watch people. This lane may be cramped and higgledy-piggledy, but you can see all sorts of people here, even big cadres. There's one big noise whose mum and dad live in that building, and sometimes he comes in with his arms full of packages to see them. He can't drive in, so he stops the car at the entrance, making all the passers-by swear.

XINRAN: But how do you know he's an important cadre?

GIRL: It may seem a mess here, but we have public security patrols every day. They say it's so that "the regulations are obeyed". If anyone else's car blocked the entrance, the PSB would put a stop to it. I've heard people say that the numbers on his car number plate are low ones, and the lower the number the higher the cadre's rank.

XINRAN: And what other kinds of people do you see?

GIRL: Just ask her. She can tell who's walking past her without even looking up. We often play "guessing people" games. She tells me what kind of a person someone might be and why. I point out to her anyone I see from far, far away, and how they walk and hold themselves. Some of them are my neighbours. She gets lots of them right. It's fun!

MRS XIE: It's just a bit of nonsense, like a dog scrabbling away at a hole, as we say. It's just a game I play with the girl to keep her entertained!

XINRAN: OK, tell me. Entertain me. Too bad that just now there's no one coming.

MRS XIE: If you think about it, I've sat here for twenty-eight years mending shoes, and that's twenty-eight years' worth of lessons, learning to watch people. Shoe size depends on the person's height, everyone knows that. OK, that's a generalisation. There are some tall people with small feet, but not many short people with big feet. Big wide shoes usually belong to someone who's done a lifetime of manual labour which has splayed their toes. He may have come up in the world, but you can tell he has lots of poor relatives. If someone has wide shoes, you should look at their trouser legs too. If their trousers hang above their ankles, they're usually old – I reckon it's because their old bellies stick out. If the trouser bottoms drag on the ground, they're either kids or nouveau riche who haven't learned how to wear their trousers properly. When it's a small foot with narrow shoes, the person's family have been city folk for generations, and their toes haven't been splayed through hard work. If they have a good life, then they have a slow gait. If they're poor, then they stride along. If they tread on someone's foot and can step back and give way, then they're educated, good people. Then there are people who don't know how to give way, people who wear designer shoes, fakes too. But human beings are not made by the clothes they wear. If they have no feelings and no talent, they're useless!

The man whose shoe I just mended only knows about what he wears, and doesn't know about people.

XINRAN: Why?

MRS XIE: His shoe was a designer fake, a particularly cheap one. If you've got learning, you can tell by looking that real and fake labels are not the same. He can't, so he falls right into the trap. Besides, does smiling at a woman make you lose face? He's been coming to have his shoes mended for a few years now, and he's never said more than a word or two to me. He wants you to understand that he's a city gent, higher up the social scale than you, and a man. But he hasn't managed to have a son. If a man wants a son, he needs to be strong-willed, he needs to be daring, and show his goodness in his face. A man who's only good at being a bully boy can only produce daughters.

XINRAN: And what can you tell from these feet? What kind of learning does this woman have?

MRS XIE: You want the truth?

XINRAN: Of course I want the truth.

MRS XIE: Then I'll tell you. As soon as I caught sight of your feet, I knew you were a poor person from a posh family.

XINRAN: A poor person from a posh family? I don't understand.

MRS XIE: You don't understand what that is? It means your forebears were posh, but you don't have any money. If you were posh now, you wouldn't have bought yourself those cheap shoes. The soles are very thin and the shape's not good. I guarantee you've got corns!

XINRAN: You're amazing! I do have corns on my feet – they've been killing me the last couple of days!

MRS XIE: I've got cream here specially for treating corns. Do you want to have a try? Don't put your feet in water for two days, and they should be better on the third day.

XINRAN: But it's thirty-nine degrees, so hot, and I sweat buckets every day! I can't put my feet in water?

MRS XIE: Well, you're not home yet . . . see how they hurt then . . .

XINRAN: And what can you tell about other women?

MRS XIE: The ones in high heels are most worth looking at. If they jab their heels into the ground as they walk, it's because they don't know how to wear them, or they've put them on for the first time. You don't need to look at them to know that they're sticking out their bums, which is really unattractive! You have to walk slowly in high heels – walking fast looks hideous. The higher the heels they're wearing, the less willing they are to give way to other people – these are shoes that can only go forwards not backwards. The high-heeled slippers that are fashionable nowadays are really funny. The foot often slips out of them, and then the slipper is just looped over the foot, which makes it completely useless. Everyone knows that women have small, delicate feet, but with these high heels now, the toes are very pointed, not for putting your foot in. It makes the whole shoe big, and a small woman striding along with a pair of big feet looks ridiculous! And something else: not a lot of women look after their feet. Sometimes you smell her perfume, what a lovely smell! But she walks past you and her feet are really ugly with yellow calluses at the back of the heels and the feet all wrinkly. If I look up, the face is bound to be plastered in thick make-up. Quite repulsive. I can't bear to see that. Then . . .

*

A man who was cycling past paused with one foot on the ground. "Hey, are you here this afternoon?" he asked. "I'm always here, in all weathers, apart from when I'm eating and sleeping. If my stall's here and I'm not, it's because I'm in the toilet." "I'll come back this afternoon then," said the man, and he cycled off.

*

XINRAN: So, in your twenty-eight years here, what changes have you seen in the shoes you've repaired?

MRS XIE: Twenty-eight years ago, the money came in a few jiao at a time, everyone was poor then. In the early days, I was mending rubber and plastic shoes for a few jiao a time, and putting plastic soles on cloth shoes. There were some leather shoes that people had for a lifetime. Leather shoes then were sturdy, not like shoes now which come in fancy styles – you only wear them a few days and the seams come apart, the glue comes unstuck and the leather gets holes. In the eighties, more people were wearing leather shoes but when they bought new shoes, they'd come and get another sole stuck on so they could wear them for longer. Still, I could only charge a few jiao, less than one yuan, each time. In the nineties, it seemed like everyone was wearing leather shoes, but a lot of it was fake leather – there wasn't much real leather – so that was a real money-earner, I was charging by the yuan. Now we're in the next century, and it seems like there's hardly any repair work for real leather shoes – people wearing real leather shoes don't come – it's almost all fake designer labels. A lot of people who bring me their shoes for repair boast how good and how expensive they were. I don't say anything, but I think, like hell these are genuine! Would a genuine label shoe be so disgustingly badly made? Would the leather be such poor quality? But what's the point of saying anything? People pay to have their shoes mended, I mend them, take the money, and we each go back to our own homes. Why go looking for trouble! *Aiya!* I must go and make lunch, my old man's waiting for me.

XINRAN: You go home at midday?

MRS XIE: Sometimes I do, sometimes I don't.

XINRAN: What do you usually eat at midday?

MRS XIE: I just buy a couple of fried pancakes or dumplings or something. [She laughs.] Nothing fancy.

XINRAN: Can the five of us come and join you for lunch today? Would that be all right? Can we share your meal?

MRS XIE: You can, though I don't have any kind of a home. There's not even anywhere to sit down. Doesn't that put you off?

XINRAN [I could see she didn't believe that we wanted to visit her home]: We really do want to go. I've got an appetite already.

MRS XIE: *Aiya!* Well then, you keep an eye on the stall for me. I'll just pop to the loo.

XINRAN: Fine, we'll be here to make sure you don't lose anything.

*

Mrs Xie trotted off, and seeing how anxious she looked, I said guiltily: "She looks like she was desperate to go." A drinks seller on a nearby stall overheard and laughed: "No one here worries about losing things if they leave their stall, because we all look after each other's stalls. There's no need to let anyone know. She'll have gone to buy food, because she can't give you pancakes and steamed bread when you get to her house!"

When I heard this, I rushed after her, and found she was indeed buying a fried chicken. I was too late – the chicken had already been cut into pieces and couldn't be given back. I knew we couldn't persuade her to let us pay, so all I could do was carry the chicken and go with her to buy vegetables.

When we followed her to her home, we were all struck dumb. We were in a small factory which had gone out of business years before. The ramshackle premises were secured by a big gate beside which stood an empty storeroom and toilet. This space, devoid of all furniture and fittings, was their home. The "bedroom" was in the triangular space under the stairs, partitioned off and just big enough to put a board down. There they slept in winter, spring and autumn. The "kitchen" was a gas cooker in the space beside the toilet. Water for washing, rinsing and drinking all came from the toilet cistern. It was stiflingly hot when she took us inside and, with some embarrassment, she moved their summer bed – a board sitting on some old wooden packing cases – outside so that she could free up a bit of "cool" space.

We sat down to eat our meal with her and her husband, who repaired students' bicycles outside a technical middle school. She made us a Hubei-style dish of meat steamed with ground rice, some fried greens and some fried dried bean curd left over from a previous meal. Then there was the fried chicken she had bought, and rice and steamed bread. Afterwards, we worked out that our meal had cost the couple what the two of them earned in a month from shoe and bicycle repairs. That was the first time I had sat on an old tyre to eat a meal. They had no stools or chairs – in fact they had no furniture at all.

After we had eaten, Mrs Xie burst out crying and said: "In twenty-eight years, no one has come to visit us or eaten a meal with us! City folk look down on us, no one respects us, in fact no one pays us any attention at all! We have nothing. We've used every penny to put our children through university! Every time my daughter comes back on holiday, she squeezes onto the plank with me to sleep, poor thing. In winter, she freezes like us; in summer, she swelters like us. If we give her money to go and stay with her grandparents for the holidays, she won't go. She says, 'My mum and dad live like this day in and day out so that we can go to university, why can't I spend the time with you?' She's very mature. She studies and has a job, and hasn't even got anywhere to go in the holidays, but we just can't do any more for them than we already do!"

Her husband had been standing beside her smiling silently. His eyes, too, reddened and he said: "As soon as our children were born, we had to leave them with our parents to bring up. We've had such a hard grind, so very, very hard. We couldn't afford to send our children to school in the city. They had to go to school in the countryside, but they both did us proud! Just like their mum, they came top in the county results. I'll never forget when my son got his offer for Xi'an Communications University and came to show it to me at my bicycle repair stand outside the school. His clothes were so tatty the students thought he was a beggar. He didn't have the money to take a train, so he'd spent several days and nights on a long-distance bus to get here. When he saw me, he didn't have the strength to be happy any more, he just said: 'Dad, I'm hungry. I've passed the university exams!' And then he collapsed. I called some students over to help, and when they saw the offer letter for Xi'an Communications University in his hand, they were flabbergasted! This is one of the key universities that they dream of getting into! My . . . son . . . is . . . fantastic!"

He was unable to say more.

As I watched them, I thought – and you could not help but think – that this couple who lived worse than refugees had produced for the Chinese people two highly talented youngsters. You could not help but think that their savings, accumulated jiao by jiao, and yuan by yuan, had saved China's educational system two student grants. And you could not help but think that these two country people, despised by everyone, had brought up a son and a daughter who aroused admiration in everyone who saw them!

We all had tears in our eyes. I knew that my crew were feeling very emotional. This couple exemplified just the kind of Chinese self-respect and pride that we had been looking for.

Before saying goodbye, I asked them my final three questions.

*

XINRAN: How did you two meet?

MRS XIE: When I couldn't go to university, I refused to get married. Then we were introduced, and he said to me: "You couldn't go to university, but if you have children, you can send them to university in your place." Intelligent, wasn't he? Among all the men I knew, none of them understood me the way he did. So I married him, and we both earned the money to send our children to university!

XINRAN: What is your next wish?

MRS XIE: To help my children do advanced studies at the best universities of the world, and to help them see the world and further increase their learning!

*

This led us to put through a long-distance call to their son, establishing how we could keep in touch. I hoped I could look into the possibilities of helping this mother realise her dreams, and also help this young man who had fought his way up from the lowest level of society to the pinnacle of Chinese academic circles see a bit of this great and colourful world for his mother.

*

XINRAN: Who's more handsome, your son or your daughter?

MRS XIE: They're both good-looking!

XINRAN: Friends who've seen your daughter all say she's very pretty.

MRS XIE: No, no, not at all. They're both ugly. Poor families don't have good-looking children!

*

Poor families don't have good-looking children! Her words pained me. In China there's a saying: "Laugh at the poor, but don't laugh at prostitutes", meaning that the poor are the lowest level of society, lower even than prostitutes, and are only worthy of ridicule. It's an old saying, which had been officially wiped out by half a century of revolution, but has now been dug up again from the rubbish heap of history. It describes the gulf which separates rich and poor as a result of the flying leaps which China's development has taken.

While I was worrying about this "putting old concepts to new use", I received an email that had been circulating on Chinese blogs from a friend in Beijing. She asked me to pass it on to the overseas Chinese who were with me, and tell them it described the kind of love which was becoming fashionable among Chinese city dwellers.

Ten true things that everyone should keep in mind.

1. On meeting a beggar: When you meet someone begging for money, give him or her a bit of food; when you meet someone begging for food, give them a bit of money.

2. If you meet an elderly or disabled person or a pregnant woman on a bus, don't raise your voice or make a song and dance about giving up your seat

to them. When you stand up, use your body to keep the space and give it to the person who needs it. Then pretend you're getting off and move away. It's a fact that too often people don't move far away. When someone thanks you, give them a smile.

3. In snow and rain, and on cold or snowy evenings, if you meet someone selling vegetables, fruit or newspapers who has just a bit left and still can't go home, buy everything if you can, and if you can't, buy something. Because eating something is still eating and reading something is still reading, and buying it means they can go home sooner.

4. If you meet an elderly man or woman or child lost on the streets, take them home if you can; if you can't, put them onto a bus or take them to the local police station. If you have a phone, then make a call for the old person or child before you go. After all, you won't miss the cost of a couple of calls.

5. If someone who's lost asks you for an address and you happen to know where it is, then go ahead and tell them. Don't back off apologetically; no one's trying to get at you.

6. If you find a purse, have a look for the owner. If you really need the money, then leave the small change behind. Phone the owner and say you found it in a toilet. Return the credit cards, ID card and driving licence to the owner. Most people won't be bothered about losing the money. Jot down the person's address in your notebook, and when you've made your money, go and say sorry and pay the money back.

7. If you come across students doing jobs to pay their school fees – especially if they're middle-school students and if they're young girls – buy a bit of whatever they're selling. If she's not from a poor family, and needed courage to go out and find work, then give her some encouragement.

8. If you see someone sitting on the pavement at night with their goods laid out on a bit of carpet, buy as much as you can and don't haggle. These things aren't expensive, and no one whose home situation is less than terrible would ever go out in the cold to sell stuff like that.

9. If you're pretty well off, don't keep a mistress. Support a few school students from poor mountain areas on the quiet. Don't let them know who you are, otherwise it will be awkward and terribly embarrassing when you meet. But you won't be on tenterhooks all the time like when you're keeping

a mistress – in fact you'll feel quite easy in yourself. If you really want to keep a mistress, then keep one, but at least do something good as well. After all, people are complicated.

10. If you have plenty of time, and you happen to feel that what I have said is right, then post an answer to my message. It's more gratifying than answering completely rubbish messages. Also if you have enough time, post this text on to a few other sites. The more good people there are, the better we will feel.

On the Road,

Interlude 5:

A Squall at the 4 May Memorial

While we were in Beijing on the final stage of our journey, we stayed in the Red Building, next to the former home of Beijing University. The Red Wall Hotel, currently "trying for three-star grading", is next to the Beijing University Museum, and next to that stands a newly erected monument to the 4 May Patriotic Movement.

The 4 May Movement marks the moment at which China embarked on a century of modern history. In 1914, Japan used the pretext of the outbreak of the First World War to declare war on Germany, and occupy Qingdao and the entire length of the Jiaoji Railway. Once in control of Shandong, Japan removed from Germany all the privileges which that country had seized in the province. At the close of the war in 1918, Germany was defeated. In January 1919, the victorious nations opened a peace conference in Paris. China, represented by a joint delegation of the Beijing government and the Guangzhou military government, attended on the side of the victors, and put forward a number of proposals. These included abolition of all of the Great Powers' concessions in China, along with abolition of the "21 Demands" unequal treaty concluded between President Yuan Shikai and the Japanese imperialists, and restitution of all powers removed from Germany in Shandong by Japan before the war. But the Great Powers manipulated the Paris Peace Conference in such a way that not only were the Chinese demands rejected, but the peace treaty with Germany proclaimed that the Shandong concessions were to be turned over in their entirety to Japan. The Beijing government was prepared to sign the treaty but the Chinese people were fiercely opposed.

On the afternoon of 4 May 1919, over three thousand students from Beijing University and twelve other universities and training colleges broke through police and army cordons and gathered in Tiananmen Square to hear speakers. Then they organised demonstrations and shouted slogans such as: "Fight for sovereignty abroad, get rid of national traitors at home", "Abolish the 21 Demands" and "Refuse to sign the peace treaty". They also demanded that the leaders of the pro-Japanese faction – Cao Rulin, Zhang Zongxiang and Lu Zongyu – be punished. The Beijing students went on strike and galvanised the entire country into resistance.

The impact of the patriotic activities of the Beijing students spread rapidly to cities such as Tianjin, Shanghai, Changsha and Guangzhou, and there was support, too, from Chinese students studying abroad and overseas Chinese. Even more students embarked on propaganda activities on 4 June and within two days nearly a thousand students had been arrested. This further aroused popular anger. From 5 June, between sixty and seventy thousand Shanghai workers held a political strike, while workers from cities such as Nanjing, Tianjin, Hangzhou, Jinan, Wuhan, Jiujiang and Wuhu held a succession of strikes and demonstrations. The Beijing government was so shaken by this activity that on 6 June it was forced to release all those students who had been arrested. On 10 June, a proclamation "approved" Cao, Zhang and Lu's "resignations". On 28 June the Chinese delegation refused to sign the peace treaty with Germany. The victorious 4 May Patriotic Movement now came to a temporary halt.

The 4 May Movement is seen as marking the end of the old Chinese democratic revolution and the beginning of the new. After the People's Republic of China was established, the Government Administration Council of the Central People's Government proclaimed in December 1949 that henceforth 4 May would be National Youth Day.

All the elderly people we had interviewed were witnesses to the history of China after the 4 May Movement. For this reason, I felt that before completing *China Witness*, we should record on camera, next to the monument, the feelings about this history evoked for me by these interviews.

However, we were interrupted by two men dressed in light grey uniforms and wearing "security guard" armbands.

*

SECURITY MEN: You're not allowed to film here!

XINRAN: Why?

SECURITY MAN A: Have you got a permit?

XINRAN: What permit? We've come to pay our respects to former generations, and to share the glory of those times ... surely we don't need a permit?

SECURITY MAN B: Why are you using a video camera?

XINRAN: To record our feelings and what we have found out about the 4 May Movement.

SECURITY MEN: It's not allowed. The rules say that the media can only film if they have permits.

XINRAN: Whose rules?

SECURITY MEN: The park administration. You're on our territory, you have to let us run it.

XINRAN: Your Huangchenggen Park, is it one of the municipal parks open to the public? Does it come under the Beijing Municipal Administration? Is it public property protected by the law of the People's Republic of China? If it is, then why can't Chinese citizens find out about one of our own historical monuments? And can't foreigners film a monument on a main street commemorating Chinese history?

SECURITY MAN A: We're not going to go into all that with you, you've got to show a permit, otherwise we'll call people to come and take you away!

XINRAN: Take us away? Why? Did you know it's breaking the law to arrest innocent people? Who's in charge of you? We'll talk to him, because you don't have the most basic municipal administration rules to back you up. What you're doing is going to be evidence for world opinion that accuses China of having no legal system or human rights. You're damaging our image of democratic freedom. Who's your boss? Get him here, or I'll go and see him!

SECURITY MAN A [pointing to B]: He's phoning the boss now.

XINRAN: Thank you. I think your boss will see I'm right.

SECURITY MAN B: The boss says he's too busy to come.

XINRAN: Then I'll speak to him on the phone. Like you said, if we've contravened your administrative regulations, then that's his job and he has to take care of it. Kindly ring him again and tell him I have an important matter to discuss with him.

*

I sounded so intransigent that Security Man B wasted no time in dialling again: "That woman insists on speaking to you!" he said.

But he did not pass the phone to me – he gave it to A who listened, and listened, and listened. All at once, he went pale. When the call ended, I could see they did not know what to do. Obviously their boss knew something about "media connections" and their fearsomeness, and wanted nothing to do with us. The poor administrators standing before us only knew that their boss was "he who must be obeyed", and they had no way of relinquishing their responsibilities.

At that moment I remembered the saying that "'face' is the lifeline of the Chinese poor". I did not want to make life too difficult for two almost uneducated young people, so I changed my tone:

*

XINRAN: Soon 2008 will be here, and this park is one of the sights of Beijing. There will be more people than ever from China and abroad who want to come and see this monument to modern Chinese history, and nowadays most travellers bring video cameras. If we keep stopping them, then it will make us look ridiculous. Go back and tell your boss to bring your administrative statutes into line with Chinese law. Otherwise the people breaking the law will be you. Your boss can't send you out into the street and wash his hands of you. He has to help you clarify some basic international rights and laws, otherwise you may become the criminals in the development of Chinese civilisation. I'm not joking. If I'd been an overseas Chinese with a foreign passport and didn't understand your sense of responsibility and patriotism, this incident today might have become a huge joke, and made us a laughing stock for foreigners. Fancy needing a news permit to video a historical monument in a Chinese street. You would become proof that there is no freedom of speech in China! [Brief pause.] What exactly are your powers and responsibilities?

SECURITY MEN [in unison]: We don't know.

XINRAN: So what regulations do you follow to enforce public security?

SECURITY MAN A: We've got documents, but I can't quote them to you.

SECURITY MAN B: They're all very old, we haven't got the new ones yet. We can't tell you, but our boss knows.

*

This was a typically Chinese answer: we don't know, our bosses know.

Do these leaders know? If they do but don't get things clear for those under them, are they real leaders? I recalled a friend quoting an old saying and complaining about people who "out of their own ignorance, clarify things for other people". That's terrible, but bamboozling other people when one understands things clearly is even more terrible.

At this point I want to quote the definition of a Chinese person taken from a British encyclopedia of 1842 . . .

A Chinaman is cold, cunning and distrustful; always ready to take advantage of those he has to deal with; extremely covetous and deceitful; quarrelsome, vindictive, but timid and dastardly. A Chinaman in office is a strange compound of insolence and meanness. All ranks and conditions have a total disregard for truth.

How much has this image of "the Chinaman" changed in the last 150 years? I don't know – I can't even tell in my own lifetime.

"I don't know" or "I've no idea" appears to be the usual response to the almost completely opposed life values expressed by our interviewees in explaining who they are, and by the sons and daughters trying to understand them. In fact, almost every Chinese person has been through the "I don't knows" and "I've no ideas" of the last hundred years. Even surviving archives of the great events of Chinese history and Chinese yearbooks differ in the way they present that history. One hundred years filled with too many wars with all the chaos and strife they bring in their wake, together with the failure of our national saviours, dramatic changes in our beliefs and confusion in moral standards, have led to a kind of "inflation and metamorphosis" both in the way Chinese people describe reality to themselves, and in the architecture of Chinese cities. In the search for their roots and for their self-respect as a nation, Chinese people have lost their way. The result is a historical map which lacks an agreed system of explanatory symbols and is forever being reprinted.

Afterword

Images of My Motherland

It was hard for me to put down my pen and "finish" this book. As I wrote, I kept asking myself: Are my experiences and even what I write also part of those "things you can't say for sure"? The reality is just that: in all my interviewing, editing and tidying, I could not bridge the gap between the historical facts of that time and the gloss put on it by the people who came after them; I could not find any universally recognised standards of right and wrong in the last few generations of China's history; I could not figure out how to experience or express the delights and excitements of their childhood, the aspirations and pleasures of their adulthood and the joys of their old age. I had even wondered whether they had had any opportunities to experience "delights". The facts proved me wrong: our parents and grandparents had not only experienced "delights" that we can understand, they had the will and the ability to search for, be moved by and comprehend delight in the midst of dire poverty and things that "cannot be said for sure".

I am in the process of searching for my heart's true motherland, among all the "can't say for sures" of several generations of Chinese.

After I returned from my travels, I found myself unable to escape the stories in the books; unable to escape the voices of those interviewees; unable to escape my country as it revealed itself to me in the cracks between the layers of history . . . I spent six months laboriously selecting, rejecting and editing 800,000 characters' worth of research, interviews and recordings into 300,000 Chinese characters. Every day I found myself in a state of emotional turmoil; it was often very hard to find textual proofs in historical sources to explain what the interviewees had experienced, for theirs was a time of history which even now has not been completed, a time which nobody can explain, much less fully document.

When after those six months I returned to my friends and appeared in public once more, many of my acquaintances were startled: "Xinran, what's happened to you? Where did all those white hairs come from?" I replied: "I got all those white hairs from months skulking at home!" But I knew that they were the sprouts of "bitter thoughts and remembrances" in my heart. The cares weighing on the hearts of the old people I had interviewed had led me to ponder deeply on the last century of China's history, and had drawn me into the arduous journey towards understanding modern China.

On this journey I met over a hundred Chinese university students who lent me their support, acting as my assistants, doing research, word processing, selecting and editing extracts. They began to develop an interest just like mine, an intense curiosity about the nature of the cultural system and historic earth our modern-day life is rooted in. Why have we not paid proper attention to the history that is right next to us, which is disappearing as our lives and even our streets are transformed in front of our eyes? The stories of our grandfathers and grandmothers are doors that will close and be destroyed one day soon: how many of them have been passed on to their children and grandchildren?

In fact, the reactions of the university students were more powerful than those of my own – their parents' – generation. First, there was the gulf of language between them. The old people's variety of different accents caused considerable embarrassment for some of the university students who came from the same part of the world – "You're from the same place, and you can't understand what that person was saying?" The scenes and objects that appeared in these narratives, things that had disappeared never to return, made life very hard for these bright students from the best universities: "I don't know how to write this word, or what that thing's for . . ."

Then there was the confusion surrounding common historical knowledge. The great joys and sorrows of the old people who had been forced together into their shared historical experiences astonished and shocked those university students, whose own historical education had been delivered in disconnected fragments, misinterpreted or overlooked: "How come we didn't know about these things?" Some of them could not even spell the names of the famous men who had ruled China and been the driving force behind major historical events . . . The old people's aspirations and sacrifice, their pure hearts and lack of personal ambition, caused the university students to ask suspiciously again and again: "How could they have invested so much faith in a political party which had no economic knowledge and no understanding of human nature?"

Another typical response from the university students was an examination of their own consciences. As one of them said: "Our own parents and grandparents have survived this time; do they have stories like these as well? Why haven't they told them to us? Once I know their stories, how will I judge their past? Will I still be proud of my widely read grandfather and my kindly, skilled grandmother?"

It is my belief that pain and questions are an overture to social progress.

In April 2007 I returned to China, for further confirmation of my experiences of a nation that was "changing and modernising with every passing day" so that I would have another chance to come to understand the disappearing older generations of Chinese.

After almost four weeks of revisits to Beijing, Shanghai, Nanjing and small villages on the edges of the big cities, and further meetings with people I had interviewed, I was left with even more, even newer "things that I couldn't say for sure". Many different images of those old people's former battles and hopes, images that seemed almost impossible to reconcile with each other, were spinning before my eyes and jostling in my thoughts:

– *A shopping street in a modern metropolis:* men dressed in Western brand-name suits and women in evening gowns were wandering about in couples in the sunlight, shopping or simply taking a stroll. Countless envious eyes were following their progress; most of those eyes were set in faces that still bore the scars of hard labour in the fields, and in bodies carved by the years.

– *A roadside snack stall in a small village:* most of the men were talking business, and the women were all discussing their children's education; but the students were all talking about how to impress people with Korean hairstyles, how to play Japanese computer games, or how to go to the city to find the jobs that made big money.

– *Vendors crying their wares in a tourist spot:* a string of three small monkeys and a Buddha statue decorated with little flashing lights, which the vendor calls "the quest of today's Chinese". Those three monkeys were said to be a folk understanding of Jiang Zemin's "Three Represents" policy. The "Three Represents" is usually summarised as: The Communist Party of China represents the requirements of China's advanced productive forces, the progressive course of China's advanced culture and the fundamental interests of the overwhelming majority of the Chinese masses. One of the three monkeys on the string was covering its eyes with both hands – don't see; one was covering its ears with both hands – don't hear; one was covering its mouth – don't speak. The seller explained to the tourists that this was the "wise" way for Chinese people to deal with Party leaders: look without seeing; turn a deaf ear; watch but don't say anything. But wisest of all was to be like the Buddha seated in the petals of a lotus – purge your mind of desire and ambition.

– *A little bookshop in a small town:* bursting with "big bargain" books, "stock-clearance crazy prices" CDs and "guaranteed genuine promotional offer" DVDs. They had everything you could ever want, ancient and modern, Chinese and foreign, so cheap that only a fool would not buy them, even more elegantly printed and bound than those in the big state-run Xinhua bookshop. On impulse I bought over thirty volumes, hoping to catch up on my "modern Chinese current affairs literature". One of the books was called *China's Twentieth-Century Disasters*, which recorded fifteen floods along China's five major waterways, five major famines in the densely populated eastern region, four major earthquakes along the eastern seaboard and many droughts and fires, all between 1910 and 1998. Were they acts of God, or were they man-made, political disasters? The book gave no comment or analysis, merely stating that in each case over 10,000 lives had been lost. I sighed inwardly: this nation had suffered so much from faction-fighting and warlords, and the common people had had to endure so many viciously cruel natural disasters as well. However, this is a nation that "wild fires cannot consume, they grow again in the spring breeze": 1.3 billion people had survived all the disasters and hardships of the century!

– *Magazines:* of all the publications in China, these are by far the fastest growing area. The major newspapers are still half official political articles, half advertising; the smaller local papers seem to have more of an "eye for the money", and have more advertisements than anything else, with the rest made up of sensational or novelty stories, and just a sprinkling of major national current affairs stories and Party news. It is very hard to understand some of the things these advertisements are offering, often in a rather peremptory manner, such as "international luxury leisure home living is the first choice for Chinese people", "if you're looking for somewhere to live, live like a tycoon", "life without a luxury house or big-brand car is not really living", and so on . . . In a mere twenty years of reform, can 1.3 billion Chinese people walk into an "international luxury life" with a single step? And does this mean that all those peasants who earn less than a hundred yuan a year are "not really living"? Is the journey from extreme socialism to extreme capitalism our only possible route to "a strong nation and a wealthy people"?

– *On Chinese television:* the country has dozens of television channels, and on all of them peak time is dominated by beauty contests, talent competitions, historical costume dramas, lectures on history by big-name historians and other such programmes. News programmes remain dominated by interminable seas of meetings and still noticeably lack current affairs analysis. This is clearly a very sensitive area: in China, the further away something is in space and time, the safer it is for the media. Sometimes it seems that every Chinese is a nutrition expert or a gourmet: these are safe topics that have neither been made risky by government or dynastic changes, nor dragged into conflicts of personalities. Radio seems a little braver than television: once-forbidden areas such as sex, an independent legal system, freedom of the press, religion and so on, all "briefly and evasively" show their faces in public; some have even become the "trademark themes" of smaller local stations. But limited international knowledge leads many presenters to express highly ludicrous attitudes, such as "only the ultimate world-quality Starbucks coffee can give the experience of true white-collar pride", "all stars of international fashionable society crave a beautiful white skin", "the USA is the cultural centre of the modern world", "every single day, all the people in the world are watching China's development", and so on and so forth. I once heard an old man phone the presenter of a radio hotline: "Mr Presenter, can you talk about what the *foreigners* admire about *us* now?"

– *The Internet and blogs:* the only places where Chinese people can express themselves fully and without reserve. I have seen Chinese people's search for and defence of their roots, as well as their eagerness to pass on the inheritance of China's culture. The increasing popularity of the Internet has been a true "cultural revolution" in Chinese society, completely remaking the old system that had lasted for millennia, where words could only travel from the top of society to the bottom in a one-way stream: Chinese people can now say whatever is on their minds without fear. To China's Internet users, the Net is not only a platform for speech, it is also a space of safety and liberation: people who suspect the gods, who question the government, who rebel against their parents, who oppose their superiors, even those who grumble about their spouses or have harsh things to say about their friends and family, whose views would once have been viewed as "rebelling against authority", "behaving inappropriately" and "betraying their own family", can let off steam here, with never a soul the wiser, not even the gods themselves. Now every town and tiny village that has electricity also has Internet cafés and bars, so full that it has become a problem, as old and young alike become addicted to the Internet. Rumour has it that a new "hot topic" among many women is how to retrieve husbands and children from the Internet café for food and sleep.

To tell the truth, I am a little nervous about visiting today's Chinese web pages – the lure of these places really is too great! Leaving aside the fascinating anecdotes, the information on cultivating the body and the sex, the dazzling variety of lifestyle advice, and looking only at the exposed secrets of history, the analysis of the great works of the ancients and of international points of conflict . . . as soon as you dive in you can easily lose yourself in all those "nobody can say for sures".

The first example: China's territory. The People's Republic of China has a land area of approximately 9,600,000 square kilometres, which makes it the third largest country in the world after only Russia and Canada (forty-two times the size of the United Kingdom). It is divided into four directly governed cities, twenty-three provinces, five autonomous regions and two Special Administrative Zones, and the capital is Beijing. China's territory spans forty-nine degrees of latitude stretching from latitude 53°30' north to 4° north, a distance of 5,500 kilometres from north to south. At its easternmost point, Chinese territory begins at 135°05' east, with its westernmost point at 73°40' east, a distance of 5,200 kilometres from east to west, spanning sixty degrees of longitude, with a time difference of more than four hours. This is a national "definition", the only thing which is recognised to be the same amid all the various "differences". Different Chinese official websites give different figures for other things: www.china.org.cn states that it borders on fifteen countries by land, and China's sea areas have an area of approximately 4,730,000 square kilometres, with about 5,400 islands and islets distributed throughout. But www.gov.cn maintains that China's sea area is about 4,700,000 square kilometres, containing 7,600 islands, and that China shares a land border with fourteen nations, and has eight neighbours by sea.

The second example: it is said that at the end of 2005 China's population was 1,306,313,812, and that it has 668 cities, of which 13 have a population of 2 million or more, 24 have a population of 1 to 2 million, 48 have half a million to a million, 205 have a population of 200,000–500,000, and 378 less than 200,000. But on 11 November 2005 the head of the Chinese Construction Ministry said that in less than ten years' time the number of China's megacities of over a million people would already have increased from 34 to 49. No matter which figure is correct, they all imply that in eight years China will have more than ten new megacities! Will these fifteen megacities come from an increase in the non-agricultural population? Will they be capable of absorbing the increase in population? Are housing, traffic, schools, social plans in general, medical protection and green spaces being developed at the same speed? Will the original inhabitants and the newcomers be able to get along and live together side by side? My research teams were unable to find any material with figures on the subject, plans for development or anything of that kind.

The third example: on 18 February 2004 at 20:31 GMT, 04:31 Beijing time, China's Xinhua News Agency released the news that Wu Yi, China's Deputy Prime Minister and Minister for Health, met Gao Yaojie, a doctor from China's Henan province. Gao Yaojie is a retired obstetrician who was subjected to many years' official harassment for exposing the truth about the AIDS situation in that province, and was refused permission by the government to travel to the United Nations to receive the Jonathan Mann Award for health and human rights. It is said that when Wu Yi and Gao Yaojie met, all local officials, including the head of the province, were ordered to leave the room, leaving only the two women behind. Wu Yi told Dr Gao to drop all formalities and speak freely, and the meeting lasted for three hours. But even after this highly significant meeting, the government still did not allow Gao Yaojie to collect her prize; it was not until early 2007 that the Chinese government notified the UN that Gao Yaojie was about to begin her journey to receive the award. Why could not even a dialogue with the Deputy Prime Minister get the doctor the support she deserved? And what had eliminated the obstacles set up by the local government after that? Could it be possible that the local government had become an entrenched power in its own right? If not, how could a single-party

Chinese government permit a local government to undermine China's international image in that way? Could it be that Henan's AIDS situation had progressed so far that it frightened the central government? Or had three years' delay had a beneficial effect on the treatment of AIDS in Henan? If so, why had the Chinese media, whose "sole duty is to utter praise", not reported it? As I understand it, by the end of 2006, Henan province had stated that it has 11,844 cases of AIDS, but medical workers and experts say that the number of AIDS carriers in Henan province may have reached 1 million.

The fourth example: in recent years, from both inside China and abroad, the calls for the Chinese Communist Party and the Chinese government to re-evaluate and officially define the Cultural Revolution have been getting louder and louder. Increasingly, the ruling party is starting to face angry recriminations for its unfairness and weak government, and their toleration and willingness to overlook Mao Zedong's crimes. However, in May 2007 I read on a Chinese official website:

24 June 2005: Official Almanac of the People's Republic of China

The "Cultural Revolution", which lasted from May 1966 to October 1976, resulted in the gravest setbacks to the Party, the nation and the people since the founding of the People's Republic. This "Cultural Revolution" was instigated and led by Mao Zedong. The course of the "Cultural Revolution" can be divided into three parts:

- From the start of the Cultural Revolution to the Party's Ninth Plenary Congress in April 1969. The guidelines and policy of the "Ninth Plenary" were erroneous in ideology, policy and organisation.

- From the Central Ninth Plenary to the Tenth Plenary Conference of the Chinese Communist Party in August 1973. The Tenth Plenary continued the Ninth Plenary's "leftist" errors, and made Wang Hongwen Deputy Central Chairman of the Chinese Communist Party. Jiang Qing, Zhang Chunqiao, Yao Wenyuan and Wang Hongwen combined in the Central Politburo to form the "Gang of Four", further increasing the strength of Jiang Qing's counter-revolutionary group.

- The "Tenth Plenary" to October 1976. In early October 1976, the Central Politburo, carrying out the will of the Party and the people, smashed Jiang Qing's revolutionary clique, and put an end to the disaster of the "Cultural Revolution". Hua Guofeng, Ye Jianying, Li Xiannian and others played an important role in this. As to the "Cultural Revolution", the major responsibility is Mao Zedong's. However, at the end of the day, Mao Zedong's errors are the mistakes of a great proletarian revolutionary.

I am baffled: how can the government "repudiate the Cultural Revolution and accept the mistakes of Mao Zedong" as part of the official almanac of national history, and yet not allow the media to embark on a full-scale condemnation of the Cultural Revolution? The government still refuses to delete or make cuts in the description of relevant records in school textbooks, and forbids the publishing of literary works on related topics. Does the constitution of a "democratic republic" allow this garbled, out-of-context history, and this emperor-like avoidance of history? Perhaps the government's silence is for the sake of those peasants who still believe that Mao Zedong is "the red sun"? Throughout the history of imperial China, many changes of dynasty began with peasant rebellions.

On 15 May 2007, just before I left China, I tried, as I had many times before, to open the Chinese web page of the BBC news, but once again I failed. I hope the day will come soon when I can read the news in my homeland: that will be a sign of China's bravery, and its courage to join the rest of the world.

On 10 August 2007 I got an email from a friend in a Chinese news work unit: the radio station where I used to work, Radio Jiangsu, had been singled out by the central government for punishment. Eight radio stations had ceased broadcasting in Jiangsu province alone, and over two hundred radio stations up and down the country had been shut down with no warning. The reason the high-ups had given was that they had been "moving too quickly, developing in ways that do not conform to recognised standards". As I understand it, this is a "political rectification" that took place countless times before 1980, but never again since then. In their discussions on the Internet, my fellow journalists held a variety of opinions. Some said that there was actually a point to this rectification: without it, people for whom the radio, which had enjoyed a mere twenty years of opening up, was a window on the world would have been destroyed by the "rubbish guidance" it was producing. Some considered that this rectification was a retrograde step for China's news, believing that the laws of the natural world and the "survival of the fittest" would assure a healthy development for China's news if it was left to itself. Others maintained that this was an "immunisation" for freedom of the press, in preparation for the relaxing of Chinese media controls for the 2008 Olympic Games. One old journalist even said that it was because of the Seventeenth Congress of the Chinese Communist Party, which was held in November 2007: "There's always rectification before a Party congress, every time, it's standard practice." I thought that a sign of social progress was the news teaching the people to be more aware of the law, not acting as a tool of the government.

In today's China, the taxi drivers have been one of my best sources of relatively up-to-date and comparatively genuine public opinion. They have seen and learned much in the broad streets and narrow alleys, and they have come to the best understanding of these "huge changes and renewals", as they constantly modify their routes amid the endless succession of traffic jams. Every time I've come back, chatting and debating with them and listening to their cursing and jokes has been a necessary lesson for me on China's newest developments.

These are some of the complaints that I heard from a group of taxi drivers in April and May 2007:

– In Beijing, a thirty-ish male taxi driver discussing Taiwan and the mainland:
Is Taiwan easier to govern than the mainland? Quite so! Had Chiang Kai-shek got more of what it takes than Mao Zedong? I don't believe it. Could Chiang Kai-shek have taken on the mainland? Impossible, he only knew how to cook food on the peasants' wood-burning stoves, holding the foreigners' cookery books in both hands – the peasants would never get a taste of it! Our Mao couldn't make peasant food, but he knew how to help peasants steal food from rich people's kitchens. Who would the peasants follow, if not him? If someone was to stand up and say to you: Follow me, I'll write off the debts that have crushed your family for generations, you'd go along with him! Debts are like leopards and wolves, taxes are like tigers – who'd be willing to live with unpaid debts?! Chinese peasants can't read or write, but they all know about title deeds, they all understand that one debt paper can crush a whole family to death! When we'd just been liberated, Mao Zedong burned all the records of their debts, and let them breathe again – of course they were going to work like donkeys for him! Now the officials just aren't as clever as Old Man Mao; if they keep on the way they're going, on making life hard for the peasants, then they'd better watch out!

— In Beijing, a male taxi driver and former Red Guard who has just been refused a tourist visa to the USA:

Are those foreigners being fair, punishing a country's citizens for the opinions of a political party, denying them the freedom to travel and see the world? It's like punishing my son and making him admit his errors over the beating, breaking and stealing I did back when I was a Red Guard! Is that fair? Are the British being punished for supporting slavery? Do the Americans get punished for massacring the Indians? Are the French punished for their role in enslaving North Africa? Are the Spanish punished for plundering Latin America? Are the Dutch punished for what they did to the North Americans? Are the Italians or the Turks punished for allowing the conquests and massacres of ancient times? God hasn't been punished for sending down a flood to drown the human race either, has He? Mao Zedong and the Communist Party are the deadly enemies of Britain and the US, but who do they think they are, trying to punish us with their foreign visas? What country has ever refused Communist Party leaders a visa when they go off on their state visits? Why do those free, democratic Western countries treat our common people like a joke?

— In Nanjing, a female taxi driver:

My niece is studying abroad in Germany. She told me on the phone that the foreigners over there say that Chinese are too greedy for territory. Who have we ever attacked? You say we've attacked Tibet? Vietnam? Korea? What about it? They were all just the same once. What developed countries in the world today haven't attacked other smaller or weaker countries? Which of them hasn't stolen China's wealth? First they fill their own pockets, then they turn round and accuse other people of having dirty hands, it's a joke! Those foreigners dare call *us* greedy for territory? That American Bush has used his power to stir up chaos in the world, there's violence everywhere, and he calls it "anti-terrorism"? I've heard that the weapons those terrorists are using were all made in America! Where have all the decent people gone, how come nobody's tried to put a stop to their violent ways? I told my niece, don't you listen to foreigners who believe bad words about China, they all bully the weak but fear the strong!

— In Shanghai, a very young male taxi driver, of about twenty:

Going to Britain to study for two years was really disappointing. Everyone in my family had wanted me go to America, but I thought America didn't have enough history or culture; besides, my grandfather said that in Shanghai the British had a better reputation than other countries. There are a lot of old houses in Shanghai that were built by the British and French in the twenties and thirties, and even some of their old servants say that the British treated their maids better than other people. You know, in the past many schools and foundling hospitals in Shanghai were built and run by British religious societies. So I thought that if the people were so good and kind when they went abroad, they would be even better to foreigners in their own country. But I was disappointed. Really very disappointed! My master's there was like I'd been put in a studying machine, not a breath of human life, just timetables, reading lists, students doing all their research together, teachers who barely showed their faces . . . The school allocated all the Chinese students rooms together, there was nobody to help you get involved with the local way of life, and by the time I'd finally learned how to integrate myself into British society, my visa had run out, so they didn't even give me a chance to put it into practice. After I came back I was very depressed; when I saw Britain on the TV I'd suddenly get struck by "Britain feelings", I thought I really did have feelings for the place. But once I'd calmed down and thought about it for a while, wasn't that just mawkish sentimentality? Those Brits don't take us Chinese seriously! Perhaps they still see us as the "losers" of the Opium War. Am I taking it too much to heart? But I really couldn't bear it. When I first came back I joined a British company, but before I'd been there a month I left to find work as a taxi driver, I was looking for a bit of equality and self-respect in the river of cars and traffic. Why did I walk out? I had a British head manager just before I quit, and when he spoke to you his voice was as cold as a freezer. We're all people, what gives you the right to be so high and mighty? Isn't it just that China's a bit more backward than the old-brand empires? Sometimes I really want to write an email to my old supervisor, saying: We're young and vigorous now, we may be a little bit naive and ignorant compared to you Brits, but the future belongs to us! Why haven't I written it? I'm afraid they'll be sick with rage!

"Words heard on the road" have always been a part of my social education, lessons that give me food for thought.

– *Wangfujing bookshop, Beijing, 18 April 2007:*
     SON: Daddy, what are these dolls for?

FATHER: They're called the Olympic Dolls, they're the mascots for the 2008 Olympics.

SON: Why do they look like that? What country are they from?

FATHER: Um . . . "world citizens", maybe? I think this must be "bringing China in line with the international community".

SON: Oh . . . I get it, our Olympic mascots are the cousins of the foreigners' Transformers!

*

— *Starbucks coffee house, next door to the presidential palace in Nanjing, 4 May 2007:*

CHINESE-SPEAKING FOREIGN CUSTOMER: Gosh, what a beautiful building.

SERVER: Isn't it? It used to be part of the presidential palace in the Republican era.

CUSTOMER: Why haven't they made it into a museum?

SERVER: That would be a waste of resources, wouldn't it? Then this house couldn't be used to make money.

CUSTOMER: It's a real pity, using such a beautiful building as a coffee house!

SERVER: No, it's not. What we're doing here is allowing the best-quality goods in the world to mingle with Chinese traditional culture.

*

— *Train from Nanjing to Shanghai, 7 May 2007:*

GIRL A: How do you know that your dad has a lover?

GIRL B: I bumped into them, yuck, they were all over each other.

GIRL A: Did you tell your mum?

GIRL B: What would be the point? She said it herself a long time ago, all men eat what's in their bowl while eyeing up what's in the wok!

GIRL A: Not necessarily, not my dad.

GIRL B: That's because you don't know. My mum says, what man with money doesn't keep a mistress these days?

GIRL A: So what're we going to do when we have men?

GIRL B: If they can keep lovers, so can we!

*

— *Ladies' toilets, Shanghai Hongqiao Domestic Airport, 11 May 2007:*

MANAGER: Why is this paper dispenser so loose?

CLEANER: I thought that it would make it more convenient for the customers.

411

MANAGER: You can't do that, it has to be tight, or it's easy for the customers to pull out a lot all at once, and we're the ones who have to pay for it. Have you wiped down all the pictures?

CLEANER: Yes, all of them, even the new ones they've just hung up. It's just that one over the soap dispenser, there's a mark on the man's face, I can't get it off.

MANAGER: Don't you scrub that off, I put that tape over the man's eyes myself. Whatever were they were thinking of, hanging a picture of a man in a ladies' toilet? How come the floor in that cubicle isn't shiny?

CLEANER: I've just mopped it.

MANAGER: Not hard enough, you should mop the floor until you can see the face of the person in the next toilet!

*

When I heard this, I congratulated myself that there was no one in the cubicles on either side of me; I could hardly imagine performing my private natural functions "face to face" with my neighbours.

*

– *Zhengda Shopping Centre, Shanghai, 12 May 2007:*

YOUNG WOMAN: This brand's no good!

YOUNG MAN: It looks really great on you.

YOUNG WOMAN: What do you know about it? Nobody takes this brand seriously, I'll crash and burn in the interview, for certain!

YOUNG MAN: Well, can't you wear that one from Next?

YOUNG WOMAN: That brand's too old-fashioned – as soon as the boss sees it he'll know that I'm behind the times.

YOUNG MAN: Things are really expensive here, and money's tight for me this month.

YOUNG WOMAN: So do you really love me?

YOUNG MAN: Of course I love you!

YOUNG WOMAN: Do you? Then you couldn't let me show up in clothes that aren't even brand names and lose face in front of a foreign boss, now, could you?

*

– *Shanghai Pudong International Airport, 15 May 2007:*

MAN A: Aren't you going to buy her that necklace?

MAN B: It's too expensive. I can't very well claim the money back at my work unit.

MAN A: Get the attendant to write you two receipts, one for books, one for souvenirs, and that'll be the end of the matter!

MAN B: That brain of yours is good for something, anyway!

MAN A: Oh, we all do it. You tell me, are there a hundred honest officials in our China, officials who've never used public funds to pay for private expenses?

MAN B: Officials who've never claimed on expenses? A hundred? Not that many.

*

On 16 May 2007 I was in the departure lounge of Shanghai International Airport, reading a Chinese newspaper and waiting for the plane for New Zealand, where I was going to start the launch tour for my fourth book, *Miss Chopsticks*. The main headline in the papers was still the China Petroleum and Gas Group's discovery of oilfields of up to 1 billion tonnes in the Tanhai area of the Bohai Gulf: apparently the Prime Minister, Wen Jiabao, had been "too excited to sleep". This reminded me of the worries Mr You had mentioned in his interview, that China's future strength and economic staying power would be determined by its oil supplies.

The most noticeable pictures in the illustrated part of the news were of the Chinese stock market, full of beaming faces after a series of rapid rises, juxtaposed with the gloomy faces of car salesmen; people were putting all their funds into the stock market. Many of the stock owners' faces were worn by the years, but the car dealers were all healthy young people who looked tasty enough to eat. By the side of a group of photos of ostentatious and extravagant "International Labour Day" marriage ceremonies was an old woman's face, full of grief and rage – another 91-year-old woman in Jiangxi province had made public her humiliating status as a Japanese "comfort woman". The old lady in the photograph looked agonised: why did they humiliate so many of us girls, and how can they still not admit it?

I put down my newspaper, and a song that was being played on the loudspeakers drifted into my ears. This song, "Dyed with my Blood", was written for the soldiers who died in the China-Vietnam War in the 1980s, and it had been forgotten by many people, before international politics had once again painted it with fresh colour:

> *Perhaps after this farewell I will never return,*
> *Will you understand? Will you see why?*
> *Perhaps I will fall and never rise again,*

Will you wait for me forever?
If that is so, do not grieve,
For the flag of the Republic will be dyed with my blood . . .

I was thinking: is not the flag of today's China dyed with the blood of our forebears in the same way? Do China's young people understand this? Will the flourishing crown of leaves and branches that has grown up from their roots, watered by China's violent storms and rains of blood, retain any memory of the roots?

*

The "Beijing Olympic torch storm" had been going on for three days in April 2008 when I did my final editing of *China Witness* with my London editor. I could see how much Chinese people had been constantly shocked and hurt by the mainly one-sided news "selected" by Western media in its coverage of China; only a very few exceptions, such as Frans-Paul van der Putten's letter in the *International Herald Tribune* on 6 April 2008, showed a real and all-too-rare understanding of China and its inherent problems in the last century.

On the BBC website, which became accessible in China just a few weeks before the Olympic torch went around the world, Chinese emails flooded in, showing the confusion and passionate hurt experienced by young Chinese:

— *The Dalai Lama supports the Beijing Olympics, as he has stated many times, and agreed that Tibet could be a part of China. Why, I wonder, do both sides, Tibetan and Chinese, never listen to him? And why does this complication almost never play a part in the news I watch in the UK?*

— *The 2008 Olympics was voted by the world democratically seven years ago; the UN recognizes China as a country including Tibet. How do we respect that democratic process, both UN and Olympic, when we see the sort of attacks on China's human rights record and democracy constantly reported in the news?*

— *What will be said, I wonder, if someone points out that the London Olympics in 2012 should be cancelled because British troops invaded Iraq, are illegally occupying it?*

— *What's the difference between "freedom fighters" and "terrorists"? By what standard are we judging? The Western news coverage on the Beijing Olympics seems to follow an agenda as clearly set as any propaganda.*

– There are hundreds of thousands, millions of people who speak English in China. I'd like to know how many British people speak Chinese. Most secondary school children in China know Shakespeare, Dickens and are aware of a wide range of Western music. How many Westerners know of Chinese books or music? Is this because of Western press controls, a deliberate policy by the government or simply arrogance?

– Why does Western media hate China so much? We are not living in the same China as our parents and grandparents had, even though under the same name as PR China. Why do none tell this difference to the world from those highly respected and luxurious-living foreign media in China?

'Why' has become not only a word or a question, but symptomatic of a deeper questioning and shock in young Chinese hearts and minds . . . It could turn China towards a better political system in the future, or, simply destroy their trust in the developed Western world.

I wonder how many people have realised that the naivety and ignorance of some Western media risks damaging the belief of young Chinese in democracy, and that it could also possibly force the Chinese authorities to slow down the faltering progress of the democracy movement which began in 2008. I don't think most Westerners have any idea how much the Chinese had suffered in the hundred years up to the late 1980s . . . Twenty years is a very short time for this nation to have the chance during relatively peaceful times to change its thinking, and to learn about freedom and democracy, including how to be with Tibet and Tibetans . . .

I believe it would be a great chance for the Chinese people to touch and feel the world through the universal language – of sport and music – if the Beijing Olympics were to succeed. Otherwise, there is a risk that young Chinese may feel the same confusion about democracy and find themselves in conflict with the Western world in the same way as the previous three generations after the Opium War, when China lost its national pride.

This world will not be in peace if we don't really understand and respect democracy everywhere, if we don't give people all of the information they need to make a choice, and then move on to a peaceful future. This is true all over the world. Humanity has paid so much for its past mistakes because we are too often taught to hate one another.

As a Chinese media person I struggled with Chinese censorship for a long time before I moved to London in 1997. Now, I feel the same sense of struggle again, but in the West, not with censorship, but with ignorance about my motherland.

Please, let us all think and work towards not producing more darkness with hate. Only light and the brightness of understanding can destroy darkness.

*

At about 10.30 p.m. on 12 May 2008, as I was going through the mountain of emails that had built up while I was at a conference in France, one subject with many exclamation marks jumped out at me.

"North Sichuan, Wenchuan, a 7.8 earthquake at 14:28 on May 12. The tremor was felt in all but three northern provinces but the whole of China has been shaken!!!!!!!!"

For the first few seconds, I couldn't believe what I had read, and then, almost immediately, I thought of the Tangshan earthquake in 1976, when nearly 300,000 people lost their lives. (Chinese government statistics list 240,000 dead, though I was told that figure does not include the military, those travelling through the area, or the un-registered migrants who worked in the coal mines.) I felt a chill through my whole body and I couldn't help my tears. Tangshan was a terrible blow to the Chinese people. In my book *The Good Women of China*, one chapter is about my interview with a group of mothers who all lost their children in that earthquake. Every single morning since then, those women have set an alarm for the time when their beloved children disappeared so that they could pray.

At the time of writing this on the 18 May 2008, over 32,000 deaths have been confirmed in this latest earthquake, and over 17,000 bodies are still covered by rubble. Thousands of children will have died because the earthquake took place at 2.28 p.m. during afternoon school time. One town, which had a population of tens of thousands, has only 2,200 survivors, and their homes have been completely destroyed. Today, China's State Council has decided that 19–21 May will be a national time of mourning for the earthquake victims of Sichuan Wenchuan. It is the first time in China's history that a natural disaster will be mourned nationwide.

I can see the huge difference from the government's response 30 years ago, when they banned news of Tansghan to save political face and refused international support out of a misplaced and distorted sense of national pride. This time, the Chinese government announced the Sichuan earthquake within 58 minutes and asked for international help immediately. The images of crying mothers in amongst the ruins of Sichuan on the front page of Western newspapers have drawn the world's attention from the political chaos of the Olympic torch and I sense a huge sympathy for China's loss. Also, many Chinese have learned and realised that human lives are far more important than any political or editorial angle, as the BBC and other Western media put the Sichuan earthquake as their top story.

The Chinese Internet is full of every kind of Chinese voice: sad laments for the lost and for those single-child families, who will never have the chance to have other children; warm thanks to the rescue teams and the People's Liberation Army who have been fighting day and night to save lives; thanks and encouragement for everyone who continues to donate to the poor victims; hatred towards those who allowed the poorly constructed buildings; anger with the millionaires who haven't stood up to help the people lost in this natural disaster; worry about the China Engineering Physics Research Institute, located in Sichuan Mianyang near Wenchuan, because the research station is responsible for China's nuclear weapons – it is hard to imagine the consequences if the reactor was damaged; and warnings about the North Sichuan Dam, which, if it were to break, could flood at least 160,000 lives.

These voices mostly come from the younger generation, I guess, because most of their parents and grandparents don't know how to use a computer – they are a generation who know, instead, of civil war, political madness, and queuing for food. In seeing those young Chinese united in such a way, in their care, their outrage and national pride, I realise I may be wrong about them. I used to think that they were too comfortable and too rich to understand China's hungry past, or those poor, uneducated peasants and the misunderstood last generations.

All of this made me think of that song "Dyed with my Blood", again: why does the national flag have to be painted with Chinese blood? I pray for my motherland – I hope there will be peace and strength, rooted in love and happy families, and with friends around the world.

Acknowledgements

Before I write every book and after I have finished it, the names of many, many people come to mind, and all of them need to be thanked. Some of them may not appear in the text or form part of the book, but they are a part of what I have become today, the Xinran who is able to write books.

Aside from my mother and the rest of my family, I probably owe most gratitude to the hands of the midwife who brought me into the world since she was dexterous enough not to drop me on my head and turn me into an idiot. Then there were the "aunties" of my kindergarten who constantly drilled into me that "tree leaves don't grow in the ground, and roots don't grow in the air". Then there were my primary and middle school teachers who taught me truths about nature like "What is red? The sun at dawn! What is black? Coal underground!" so I learned that as well as people, there were other lives that shared our earth. From them, I acquired basic facts such as that while I was fast asleep, there were other people busy labouring away. There is a Chinese orphan whom I can never thank enough: Yinda had never had a home, but he taught me that by imagining what people were doing behind every door, I could rid myself of the misery of being bullied. Then there are those chattering and twittering flocks of friends at university: among them, the weeping, snivelling "bad girls", severely punished for transgressing the rules, who were a spur to me to work hard to become a good Chinese woman. They all helped my Chinese heart become reflective and mature.

When I was at the radio station in China, it was those listeners who felt I was talking only to them from their radio set that made me understand that China which I had never seen and of which I had no knowledge.

As for my son, Panpan Xue, from the first Chinese sentence he babbled as a baby, to the first book in English he read about China; from the time, at the age of three, that he asked what China was, to his return to China as a fifteen-year-old volunteer, to teach English to poor mountain children; it was through his growing up that I explored my ability to be a Chinese mother. I want to thank him for being my assistant on the project.

Then there is my husband, Toby Eady, who, although he can say only five things in Chinese (and one of those is a swear word), has gone in search of China's culture and history, and understands, encourages and supports my "China complex". Without him, I would probably never have had the strength to finish *China Witness*.

All in all, the list of people whom I want to thank is enormously long. You could say that what these names make up is a book of my own life. When I thought that I might be able to write a book like this, I shouted my thanks – to life, to every tiny little bit, breath and ray of light around me.

There is one other factor in these necessary thanks: what exactly is my role in this book? The author with twenty years of investigative achievements to her credit? The scholar who believes she understands China? A guide along the motorways with their forest of signposts? Or an attentive student and listener who, by dint of her familiarity with Chinese culture and her passion for its people, has opened one or two doors for Westerners, and walked into China with them? My head still teems, night and day, with the multitudes of things I saw, books I read and things I experienced. So what am I in this book? What is the information which I am so keen to give my readers? What do I hope that they will feel after they have made their journey through it?

I am actually saying to those who want so much to understand and have things explained to them that time not only forms the construct of our lives, it creates space and clarifies our memories. What has actually happened is that an increasingly clear memory has taken me to the answer to these questions. In May 2006, Toby and I were invited to attend a workshop on literary translation in Holland. For two days, publishers, translators, writers and reporters from thirty-odd countries discussed our different national literatures and argued back and forth about how to get translated works published for the rest of the world to enjoy. The event, enthusiastic, liberating and endlessly thought-provoking, was organised by the NLPVF (the Foundation for the Production and Translation of Dutch Literature) and the chairman who brought us into this space and made it possible for us to enjoy it was Maarten Asscher, a Dutch scholar. As we embarked on the day's agenda, and more and more people launched into what became a single-minded debate on literary issues, I realised that it was our conference "maestro" Maarten Asscher who was guiding and controlling the way in which our three-sided discussions – on literature, translation and publishing – developed. Yet quite unlike most politicians, teachers and other figures of importance so keen to display their wisdom, he was entirely self-effacing. Instead, he became our "general", allowing each participant's enthusiasm for literature, translation or publishing to blend with his plans, and the needs of world literary thinking to be absorbed by Dutch scholarship. Two days of this and, thanks to Maarten, my memory was steeped in debate – and I was just a foreigner and a novice! Through him, I learned to "mediate" my awareness of other cultures, and to contribute my own building blocks to a shared cultural "bridge-building".

Through this book, I hope my own readers, standing like me outside the door looking in at China and its history, will experience these memories of China for themselves. I long for my readers to empathise with the people in this book and their families' stories; and to see how a people have risen from poverty and conflict to assume a new self-respect. And it will not be me – limited as I am to existing within a single moment, a Chinese cell with a single function – it will be the China witnesses who, with their stories, have the real power to persuade.

China Witness is a crystallisation, too, of numerous people's combined efforts. Without the help of the following, this book would never have seen the light of day now: in Beijing, Chen Linfei and Cheng Lu ran the research side; in Nanjing, Zhang Ye and Leo Hao Chong coordinated the collection of background information; Yang Ji, Kate Shortt and others filmed and recorded; Julie from Jindian travel agency did the planning and organising; London office volunteers John and Li Yi did the email communications work, led by Mothers' Bridge of Love (MBL) CEO Wendy Wu; and Xiao Shenshen (Beijing University), Wei Xuan (Beijing Broadcasting University), Pan Zhigang (Nanjing University Web) and more than fifty students from Shanghai's Fudan University helped with documentation.

Without Esther Tyldesley, Nicky Harman and Julia Lovell, who translated this book from Chinese into English (putting Chinese clouds into an English box, as Esther says); without my two editors, Dan Frank at Pantheon Books, who formed my writing into a readable book, and Alison Samuel, who has done so much not only for this book but also my other books published by her Chatto & Windus team; without those Random House people who have worked on this book, and many friends in different countries and the wisdom and dedication they have brought to the project – without all of them these Chinese stories would still be gathering dust in my Chinese memory or even left in the past of China.

Please do not think that I have simply given you a long list of names. In fact, they are not only a part of this book, they are part of China's witnesses today. I thank them, as China will thank them in the future, because they gathered together for us these precious historical records. Every book is imbued with the blood, sweat and reflections of so many people, and forms a building block in the Long March of literature.

Chinese Assistants:
What *China Witness* Meant to Them

My thanks go to all the following for their help:

Wendy Wu, MBL CEO and *China Witness* supporter: *As CEO of Mothers' Bridge of Love (MBL), I feel that the book opens a door for exploring a cultural journey for Chinese children, for those who were adopted by Western families and for those Chinese who now live in the West.*

Leo Hao Chong, *China Witness* Nanjing research team leader: *I realised, as I worked with the team, that the stories the book told were going to be very different from those in our school history textbooks.*

Julie Zhu, *China Witness* travel and office assistant: *This experience helps me and many others understand our parents' and grandparents' lives, with their tears and suffering, and their happiness which is different from ours.*

Chen Linfei, Beijing research team leader: *These witnesses have put up with such immense hardship and yet still stand miraculously tall . . .*

Li Yi, London MBL office and media assistant: *These people and their lives are both very distant and very close to us. I discovered a very simple fact: China is very big. They truly have testified to this most ordinary and yet most important fact about China.*

Yang Ji, *China Witness* media assistant and cameraman: *I never thought about what my parents' and grandparents' generation had lived through before this.*

Xuan Xuan, *China Witness* media assistant: *Ordinary people emit a very uncommon strength. Our self-restraint cannot conceal this expression of our national self-respect.*

Panpan Xue, *China Witness* media assistant: *The stories were different but the witnesses all felt relieved that someone was there to listen to them, to comfort them. I hope that people reading this book will reach a new level of understanding and be educated in the same way as I was.*

Jiang Wei, *China Witness* media assistant: *This project has awakened my interest in discovering the untold story of my own family.*

Li Xu, *China Witness* media assistant: *Now, wherever I am, I can say with complete confidence: "I am proud of my country and her people!"*

Li Yuan, *China Witness* media assistant: *I feel I have grown up by working on these stories about the kind of lives which I had never encountered in my life before . . .*

Xu Ke, *China Witness* TV assistant: *I had never been so moved as when I listened to those old people tell of the joys and sorrows of their lives. Now the whole world will listen to these hidden voices.*

Kenny Renhu, *China Witness* research support: *I gave my parents traditional respect, but I didn't learn about their history or try to understand them. My mother told me that she would not allow me to suffer the way she did.*

Pan Zhigang, *China Witness* assistant manager, Nanjing
Shen Wei, *China Witness* assistant manager, Beijing
Cheng Lu, *China Witness* research assistant, Beijing
Xiao Shenshen, *China Witness* research assistant, Beijing
Yan Yan, *China Witness* research supporter, Beijing
Tea, *China Witness* research supporter, Nanjing
Xin Meng, *China Witness* research supporter, Nanjing
Liang Qin, *China Witness* research supporter, Henan
Wu Suiping, *China Witness* research supporter, Henan
Yi Zhang, *China Witness* research supporter, Xinjiang
Lin Xue & Ping, *China Witness* research supporter, Sichuan
Zhang Yongmin, *China Witness* research supporter, Shanghai
Zhong Jane, *China Witness* research supporter, Shanghai
Liu Tong, *China Witness* research supporter, Gansu
Zha Xi Liu & Pu Er Min, *China Witness* research supporters, Anhui
Xi Fenglan, *China Witness* research supporters, Guizhou
Li Lin, *China Witness* research supporter, Shandong
Gao Feng, *China Witness* research supporter, Shanxi
Hu Feibao, *China Witness* research supporter, Silk Road
Wu Fan, *China Witness* research supporter, Guangdong
Kate Shortt, *China Witness* photographer

What we have done together with Xinran is so that Chinese history will not be forgotten, and so that our history will be known and remembered throughout the world.

Index

ALSO BY

XINRAN

THE GOOD WOMEN OF CHINA
Hidden Voices

When Deng Xiaoping's efforts to "open up" China took root in the late 1980s, Xinran recognized an invaluable opportunity. As an employee for the state radio system, she had long wanted to help improve the lives of Chinese women. But when she was given clearance to host a radio call-in show, she barely anticipated the enthusiasm it would quickly generate. Operating within the constraints imposed by government censors, "Words on the Night Breeze" sparked a tremendous outpouring, and the hours of tape on her answering machines were soon filled every night. Whether angry or muted, posing questions or simply relating experiences, these anonymous women bore witness to decades of civil strife, and of halting attempts at self-understanding in a painfully restrictive society. In this collection, by turns heartrending and inspiring, Xinran brings us the stories that affected her most, and offers a graphically detailed, altogether unprecedented work of oral history.

Current Affairs/Women's Studies

ALSO AVAILABLE
Sky Burial

ANCHOR BOOKS
Available wherever books are sold.
www.anchorbooks.com

CHINA IN TEN WORDS
by Yu Hua

Framed by ten phrases common in the Chinese vernacular, *China in Ten Words* uses personal stories and astute analysis to reveal as never before the world's most populous yet oft-misunderstood nation. In "Disparity," for example, Yu Hua illustrates the expanding gaps that separate citizens of the country. In "Copycat," he depicts the escalating trend of piracy and imitation as a creative new form of revolutionary action. And in "Bamboozle," he describes the increasingly brazen practices of trickery, fraud, and chicanery that are, he suggests, becoming a way of life at every level of society. Witty, insightful, and courageous, this is a refreshingly candid vision of the "Chinese miracle" and all of its consequences.

History/Asian Studies

RED CHINA BLUES
My Long March from Mao to Now
by Jan Wong

Red China Blues is Jan Wong's startling—and ironic—memoir of her rocky six-year romance with Maoism (which crumbled as she became aware of the harsh realities of Chinese communism); her dramatic firsthand account of the devastating Tiananmen Square uprising; and her engaging portrait of the individuals and events she covered as a correspondent in China during the tumultuous era of capitalist reform under Deng Xiaoping. In setting out to show readers in the Western world what life is like in China—and why we should care, she reacquaints herself with the old friends and enemies of her radical past and comes to terms with the legacy of her ancestral homeland.

Memoir

THE CORPSE WALKER
Real-Life Stories: China From the Bottom Up
by Liao Yiwu

The Corpse Walker introduces us to regular men and women at the bottom of Chinese society, most of whom have been battered by life but have managed to retain their dignity: a professional mourner, a human trafficker, a public toilet manager, a leper, a grave robber, and a Falun Gong practitioner, among others. By asking challenging questions with respect and empathy, Liao Yiwu managed to get his subjects to talk openly and sometimes hilariously about their lives, desires, and vulnerabilities, creating a book that is an instance par excellence of what was once upon a time called "The New Journalism." *The Corpse Walker* reveals a fascinating aspect of modern China, describing the lives of normal Chinese citizens in ways that constantly provoke and surprise.

Sociology

THE LONG MARCH
The True History of Communist China's Founding Myth
by Sun Shuyun

The Long March uncovers the true story behind the mythic march of Mao's soldiers across China, exposing the famine, disease, and desertion behind the legend. In 1934, in the midst of civil war, the Communist party and its 200,000 soldiers were forced from their bases by Chiang Kai-shek and his Nationalist troops. Led by Mao Tse Tung, they set off on a strategic retreat to the barren north of China. As Sun Shuyun travels along the march route, her interviews with survivors and villagers show that the forces at work during the days of the revolution—poverty, sickness, and Mao's use of terror, propaganda, and ruthless purges—have shaped modern China irrevocably. Uncovering the forced recruitment, political infighting, and futile deaths behind the myth, Shuyun creates a compelling narrative of a turning point in modern Chinese history.

History/China

"SOCIALISM IS GREAT!"
A Worker's Memoir of the New China
by Lijia Zhang

With a great charm and spirit, *"Socialism Is Great!"* recounts Lijia Zhang's rebellious journey from disillusioned factory worker to organizer in support of the Tiananmen Square demonstrators to eventually become the writer and journalist she always determined to be. Her memoir is like a brilliant miniature illuminating the sweeping historical forces at work in China after the Cultural Revolution as the country moved from one of stark repression to a vibrant, capitalist economy.

Memoir/China

RED AZALEA
by Anchee Min

A revelatory and disturbing portrait of China, this is Anchee Min's celebrated memoir of growing up in the last years of Mao's China. As a child, Min was asked to publicly humiliate a teacher; at seventeen, she was sent to work at a labor collective. Forbidden to speak, dress, read, write, or love as she pleased, she found a lifeline in a secret love affair with another woman. Miraculously selected for the film version of one of Madame Mao's political operas, Min's life changed overnight. Then Chairman Mao suddenly died, taking with him an entire world. This national bestseller and *New York Times* Notable Book is exceptional for its candor, its poignancy, its courage, and for its prose which *Newsweek* calls "as delicate and evocative as a traditional Chinese brush painting."

Memoir

ANCHOR BOOKS
Available wherever books are sold.
www.anchorbooks.com

Meet with Interesting People
Enjoy Stimulating Conversation
Discover Wonderful Books

VINTAGE BOOKS / ANCHOR BOOKS

Reading Group Center
THE READING GROUP SOURCE FOR BOOK LOVERS

Visit ReadingGroupCenter.com where you'll find great reading choices—award winners, bestsellers, beloved classics, and many more—and extensive resources for reading groups such as:

Author Chats

Exciting contests offer reading groups the chance to win one-on-one phone conversations with Vintage and Anchor Books authors.

Extensive Discussion Guides

Guides for over 450 titles as well as non–title specific discussion questions by category for fiction, nonfiction, memoir, poetry, and mystery.

Personal Advice and Ideas

Reading groups nationwide share ideas, suggestions, helpful tips, and anecdotal information. Participate in the discussion and share your group's experiences.

Behind the Book Features

Specially designed pages which can include photographs, videos, original essays, notes from the author and editor, and book-related information.

Reading Planner

Plan ahead by browsing upcoming titles, finding author event schedules, and more.

Special for Spanish-language reading groups
www.grupodelectura.com

A dedicated Spanish-language content area complete with recommended titles from Vintage Español.

A selection of some favorite reading group titles from our list

Atonement by Ian McEwan
Balzac and the Little Chinese Seamstress by Dai Sijie
The Blind Assassin by Margaret Atwood
The Devil in the White City by Erik Larson
Empire Falls by Richard Russo
The English Patient by Michael Ondaatje
A Heartbreaking Work of Staggering Genius by Dave Eggers
The House of Sand and Fog by Andre Dubus III
A Lesson Before Dying by Ernest J. Gaines

Lolita by Vladimir Nabokov
Memoirs of a Geisha by Arthur Golden
Midnight in the Garden of Good and Evil by John Berendt
Midwives by Chris Bohjalian
Push by Sapphire
The Reader by Bernhard Schlink
Snow by Orhan Pamuk
An Unquiet Mind by Kay Redfield Jamison
Waiting by Ha Jin
A Year in Provence by Peter Mayle

Printed in the United States
by Baker & Taylor Publisher Services